Selected Writings

Thomas Jefferson

Selected Writings

WITH AN INTRODUCTION BY

Tom Wicker

LIBRARY OF AMERICA PAPERBACK CLASSICS

Contents

Each section has its own table of contents.

INTRODUCTION

by Tom Wicker

For Americans accustomed to the limitations of modern politicians, with their muddled syntax, innocence of history, and narrow view, the range of Thomas Jefferson's interests and intellect is difficult to comprehend. Which President of the twentieth century, for instance, could be called truly a learned person? Not merely well-read, able professionally, or wise and experienced in the ways of man—but accomplished in literature, law, science, music, languages, government, philosophy, agriculture, mathematics, even enology? Which recent occupant of the President's house in Washington could have designed such a building, let alone a house of his own so ingenious and pleasing as Monticello? President Kennedy's remark to a group of Nobel Prize winners—that so many distinguished persons had not been gathered in the White House since Jefferson dined alone—was not only witty but almost literally true. On March 3, 1797, for only one example, the great Virginian was installed as president of the American Philosophical Society; the next day he was sworn in as vice-president of the United States; and one week later he presented the Philosophical Society with a paper on megalonyx, describing recent fossil discoveries in his home state.

Jefferson's interests seem to have been as limitless as the American land he sent Lewis and Clark to explore; but he was not a dilettante. In this handy sampling of his more notable papers, the depth and sweep of his knowledge is often shown—perhaps most graphically in a disquisition on weights, measures, and coinage, distinguished historically as well as scientifically, that had been requested from him by Congress while he served as the first secretary of state.

Most foreign ambassadors were content to watch the French Revolution from the privileged sanctuaries of their embassies. Not Jefferson, the lawyer-diplomat who then represented the United States in Paris. He became so deeply involved in the events exploding around him that he tried to persuade King Louis to proclaim a "charter of rights" not unlike the Bill of Rights Jefferson already had been instrumental in attaching to the new Constitution of the United States. The Marquis de Lafayette was persuaded, but Louis turned to his nobles instead, rejected Jefferson's proposal, and ended up on the guillotine. Perhaps he would have anyway.

Jefferson's intellectual curiosity, whether in passing or in directed study, was insatiable. While traveling in Europe he noticed and wrote down more than most scholars learn in a lifetime—much of it reprinted in this volume. The scientist Jefferson, it will be seen, made an intricate drawing of an "Archimedes' screw" for raising water above its level; the architect carefully recorded details of a window that admitted air but not rain because "the upper sash opens on a horizontal axis, or pins in the centre of the sides, the lower sash slides up"; the tinkerer sketched out an elongated Dutch wheelbarrow "very convenient for loading and unloading"; the artist observed that in Dusseldorf "the gallery of paintings is sublime"; and the progressive farmer was interested to learn that the famous Westphalian ham was cut from a hog with "heavy lop ears," fed on acorns, and required 4 pounds of "fine Holland salt" to 100 pounds of pork before being smoked in a room with no chimney and sold at eight and a half pence sterling per pound. Such examples are multiplied in this fascinating volume.

When on these European travels Jefferson sampled the wines of the Moselle Valley, he could compare the "Crach of 1783 with Baron Burrhesheim's of the same year" and confidently report to his journal that "the latter is quite clear of acid, stronger, and very sensibly the best." His attention to European wines and cuisine was acute, and he acquired an impressive cellar for Monticello, also bringing back recipes that—I can testify as an amateur cook—will turn out splendidly in today's kitchens.

Always the good husbandman and a true child of the land, Jefferson attempted by importing the necessary plants to establish an olive-growing industry in South Carolina and Georgia; and he brought in upland rice from Africa ("about lat. 9° 30′ North"), hoping it "might supersede the culture of the wet rice, which renders South Carolina and Georgia so pestilential through the summer."

Here is part of his advice, hardly commonplace for traveling VIPs, to friends about to go abroad: "Take every possible occasion for entering into the houses of the laborers, and especially at the moments of their repast; see what they eat, how they are clothed, whether they are obliged to work too hard; whether the government or their landlord takes from them an unjust proportion of their labor; on what footing stands the property they call their own, their personal liberty, &c., &c."

He read and wrote Latin and Greek, enjoyed verse in these languages as well as in French and English, and was an erudite literary critic—so much so that he was willing to challenge Samuel Johnson's classification of the poetic feet, praising its simplicity but in the same sentence remarking upon "the doubtfulness, if not the error, on which it was founded." Though he has little to say about rhyme in his "Thoughts on English Prosody" (here printed in full), he makes brief but telling judgment on poets whose work shows "the loss of regular measure." Their pieces, he remarks, "are seldom read twice."

When Jefferson turned seriously to a subject—virtually any subject—he could exhaust it. In *Observations on the Whale-Fishery,* included here and written during his service in Paris, he displayed a comprehensive grasp of the whaling industry, the virtues and deficiencies of its product (spermaceti whale coagulates at 41 degrees Fahrenheit but oil of the "Groenland" whale remains liquid to 36 degrees), the economic advantages to France of opening its ports to American whalers, the self-defeating folly of French protectionism, the shrewd British effort to subsidize and corner the whale oil market, and the U.S. interest in keeping its whalers at work while trading their product for French cloth goods.

It's hard to think of a contemporary political figure who could produce such a lucidly detailed paper on *any* subject—certainly not one so esoteric—without the aid of the ubiquitous staff persons that swarm about them. Jefferson did it alone, and within a year of having written and published the book-length *Notes on the State of Virginia,* a magisterial description of that state's flora, fauna, soil, climate, mountains, farms, ports, and other natural and manmade conditions.

This remarkable man even had a hand, for better or for worse, in introducing the prison to America: "Public labor was thought the best punishment to be substituted for death. But while I was in France, I heard of a society in England, who had successfully introduced solitary confinement, and saw the drawing of a prison at Lyons." Jefferson sent the drawing, and one he adapted for American conditions, to the governor of Virginia, who accepted the idea. Labor in confinement was thus substituted in that state, as it already had been in Philadelphia, for public labor as penance for crime. Corrections apparently was one of Jefferson's myriad interests; for as early as 1779, he had proposed "A Bill for Proportioning Crimes and Punishments," which the Virginia legislature failed by only one vote to adopt.

In that document, and in a draft constitution he earlier had drawn up for the state, capital punishment was to be abolished for all crimes except murder and treason—a radical advance for that time and place. He had, moreover, a most modern idea of deterrence, reckoning it best accomplished if "men while contemplating to perpetrate a crime would see their punishment ensuing as necessarily as effects follow their causes"—or, as would be said today, "swift and certain punishment."

Jefferson was more than usually advanced, too, in his concern for the rights of women. In the draft constitution he proposed for Virginia, he provided that 'females shall have equal rights with males" in determining inheritances. In a later bill for "the more general diffusion of knowledge," Jefferson not only proposed for Virginia a clear forerunner of what became the free public school system but specified that in each school district free tuition should be provided for three years of instruction in reading, writing, and arithmetic, as well as Greek, Roman, English, and American history, "for all the free children, male and female," residing there.

"Free children" meant, of course, that Jefferson was not prepared to interfere with the institution of slavery, and his larger view of women's rights narrowed abruptly when he went on to provide for free tuition for certain superior scholars—males only—at William and Mary College. As much a man ahead of his time as any American ever was, Jefferson

nevertheless showed in his papers that he either observed or
never realized certain limitations of the age; though enlightened about capital punishment, he proposed other penalties
that would be deemed cruel and unusual today—castration
for rape, a hole bored through the nose of a woman caught
in polygamy or homosexuality, maiming and mutilation for
those who maimed or mutilated.

These pages make no effort to convey the quality of Jefferson's musicianship, though to judge by his other talents he
probably was a violinist worth hearing. His remarkable ability
as a writer, however, is everywhere on display. Save only Lincoln, no American President—perhaps no American public
man—can approach Jefferson's felicity with words (the Declaration of Independence being only the most famous example) or the relentless logic he could marshal in support of a
point.

For example, in denying the constitutionality of Alexander
Hamilton's proposed national bank, Secretary of State Jefferson (before constitutional interpretation became a task for the
Supreme Court) could call upon a lawyer's learning, a politi-
cian's instinct, and a writer's pen. No justification for the
bank, he contended, could be found in the Constitution's
grant of power to Congress to lay taxes for the general welfare of the United States—

> that is to say, "to lay taxes for *the purpose* of providing
> for the general welfare." For the laying of taxes is the *power,*
> and the general welfare the *purpose* for which the power is
> to be exercised. They are not to lay taxes *ad libitum for any
> purpose they please*; but only *to pay the debts or provide for the
> welfare of the Union*. In like manner, they are not *to do any-
> thing they please* to provide for the general welfare, but only
> to *lay taxes* for that purpose. To consider the latter phrase,
> not as describing the purpose of the first, but as giving a
> distinct and independent power to do any act they please,
> which might be for the good of the Union, would render
> all the preceding and subsequent enumerations of power
> completely useless.
>
> It would reduce the whole instrument to a single phrase,
> that of instituting a Congress with power to do whatever

would be for the good of the United States; and, as they would be the sole judges of the good or evil, it would be also a power to do whatever evil they please.

Jefferson was here arguing against what later came to be the accepted but not unchallenged constitutional doctrine of "implied powers," and in the same brief he raised questions about the power of veto that the Constitution granted to the President:

> If the pro and the con hang so even as to balance his judgment, a just respect for the wisdom of the legislature would naturally decide the balance in favor of their opinion. It is chiefly for cases where they are *clearly misled by error, ambition, or interest,* that the Constitution has placed a check in the negative of the President. (Emphasis added.)

The President was not, in this view, to wield the veto because of a mere policy disagreement with the legislature, or when the legislative case was as strong as his, but only when the wrong to be vetoed was clear and perhaps venal. Jefferson's argument against the bank, therefore, reflects an almost constant theme in these pages—the necessity to restrain the power of the central government and to guard against those who would clothe the executive in "monarchical" powers. Even in his first inaugural address (available here in its entirety), Jefferson stated the "sacred principle, that though the will of the majority is in all cases to prevail, that will to be rightful must be reasonable; that the minority possess their equal rights, which equal law must protect, and to violate would be oppression."

Such a view of power makes it one of the renowned ironies of American history that, in the two terms he served following Washington and John Adams, Jefferson became of necessity one of the strongest of our Presidents—witness the Louisiana Purchase, presented to Congress as an executive *fait accompli.* And though he was a leader in the emergence of political factions—his own being the forebear of the present Democratic party—he warned in that same first inaugural (one of the best of any President, though contemporaries said it had been mumbled almost inaudibly): "Every difference of opinion is not a difference of principle. We have called by different names brethren of the same principle. We are all Republicans, we are all Federalists. If there be any among us who would wish to dissolve this Union or to change its republican form, let them stand undisturbed as monuments of the safety with which error of opinion may be tolerated where reason is left free to combat it." Conservatives and liberals of today, take note.

On one question of power and the state, Jefferson never wavered from the standard he set in 1779 in his seminal "Bill for Establishing Religious Freedom" in Virginia (also reprinted here): "No man shall be compelled to frequent or support any religious worship, place, or ministry whatsoever, nor shall be enforced, restrained, molested, or burthened in his body or goods, nor shall otherwise suffer, on account of his religious opinions or belief; but that all men shall be free to profess, and by argument to maintain, their opinions in matters of religion, and that the same shall in no wise diminish, enlarge, or affect their civil capacities." So much for those who insist that the republic was founded as a "Christian nation" and must so remain.

Like all Presidents, however, Jefferson developed by the time of his second inaugural some darker, rather Nixonian thoughts on what he called "the artillery of the press . . . levelled against us, charged with whatsoever its licentiousness could devise or dare." Even so, he proposed no punishments or limitation, "since truth and reason have maintained their ground against false opinions in league with false facts" and therefore "the press, confined to truth, needs no other legal restraint . . . no other definite line can be drawn between the inestimable liberty of the press and its demoralizing licentiousness."

In the famous epitaph he wrote for himself (to be inscribed on a monument of his own design), he chose with precision those of his many achievements that would stand all tests of time and circumstance: "Author of the Declaration of American Independence, of the Statute of Virginia for religious freedom, & Father of the University of Virginia." Note that none of these are *presidential* achievements, a fact that might serve to put in proper perspective the more exalted and all too adulatory view Americans today tend to take toward their elected leaders. It may be too much to expect, in modern circumstances, that any President could match Jefferson's learning and intellectual reach, but aspirants to that office he did so much to establish might well be measured for their understanding of the "palpable truth" he set down, with characteristic clarity, in a letter written in the last weeks of a lengthy life: "The mass of mankind has not been born with saddles on their backs, nor a favored few booted and spurred, ready to ride them legitimately, by the grace of God."

Public Papers

Contents

Resolutions of Congress on Lord North's Conciliatory Proposal

In Congress

THE SEVERAL Assemblies of NEW JERSEY, PENNSYLVANIA and VIRGINIA, having referred to the Congress a resolution of the House of Commons of GREAT BRITAIN, which resolution is in these words, viz.

Lunae, 20° die Feb. 1775.
The House in a Committee on the American papers. Motion made, and question proposed.

THAT *it is the opinion of this Committee, that when the General Council and Assembly, or General Court of any of his Majesty's provinces, or colonies in America, shall propose to make provision, according to the condition, circumstance, or situation of such province or colony, for contributing their proportion to the common defence (such proportion to be raised under the authority of the General Court, or General Assembly of such province or colony, and disposable by Parliament) and shall engage to make provision also, for the support of the civil government, and the Administration of justice in such province or colony, it will be proper if such proposal shall be approved by his Majesty and the two Houses of Parliament; and for so long as such provision shall be made accordingly, to forbear in respect of such province or colony, to lay any duty, tax, or assessment, or to impose any further duty, tax or assessment, except only such duties as it may be expedient to continue to levy or impose, for the regulation of commerce, the net produce of the duties last mentioned, to be carried to the account of such province or colony respectively.*

The Congress took the said resolution into consideration, and are thereupon of opinion:

That the colonies of America are entitled to the sole and exclusive privilege of giving and granting their own money; that this involves a right of deliberating whether they will make any gift, for what purposes it shall be made, and what shall be it's amount; and that it is a high breach of this privilege for any body of men, extraneous to their constitutions, to prescribe the purposes for which money shall be levied on them, to take to themselves the authority of judging of their conditions, circumstances and situations; and of determining the amount of the contribution to be levied.

That as the colonies possess a right of appropriating their gifts, so are they entitled at all times to enquire into their application, to see that they be not wasted among the venal and corrupt for the purpose of undermining the civil rights of the givers, nor yet be diverted to the support of standing armies, inconsistent with their freedom and subversive of their quiet. To propose therefore, as this resolution does, that the monies given by the colonies shall be subject to the disposal of parliament alone, is to propose that they shall relinquish this right of enquiry, and put it in the power of others to render their gifts, ruinous, in proportion as they are liberal.

That this privilege of giving or of withholding our monies is an important barrier against the undue exertion of prerogative, which if left altogether without controul may be exercised to our great oppression; and all history shews how efficacious is its intercession for redress of grievances and re-establishment of rights, and how improvident it would be to part with so powerful a mediator.

We are of opinion that the proposition contained in this resolution is unreasonable and insidious: unreasonable, because, if we declare we accede to it, we declare without reservation, we will purchase the favour of Parliament, not knowing at the same time at what price they will please to estimate their favor: It is insidious, because, individual colonies, having bid and bidden again, till they find the avidity of the seller too great for all their powers to satisfy; are then to return into opposition, divided from their sister colonies whom the minister will have previously detached by a grant of easier terms, or by an artful procrastination of a definitive answer.

That the suspension of the exercise of their pretended power of taxation being expressly made commensurate with the continuance of our gifts, these must be perpetual to make that so. Whereas no experience has shewn that a gift of perpetual revenue secures a perpetual return of duty or of kind disposition. On the contrary, the Parliament itself, wisely attentive to this observation, are in the established practice of granting their supplies from year to year only.

Desirous and determined as we are to consider in the most dispassionate view every seeming advance towards a reconciliation made by the British Parliament, let our brethren of Britain reflect what would have been the sacrifice to men of free spirits had even fair terms been proffered, as these insidious proposals were with circumstances of insult and defiance. A proposition to give our money, accompanied with large fleets and armies, seems addressed to our fears rather than to our freedom. With what patience would Britons have received articles of treaty from any power on earth when borne on the point of a bayonet by military plenipotentiaries?

We think the attempt unnecessary to raise upon us by force or by threats our proportional contributions to the common defence, when all know, and themselves acknowledge we have fully contributed, whenever called upon to do so in the character of freemen.

We are of opinion it is not just that the colonies should be required to oblige themselves to other contributions, while Great Britain possesses a monopoly of their trade. This of itself lays them under heavy contribution. To demand therefore, additional aids in the form of a tax, is to demand the double of their equal proportion, if we are to contribute equally with the other parts of the empire, let us equally with them enjoy free commerce with the whole world. But while the restrictions on our trade shut to us the resources of wealth, is it just we should bear all other burthens equally with those to whom every resource is open.

We conceive that the British Parliament has no right to intermeddle with our provisions for the support of civil government, or administration of justice. The provisions we have made are such as please ourselves, and are agreeable to our own circumstances; they answer the substantial purposes of government and of justice, and other purposes than these should not be answered. We do not mean that our people shall be burthened with oppressive taxes to provide sinecures for the idle or the wicked, under colour of providing for a civil list. While Parliament pursue their plan of civil government within their own jurisdiction, we also hope to pursue ours without molestation.

We are of opinion the proposition is altogether unsatisfactory because it imports only a suspension of the mode, not a renunciation of the pretended right to tax us: Because too it does not propose to repeal the several Acts of Parliament passed for the purposes of restraining the trade and altering the form of government of one of our Colonies; extending the boundaries and changing the government of Quebec; enlarging the jurisdiction of the Courts of Admiralty and Vice Admiralty; taking from us the rights of trial by a Jury of the vicinage in cases affecting both life and property; transporting us into other countries to be tried for criminal offences; exempting by mock-trial the murderers of Colonists from punishment; and quartering soldiers on us in times of profound peace. Nor do they renounce the power of suspending our own Legislatures, and of legislating for us themselves in all cases whatsoever. On the contrary, to shew they mean no discontinuance of injury, they pass acts, at the very time of holding out this proposition, for restraining the commerce and fisheries of the Provinces of New-England, and for interdicting the trade of other Colonies with all foreign nations and with each other. This proves unequivocally they mean not to relinquish the exercise of indiscriminate legislation over us.

Upon the whole, this proposition seems to have been held up to the world, to deceive it into a belief that there was nothing in dispute between us but the *mode* of levying taxes; and that the Parliament having now been so good as to give up this, the Colonies are unreasonable if not perfectly satisfied: Whereas in truth, our adversaries still claim a right of demanding *ad libitum*, and of taxing us themselves to the full amount of their demand, if we do not comply with it. This leaves us without any thing we can call property. But, what is of more importance, and what in this proposal they keep out of sight, as if no such point was now in contest between us, they claim a right to alter our Charters and established laws, and leave us without any security for our Lives or Liberties. The proposition seems also to have been calculated more particularly to lull into fatal security our well-affected fellow subjects on the other side the water, till time should be given for the operation of those arms, which a British Minister pronounced would instantaneously reduce the "cowardly" sons of America to unreserved submission. But when the world reflects, how inadequate to justice are these vaunted terms; when it attends to the rapid and bold succession of injuries, which, during a course of eleven years, have been aimed at these Colonies; when it reviews the pacific and respectful expostulations, which, during that whole time, were the sole arms we opposed to them; when it observes that our complaints were either not heard at all, or were answered with new and accumulated injury; when it recollects that the Minister himself on an early occasion declared, "that he would never treat with America, till he had brought her to his feet," and that an avowed partisan of Ministry has more lately denounced against us the dreadful sentence *"delenda est Carthago,"* that this was done in presence of a British Senate, and being unreproved by them, must be taken to be their own sentiment, (especially as the purpose has already in part been carried into execution by their treatment of Boston, and burning of Charlestown) when it considers the great armaments with which they have invaded us, and the circumstances of cruelty with which these have commenced and prosecuted hostilities; when these things, we say, are laid together, and attentively considered, can the world be deceived into an opinion that we are unreasonable, or can it hesitate to believe with us, that nothing but our own exertions may defeat the ministerial sentence of death or abject submission.

By Order of the Congress,

JOHN HANCOCK, *President.*

Philadelphia, July 31, 1775.

Draft Constitution for Virginia
[*June, 1776.*]

FAIR COPY

[*A Bil*]l for new-modelling the form of Government and for establishing the Fundamental principles thereof in future.

Whereas George
Guelf king of Great Britain and Ireland and Elector of Hanover, heretofore entrusted with the exercise of the kingly office in this government hath endeavored to pervert the same into a detestable and insupportable tyranny;

by putting his negative on laws the most wholesome & necessary for ye public good;

by denying to his governors permission to pass laws of immediate and pressing importance, unless suspended in their operations for his assent, and, when so suspended, neglecting to attend to them for many years;

by refusing to pass certain other laws, unless the person to be benefited by them would relinquish the inestimable right of representation in the legislature

by dissolving legislative assemblies repeatedly and continually for opposing with manly firmness his invasions on the rights of the people;

when dissolved, by refusing to call others for a long space of time, thereby leaving the political system without any legislative head;

by endeavoring to prevent the population of our country, & for that purpose obstructing the laws for the naturalization of foreigners & raising the condition [*lacking appro*]priations of lands;

[*by keeping among u*]s, in times of peace, standing armies and ships of war;

[*lacking*]ing to render the military independent of & superior to the civil power;

by combining with others to subject us to a foreign jurisdiction, giving his assent to their pretended acts of legislation.

for quartering large bodies of troops among us;

for cutting off our trade with all parts of the world;

10

for imposing taxes on us without our consent;

for depriving us of the benefits of trial by jury;

for transporting us beyond seas to be tried for pretended offences; and

for suspending our own legislatures & declaring themselves invested with power to legislate for us in all cases whatsoever;

by plundering our seas, ravaging our coasts, burning our towns and destroying the lives of our people;

by inciting insurrections of our fellow subjects with the allurements of forfeiture & confiscation;

by prompting our negroes to rise in arms among us; those very negroes whom ~~he hath from time to time~~ by an inhuman use of his negative he hath refused permission to exclude by law;

by endeavoring to bring on the inhabitants of our frontiers the merciless Indian savages, whose known rule of warfare is an undistinguished destruction of all ages, sexes, & conditions of existence;

by transporting at this time a large army of foreign mercenaries [*to complete*] the works of death, desolation & tyranny already begun with circum[*stances*] of cruelty & perfidy so unworthy the head of a civilized nation;

by answering our repeated petitions for redress with a repetition of injuries;

and finally by abandoning the helm of government and declaring us out of his allegiance & protection;

by which several acts of misrule the said George

Guelf has forfeited the kingly office and has rendered it necessary for the preservation of the people that he should be immediately deposed from the same, and divested of all its privileges, powers, & prerogatives:

And forasmuch as the public liberty may be more certainly secured by abolishing an office which all experience hath shewn to be inveterately inimical thereto ~~or which~~ and it will thereupon become further necessary to re-establish such ancient principles as are friendly to the rights of the people and to declare certain others which may co-operate with and fortify the same in future.

Be it therefore enacted by the authority of the people that

the said, George   Guelf be, and he hereby is deposed
from the kingly office within this government and absolutely
divested of all it's rights, powers, and prerogatives: and that
he and his descendants and all persons acting by or through
him, and all other persons whatsoever shall be and forever
remain incapable of the same: and that the said office shall
henceforth cease and never more either in name or substance
be re-established within this colony.

And be it further enacted by the authority aforesaid that
the following fundamental laws and principles of government
shall henceforth be established.

The Legislative, Executive and Judiciary offices shall be
kept forever separate; no person exercising the one shall be
capable of appointment to the others, or to either of them.

I. LEGISLATIVE.

Legislation shall be exercised by two separate houses, to wit
a house of Representatives, and a house of Senators, which
shall be called the General Assembly of Virginia.

Ho. of Represen-tatives The sd house of Representatives shall be composed of persons chosen by the people annually on
the [1st day of October] and shall meet in General
assembly on the [1st day of November] following and so from
time to time on their own adjournments, or at any time when
summoned by the Administrator and shall continue sitting so
long as they shall think the publick service requires.

Vacancies in the said house by death or disqualification
shall be filled by the electors under a warrant from the
Speaker of the said house.

Electors All male persons of full age and sane mind having
a freehold estate in [one fourth of an acre] of land
in any town, or in [25] acres of land in the country, and all
Elected persons resident in the colony who shall have paid
scot and lot to government the last [two years] shall
have right to give their vote in the election of their respective
representatives. And every person so qualified to elect shall be
capable of being elected, provided he shall have given no
bribe either directly or indirectly to any elector, and shall take
an oath of fidelity to the state and of duty in his office, before

he enters on the exercise thereof. During his continuance in the said office he shall hold no public pension nor post of profit, either himself, or by another for his use.

The number of Representatives for each county or borough shall be so proportioned to the numbers of it's qualified electors that the whole number of representatives shall not exceed [300] nor be less than [125.] for the present there shall be one representative for every [   ] qualified electors in each county or borough: but whenever this or any future proportion shall be likely to exceed or fall short of the limits beforementioned, it shall be again adjusted by the house of representatives.

The house of Representatives when met shall be free to act according to their own judgment and conscience.

The Senate shall consist of not less than [15] nor more than [50] members who shall be appointed by the house of Representatives. One third of them shall be removed out of office by lot at the end of the first [three] years and their places be supplied by a new appointment; one other third shall be removed by lot in like manner at the end of the second [three] years and their places be supplied by a new appointment; after which one third shall be removed annually at the end of every [three] years according to seniority. When once removed, they shall be forever incapable of being reappointed to that house. Their qualifications shall be an oath of fidelity to the state, and of duty in their office, the being [31] years of age at the least, and the having given no bribe directly or indirectly to obtain their appointment. While in the senatorial office they shall be incapable of holding any public pension or post of profit either themselves, or by others for their use.

Senate

The judges of the General court and of the High court of Chancery shall have session and deliberative voice, but not suffrage in the house of Senators.

The Senate and the house of representatives shall each of them have power to originate and amend bills; save only that bills for levying money bills shall be originated and amended by the representatives only: the assent of both houses shall be requisite to pass a law.

The General assembly shall have no power to pass any law

inflicting death for any crime, excepting murder, & ~~such~~ those offences in the military service for which they shall think punishment by death absolutely necessary: and all capital punishments in other cases are hereby abolished. Nor shall they have power to prescribe torture in any case whatever: nor shall there be power anywhere to pardon crimes or to remit fines or punishments: nor shall any law for levying money be in force longer than [ten years] from the time of its commencement.

[Two thirds] of the members of either house shall be a Quorum to proceed to business.

II. Executive.

The executive powers shall be exercised in manner following.

Adminis-   One person to be called the [Administrator] shall
trator   be annually appointed by the house of Representatives on the second day of their first session, who after having acted [one] year shall be incapable of being again appointed to that office until he shall have been out of the same [three] years.

Deputy   Under him shall be appointed by the same house
Admr.   and at the same time, a Deputy-Administrator to assist his principal in the discharge of his office, and to succeed, in case of his death before the year shall have expired, to the whole powers thereof during the residue of the year.

The administrator shall possess the power formerly held by the king: save only that, he shall be bound by acts of legislature tho' not expressly named;

he shall have no negative on the bills of the Legislature;

he shall be liable to action, tho' not to personal restraint for private duties or wrongs;

he shall not possess the prerogatives;

of dissolving, proroguing or adjourning either house of Assembly;

of declaring war or concluding peace;

of issuing letters of marque or reprisal;

of raising or introducing armed forces, building armed vessels, forts or strongholds;

of coining monies or regulating their values;

of regulating weights and measures;

of erecting courts, offices, boroughs, corporations, fairs, markets, ports, beacons, lighthouses, seamarks.

of laying embargoes, or prohibiting the exportation of any commodity for a longer space than [40] days.

of retaining or recalling a member of the state but by legal process pro delicto vel contractu.

of making denizens.

of pardoning crimes, or remitting fines or punishments.

of creating dignities or granting rights of precedence.

but these powers shall be exercised by the legislature alone, and excepting also those powers which by these fundamentals are given to others, or abolished.

A Privy council shall be annually appointed by the house of representatives whose duties it shall be to give advice to the Administrator when called on by him. With them the Deputy Administrator shall have session and suffrage. Privy Council

Delegates to represent this colony in the American Congress shall be appointed when necessary by the house of Representatives. After serving [one] year in that office they shall not be capable of being re-appointed to the same during an interval of [one] year. Delegates

A Treasurer shall be appointed by the house of Representatives who shall issue no money but by authority of both houses. Treasurer

An Attorney general shall be appointed by the house of Representatives Attorney Genrl.

High Sheriffs and Coroners of counties shall be annually elected by those qualified to vote for representatives: and no person who shall have served as high sheriff [one] year shall be capable of being re-elected to the said office in the same county till he shall have been out of office [five] years. High Sheriffs, &c.

All other Officers civil and military shall be appointed by the Administrator; but such appoint- Other Officers ment shall be subject to the negative of the Privy council, saving however to the Legislature a power of transferring to any other persons the appointment of such officers or any of them.

III. JUDICIARY.

The Judiciary powers shall be exercised
First, by County courts and other inferior jurisdictions:
Secondly, by a General court & a High court of Chancery:
Thirdly, by a Court of Appeals.

County Courts, &c. The judges of the county courts and other inferior jurisdictions shall be appointed by the Administrator, subject to the negative of the privy council. They shall not be fewer than [five] in number. Their jurisdictions shall be defined from time to time by the legislature: and they shall be removable for misbehavior by the court of Appeals.

Genl. Court and High Ct. of Chancery The Judges of the General court and of the High court of Chancery shall be appointed by the Administrator and Privy council. If kept united they shall be [5] in number, if separate, there shall be [5] for the General court & [3] for the High court of Chancery. The appointment shall be made from the faculty of the law, and of such persons of that faculty as shall have actually exercised the same at the bar of some court or courts of record within this colony for [seven] years. They shall hold their commissions during good behavior, for breach of which they shall be removable by the court of Appeals. Their jurisdiction shall be defined from time to time by the Legislature.

Court of Appeals The Court of Appeals shall consist of not less than [7] nor more than [11] members, to be appointed by the house of Representatives: they shall hold their offices during good behavior, for breach of which they shall be removable by an act of the legislature only. Their jurisdiction shall be to determine finally all causes removed before them from the General Court or High Court of Chancery, or of the county courts or other inferior jurisdictions for misbehavior: [to try impeachments against high offenders lodged before them by the house of representatives for such crimes as shall hereafter be precisely defined by the Legislature, and for the punishment of which, the said legislature shall have previously prescribed certain and determinate pains.] In this court the judges of the General court and High court of Chancery shall have session and deliberative voice, but no suffrage.

All facts in causes whether of Chancery, Common, Ecclesiastical, or Marine law, shall be tried by **Juries** a jury upon evidence given vivâ voce, in open court: but where witnesses are out of the colony or unable to attend through sickness or other invincible necessity, their deposition may be submitted to the credit of the jury.

All Fines or Amercements shall be assessed, & **Fines, &c.** Terms of imprisonment for Contempts & Misdemeanors shall be fixed by the verdict of a Jury.

All Process Original & Judicial shall run in the **Process** name of the court from which it issues.

Two thirds of the members of the General court, **Quorum** High court of Chancery, or Court of Appeals shall be a Quorum to proceed to business.

IV. RIGHTS, PRIVATE AND PUBLIC.

Unappropriated or Forfeited lands shall be appro- **Lands** priated by the Administrator with the consent of the Privy council.

Every person of full age neither owning nor having owned [50] acres of land, shall be entitled to an appropriation of [50] acres or to so much as shall make up what he owns or has owned [50] acres in full and absolute dominion. And no other person shall be capable of taking an appropriation.

Lands heretofore holden of the crown in fee simple, and those hereafter to be appropriated shall be holden in full and absolute dominion, of no superior whatever.

No lands shall be appropriated until purchased of the Indian native proprietors; nor shall any purchases be made of them but on behalf of the public, by authority of acts of the General assembly to be passed for every purchase specially.

The territories contained within the charters erecting the colonies of Maryland, Pennsylvania, North and South Carolina, are hereby ceeded, released, & forever confirmed to the people of those colonies respectively, with all the rights of property, jurisdiction and government and all other rights whatsoever which might at any time heretofore have been claimed by this colony. The Western and Northern extent of this country shall in all other respects stand as fixed by the charter of*

until by act of the Legislature one or more territories shall be laid off Westward of the Alleghaney mountains for new colonies, which colonies shall be established on the same fundamental laws contained in this instrument, and shall be free and independent of this colony and of all the world.

Descents shall go according to the laws Gavelkind, save only that females shall have equal rights with males.

Slaves   No person hereafter coming into this county shall be held within the same in slavery under any pretext whatever.

Naturalization   All persons who by their own oath or affirmation, or by other testimony shall give satisfactory proof to any court of record in this colony that they propose to reside in the same [7] years at the least and who shall subscribe the fundamental laws, shall be considered as residents and entitled to all the rights of persons natural born.

Religion   All persons shall have full and free liberty of religious opinion; nor shall any be compelled to frequent or maintain any religious institution.

Arms   No freeman shall be debarred the use of arms [within his own lands].

Standing Armies   There shall be no standing army but in time of actual war.

Free Press   Printing presses shall be free, except so far as by commission of private injury cause may be given of private action.

Forfeitures   All Forfeitures heretofore going to the king, shall go the state; save only such as the legislature may hereafter abolish.

*Gaps here and elsewhere in the text reflect unfinished portions of the original manuscript.

The royal claim to Wrecks, waifs, strays, treasure- **Wrecks**
trove, royal mines, royal fish, royal birds, are declared to have been usurpations on common right.

No Salaries or Perquisites shall be given to any **Salaries**
officer but by some future act of the legislature. No
salaries shall be given to the Administrator, members of the
legislative houses, judges of the court of Appeals, judges of
the County courts, or other inferior jurisdictions, Privy counsellors, or Delegates to the American Congress: but the reasonable expences of the Administrator, members of the house
of representatives, judges of the court of Appeals, Privy counsellors, & Delegates for subsistence while acting in the duties
of their office, may be borne by the public, if the legislature
shall so direct.

No person shall be capable of acting in any office **Qualifica-**
Civil, Military [or Ecclesiastical] ~~The Qualifications~~ **tions**
~~of all not otherwise directed, shall be an oath of fidelity to~~
~~state and the having given no bribe to obtain their office~~ who
shall have given any bribe to obtain such office, or who shall
not previously take an oath of fidelity to the state.

None of these fundamental laws and principles of government shall be repealed or altered, but by the personal consent
of the people on summons to meet in their respective counties on one and the same day by an act of Legislature to be
passed for every special occasion: and if in such county meetings the people of two thirds of the counties shall give their
suffrage for any particular alteration or repeal referred to
them by the said act, the same shall be accordingly repealed
or altered, and such repeal or alteration shall take it's place
among these fundamentals and stand on the same footing
with them, in lieu of the article repealed or altered.

The laws heretofore in force in this colony shall remain in
force, except so far as they are altered by the foregoing fundamental laws, or so far as they may be hereafter altered by
acts of the Legislature.

A Bill for Establishing Religious Freedom

SECTION I. Well aware that the opinions and belief of men depend not on their own will, but follow involuntarily the evidence proposed to their minds; that Almighty God hath created the mind free, and manifested his supreme will that free it shall remain by making it altogether insusceptible of restraint; that all attempts to influence it by temporal punishments, or burthens, or by civil incapacitations, tend only to beget habits of hypocrisy and meanness, and are a departure from the plan of the holy author of our religion, who being lord both of body and mind, yet chose not to propagate it by coercions on either, as was in his Almighty power to do, but to extend it by its influence on reason alone; that the impious presumption of legislators and rulers, civil as well as ecclesiastical, who, being themselves but fallible and uninspired men, have assumed dominion over the faith of others, setting up their own opinions and modes of thinking as the only true and infallible, and as such endeavoring to impose them on others, hath established and maintained false religions over the greatest part of the world and through all time: That to compel a man to furnish contributions of money for the propagation of opinions which he disbelieves and abhors, is sinful and tyrannical; that even the forcing him to support this or that teacher of his own religious persuasion, is depriving him of the comfortable liberty of giving his contributions to the particular pastor whose morals he would make his pattern, and whose powers he feels most persuasive to righteousness; and is withdrawing from the ministry those temporary rewards, which proceeding from an approbation of their personal conduct, are an additional incitement to earnest and unremitting labours for the instruction of mankind; that our civil rights have no dependance on our religious opinions, any more than our opinions in physics or geometry; that therefore the proscribing any citizen as unworthy the public confidence by laying upon him an incapacity of being called to offices of trust and emolument, unless he profess or renounce this or that religious opinion, is depriving him injuriously of those privileges and advantages to which, in common with his fellow citizens, he has a natural right; that it tends also to corrupt the principles of that very religion it is meant to encourage, by bribing, with a monopoly of worldly honours and emoluments, those who will externally profess and conform to it; that though indeed these are criminal who do not withstand such temptation, yet neither are those innocent who lay the bait in their way; that the opinions of men are not the object of civil government, nor under its jurisdiction; that to suffer the civil magistrate to intrude his powers into the field of opinion and to restrain the profession or propagation of principles on supposition of their ill tendency is a dangerous falacy, which at once destroys all religious liberty, because he being of course judge of that tendency will make his opinions the rule of judgment, and approve or condemn the sentiments of others only as they shall square with or differ from his own; that it is time enough for the rightful purposes of civil government for its officers to interfere when principles break out into overt acts against peace and good order; and finally, that truth is great and will prevail if left to herself; that she is the proper and sufficient antagonist to error, and has nothing to fear from the conflict unless by human interposition disarmed of her natural weapons, free argument and debate; errors ceasing to be dangerous when it is permitted freely to contradict them.

SECT. II. WE the General Assembly of Virginia do enact that no man shall be compelled to frequent or support any religious worship, place, or ministry whatsoever, nor shall be enforced, restrained, molested, or burthened in his body or goods, nor shall otherwise suffer, on account of his religious opinions or belief; but that all men shall be free to profess, and by argument to maintain, their opinions in matters of religion, and that the same shall in no wise diminish, enlarge, or affect their civil capacities.

SECT. III. AND though we well know that this Assembly, elected by the people for the ordinary purposes of legislation only, have no power to restrain the acts of succeeding Assemblies, constituted with powers equal to our own, and that therefore to declare this act irrevocable would be of no effect in law; yet we are free to declare, and do declare, that the rights hereby asserted are of the natural rights of mankind, and that if any act shall be hereafter passed to repeal the present or to narrow its operation, such act will be an infringement of natural right.

A Bill for Proportioning Crimes and Punishments

SECTION I. Whereas it frequently happens that wicked and dissolute men, resigning themselves to the dominion of inordinate passions, commit violations on the lives, liberties, and property of others, and the secure enjoyment of these having principally induced men to enter into society, government would be defective in its principal purpose, were it not to restrain such criminal acts by inflicting due punishments on those who perpetrate them; but it appears at the same time equally deducible from the purposes of society, that a member thereof, committing an inferior injury, does not wholly forfeit the protection of his fellow citizens, but after suffering a punishment in proportion to his offence, is entitled to their protection from all greater pain, so that it becomes a duty in the Legislature to arrange in a proper scale the crimes which it may be necessary for them to repress, and to adjust thereto a corresponding gradation of punishments. And whereas the reformation of offenders, though an object worthy the attention of the laws, is not effected at all by capital punishments which exterminate instead of reforming, and should be the last melancholy resource against those whose existence is become inconsistent with the safety of their fellow citizens; which also weaken the State by cutting off so many, who, if reformed, might be restored sound members to society, who, even under a course of correction, might be rendered useful in various labours for the public, and would be, living, and long-continued spectacles to deter others from committing the like offences. And forasmuch as the experience of all ages and countries hath shewn, that cruel and sanguinary laws defeat their own purpose, by engaging the benevolence of mankind to withhold prosecutions, to smother testimony, or to listen to it with bias; and by producing in many instances a total dispensation and impunity under the names of pardon and privilege of clergy; when, if the punishment were only proportioned to the injury, men would feel it their inclination, as well as their duty, to see the laws observed; and the power of dispensation, so dangerous

and mischievous, which produces crimes by holding up a
hope of impunity, might totally be abolished, so that men
while contemplating to perpetrate a crime would see their
punishment ensuing as necessarily as effects follow their
causes; for rendering crimes and punishments, therefore,
more proportionate to each other,

SECT. II. Be it enacted by the General Assembly, that no
crime shall be henceforth punished by the deprivation of life
or limb,* except those herein after ordained to be so punished.

SECT. III.† If a man do levy war‡ against the Commonwealth *in the same*, or be adherent to the enemies of the Commonwealth *within the same*,§ giving to them aid or comfort
in the Commonwealth, or elsewhere, and thereof be convicted, of open deed, by the evidence of two sufficient and
lawful witnesses, or his own voluntary confession, the said
cases, and no‖ others, shall be adjudged treasons which extend

*This takes away the punishment of cutting off the hand of a person strik-
ing another, or drawing his sword in one of the superior courts of justice.
Stamf. P. C. 38. 33. H. 8. c. 12. In an earlier stage of the Common law, it was
death. Gif hwa gefeohte on Cyninges huse sy he scyldig ealles his yrfes, and
sy on Cyninges dome hwæther he lif age de nage; si quis in regis domo
pugnet, perdat omnem suam hæreditatem, et in regis sit arbitrio, possideat
vitam an non possideat. Ll. Inae. 6. Gif hwa on Cyninges healle gefeohte,
oththe his wæpne gebrede, and hine mon gefo, sy thæt on Cyninges dome
swa death, swa lif, swa he him forgyfan wille: si quis in aula regia pugnet,
vel arma sua extrahat et capiatur, sit in regis arbitrio tam mors quam vita,
sicut ei condonare voluerit. Ll. Alfr. 7, Gif hwa on Cyninges hirede gefeohte
tholige thæt lifes, buton se Cyning him gearian wille: si quis in regia dimicat,
perdat vitam, nisi rex hoc illi condonare velit. Ll. Cnuti. 56. 4. Bl. 125.

†25. E. 3. st. 5. c. 2. 7. W. 3. c. 3. § 2.

‡Though the crime of an accomplice in treason is not here described, yet,
Lord Coke says, the partaking and maintaining a treason herein described,
makes him a principal in that treason: it being a rule that in treason all are
principals. 3 Inst. 138. 2 Inst. 590. 1 H. 6. 5.

§These words in the English statute narrow its operation. A man adhering
to the enemies of the Commonwealth, in a foreign country, would certainly
not be guilty of treason with us, if these words be retained. The convictions
of treason of that kind in England have been under that branch of the statute
which makes the compassing the king's death treason. Foster 196, 197. But as
we omit that branch, we must by other means reach this flagrant case.

‖The stat. 25. E. 3. directs all other cases of treasons to await the opinion
of Parliament. This has the effect of negative words, excluding all other treasons. As we drop that part of the statute, we must, by negative words, pre-

to the commonwealth, and the person so convicted shall suffer death, by hanging,* and shall forfeit his lands and goods to the commonwealth.

SECT. IV. If any person commit petty treason, or a husband murder his wife, a parent† his child, or a child his parent, he shall suffer death, by hanging, and his body be delivered to Anatomists to be dissected.

SECT. V. Whosoever committeth murder by poisoning, shall suffer death by poison.

SECT. VI. Whosoever committeth murder by way of duel, shall suffer death by hanging; and if he were the challenger,

---

vent an inundation of common law treasons. I strike out the word "it," therefore, and insert "the said cases, and no others." Quære, how far those negative words may effect the case of accomplices above mentioned? Though if their case was within the statute, so as that it needed not await the opinion of Parliament, it should seem to be also within our act, so as not be ousted by the negative words.

*This implies "by the neck." See 2 Hawk. 544 notes n. o.

† By the stat. 21. Jac. 1. c. 27. and Act Ass. 1170. c. 12. concealment by the mother of the death of a bastard child is made murder. In justification of this, it is said, that shame is a feeling which operates so strongly on the mind, as frequently to induce the mother of such a child to murder it, in order to conceal her disgrace. The act of concealment, therefore, proves she was influenced by shame, and that influence produces a presumption that she murdered the child. The effect of this law then is, to make what, in its nature, is only presumptive evidence of a murder conclusive of that fact. To this I answer, 1. So many children die before or soon after birth, that to presume all those murdered who are found dead, is a presumption which will lead us oftener wrong than right, and consequently would shed more blood than it would save. 2. If the child were born dead, the mother would naturally choose rather to conceal it, in hopes of still keeping a good character in the neighborhood. So that the act of concealment is far from proving the guilt of murder on the mother. 3. If shame be a powerful affection of the mind, is not parental love also? Is it not the strongest affection known? Is it not greater than even that of self-preservation? While we draw presumptions from shame, one affection of the mind against the life of the prisoner, should we not give some weight to presumptions from parental love, an affection at least as strong, in favor of life? If concealment of the fact is a presumptive evidence of murder, so strong as to overbalance all other evidence that may possibly be produced to take away the presumption, why not trust the force of this incontestable presumption to the jury, who are, in a regular course, to hear presumptive, as well as positive testimony? If the presumption arising from the act of concealment, may be destroyed by proof positive or circumstantial to the contrary, why should the legislature preclude that contrary proof? Objection. The crime is difficult to prove, being usually committed in

his body, after death, shall be gibbetted.* He who removeth
it from the gibbet shall be guilty of a misdemeanor, and the
officer shall see that it be replaced.

SECT. VII. Whosoever shall commit murder in any other
way shall suffer death by hanging.

SECT. VIII. And in all cases of Petty treason and murder,
one half of the lands and goods of the offender shall be forfeited to the next of kin to the person killed, and the other
half descend and go to his own representatives. Save only,
where one shall slay the challenger in a duel,† in which case,
no part of his lands or goods shall be forfeited to the kindred
of the party slain, but instead thereof, a moiety shall go to
the commonwealth.

SECT. IX. The same evidence‡ shall suffice, and order and
course§ of trial be observed in cases of Petty treason as in
those of other‖ murders.

---

secret. Answer. But circumstantial proof will do; for example, marks of violence, the behavior, countenance, &c. of the prisoner, &c. And if conclusive
proof be difficult to be obtained, shall we therefore fasten irremovably upon
equivocal proof? Can we change the nature of what is contestable, and make
it incontestable? Can we make that conclusive which God and nature have
made inconclusive? Solon made no law against parricide, supposing it impossible that any one could be guilty of it; and the Persians, from the same
opinion, adjudged all who killed their reputed parents to be bastards; and
although parental be yet stronger than filial affection, we admit saticide
proved on the most equivocal testimony, whilst they rejected all proof of an
act certainly not more repugnant to nature, as of a thing impossible, unprov-
able. See Beccaria, § 31.

*25. G. 2. c. 37.

†Quære, if the estates of both parties in a duel, should not be forfeited?
The deceased is equally guilty with a suicide.

‡Quære, if these words may not be omitted? By the Common law, one
witness in treason was sufficient. Foster 233. Plowd. 8. a. Mirror c. 3. § 34.
Waterhouse on Fortesc. de laud. 252. Carth. 144. per Holt. But Lord Coke,
contra 3 inst. 26. The stat. 1. E. 6. c. 12. & 5. E. 6. c. 11. first required two
witnesses in treason. The clause against high treason supra, does the same as
to high treason; but it seems if 1st and 5th E. 6. are dropped, Petty treason
will be tried and proved, as at Common law, by one witness. But quære,
Lord Coke being contra, whose opinion it is ever dangerous to neglect.

§These words are intended to take away the peremptory challenge of
thirty-five jurors. The same words being used 1. 2. Ph. & M. c. 10. are deemed
to have restored the peremptory challenge in high treason; and consequently
are sufficient to take it away. Foster 237.

‖Petty treason is considered in law only as an aggravated murder. Foster

SECT. X. Whosoever shall be guilty of manslaughter,* shall, for the first offence, be condemned to hard† labour for seven years in the public works; shall forfeit one half of his lands and goods to the next of kin to the person slain; the other half to be sequestered during such term, in the hands, and to the use, of the commonwealth, allowing a reasonable part of the profits for the support of his family. The second offence shall be deemed murder.

SECT. XI. And where persons meaning to commit a trespass‡ only, or larceny, or other unlawful deed, and doing an act from which involuntary homicide hath ensued, have heretofore been adjudged guilty of manslaughter or of murder, by transferring such their unlawful intention to an act, much more penal than they could have in probable contemplation; no such case shall hereafter be deemed manslaughter unless manslaughter was intended, nor murder, unless murder was intended.

SECT. XII. In other cases of homicide the law will not add to the miseries of the party, by punishments or forfeitures.§

---

107. 323. A pardon of all murders, pardons Petty treason. 1 Hale P. C. 378. see 2 H. P. C. 340. 342. It is also included in the word "felony," so that a pardon of all felonies, pardons Petty treason.

*Manslaughter is punishable at law, by burning in the hands, and forfeiture of chattels.

†It is best, in this act, to lay down principles only, in order that it may not forever be undergoing change; and, to carry into effect the minuter parts of it, frame a bill "for the employment and government of felons, or malefactors, condemned to labor for the Commonwealth," which may serve as an Appendix to this, and in which all the particulars requisite may be directed; and as experience will, from time to time, be pointing out amendments, these may be made without touching this fundamental act. See More's Utopia p. 50. for some good hints. Fugitives might, in such a bill, be obliged to work two days for every one they absent themselves.

‡The shooting at a wild fowl, and killing a man, is homicide by misadventure. Shooting at a pullet, without any design to take it away, is manslaughter; and with a design to take it away, is murder. 6 Sta. tr. 222. To shoot at the poultry of another, and thereby set fire to his house, is arson, in the opinion of some. Dalt. c. 116. 1. Hale's P. C. 569. c. contra.

§Beccaria. § 32. Suicide. Homicides are, 1. Justifiable. 2. Excusable. 3. Felonious. For the last, punishments have been already provided. The first are held to be totally without guilt, or rather commendable. The second are in some cases not quite unblamable. These should subject the party to marks of contrition; viz., the killing of a man in defence of property; so also in defence

SECT. XIII. Whenever sentence of death shall have been pronounced against any person for treason or murder, execution thereof shall be done on the next day but one, after

---

of one's person, which is a species of excusable homicide; because, although cases may happen where these also are commendable, yet most frequently they are done on too slight appearance of danger; as in return for a blow, kick, fillip, &c.; or on a person's getting into a house, not animo furandi, but perhaps veneris causa, &c. Bracton says, "si quis furem nocturnum occident, ita demum impune foret, si parcere ei sine periculo suo non potuit, si autem potuit, aliter erit." "Item erit si quis hamsokne quæ dicitur invasio domus contra pacem domini regis in domo sua se defenderit, et invasor occisus fuerit; impersecutus et insultus remanebit, si ille quem invasit aliter se defendere non potuit; dicitur enim quod non est dignus habere pacem qui non vult observare eam." L. 3. c. 23. § 3. "Qui latronem occiderit, non tenetur, nocturnum vel diurum, si aliter periculum evadere non possit; tenetur tamen si possit. Item non tenetur si per infortunium, et non animo et voluntate occidendi, nec dolus, nec culpa ejus inveniatur." L. 3. c. 36. § 1. The stat. 24. H. 8. c. 5. is therefore merely declaratory of the Common law. See on the general subject Puffend. 2. 5. § 10. 11. 12. 16. 17. Excusable homicides are by misadventure, or in self-defence. It is the opinion of some lawyers, that the Common law punished these with death, and that the statute of Marlbridge c. 26. and Gloucester, c. 9. first took away this by giving them title to a pardon, as matter of right, and a writ of restitution of their goods. See 2. Inst. 148. 315. 3. Inst. 55. Bracton L. 3. c. 4. § 2. Fleta L. 1. c. 23. § 14. 15. 21. E. 3. 23. But it is believed never to have been capital. 1. H. P. C. 425. 1 Hawk. 75. Foster, 282. 4. Bl. 188. It seems doubtful also, whether at Common law, the party forfeited all his chattels in this case, or only paid a weregild. Foster, ubi supra, doubts, and thinks it of no consequence, as the statute of Gloucester entitles the party to Royal grace, which goes as well to forfeiture as life. To me there seems no reason for calling these excusable homicides, and the killing a man in defence of property, a justifiable homicide. The latter is less guiltless than misadventure or self-defence.

Suicide is by law punishable by forfeiture of chattels. This bill exempts it from forfeiture. The suicide injures the State less than he who leaves it with his effects. If the latter then be not punished, the former should not. As to the example, we need not fear its influence. Men are too much attached to life, to exhibit frequent instances of depriving themselves of it. At any rate, the quasi-punishment of confiscation will not prevent it. For if one be found who can calmly determine to renounce life, who is so weary of his existence here, as rather to make experiment of what is beyond the grave, can we suppose him, in such a state of mind, susceptible of influence from the losses to his family from confiscation? That men in general, too, disapprove of this severity, is apparent from the constant practice of juries finding the suicide in a state of insanity; because they have no other way of saving the forfeiture. Let it then be done away.

such sentence, unless it be Sunday, and then on the Monday following.*

SECT. XIV. Whosoever shall be guilty of rape,† *polygamy*,‡

*Beccaria. § 19. 25. G. 2. c. 37.

†13. E. 1. c. 34. Forcible abduction of a woman having substance is felony by 3. H. 7. c. 2. 3 Inst. 61. 4 Bl. 208. If goods be taken, it will be felony as to them, without this statute; and as to the abduction of the woman, quære if not better to leave that, and also kidnapping, 4. Bl. 219. to the Common law remedies, viz., fine, imprisonment, and pillory, Raym. 474. 2 Show. 221. Skin. 47. Comb. 10. the writs of Homine replegiando, Capias in Withernam, Habeas corpus, and the action of trespass? Rape was felony at the Common law. 3. Inst. 60. but see 2. Inst. 181. further—for its definition see 2. Inst. 180. Bracton, L. 3. c. 28. § 1. says the punishment of rape is "amissio membrorum, ut sit membrum pro membro, quia virgo, cum corrumpitur, membrum amittit, et ideo corruptor puniatur in eo in quo deliquit; oculus igitur amittat propter aspectum decoris quo virginem concupivit; amittat et testiculos qui calorem stupri induxerunt. Olim quidem corruptores virginitatis et castitatis suspendebantur et eorum fautores, &c. Modernis tamen temporibus aliter observatur," &c. And Fleta, "solet justiciarius pro quolibet mahemio ad amissionem testiculorum vel oculorum convictum condemnare, sed non sine errore, eo quod id judicium nisi in corruptione virginum tantum competebat; nam pro virginitatis corruptione solebant abscidi et merito judiciari, ut sic pro membro quod abstulit, membrum per quod deliquit amitteret, viz., testiculos, qui calorem stupri induxerunt," &c. Fleta, L. 1. c. 40. § 4. "Gif theow man theowne to nydhed genyde, gabte mid his eowende:" "Si servus servam ad stuprum coegerit, compenset hoc virga sua virili. Si quis puellam," &c. Ll. Aelfridi. 25. "Hi purgist femme per forze forfait ad les membres." Ll. Gul. conq. 19. In Dyer, 305, a man was indicted, and found guilty of a rape on a girl of seven years old. The court "doubted of the rape of so tender a girl; but if she had been nine years old, it would have been otherwise." 14. Eliz. Therefore the statute 18. Eliz. c. 6. says, "For plain declaration of law, be it enacted, that if any person shall unlawfully and carnally know and abuse any woman child, under the age of ten years, &c., he shall suffer as a felon, without allowance of clergy." Lord Hale, however, 1. P. C. 630. thinks it rape independent of that statute, to know carnally, a girl under twelve, the age of consent. Yet 4. Bl. 212. seems to neglect this opinion; and as it was founded on the words of 3. E. 1. c. 13. and this is with us omitted, the offence of carnally knowing a girl under twelve, or ten years of age, will not be distinguished from that of any other.

‡1. Jac. 1. c. 11. Polygamy was not penal till the statute 1. Jac. The law contented itself with the nullity of the act. 4. Bl. 163. 3. Inst. 88.

But no one shall be punished for Polygamy, who shall have married after probable information of the death of his or her husband or wife, or after his or her husband or wife, hath absented him or herself, so that no notice of his or her being alive hath reached such person for seven years together, or hath suffered the punishments before prescribed for rape, polygamy, or sodomy.

or sodomy* with man or woman, shall be punished; if a man, by castration,† a woman, by boring through the cartilage of her nose a hole of one half inch in diameter at the least.

SECT. XV. Whosoever on purpose,‡ shall disfigure another, by cutting out or disabling the tongue, slitting or cutting off a nose, lip, or ear, branding, or otherwise, shall be maimed, or disfigured in like§ sort; or if that cannot be, for want of the same part, then as nearly as may be, in some other part of at least equal value and estimation, in the opinion of a jury, and moreover, shall forfeit one half of his lands and goods to the sufferer.

---

*§ 25. H. 8. c. 6. Buggery is twofold. 1. With mankind, 2. with beasts. Buggery is the Genus, of which Sodomy and Bestiality, are the species. 12. Co. 37. says, "note that Sodomy is with mankind." But Finch's L. B. 3. c. 24. "Sodomiary is a carnal copulation against nature, to wit, of man or woman in the same sex, or of either of them with beasts." 12. Co. 36. says, "it appears by the ancient authorities of the law that this was felony." Yet the 25. H. 8. declares it felony, as if supposed not to be so. Britton, c. 9. says, that Sodomites are to be burnt. F. N. B. 269. b. Fleta, L. 1. c. 37. says, "pecorantes et Sodomitæ in terra vivi confodiantur." The Mirror makes it treason. Bestiality can never make any progress; it cannot therefore be injurious to society in any great degree, which is the true measure of criminality in foro civili, and will ever be properly and severely punished, by universal derision. It may, therefore, be omitted. It was anciently punished with death, as it has been latterly. Ll. Aelfrid. 31. and 25. H. 8. c. 6. see Beccaria. § 31. Montesq.

† Bracton, Fleta, &c.

‡ 22. 23. Car. 2. c. 1. Maiming was felony at the Common law. Britton, c. 25. 'Mahemium autem dici poteri, aubia aliquis in aliqua parte sui corporis læsionem acceperit, per quam affectus sit inutilis ad pugnandum: ut si manus amputetur, vel pes, oculus privetur, vel scerda de osse capitis laveter, vel si quis dentes præcisores amiserit, vel castratus fuerit, et talis pro mahemiato poterit adjudicari.' Fleta L. 1. c. 40. 'Et volons que nul maheme ne soit tenus forsque de membre tollet dount home es plus feble a combatre, sicome del oyl, ou de la mayn, ou del pie, ou de la tete debruse, ou de les dentz devant.' Britton, c. 25. For further definitions, see Bracton, L. 3. c. 24 § 3. 4. Finch L. B. 3. c. 12. Co. L. 126. a. b. 288. a. 3. Bl. 121. 4. Bl. 205. Stamf. P. C. L. 1. c. 41. I do not find any of these definitions confine the offence to wilful and malicious perpetrations of it. 22. 23. Car. 2. c. 1. called the Coventry act, has the words 'on purpose and of malice forethought.' Nor does the Common law prescribe the same punishment for disfiguring, as for maiming.

§ The punishment was by retaliation. "Et come ascun appele serra de tele felonie atteint et attende jugement, si soit le jugement tiel que il perde autriel membre come il avera tollet al pleintyfe. Et sy la pleynte soi faite de femme que avera tollet a home ses membres, en tiel cas perdra la femme la une meyn

SECT. XVI. Whosoever shall counterfeit* any coin current by law within this commonwealth, or any paper bills issued in the nature of money, or of certificates of loan, on the credit of this commonwealth, or of all or any of the United States of America, or any Inspectors' notes for tobacco, or shall pass any such counterfeited coin, paper bills, or notes, knowing them to be counterfeit; or, for the sake of lucre, shall diminish† each, or any such coin, shall be condemned to hard labour six years in the public works, and shall forfeit all his lands and goods to the commonwealth.

SECT. XVII. The making false any such paper bill, or note, shall be deemed counterfeiting.

SECT. XVIII.‡ Whosoever committeth arson, shall be con-

---

par jugement, come le membre dount ele axera trespasse." Britton, c. 25. Fleta, B. 1. c. 40. Ll. Ælfr. 19. 40.

*25. E. 3. st. 5 c. 2. 5. El. c. 11. 18. El. c. 1. 8. 9. W. 3. c. 26. 15. 16. G. 2. c. 28. 7. Ann. c. 25. By the laws of Æthelstan and Canute, this was punished by cutting off the hand. "Gif se mynetere ful wurthe slea man tha hand of, the he that ful mid worthe and sette uppon tha mynet smiththan." In English characters and words "if the minter foul [criminal] wert, slay the hand off, that he the foul [crime] with wrought, and set upon the mint-smithery." Ll. Aethelst. 14. "Et si quis praeter hanc, falsam fecerit, perdat manum quacum falsam confecit." Ll. Cnuti. 8. It had been death by the Ll. Æthelredi sub fine. By those of H. 1. "si quis cum falso denario inventus fuerit—fiat justitia mea, saltem de dextro pugno et de testiculis." Anno 1108. Operæ pretium vero est audire quam severus rex fuerit in pravos. Monetarios enim fere omnes totius Angliæ fecit ementulari, et manus dextras abscindi, quia mone-tam furtive corruperant. Wilkins ib. et anno 1125. When the Common law became settled, it appears to have been punishable by death. "Est aliud genus criminis quod sub nomine falsi continetur, et tangit coronam domini regis, et ultimum inducit supplicium, sicut de illis qui falsam fabricant monetam, et qui de re non reproba, faciunt reprobam; sicut sunt retonsores denariorum." Bract. L. 3. c § 2. Fleta, L. 1. c. 22. § 4. Lord Hale thinks it was deemed petty treason at common law. 1. H. P. C. 220. 224. The bringing in false money with *intent* to merchandize, and make payment of it, is treason, by 25. E. 3. But the best proof of the intention, is the act of passing it, and why not leave room for repentance here, as in other cases of felonies intended? 1. H. P. C. 229.

†Clipping, filing, rounding, impairing, scaling, lightening, (the words in the statutes) are included in "diminishing;" gilding, in the word "casing;" coloring in the word "washing;" and falsifying, or making, is "counter-feiting."

‡43 L. c. 13. confined to four counties. 22. 23. Car. 2. c. 7. 9. G. 1. c. 22. 9. G. 3. c. 29.

demned to hard labour five years in the public works, and shall make good the loss of the sufferers threefold.*

SECT. XIX. If any person shall, within this Commonwealth, or, being a citizen thereof, shall without the same, wilfully destroy† or run‡ away with any sea-vessel, or goods laden on board thereof, or plunder or pilfer any wreck, he shall be condemned to hard labour five years in the public works, and shall make good the loss of the sufferers threefold.

SECT. XX. Whosoever committeth a robbery,§ shall be condemned to hard labour four years in the public works, and shall make double reparation to the persons injured.

SECT. XXI. Whatsoever act, if committed on any mansion-

---

*Arson was a felony at Common law—3. Inst. 66; punished by a fine, Ll. Aethelst. 6. But Ll. Cnuti, 61. make it a "scelus inexpiable." "Hus brec and bærnet and open thyfth æberemorth and hlaford swice æfter woruld laga is botleds." Word for word, "house break and burnt, and open theft, and manifest murther, and lord-treachery, afterworld's law is bootless." Bracton says it was punished by death. "Si quis turbida seditione incendium fecerit nequiter et in felonia, vel ob inimicitias, vel praedandi causa, capitali puniatur poena vel sententia." Bract. L. 3. 27. He defines it as commissible by burning "aedes alienas." Ib. Britton, c. 9. "Ausi soit enquis de ceux que felonisement en temps de pees eient autre *blees* ou autre *mesons* ars, et ceux que serrount de ceo atteyntz, soient ars issint que eux soient punys par mesme cele chose dount ilz pecherent." Fleta, L. 1. c. 37. is a copy of Bracton. The Mirror c. 1. § 8. says, "Ardours sont que ardent citie, ville, maison home, maison beast, ou auters chatelx, de lour felonie en temps de pace pour haine ou vengeance." Again, c. 2. § 11. pointing out the words of the appellor "jeo dise que Sebright, &c., entiel meason ou *biens* mist de feu." Coke 3. Inst. 67. says, "the ancient authors extended this felony further than houses, viz., to sacks of corn, waynes or carts of coal, wood or other goods." He denies it as commissible, not only on the inset houses, parcel of the mansion house, but the outset also, as barn, stable, cowhouse, sheep house, dairy house, mill house, and the like, parcel of the mansion house. But "burning of a barn, being no parcel of a mansion house, is no felony," unless there be corn or hay within it. Ib. The 22. 23. Car. 2. and 9. G. 1. are the principal statutes against arson. They extend the offence beyond the Common law.

†1. Ann. st. 2. c. 9. 12. Ann. c. 18. 4. G. 1. c. 12. 26. G. 2. c. 19.

‡11. 12. W. 3. c. 7.

§Robbery was a felony at Common law. 3 Inst. 68. "Scelus inexpiable," by the Ll. Cnuti. 61. [See before in Arson.] It was punished with death. Britt. c. 15, "de robbours et de larouns et de semblables mesfesours, soit ausi ententivement enquis—et tauntost soient ceux robbours juges a la mort." Fleta says, "si quis convictus fuerit de bonis viri robbatis vel asportatis ad sectam regis judicium capitale subibit." L. 1. c. 39. See also Bract. L. 3. c. 32. § 1.

house, would be deemed a burglary,* shall be burglary, if committed on any other house; and he who is guilty of burglary, shall be condemned to hard labour four years in the public works, and shall make double reparation to the persons injured.

SECT. XXII. Whatsoever act, if committed in the night time, shall constitute the crime of burglary, shall, if committed in the day, be deemed house-breaking†; and whoever is

*Burglary was felony at the Common law. 3 Inst. 63. It was not distinguished by ancient authors, except the Mirror, from simple House-breaking, ib. 65. Burglary and House-breaking were called "Hamsockne diximus etiam de pacis violatione et de immunitatibus domus, si quis hoc in posterum fecerit ut perdat omne quod habet, et sit in regis arbitrio utrum vitam habeat. Eac we quædon be mundbryce and be ham socnum, sethe hit ofer this do thæt he dolie ealles thæs the age, and sy on Cyninges dome hwæther he life age; and we quoth of mound-breach, and of home-seeking he who it after this do, that he dole all that he owe [owns], and is in king's doom whether he life owes [owns.]" Ll. Eadmundi, c. 6. and see Ll. Cnuti. 61. "hus brec," in notes on Arson. ante. A Burglar was also called a Burgessor. "Et soit enquis de Burgessours et sunt tenus Burgessours trestous ceux que *felonisement* en temps de pees debrusont esglises ou auter mesons, ou murs ou portes de nos cytes, ou de nos Burghes." Britt. c. 10. "Burglaria est nocturna diruptio habitaculi alicu jus, vel ecclesiæ, etiam murorum, partarumve civitatis aut burgi, ad feloniam aliquam perpetrandam. *Noctanter* dico, recentiores secutus; veteres enim hoc non adjungunt." Spelm. gloss. verb. Burglaria. It was punished with death. Ib. citn. from the office of a Coroner. It may be committed in the outset houses, as well as inset. 3 Inst. 65. though not under the same roof or contiguous, provided they be within the Curtilage or Homestall. 4 Bl. 225. As by the Common law, all felonies were clergiable, the stat. 23 H. 8. c. 1. 5. E. 6. c. 9. and 18 El. c. 7. first distinguished them, by taking the clerical privilege of impunity from the principals, and 3. 4. W. M. c. 9. from accessories before the fact. No *statute* defines what Burglary is. The 12 Ann. c. 7. decides the doubt whether, where breaking is subsequent to entry, it is Burglary. Bacon's Elements had affirmed, and 1. H. P. C. 554. had denied it. Our bill must distinguish them by different degrees of punishment.

†At the Common law, the offence of Housebreaking was not distinguished from Burglary, and neither of them from any other larceny. The statutes at first took away clergy from Burglary, which made a leading distinction between the two offences. Later statutes, however, have taken clergy from so many cases of Housebreaking, as nearly to bring the offences together again. These are 23 H. 8. c. 1. 1 E. 6. c. 12. 5 and 6 E. 6. c. 9. 3 and 4 W. M. c. 9. 39 El. c. 15. 10 and 11 W. 3 c. 23. 12 Ann. c. 7. See Barr. 428. 4 Bl. 240. The circumstances which in these statutes characterize the offence, seem to have been occasional and unsystematical. The houses on which Burglary may be committed, and the circumstances which constitute that crime being ascertained, it will be better to define Housebreaking by the same subjects and

guilty thereof, shall be condemned to hard labour three years in the public works, and shall make reparation to the persons injured.

SECT. XXIII. Whosoever shall be guilty of horse-stealing,* shall be condemned to hard labour three years in the public works, and shall make reparation to the person injured.

SECT. XXIV. Grand larceny† shall be where the goods stolen are of the value of five dollars; and whosoever shall be guilty thereof, shall be forthwith put in the pillory for one half hour, shall be condemned to hard labour‡ two years in the public works, and shall make reparation to the person injured.

---

circumstances, and let the crimes be distinguished only by the hour at which they are committed, and the degree of punishment.

*The offence of Horse-stealing seems properly distinguishable from other larcenies, here, where these animals generally run at large, the temptation being so great and frequent, and the facility of commission so remarkable. See 1 E. 6. c. 12. 23 E. 6. c. 33. 31 El. c. 12.

† The distinction between grand and petty larceny, is very ancient. At first 8d. was the sum which constituted grand larceny. Ll. Æthelst. c. 1. "Ne parcatur ulli furi, qui furtum manutenens captus sit, supra 12. annos nato, et supra 8. denarios." Afterwards, in the same king's reign it was raised to 12d. "non parcatur alicui furi ultra 12 denarios, et ultra 12 annos nato—ut occidemus illum et capiamus omne quod possidet, et imprimis sumamus rei furto ablatæ pretium ab hærede, ac dividatur postea reliquum in duas partes, una pars uxori, si munda, et facinoris conscia non sit; et residuum in duo, dimidium capiat rex, dimidium societas." Ll. Aethelst. Wilkins, p. 65.

‡Ll. Inae. c. 7. "Si quis furetur ita ut uxor ejus et infans ipsius nesciant, solvat 60. solidos pœnæ loco. Si autem furetur testantibus omnibus hæredibus suis, *abeant omnes in servitutem*." Ina was king of the West-Saxons, and began to reign A. C. 688. After the union of the Heptarchy, i. e. temp. Æthelst, inter 924 and 940, we find it punishable with death as above. So it was inter 1017 and 1035, i. e. temp. Cnuti. Ll. Cnuti. 61. cited in notes on Arson. In the time of William the conqueror, it seems to have been made punishable by fine only. Ll. Gul. conq. apud Wilk. p. 218, 220. This commutation, however, was taken away by Ll. H. 1. anno 1108. "Si quis in furto vel latrocinio deprehensus fuisset, suspenderetur; sublata wirgildorum, id est, pecuniaræ redemptionis lege." Larceny is the felonious taking and carrying away of the personal goods of another. 1. As to the taking, the 3. 4. W. M. c. 9 § 5. is not additional to the Common law, but declaratory of it; because where only the care or use, and not the possession, of things is delivered, to take them was larceny at the Common law. The 33 H. 6. c. 1. and 21, H. 8. c. 7. indeed, have added to the Common law, by making it larceny in a servant to convert things of his master's. But quære, if they should be imitated more than as to other breaches of trust in general. 2. As to the subject of larceny,

SECT. XXV. Petty larceny shall be, where the goods stolen are of less value than five dollars; whosoever shall be guilty thereof, shall be forthwith put in the pillory for a quarter of an hour, shall be condemned to hard labour for one year in the public works, and shall make reparation to the persons injured.

SECT. XXVI. Robbery* or larceny of bonds, bills obligatory, bills of exchange, or promissory notes, for the payment of money or tobacco, lottery tickets, paper bills issued in the nature of money, or certificates of loan on the credit of this commonwealth, or of all or any of the United States of America, or inspectors notes for tobacco, shall be punished in the same manner as robbery or larceny of the money or tobacco due on, or represented by such papers.

SECT. XXVII. Buyers† and receivers of goods taken by way of robbery or larceny, knowing them to have been so taken, shall be deemed accessaries to such robbery or larceny after the fact.

SECT. XXVIII. Prison-breakers,‡ also, shall be deemed accessaries after the fact, to traitors or felons whom they enlarge from prison.§

---

4 G. 2. c. 32. 6 G. 3. c. 36. 48. 45. El. c. 7. 15 Car. 2. c. 2. 23 G. 2. c. 26. 31 G. 2. c. 35. 9 G. 3. c. 41. 25 G. 2. c. 10. have extended larceny to things of various sorts either real, or fixed to the reality. But the enumeration is unsystematical, and in this country, where the produce of the earth is so spontaneous, as to have rendered things of this kind scarcely a breach of civility or good manners, in the eyes of the people, quære, if it would not too much enlarge the field of Criminal law? The same may be questioned of 9 G. 1. c. 22. 13 Car. 2. c. 10. 10 G. 2. c. 32. 5 G. 3. c. 14. 22 and 23 Car. 2. c. 25. 37 E. 3. c. 19. making it felony to steal animals feræ naturæ.

*2 G. 2. c. 25 § 3. 7 G. 3. c. 50.

†3. 4. W. M. c. 9. § 4. 5 Ann. c. 31. § 5. 4 G. 1. c. 11. § 1.

‡1 E. 2.

§ Breach of prison at the Common law was capital, without regard to the crime for which the party was committed. "Cum pro criminis qualitate in carcerem recepti fuerint, conspiraverint (ut ruptis vinculis aut fracto carcere) evadant, amplius (quam causa pro qua recepti sunt exposeit) puniendi sunt, videlicet ultimo supplicio, quamvis ex eo crimine innocentes inveniantur, propter quod inducti sunt in carcerem et imparcati." Bracton L. 3. c. 9. § 4. Britt. c. 11. Fleta, L. 1. c. 26. § 4. Yet in the Y. B. Hill. 1. H. 7. 2. Hussey says, that by the opinion of Billing and Coke, and all the justices, it was a felony in strangers only, but not in the prisoner himself. S. C. Fitz. Abr.

SECT. XXIX. All attempts to delude the people, or to abuse their understanding by exercise of the pretended arts of witchcraft, conjuration, enchantment, or sorcery, or by pretended prophecies, shall be punished by ducking and whipping, at the discretion of a jury, not exceeding fifteen stripes.*

SECT. XXX. If the principal offenders be fled,† or secreted from justice, in any case not touching life or member, the accessaries may, notwithstanding, be prosecuted as if their principal were convicted.‡

Coron. 48. They are the principal felons, not accessaries. ib. Whether it was felony in the prisoner at Common law, is doubted. Stam. P. C. 30. b. The Mirror c. 5. § 1, says "abusion est a tener escape de prisoner, ou de bruserie del gaole pur peche mortell, car cel usage nest garrant per nul ley, ne in nul part est use forsque in cest realme, et en France, eins [mais] est leu garrantie de ceo faire per la ley de nature." 2 Inst. 589. The stat. 1. E. 2. de fraugentibus prisonam, restrained the judgment of life and limb for prison breaking, to cases where the offence of the prisoner required such judgment.

It is not only vain, but wicked, in a legislator to frame laws in opposition to the laws of nature, and to arm them with the terrors of death. This is truly creating crimes in order to punish them. The law of nature impels every one to escape from confinement; it should not, therefore, be subjected to punishment. Let the legislator restrain his criminal by walls, not by parchment. As to strangers breaking prison to enlarge an offender, they should, and may be fairly considered as accessaries after the fact. This bill says nothing of the prisoner releasing himself by breach of jail, he will have the benefit of the first section of the bill, which repeals the judgment of life and death at the common law.

*Gif wiccan owwe wigleras nansworan, owwe morthwyrhtan owwe fule afylede æbere horcwenan ahwhar on lande wurthan agytene, thonne fyrsie man of earde and clænsie tha theode, owwe on earde forfare hi mid ealle, buton hi geswican and the deoper gebetan: if witches, or weirds, man-swearers, murther-wroughters, or foul, defiled, open whore-queens, anywhere in the land were gotten, then force them off earth, and cleanse the nation, or in earth forth-fare them withal, but on they beseech, and deeply better. Ll. Ed. et Guthr. c. 11. "Sagæ, mulieres barbara, factitantes sacrificia, aut pestiferi, si cui mortem intulerint, neque id inficiari poterint, capitis poena esto." Ll. Æthelst. c. 6. apud Lambard. Ll. Aelfr. 30. Ll. Cnuti. c. 4. "Mesme cel jugement (d'etrears) eyent sorcers, et sorceresses, &c. ut supra. Fleta ut et ubi supra." 3. Inst. 44. Trial of witches before Hale in 1664. The statutes 33 H. 8. c. 8. 5 El. c. 16 and 1 Jac. 1. c. 12. seem to be only in confirmation of the Common law. 9 G. 2. c. 25. punishes them with pillory, and a year's imprisonment. 3 E. 6. c. 15. 5 El. c. 15. punish fond, fantastical and false prophecies, by fine and imprisonment.

†1 Ann. c. 9. § 2.

‡As every treason includes within it a misprision of treason, so every felony

SECT. XXXI. If any offender stand mute of obstinacy,* or challenge peremptorily more of the jurors than by law he may, being first warned of the consequence thereof, the court shall proceed as if he had confessed the charge.†

SECT. XXXII. Pardon and privilege of clergy, shall henceforth be abolished, that none may be induced to injure through hope of impunity. But if the verdict be against the defendant, and the court, before whom the offence is heard and determined, shall doubt that it may be untrue for default of testimony, or other cause, they may direct a new trial to be had.‡

---

includes a misprision, or misdemeanor. 1 Hale P. C. 652. 708. "Licet fuerit felonia, tamen in eo continetur misprisio." 2 R. 3. 10. Both principal and accessary, therefore, may be proceeded against in any case, either for felony or misprision, at the Common law. Capital cases not being mentioned here, accessaries to them will of course be triable for misprisions, if the offender flies.

*E. 1. c. 12.

†Whether the judgment of penance lay at Common law. See 2 Inst. 178. 2 H. P. C. 321. 4 Bl. 322. It was given on standing mute; but on challenging more than the legal number, whether that sentence, or sentence of death is to be given, seems doubtful. 2 H. P. C. 316. Quære, whether it would not be better to consider the supernumerary challenge as merely void, and to proceed in the trial? Quære too, in case of silence?

‡"Cum Clericus sic de crimine convictus degradetur non sequitur alia pœna pro uno delicto, vel pluribus ante degradationem perpetratis. Satis enim sufficit ei pro pœna degradatio, quæ est magna capitis diminutio, nisi forte convictus fuerit de apostatia, quia hinc primo degradetur, et postea per manum laicalem comburetur, secundum quod accidit in concilio Oxoni celebrato a bonæ memoriæ S. Cantuanen. Archiepiscopo de quodam diacono, qui se apostatavit pro quadam Judaæ; qui cum esset per episcopum degradatus, statim fuit igni traditus per manum laicalem." Bract. L. 3. c. 9. § 2. "Et mesme cel jugement (i. e. qui ils soient ars eyent) sorcers et sorceresses, et sodomites et mescreauntz apertement atteyntz." Britt. c. 9. "Christiani autem Apostatæ, sortilegii, et hujusmodi detractari debent et comburi." Fleta, L. 1. c. 37. § 2 see 3. Inst. 39. 12. Rep. 92. 1 H. P. C. 393. The extent of the clerical privilege at the Common law. 1. As to the crimes, seems very obscure and uncertain. It extended to no case where the judgment was not of life, or limb. Note in 2. H. P. C. 326. This therefore excluded it in trespass, petty larceny, or killing se defendendo. In high treason against the person of the King, it seems not to have been allowed. Note 1. H. P. C. 185. Treasons, therefore, not against the King's person immediately, petty treasons and felonies, seem to have been the cases where it was allowed; and even of those, not for insidiatio varium, depopulatio agrorum, or combustio domorum. The statute

SECT. XXXIII. No attainder shall work corruption of blood in any case.

SECT. XXXIV. In all cases of forfeiture, the widow's dower shall be saved to her, during her title thereto; after which it shall be disposed of as if no such saving had been.

SECT. XXXV. The aid of Counsel,* and examination of their witnesses on oath, shall be allowed to defendants in criminal prosecutions.

SECT. XXXVI. Slaves guilty of any offence† punishable in others by labour in the public works, shall be transported to such parts in the West-Indies, South-America, or Africa, as the Governor shall direct, there to be continued in slavery.

---

de Clero, 25 E. 3. st. 3. c. 4. settled the law on this head. 2. As to the persons, it extended to all clerks, always, and toties quoties. 2 H. P. C. 374. To nuns also. Fitz. Abr. Corone. 461. 22. E. 3. The clerical habit and tonsure were considered as evidence of the person being clerical. 26. Assiz. 19. 20. E. 2. Fitz. Corone. 233. By the 9 E. 4. 28. b. 34. H. 6. 49 a. b. a simple reading became the evidence. This extended impunity to a great number of laymen, and toties quoties. The stat. 4 H. 7. c. 13. directed that real clerks should, upon a second arraignment, produce their orders, and all others to be burnt in the hand with M. or T. on the first allowance of clergy, and not to be admitted to it a second time. A heretic, Jew, or Turk (as being incapable of orders) could not have clergy. 11. Co. Rep. 29 b. But a Greek, or other alien, reading in a book of his own country, might. Bro. Clergie. 20. So a blind man, if he could speak Latin. Ib. 21. qu. 11. Rep. 29. b. The orders entitling the party, were bishops, priests, deacons and subdeacons, the inferior being reckoned Clerici in minoribus. 2. H. P. C. 373. Quære, however, if this distinction is not founded on the stat. 23 H. 8. c. 1. 25 H. 8. c. 32. By merely dropping all the statutes, it should seem that none but clerks would be entitled to this privilege, and that they would, toties quoties.

*1 Ann. c. 9.

†Manslaughter, counterfeiting, arson, asportation of vessels, robbery, burglary, house-breaking, horse-stealing, larceny.

A Bill for the More General Diffusion of Knowledge

SECTION I. WHEREAS it appeareth that however certain forms of government are better calculated than others to protect individuals in the free exercise of their natural rights, and are at the same time themselves better guarded against degeneracy, yet experience hath shewn, that even under the best forms, those entrusted with power have, in time, and by slow operations, perverted it into tyranny; and it is believed that the most effectual means of preventing this would be, to illuminate, as far as practicable, the minds of the people at large, and more especially to give them knowledge of those facts, which history exhibiteth, that, possessed thereby of the experience of other ages and countries, they may be enabled to know ambition under all its shapes, and prompt to exert their natural powers to defeat its purposes; And whereas it is generally true that the people will be happiest whose laws are best, and are best administered, and that laws will be wisely formed, and honestly administered, in proportion as those who form and administer them are wise and honest; whence it becomes expedient for promoting the publick happiness that those persons, whom nature hath endowed with genius and virtue, should be rendered by liberal education worthy to receive, and able to guard the sacred deposit of the rights and liberties of their fellow citizens, and that they should be called to that charge without regard to wealth, birth or other accidental condition or circumstance; but the indigence of the greater number disabling them from so educating, at their own expence, those of their children whom nature hath fitly formed and disposed to become useful instruments for the public, it is better that such should be sought for and educated at the common expence of all, than that the happiness of all should be confided to the weak or wicked:

SECT. II. BE it therefore enacted by the General Assembly, that in every county within this commonwealth, there shall be chosen annually, by the electors qualified to vote for Delegates, three of the most honest and able men of their county, to be called the Aldermen of the county; and that the election of the said Aldermen shall be held at the same time and place, before the same persons, and notified and conducted in the same manner as by law is directed for the annual election of Delegates for the county.

SECT. III. THE person before whom such election is holden shall certify to the court of the said county the names of the Aldermen chosen, in order that the same may be entered of record, and shall give notice of their election to the said Aldermen within a fortnight after such election.

SECT. IV. THE said Aldermen on the first Monday in October, if it be fair, and if not, then on the next fair day, excluding Sunday, shall meet at the court-house of their county, and proceed to divide their said county into hundreds, bounding the same by water courses, mountains, or limits, to be run and marked, if they think necessary, by the county surveyor, and at the county expence, regulating the size of the said hundreds, according to the best of their discretion, so as that they may contain a convenient number of children to make up a school, and be of such convenient size that all the children within each hundred may daily attend the school to be established therein, distinguishing each hundred by a particular name; which division, with the names of the several hundreds, shall be returned to the court of the county and be entered of record, and shall remain unaltered until the increase or decrease of inhabitants shall render an alteration necessary, in the opinion of any succeeding Aldermen, and also in the opinion of the court of the county.

SECT. V. THE electors aforesaid residing within every hundred shall meet on the third Monday in October after the first election of Aldermen, at such place, within their hundred, as the said Aldermen shall direct, notice thereof being previously given to them by such person residing within the hundred as the said Aldermen shall require who is hereby enjoined to obey such requisition, on pain of being punished by amercement and imprisonment. The electors being so assembled shall choose the most convenient place within their hundred for building a school-house. If two or more places, having a greater number of votes than any others, shall yet be equal between themselves, the Aldermen, or such of them as are not of the same hundred, on information thereof, shall decide between them. The said Aldermen shall forthwith proceed to have a school-house built at the said place, and shall see that the same be kept in repair, and, when necessary, that it be rebuilt; but whenever they shall think necessary that it be rebuilt, they shall give notice as before directed, to the electors of the hundred to meet at the said school-house, on such day as they shall appoint, to determine by vote, in the manner before directed, whether it shall be rebuilt at the same, or what other place in the hundred.

SECT. VI. AT every of these schools shall be taught reading, writing, and common arithmetick, and the books which shall be used therein for instructing the children to read shall be such as will at the same time make them acquainted with Græcian, Roman, English, and American history. At these schools all the free children, male and female, resident within the respective hundred, shall be intitled to receive tuition gratis, for the term of three years, and as much longer, at their private expence, as their parents, guardians or friends, shall think proper.

SECT. VII. OVER ten of these schools (or such other number nearest thereto, as the number of hundreds in the county will admit, without fractional divisions) an overseer shall be appointed annually by the Aldermen at their first meeting, eminent for his learning, integrity, and fidelity to the commonwealth, whose business and duty it shall be, from time to time, to appoint a teacher to each school, who shall give assurance of fidelity to the commonwealth, and to remove him as he shall see cause; to visit every school once in every half year at the least, to examine the schollars; see that any general plan of reading and instruction recommended by the visiters of William and Mary College shall be observed; and to superintend the conduct of the teacher in every thing relative to his school.

SECT. VIII. EVERY teacher shall receive a salary of by the year, which, with the expences of building and repairing the school houses, shall be provided in such manner as other county expences are by law directed to be provided and shall also have his diet, lodging, and washing found him, to be levied in like manner, save only that such levy shall be on the inhabitants of each hundred for the board of their own teacher only.

SECT. IX. AND in order that grammer schools may be rendered convenient to the youth in every part of the commonwealth, BE it farther enacted, that on the first Monday in November, after the first appointment of overseers for the hundred schools, if fair, and if not, then on the next fair day, excluding Sunday, after the hour of one in the afternoon, the said overseers appointed for the schools in the counties of Princess Ann, Norfolk, Nansemond and Isle-of-Wight, shall meet at Nansemond court house; those for the counties of Southampton, Sussex, Surry and Prince George, shall meet at Sussex court-house; those for the counties of Brunswick, Mecklenburg and Lunenburg, shall meet at Lunenburg courthouse; those for the counties of Dinwiddie, Amelia and Chesterfield, shall meet at Chesterfield court-house; those for the counties of Powhatan, Cumberland, Goochland, Henrico and Hanover, shall meet at Henrico court-house; those for the counties of Prince Edward, Charlotte and Halifax, shall meet at Charlotte court-house; those for the counties of Henry, Pittsylvania and Bedford, shall meet at Pittsylvania courthouse; those for the counties of Buckingham, Amherst, Albemarle and Fluvanna, shall meet at Albemarle court-house; those for the counties of Botetourt, Rockbridge, Montgomery, Washington and Kentucky, shall meet at Botetourt courthouse; those for the counties of Augusta, Rockingham and Greenbrier, shall meet at Augusta court-house; those for the counties of Accomack and Northampton, shall meet at Accomack court-house; those for the counties of Elizabeth City, Warwick, York, Gloucester, James City, Charles City and New

Kent, shall meet at James City court-house; those for the counties of Middlesex, Essex, King and Queen, King William and Caroline, shall meet at King and Queen court-house; those for the counties of Lancaster, Northumberland, Richmond and Westmoreland, shall meet at Richmond court-house; those for the counties of King George, Stafford, Spotsylvania, Prince William and Fairfax, shall meet at Spotsylvania court-house; those for the counties of Loudoun and Fauquier, shall meet at Loudoun court-house; those for the counties of Culpeper, Orange and Louisa, shall meet at Orange court-house; those for the counties of Shenandoah and Frederick, shall meet at Frederick court-house; those for the counties of Hampshire and Berkeley, shall meet at Berkeley court house; and those for the counties of Yohogania, Monongalia and Ohio, shall meet at Monongalia court-house; and shall fix on such place in some one of the counties in their district as shall be most proper for situating a grammar school-house, endeavouring that the situation be as central as may be to the inhabitants of the said counties, that it be furnished with good water, convenient to plentiful supplies of provision and fuel, and more than all things that it be healthy. And if a majority of the overseers present should not concur in their choice of any one place proposed, the method of determining shall be as follows: If two places only were proposed, and the votes be divided, they shall decide between them by fair and equal lot; if more than two places were proposed, the question shall be put on those two which on the first division had the greater number of votes; or if no two places had a greater number of votes than the others, as where the votes shall have been equal between one or both of them and some other or others, then it shall be decided by fair and equal lot (unless it can be agreed by a majority of votes) which of the places having equal numbers shall be thrown out of the competition, so that the question shall be put on the remaining two, and if on this ultimate question the votes shall be equally divided, it shall then be decided finally by lot.

SECT. X. THE said overseers having determined the place at which the grammer school for their district shall be built, shall forthwith (unless they can otherwise agree with the proprietors of the circumjacent lands as to location and price) make application to the clerk of the county in which the said house is to be situated, who shall thereupon issue a writ, in the nature of a writ of ad quod damnum, directed to the sheriff of the said county commanding him to summon and impannel twelve fit persons to meet at the place, so destined for the grammer school-house, on a certain day, to be named in the said writ, not less than five, nor more than ten, days from the date thereof; and also to give notice of the same to the proprietors and tenants of the lands to be viewed, if they be to be found within the county, and if not, then to their agents therein if any they have. Which freeholders shall be charged by the said sheriff impartially, and to the best of their skill and judgement to view the lands round about the said place, and to locate and circumscribe, by certain metes and bounds, one hundred acres thereof, having regard therein principally to the benefit and convenience of the said school, but respecting in some measure also the convenience of the said proprietors, and to value and appraise the same in so many several respective interests and estates therein. And after such location and appraisement so made, the said sheriff shall forthwith return the same under the hands and seals of the said jurors, together with the writ, to the clerk's office of the said county and the right and property of the said proprietors and tenants in the said lands so circumscribed shall be immediately devested and be transferred to the commonwealth for the use of the said grammar school, in full and absolute dominion, any want of consent or disability to consent in the said owners or tenants notwithstanding. But it shall not be lawful for the said overseers so to situate the said grammar school-house, nor to the said jurors so to locate the said lands, as to include the mansion-house of the proprietor of the lands, nor the offices, curtilage, or garden, thereunto immediately belonging.

Sect. XI. The said overseers shall forthwith proceed to have a house of brick or stone, for the said grammar school, with necessary offices, built on the said lands, which grammer school-house shall contain a room for the school, a hall to dine in, four rooms for a master and usher, and ten or twelve lodging rooms for the scholars.

SECT. XII. To each of the said grammar schools shall be allowed out of the public treasury, the sum of pounds, out of which shall be paid by the Treasurer, on warrant from the Auditors, to the proprietors or tenants of the lands located, the value of their several interests as fixed by the jury, and the balance thereof shall be delivered to the said overseers to defray the expence of the said buildings.

SECT. XIII. IN these grammar schools shall be taught the Latin and Greek languages, English grammar, geography, and the higher part of numerical arithmetick, to wit, vulgar and decimal fractions, and the extraction of the square and cube roots.

SECT. XIV. A visiter from each county constituting the district shall be appointed, by the overseers, for the county, in the month of October annually, either from their own body or from their county at large, which visiters or the greater part of them, meeting together at the said grammar school on the first Monday in November, if fair, and if not, then on the next fair day, excluding Sunday, shall have power to choose their own Rector, who shall call and preside at future meetings, to employ from time to time a master, and if necessary, an usher, for the said school, to remove them at their will, and to settle the price of tuition to be paid by the scholars. They shall also visit the school twice in every year at the least, either together or separately at their discretion, examine the scholars, and see that any general plan of instruction recommended by the visiters of William and Mary College shall be observed. The said masters and ushers, before they enter on the execution of their office, shall give assurance of fidelity to the commonwealth.

SECT. XV. A steward shall be employed, and removed at will by the master, on such wages as the visiters shall direct; which steward shall see to the procuring provisions, fuel, servants for cooking, waiting, house cleaning, washing, mending, and gardening on the most reasonable terms; the expence of which, together with the steward's wages, shall be divided equally among all the scholars boarding either on the public or private expence. And the part of those who are on private expence, and also the price of their tuitions due to the master or usher, shall be paid quarterly by the respective scholars, their parents, or guardians, and shall be recoverable, if withheld, together with costs, on motion in any Court of Record, ten days notice thereof being previously given to the party, and a jury impannelled to try the issue joined, or enquire of the damages. The said steward shall also, under the direction of the visiters, see that the houses be kept in repair, and necessary enclosures be made and repaired, the accounts for which, shall, from time to time, be submitted to the Auditors, and on their warrant paid by the Treasurer.

SECT. XVI. EVERY overseer of the hundred schools shall, in the month of September annually, after the most diligent and impartial examination and enquiry, appoint from among the boys who shall have been two years at the least at some one of the schools under his superintendance, and whose parents are too poor to give them farther education, some one of the best and most promising genius and disposition, to proceed to the grammar school of his district; which appointment shall be made in the court-house of the county, on the court day for that month, if fair, and if not, then on the next fair day, excluding Sunday, in the presence of the Aldermen, or two of them at the least, assembled on the bench for that purpose, the said overseer being previously sworn by them to make such appointment, without favor or affection, according to the best of his skill and judgment, and being interrogated by the said Aldermen, either on their own motion, or on suggestions from the parents, guardians, friends, or teachers of the children, competitors for such appointment; which teachers shall attend for the information of the Aldermen. On which interrogatories the said Aldermen, if they be not satisfied with the appointment proposed, shall have right to negative it; whereupon the said visiter may proceed to make a new appointment, and the said Aldermen again to interrogate and negative, and so toties quoties until an appointment be approved.

SECT. XVII. EVERY boy so appointed shall be authorised to proceed to the grammar school of his district, there to be educated and boarded during such time as is hereafter limited; and his quota of the expences of the house together with a compensation to the master or usher for his tuition, at the rate of twenty dollars by the year, shall be paid by the Treasurer quarterly on warrant from the Auditors.

SECT. XVIII. A visitation shall be held, for the purpose of probation, annually at the said grammar school on the last Monday in September, if fair, and if not, then on the next fair day, excluding Sunday, at which one third of the boys sent thither by appointment of the said overseers, and who shall have been there one year only, shall be discontinued as public foundationers, being those who, on the most diligent examination and enquiry, shall be thought to be of the least promising genius and disposition; and of those who shall have been there two years, all shall be discontinued, save one only the best in genius and disposition, who shall be at liberty to continue there four years longer on the public foundation, and shall thence forward be deemed a senior.

SECT. XIX. THE visiters for the districts which, or any part of which, be southward and westward of James river, as known by that name, or by the names of Fluvanna and Jackson's river, in every other year, to wit, at the probation meetings held in the years, distinguished in the Christian computation by odd numbers, and the visiters for all the other districts at their said meetings to be held in those years, distinguished by even numbers, after diligent examination and enquiry as before directed, shall chuse one among the said seniors, of the best learning and most hopeful genius and disposition, who shall be authorised by them to proceed to William and Mary College, there to be educated, boarded, and clothed, three years; the expence of which annually shall be paid by the Treasurer on warrant from the Auditors.

A Bill Declaring Who Shall Be Deemed
Citizens of this Commonwealth

SECTION I. BE it enacted by the General Assembly, that all white persons born within the territory of this commonwealth and all who have resided therein two years next before the passing of this act, and all who shall hereafter migrate into the same; and shall before any court of record give satisfactory proof by their own oath or affirmation, that they intend to reside therein, and moreover shall give assurance of fidelity to the commonwealth; and all infants wheresoever born, whose father, if living, or otherwise, whose mother was, a citizen at the time of their birth, or who migrate hither, their father, if living, or otherwise their mother becoming a citizen, or who migrate hither without father or mother, shall be deemed citizens of this commonwealth, until they relinquish that character in manner as herein after expressed: And all others not being citizens of any the United States of America, shall be deemed aliens. The clerk of the court shall enter such oath of record, and give the person taking the same a certificate thereof, for which he shall receive the fee of one dollar. And in order to preserve to the citizens of this commonwealth, that natural right, which all men have of relinquishing the country, in which birth, or other accident may have thrown them, and, seeking subsistance and happiness wheresoever they may be able, or may hope to find them: And to declare unequivocally what circumstances shall be deemed evidence of an intention in any citizen to exercise that right, it is enacted and declared, that whensoever any citizen of this commonwealth, shall by word of mouth in the presence of the court of the county, wherein he resides, or of the General Court, or by deed in writing, under his hand and seal, executed in the presence of three witnesses, and by them proved in either of the said courts, openly declare to the same court, that he relinquishes the character of a citizen, and shall depart the commonwealth; or whensoever he shall without such declaration depart the commonwealth and enter into the service of any other state, not in enmity with this, or any other of the United States of America, or do any act whereby he shall become a subject or citizen of such state, such person shall be considered as having exercised his natural right of expatriating himself, and shall be deemed no citizen of this commonwealth from the time of his departure. The free white inhabitants of every of the states, parties to the American confederation, paupers, vagabonds and fugitives from justice excepted, shall be intitled to all rights, privileges, and immunities of free citizens in this commonwealth, and shall have free egress, and regress, to and from the same, and shall enjoy therein, all the privileges of trade, and commerce, subject to the same duties, impositions and restrictions as the citizens of this commonwealth. And if any person guilty of, or charged with treason, felony, or other high misdemeanor, in any of the said states, shall flee from justice and be found in this commonwealth, he shall, upon demand of the Governor, or Executive power of the state, from which he fled, be delivered up to be removed to the state having jurisdiction of his offence. Where any person holding property, within this commonwealth, shall be attainted within any of the said states, parties to the said confederation, of any of those crimes, which by the laws of this commonwealth shall be punishable by forfeiture of such property, the said property shall be disposed of in the same manner as it would have been if the owner thereof had been attainted of the like crime in this commonwealth.

Report on Government for Western Territory

March 1, 1784

THE COMMITTEE appointed to prepare a plan for the temporary Government of the Western territory have agreed to the following resolutions:

Resolved that the territory ceded or to be ceded by Individual States to the United States whensoever the same shall have been purchased of the Indian Inhabitants & offered for sale by the U. S. shall be formed into distinct States bounded in the following manner as nearly as such cessions will admit, that is to say; Northwardly & Southwardly by parallels of latitude so that each state shall comprehend from South to North two degrees of latitude beginning to count from the completion of thirty-one degrees North of the equator, but any territory Northwardly of the 47.th degree shall make part of the state—next below, and Eastwardly & Westwardly they shall be bounded, those on the Mississippi by that river on one side and the meridian of the lowest point of the rapids of Ohio on the other; and those adjoining on the East by the same meridian on their Western side, and on their eastern by the meridian of the Western cape of the mouth of the Great Kanhaway. And the territory eastward of this last meridian between the Ohio, Lake Erie & Pennsylvania shall be one state.

That the settlers within the territory so to be purchased & offered for sale shall, either on their own petition, or on the order of Congress, receive authority from them, with appointments of time and place for their free males of full age to meet together for the purpose of establishing a temporary government, to adopt the constitution & laws of any one of these states, so that such laws nevertheless shall be subject to alteration by their ordinary legislature, and to erect, subject to a like alteration counties or townships for the election of members for their legislature.

That such temporary government shall only continue in force in any state until it shall have acquired 20,000 free inhabitants, when, giving due proof thereof to Congress, they shall receive from them authority with appointments of time and place to call a Convention of representatives to establish a permanent Constitution & Government for themselves.

Provided that both the temporary & permanent Governments be established on these principles as their basis. 1, That they shall forever remain a part of the United States of America. 2, That in their persons, property & territory, they shall be subject to the Government of the United States in Congress assembled and to the articles of confederation in all those cases in which the original states shall be so subject. 3, That they shall be subject to pay a part of the federal debts contracted or to be contracted to be apportioned on them by Congress, according to the same common rule and measure by which apportionments thereof shall be made on the other states. 4, That their respective Governments shall be in republican forms, and shall admit no person to be a citizen, who holds any hereditary title. 5, That after the year 1800 of the Christian æra, there shall be neither slavery nor involuntary servitude in any of the said states, otherwise than in punishment of crimes, whereof the party shall have been duly convicted to have been personally guilty.

That whenever any of the sd states shall have, of free inhabitants as many as shall then be in any one the least numerous of the thirteen original states, such state shall be admitted by it's delegates into the Congress of the United States, on an equal footing with the said original states: After which the assent of two thirds of the United States in Congress assembled shall be requisite in all those cases, wherein by the Confederation the assent of nine States is now required. Provided the consent of nine states to such admission may be obtained according to the eleventh of the Articles of Confederation. Until such admission by their delegates into Congress, any of the said states, after the establishment of their temporary Government, shall have authority to keep a sitting Member in Congress, with a right of debating, but not of voting.

That the territory Northward of the 45th degree, that is to say of the completion of 45° from the Equator & extending to the Lake of the Woods, shall be called SYLVANIA:

That of the territory under the 45th & 44th degrees that which lies Westward of Lake Michigan shall be called MICHIGANIA, and that which is Eastward thereof within the peninsula formed by the lakes & waters of Michigan, Huron, St. Clair and Erie, shall be called CHERRONESUS, and shall include any part of the peninsula which may extend above the 45th degree.

Of the territory under the 43^d & 42^d degrees, that to the Westward thro' which the Assenisipi or Rock river runs shall be called ASSENISIPIA, and that to the Eastward in which are the fountains of the Muskingum, the two Miamis of Ohio, the Wabash, the Illinois, the Miami of the lake and Sandusky rivers, shall be called METROPOTAMIA.

Of the territory which lies under the 41st & 40th degrees the Western, thro which the river Illinois runs, shall be called ILLINOIA; that next adjoining to the Eastward SARA-TOGA, and that between this last & Pennsylvania & extending from the Ohio to Lake Erie shall be called WASHINGTON.

Of the territory which lies under the 39th & 38th degrees to which shall be added so much of the point of land within the fork of the Ohio & Missisipi as lies under the 37th degree, that to the Westward within & adjacent to which are the confluences of the rivers Wabash, Shawanee, Tanisse, Ohio, Illinois, Missisipi & Missouri, shall be called POLYPOTAMIA, and that to the Eastward farther up the Ohio otherwise called the PELISIPI shall be called PELISIPIA.

That the preceding articles shall be formed into a charter of Compact, shall be duly executed by the President of the U. S. in Congress assembled under his hand and the seal of the United States, shall be promulgated, and shall stand as fundamental constitutions between the thirteen original States, & those now newly described unalterable but by the joint consent of the U. S. in Congress assembled and of the particular state within which such alteration is proposed to be made.

Observations on the Whale-Fishery

WHALE OIL enters, as a raw material, into several branches of manufacture, as of wool, leather, soap: it is used also in painting, architecture and navigation. But its great consumption is in lighting houses and cities. For this last purpose however it has a powerful competitor in the vegetable oils. These do well in warm, still weather, but they fix with cold, they extinguish easily with the wind, their crop is precarious, depending on the seasons, and to yield the same light, a larger wick must be used, and greater quantity of oil consumed. Estimating all these articles of difference together, those employed in lighting cities find their account in giving about 25 per cent. more for whale than for vegetable oils. But higher than this the whale oil, in its present form, cannot rise; because it then becomes more advantageous to the city-lighters to use others. This competition then limits its price, higher than which no encouragement can raise it, and becomes, as it were, a law of its nature, but, at this low price, the whale fishery is the poorest business into which a merchant or sailor can enter. If the sailor, instead of wages, has a part of what is taken, he finds that this, one year with another, yields him less than he could have got as wages in any other business. It is attended too with great risk, singular hardships, and long absences from his family. If the voyage is made solely at the expence of the merchant, he finds that, one year with another, it does not reimburse him his expences. As, for example, an English ship of 300 ton, and 42. hands brings home, communibus annis, after a four months voyage, 25. ton of oil, worth 437l. 10s. sterl. but the wages of the officers and seamen will be 400l. The Outfit then and the merchant's profit must be paid by the government. And it is accordingly on this idea that the British bounty is calculated. From the poverty of this business then it has happened that the nations, who have taken it up, have successively abandoned it. The Basques began it. But, tho' the most economical and enterprising of the inhabitants of France, they could not continue it; and it is said they never employed more than 30. ships a year. The Dutch and Hanse towns succeeded them. The latter gave it up long ago tho' they have continued to lend their name to British and Dutch oils. The English carried it on, in competition with the Dutch, during the last, and beginning of the present century. But it was too little profitable for them in comparison with other branches of commerce open to them. In the mean time too the inhabitants of the barren Island of Nantucket had taken up this fishery, invited to it by the whales presenting themselves on their own shore. To them therefore the English relinquished it, continuing to them, as British subjects, the importation of their oils into England duty free, while foreigners were subject to a duty of 18l. 5s. sterl. a ton. The Dutch were enabled to continue it long, because, 1. They are so near the northern fishing grounds, that a vessel begins her fishing very soon after she is out of port. 2. They navigate with more economy than the other nations of Europe. 3. Their seamen are content with lower wages: and 4. their merchants with a lower profit on their capital. Under all these favorable circumstances however, this branch of business, after long languishing, is at length nearly extinct with them. It is said they did not send above half a dozen ships in pursuit of the whale this present year. The Nantuckois then were the only people who exercised this fishery to any extent at the commencement of the late war. Their country, from its barrenness, yielding no subsistence, they were obliged to seek it in the sea which surrounded them. Their economy was more rigorous than that of the Dutch. Their seamen, instead of wages, had a share in what was taken. This induced them to fish with fewer hands, so that each had a greater dividend in the profit. It made them more vigilant in seeking game, bolder in pursuing it, and parcimonious in all their expences. London was their only market. When therefore, by the late revolution, they became aliens in great Britain, they became subject to the alien duty of 18l. 5s. the ton of oil, which being more than equal to the price of the common whale oil, they were obliged to abandon that fishery. So that this people, who before the war had employed upwards of 300 vessels a year in the whale fishery, (while great Britain had herself never employed one hundred) have now almost ceased to exercise it. But they still had the seamen, the most important material for this fishery; and they still retained the spirit of fishing: so that at the reestablishment of peace they were capable in a very short time of reviving their fishery in all its splendor. The British government saw that the moment was critical. They knew that their own share in that fishery was as nothing. That the great mass of fishermen was left with a nation now separated from them: that these fishermen however had lost their ancient market, had no other resource within their country to which they could turn, and they hoped therefore they might, in the present moment of distress, be decoyed over to their establishments, and be added to the mass of their seamen. To effect this they offered extravagant advantages to all persons who should exercise the whale fishery from British establishments. But not counting with much confidence on a long connection with their remaining possessions on the continent of America, foreseeing that the Nantuckois would settle in them preferably, if put on an equal footing with those of great Britain, and that thus they might have to purchase them a second time, they confined their high offers to settlers in Great Britain. The Nantuckois, left without resource by the loss of their market, began to think of removing to the British dominions: some to Nova Scotia, preferring smaller advantages, in the neighbourhood of their ancient country and friends; others to great Britain postponing country and friends to high premiums. A vessel was already arrived from Halifax to Nantucket to take off some of those who proposed to remove; two families had gone on board and others were going, when a letter was received there, which had been written by Monsieur le Marquis de la Fayette to a gentleman in Boston, and transmitted by him to Nantucket. The purport of the letter was to dissuade their accepting the British proposals, and to assure them that their friends in France would endeavour to do something for them. This instantly suspended their design: not another went on board, and the vessel returned to Halifax with only the two families.

In fact the French Government had not been inattentive to the views of the British, nor insensible of the crisis. They saw the danger of permitting five or six thousand of the best seamen existing to be transferred by a single stroke to the marine strength of their enemy, and to carry over with them an art which they possessed almost exclusively. The counterplan which they set on foot was to tempt the Nantuckois by high offers to come and settle in France. This was in the year 1785. The British however had in their favour a sameness of language, religion, laws, habits and kindred. 9 families only, of 33 persons in the whole came to Dunkirk; so that this project was not likely to prevent their emigration to the English establishments, if nothing else had happened.

France had effectually aided in detaching the U. S. of America from the *force* of Great Britain. But as yet they seemed to have indulged only a silent wish to detach them from her *commerce*. They had done nothing to induce that event. In the same year 1785, while M. de Calonne was in treaty, with the Nantuckois, an estimate of the commerce of the U. S. was submitted to the count de Vergennes, and it was shewn that, of 3. millions of pounds sterling to which their exports amounted, one third might be brought to France and exchanged against her productions and manufactures advantageously for both nations, provided the obstacles of prohibition, monopoly, and duty were either done away or moderated as far as circumstances would admit. A committee, which had been appointed to investigate a particular one of these subjects, was thereupon instructed to extend its researches to the whole, and see what advantages and facilities the Government could offer for the encouragement of a general commerce with the United States. The Committee was composed of persons well skilled in commerce; and, after labouring assiduously for several months, they made their report: the result of which was given in the letter of his Majesty's Comptroller General of the 2d of Octob. 1786. wherein he stated the principles which should be established for the future regulation of the commerce between France and the United States. It was become tolerably evident, at the date of this letter, that the terms offered to the Nantuckois would not produce their emigration to Dunkirk; and that it would be safest in every event to offer some other alternative which might prevent their acceptance of the British offers. The obvious one was to open the ports of France to their oils, so that they might still exercise their fishery, remaining in their native country, and find a new market for its produce instead of that which they had lost. The article of Whale oil was accordingly distinguished, in the letter of M. de Calonne, by an immediate abatement of duty, and promise of further abatement after the year 1790. This letter was instantly sent to America, and bid fair to produce there the effect intended, by determining the fishermen to carry on their trade from their own homes, with the advantage only of a free market in France, rather than remove to Great Britain where a free market and great bounty were offered them. An Arret was still to be prepared to give legal sanction to the letter of M. de Calonne. M. Lambert, with a patience and assiduity almost unexampled, went through all the investigations necessary to assure himself that the conclusions of the Committee had been just. Frequent conferences on this subject were held in his presence; the Deputies of the Chambers of Commerce were heard, and the result was the Arret of Dec. 29. 1787. confirming the abatements of duty present and future, which the letter of Octob. 1786. had promised, and reserving to his Majesty to grant still further favours to that production, if on further information he should find it for the interest of the two Nations.

The English had now begun to deluge the markets of France with their whale oils: and they were enabled by the great premiums given by their Government to undersell the French fisherman, aided by feebler premiums, and the American aided by his poverty alone. Nor is it certain that these speculations were not made at the risk of the British Government, to suppress the French and American fishermen in their only market. Some remedy seemed necessary. Perhaps it would not have been a bad one to subject, by a general law, the merchandize of every nation and of every nature to pay additional duties in the ports of France exactly equal to the premiums and drawbacks given on the same merchandise by their own government. This might not only counteract the effect of premium in the instance of whale oils, but attack the whole British system of bounties and drawbacks by the aid of which they make London the center of commerce for the whole earth. A less general remedy, but an effectual one, was to prohibit the oils of all *European* nations: the treaty with England requiring only that she should be treated as well as the most favoured *European* nation. But the remedy adopted was to prohibit all oils without exception.

To know how this remedy will operate we must consider the quantity of whale oil which France consumes annually, the quantity she obtains from her own fishery; and if she obtains less than she consumes, we are to consider what will follow this prohibition.

The annual consumption of France, as stated by a person who has good opportunities of knowing it, is as follows.

	pesant.	*quintaux.*	*tons.*
Paris according to the registers of 1786.	2,800,000	28,000	1750
27. other cities lighted by M. Sangrain	800,000	8,000	500
Rouen.	500,000	5,000	312½
Bordeaux.	600,000	6,000	375
Lyon	300,000	3,000	187½
Other cities, leather and light	3,000,000	30,000	1875
	8,000,000	80,000	5000

Other calculations, reduce the consumption to about half this. It is treating these with sufficient respect to place them on an equal footing with the estimate of the person before alluded to, and to suppose the truth half way between them. We will call then the present consumption of France only 60,000 quintals, or 3750 ton a year. This consumption is increasing fast as the practice of lighting cities is becoming more general, and the superior advantages of lighting them with whale oil are but now beginning to be known.

What do the fisheries of France furnish? she has employed this year 15. vessels in the Southern, and 2 in the Northern fishery, carrying 4500 tons in the whole or 265 each on an average. The English ships, led by Nantuckois as well as the French, have as I am told never averaged, in the Southern fishery, more than one fifth of their burthen, in the best year. The 15 ships of France, according to this ground of calculation, and supposing the present to have been one of the best years, should have brought, one with another, one fifth of 265 tons, or 53 tons each. But we are told they have brought near the double of that, to wit 100 tons each and 1500 tons in the whole. Supposing the 2. Northern vessels to have brought home the cargo which is common from the Northern fishery, to wit, 25 tons each, the whole produce this year will then be 1550 tons. This is 5½ months provision or two fifths of the annual consumption. To furnish for the whole year, would require 40 ships of the same size, in years as fortunate as the present, and 85 communibus annis, 44 tons, or one sixth of the burthen, being as high an average as should be counted on, one year with another: and the number must be increased with the increasing consumption. France then is evidently not yet in a condition to supply her own wants. It is said indeed she has a large stock on hand unsold occasioned by the English competition. 33,000 quintals, including this year's produce, are spoken of. This is between 6. and 7. months provision: and supposing, by the time this is exhausted, that the next year's supply comes in, that will enable her to go on 5. or 6. months longer; say a twelvemonth in the whole. But, at the end of the twelvemonth, what is to be done? The Manufactures depending on this article cannot maintain their competition against those of other countries, if deprived of their equal means. When the alternative then shall be presented of letting them drop, or opening the ports to foreign whale oil, it is presumable the latter will be adopted, as the lesser evil. But it will be too late for America: her fishery, annihilated during the late war, only began to raise its head on the prospect of market held out by this country. Crushed by the Arret of Sept. 28. in its first feeble effort to revive, it will rise no more. Expeditions, which require the expence of the outfit of vessels, and from 9. to 12 months navigation, as the Southern fishery does, most frequented by the Americans, cannot be undertaken in sole reliance on a market which is opened and shut from one day to another, with little or no warning. The English alone then will remain to furnish these supplies, and they must be received even from them. We must accept bread from our enemies, if our friends cannot furnish it. This comes exactly to the point to which that government has been looking. She fears no rival in the whale fishery but America. Or rather, it is the whale fishery of America of which she is endeavouring to possess herself. It is for this object she is making the present extraordinary efforts by bounties and other encouragements: and her success so far is very flattering. Before the war she had not 100 vessels in the whale trade, while America employed 309. In 1786. Great Britain employed 151 vessels, in 1787. 286. in 1788. 314. nearly the ancient American number; while the latter is fallen to about 80. They have just changed places then, England having gained exactly what America has lost. France by her ports and markets holds the balance between the two contending parties, and gives the victory, by opening and shutting them, to which she pleases. We have still precious remains of seamen educated in this fishery, and capable by their poverty, their boldness and address, of recovering it from the English, in spite of their bounties. But this Arret endangers the transferring to Great Britain every man of them who is not invincibly attached to his native soil. There is no other nation in present condition to maintain a competition with Great Britain in the whale fishery. The expence at which it is supported on her part seems enormous. 255 vessels, of 75,436 tons, employed by her this year in the Northern fishery, at 42 men each; and 59. in the Southern at 18 men each makes 11,772 men. These are known to have cost the government 15l. each, or 176,580l. in the whole, and that to employ the principal part of them from 3. to 4. months only. The Northern ships have brought home 20. and the Southern 60. tons of oil on an average, making 8,640 tons, every ton of oil then has cost the government 20l. in bounty. Still, if they can beat us out of the field and have it to themselves, they will think their money well employed. If France undertakes solely the competition against them, she must do it at equal expence. The trade is too poor to support itself. The 85 ships necessary to supply even her present consumption, bountied as the English are, will require a sacrifice of 1,285,200 livres a year, to maintain 3,570 seamen, and that a part of the year only. And if she will push it to 12,000 men in competition with England, she must sacrifice, as they do, 4. or 5. millions a year. The same number of men might, with the same bounty, be kept in as constant employ carrying stone from Bayonne to Cherburg, or coal from Newcastle to Havre, in which navigations they would be always at hand, and become as good seamen. The English consider among their best sailors those employed in carrying coal from New-castle to London. France cannot expect to raise her fishery, even to the supply of her own consumption, in one year or in several years. Is it not better then, by keeping her ports open to the U. S. to enable them to aid in maintaining the field against the common adversary, till she shall be in condition to take it herself, and to supply her own wants? Otherwise her supplies must aliment that very force which is keeping her under. On our part, we can never be dangerous competitors to France. The extent to which we can exercise this fishery is limited to that of the barren island of Nantucket, and a few similar barren spots; its duration to the pleasure of this government, as we have no other market.

A material observation must be added here. Sudden vicissitudes of opening and shutting ports, do little injury to merchants settled on the opposite coast, watching for the opening, like the return of a tide, and ready to enter with it. But they ruin the adventurer whose distance requires 6 months notice. Those who are now arriving from America, in consequence of the Arret of Dec. 29. will consider it as the false light which has led them to their ruin. They will be apt to say that they come to the ports of France by invitation of that Arret, that the subsequent one of Sept. 28. which drives them from those ports, founds itself on a single principle, viz. 'that the prohibition of foreign oils is the most useful encouragement which can be given to that branch of industry.' They will say that, if this be a true principle, it was as true on the 29th. of Dec. 1787. as on the 28th. of Sept. 1788. It was then weighed against other motives, judged weaker, and over-ruled, and it is hard it should be now revived to ruin them.

The Refinery for whale oil lately established at Rouen, seems to be an object worthy of national attention. In order to judge of its importance, the different qualities of whale oil must be noted. Three qualities are known in the American and English markets. 1. That of the Spermaceti whale. 2. Of the Groenland whale. 3. Of the Brazil whale. 1. The Spermaceti whale found by the Nantucketmen in the neighbourhood of the western Islands, to which they had gone in pursuit of other whales, retired thence to the coast of Guinea, afterwards to that of Brazil, and begins now to be best found in the latitude of the cape of good hope, and even of cape Horn. He is an active, fierce animal and requires vast address and boldness in the fisherman. The inhabitants of Brazil make little expeditions from their coast, and take some of these fish. But the Americans are the only distant people who have been in the habit of seeking and attacking them in numbers. The British however, led by the Nantuckois whom they have decoyed into their service, have begun this fishery. In 1785 they had 18 ships in it; in 1787, 38: in 1788, 54. or as some say 64. I have calculated on the middle number 59. Still they take but a very small proportion of their own demand. We furnish the rest. Theirs is the only market to which we carry that oil, because it is the only one where its properties are known. It is luminous, resists coagulation by cold to the 41st. degree of Farenheit's thermometer, and 4th. of Reaumur's, and yields no smell at all. It is used therefore within doors to lighten shops, and even in the richest houses for antichambers, stairs, galleries, &c. it sells at the London market for treble the price of common whale oil. This enables the adventurer to pay the duty of 18l. 5s. sterl. the ton, and still to have a living profit. Besides the mass of oil produced from the whole body of the whale, his head yields 3. or 4. barrels of what is called head-matter, from which is made the solid Spermaceti used for medicine and candles. This sells by the pound at double the price of the oil. The disadvantage of this fishery is that the sailors are from 9. to 12. months absent on the voyage, of course they are not at hand on any sudden emergency, and are even liable to be taken before they know that a war is begun. It must be added on the subject of this whale, that he is rare, and shy, soon abandoning the grounds where he is hunted. This fishery being less losing than the other, and often profitable, will occasion it to be so thronged soon, as to bring it on a level with the other. It will then require the same expensive support, or to be abandoned.

2. The Groenland whale oil is next in quality. It resists coagulation by cold to 36°. of Farenheit and 2°. of Reaumur; but it has a smell insupportable within doors, and is not luminous. It sells therefore in London at about 16l. the ton. This whale is clumsy and timid, he dives when struck, and comes up to breathe by the first cake of ice, where the fisher-

men need little address or courage to find and take him. This is the fishery mostly frequented by European nations; it is this fish which yields the fin in quantity, and the voyages last about 3. or 4. months.

3. The third quality is that of the small Brazil whale. He was originally found on the coast of Nantucket, and first led that people to this pursuit. He retired first to the banks of Newfoundland, then to the western islands; and is now found within soundings on the coast of Brazil, during the months of December, January, February and March. This oil chills at 50°. of Farenheit and 8°. of Reaumur, is black and offensive, worth therefore but 13l. the ton in London. In warm summer nights however it burns better than the Groenland oil.

The qualities of the oils thus described, it is to be added that an individual has discovered methods 1. of converting a great part of the oil of the spermaceti whale into the solid substance called spermaceti, heretofore produced from his head alone. 2. Of refining the Groenland whale oil, so as to take from it all smell and render it limpid and luminous, as that of the spermaceti whale. 3. of curdling the oil of the Brazil whale into tallow, resembling that of the beef, and answering all its purposes. This person is engaged by the company which has established the Refinery at Rouen: their works will cost them half a million of livres, will be able to refine all the oil which can be used in the kingdom, and even to supply foreign markets.—The effect of this refinery then would be 1. to supplant the solid spermaceti of all other nations by theirs of equal quality and lower price. 2. to substitute, instead of spermaceti oil, their black whale oil, refined, of equal quality and lower price. 3. to render the worthless oil of the Brazil whale equal in value to tallow: and 4. by accomodating these oils to uses, to which they could never otherwise have been applied, they will extend the demand beyond its present narrow limits to any supply which can be furnished, and thus give the most effectual encouragement and extension to the whale fishery. But these works were calculated on the Arret of Dec. 29. which admitted here freely and fully the produce of the American fishery. If confined to that of the French fishery alone, the enterprise may fail for want of matter to work on.

After this review of the whale fishery as a Political institution, a few considerations shall be added on its produce as a basis of Commercial exchange between France and the United-States. The discussions it has undergone on former occasions, in this point of view, leaves little new to be now urged.

The United-States not possessing mines of the precious metals, they can purchase necessaries from other nations so far only as their produce is received in exchange. Without enumerating our smaller articles, we have three of principal importance, proper for the French market, to wit, Tobacco, whale oil, and rice. The first and most important is Tobacco. This might furnish an exchange for 8. millions of the productions of this country: but it is under a monopoly, and that not of a mercantile, but a financiering company, whose interest is to pay in money, and not in merchandise; and who are so much governed by the spirit of simplifying their purchases and proceedings, that they find means to elude every endeavour on the part of government to make them diffuse their purchases among the merchants in general. Little profit is derived from this then as an article of exchange for the produce and manufactures of France. Whale oil might be next in importance; but that is now prohibited. American Rice is not yet of great, but it is of growing consumption in France, and being the only article of the three which is free, it may become a principal basis of exchange. Time and trial may add a fourth, that is, timber. But some essays, rendered unsuccessful by unfortunate circumstances, place that at present under a discredit, which it will be found hereafter not to have merited. The English know its value, and were supplied with it before the war. A spirit of hostility, since that event, led them to seek Russian rather than American supplies. A new spirit of hostility has driven them back from Russia, and they are now making contracts for American timber. But of the three articles before mentioned, proved by experience to be suitable for the French market, one is prohibited, one under monopoly, and one alone free, and that the smallest and of very limited consumption. The way to encourage purchasers is to multiply their means of payment. Whale oil might be an important one. In one scale is the interest of the millions who are lighted, shod or clothed with the help of it, and the thousands of labourers and manufacturers who would be employed in producing the articles which might be given in exchange for it, if received from America. In the other scale are the interests of the adventurers in the whale fishery; each of whom indeed, politically considered may be of more importance to the state than a simple labourer or manufacturer: but to make the estimate with the accuracy it merits, we should multiply the numbers in each scale into their individual importance, and see which preponderates.

Both governments have seen with concern that their commercial intercourse does not grow as rapidly as they would wish. The system of the United States is to use neither prohibitions nor premiums. Commerce there regulates itself freely, and asks nothing better. Where a government finds itself under the necessity of undertaking that regulation, it would seem that it should conduct it as an intelligent merchant would: that is to say, invite customers to purchase, by facilitating their means of payment, and by adapting goods to their taste. If this idea be just, government here has two operations to attend to, with respect to the commerce of the United States. 1. To do away, or to moderate, as much as possible, the prohibitions and monopolies of their materials for payment. 2. To encourage the institution of the principal manufactures which the necessities, or the habits of their new customers call for. Under this latter head a hint shall be suggested which must find its apology in the motive from which it flows, that is, a desire of promoting mutual interests and close friendship. 600,000 of the labouring poor of America, comprehending slaves under that denomination, are clothed in three of the simplest manufactures possible, to wit, Oznabrigs, Plains, and Duffel blankets. The first is a linen, the two last woollens. It happens too that they are used exactly by those who cultivate the tobacco and rice and in a good degree by those employed in the whale fishery. To these manufactures they are so habituated, that no substitute will be received. If the vessels which bring tobacco, rice and whale oil, do not find them in the ports of delivery, they must be sought where they can be found. That is in England at present. If they were made in France they would be gladly taken in exchange there. The quantities annually used by this description of people, and their value are as follows.

Oznabrigs 2,700,000 aunes a 16. sous the aune worth	2,160,000l.
Plains 1,350,000 aunes a 2. livres the aune . .	2,700,000
Duffel blankets 300,000 a 7livres. 4sous. each .	2,160,000
	7,020,000

It would be difficult to say how much should be added for the consumption of inhabitants of other descriptions. A great deal surely. But the present view shall be confined to the one description named. 7 millions of livres, are 9 millions of days work of those who raise card, spin and weave the wool and flax; and at 300 working days to the year, would maintain 30,000 people. To introduce these simple manufactures suppose government to give 5 per cent. on the value of what should be exported of them, for 10. years to come. If none should be exported, nothing would be to be paid; but on the other hand, if the manufactures, with this encouragement should rise to the full demand, it will be a sacrifice of 351,000livres. a year for 10. years only, to produce a perpetual subsistence for more than 30,000 people, (for the demand will grow with our population) while she must expend perpetually 1,285,000livres. a year to maintain the 3,570 seamen, who would supply her with whale oil: that is to say, for each seaman as much as for 30. labourers and manufacturers.

But to return to our subject, and to conclude.

Whether then we consider the Arret of Sept. 28. in a political or a commercial light, it would seem that the U. S. should be excepted from its operation. Still more so when they invoke against it the amity subsisting between the two nations, the desire of binding them together by every possible interest and connection, the several acts in favour of this exception, the dignity of legislation which admits not of changes backwards and forwards, the interests of commerce which require steady regulations, the assurances of the friendly motives which have led the king to pass these acts, and the hope that no cause will arise to change either his motives or his measures towards us.

Plan for Establishing Uniformity in the Coinage, Weights, and Measures of the United States

COMMUNICATED TO THE HOUSE OF REPRESENTATIVES, JULY 13, 1790

New York, July 4, 1790

SIR:—In obedience to the order of the House of Representatives of January 15th, I have now the honor to enclose you a report on the subject of measures, weights, and coins. The length of time which intervened between the date of the order and my arrival in this city, prevented my receiving it till the 15th of April; and an illness which followed soon after added, unavoidably, some weeks to the delay; so that it was not till about the 20th May that I was able to finish the report. A desire to lessen the number of its imperfections induced me still to withhold it awhile, till, on the 15th of June, came to my hands, from Paris, a printed copy of a proposition made by the Bishop of Autun, to the National Assembly of France, on the subject of weights and measures; and three days afterwards I received, through the channel of the public papers, the speech of Sir John Riggs Miller, of April 13th, in the British House of Commons, on the same subject. In the report which I had prepared, and was then about to give in, I had proposed the latitude of 38°, as that which should fix our standard, because it was the medium latitude of the United States; but the proposition before the National Assembly of France, to take that of 45° as being a middle term between the equator and both poles, and a term which consequently might unite the nations of both hemispheres, appeared to me so well chosen, and so just, that I did not hesitate a moment to prefer it to that of 38°. It became necessary, of course, to conform all my calculations to that standard—an operation which has been retarded by my other occupations.

These circumstances will, I hope, apologize for the delay which has attended the execution of the order of the House; and, perhaps, a disposition on their part to have due regard for the proceedings of other nations, engaged on the same subject, may induce them still to defer deciding ultimately on it till their next session. Should this be the case, and should any new matter occur in the meantime, I shall think it my duty to communicate it to the House, as supplemental to the present report.

I have the honor to be, with sentiments of the most profound respect,

Sir, your most obedient and most humble servant.

The Secretary of State, to whom was referred, by the House of Representatives, to prepare and report a proper plan or plans for establishing uniformity in the currency, weights, and measures of the United States, in obedience thereto, makes the following report:—

To obtain uniformity in measures, weights, and coins, it is necessary to find some measure of invariable length, with which, as a standard, they may be compared.

There exists not in nature, as far as has been hitherto observed, a single subject or species of subject, accessible to man, which presents one constant and uniform dimension.

The globe of the earth itself, indeed, might be considered as invariable in all its dimensions, and that its circumference would furnish an invariable measure; but no one of its circles, great or small, is accessible to admeasurement through all its parts, and the various trials to measure definite portions of them, have been of such various result as to show there is no dependence on that operation for certainty.

Matter, then, by its mere extension, furnishing nothing invariable, its motion is the only remaining resource.

The motion of the earth round its axis, though not absolutely uniform and invariable, may be considered as such for every human purpose. It is measured obviously, but unequally, by the departure of a given meridian from the sun, and its return to it, constituting a solar day. Throwing together the inequalities of solar days, a mean interval, or day, has been found, and divided, by very general consent, into 86,400 equal parts.

A pendulum, vibrating freely, in small and equal arcs, may be so adjusted in its length, as, by its vibrations, to make this division of the earth's motion into 86,400 equal parts, called seconds of mean time.

Such a pendulum, then, becomes itself a measure of determinate length, to which all others may be referred to as to a standard.

But even a pendulum is not without its uncertainties.

1. The difficulty of ascertaining, in practice, its centre of oscillation, as depending on the form of the bob, and its distance from the point of suspension; the effect of the weight of the suspending wire towards displacing the centre of oscillation; that centre being seated within the body of the bob, and therefore inaccessible to the measure, are sources of considerable uncertainty.

2. Both theory and experience prove that, to preserve its isochronism, it must be shorter towards the equator, and longer towards the poles.

3. The height of the situation above the common level, as being an increment to the radius of the earth, diminishes the length of the pendulum.

4. The pendulum being made of metal, as is best, it varies its length with the variations in the temperature of the atmosphere.

5. To continue small and equal vibrations, through a sufficient length of time, and to count these vibrations, machinery and a power are necessary, which may exert a small but constant effort to renew the waste of motion; and the difficulty is so to apply these, as that they shall neither retard or accelerate the vibrations.

1. In order to avoid the uncertainties which respect the centre of oscillation, it has been proposed by Mr. Leslie, an ingenious artist of Philadelphia, to substitute, for the pendulum, a uniform cylindrical rod, without a bob.

Could the diameter of such a rod be infinitely small, the centre of oscillation would be exactly at two-thirds of the whole length, measured from the point of suspension. Giving it a diameter which shall render it sufficiently inflexible, the centre will be displaced, indeed; but, in a second rod not the (1) six hundred thousandth part of its length, and not the hundredth part as much as in a second pendulum with a spherical bob of proper diameter. This displacement is so infinitely minute, then, that we may consider the centre of oscillation, for all practical purposes, as residing at two-thirds of the length from the centre of suspension. The distance between these two centres might be easily and accurately ascertained in practice. But the whole rod is better for a standard than any portion of it, because sensibly defined at both its extremities.

2. The uncertainty arising from the difference of length requisite for the second pendulum, or the second rod, in different latitudes, may be avoided by fixing on some one latitude, to which our standard shall refer. That of 38°, as being the middle latitude of the United States, might seem the most convenient, were we to consider ourselves alone; but connected with other nations by commerce and science, it is better to fix on that parallel which bids fairest to be adopted by them also. The 45th, as being the middle term between the equator and pole, has been heretofore proposed in Europe, and the proposition has been lately renewed there under circumstances which may very possibly give it some effect. This parallel is distinguished with us also as forming our principal northern boundary. Let the completion of the 45th degree, then, give the standard for our union, with the hope that it may become a line of union with the rest of the world.

The difference between the second rod for 45° of latitude, and that for 31°, our other extreme, is to be examined.

The second *pendulum* for 45° of latitude, according to Sir Isaac Newton's computation, must be of (2) 39.14912 inches English measure; and a *rod*, to vibrate in the same time, must be of the same length between the centres of suspension and oscillation; and, consequently, its whole length 58.7 (or, more exactly, 58.72368) inches. This is longer than the rod which shall vibrate seconds in the 31° of latitude, by about ⅟679 part of its whole length; a difference so minute, that it might be neglected, as insensible, for the common purposes of life, but, in cases requiring perfect exactness, the second rod, found by trial of its vibrations in any part of the United States, may be corrected by computation for the (3) latitude of the place, and so brought exactly to the standard of 45°.

3. By making the experiment in the level of the ocean, the

difference will be avoided, which a higher position might occasion.

4. The expansion and contraction of the rod with the change of temperature, is the fourth source of uncertainty before mentioned. According to the high authority so often quoted, an iron rod, of given length, may vary, between summer and winter, in temperate latitudes, and in the common exposure of house clocks, from $\frac{1}{1728}$ to $\frac{1}{2592}$ of its whole length, which, in a rod of 58.7 inches, will be from about two to three hundredths of an inch. This may be avoided by adjusting and preserving the standard in a cellar, or other place, the temperature of which never varies. Iron is named for this purpose, because the least expansible of the metals.

5. The practical difficulty resulting from the effect of the machinery and moving power is very inconsiderable in the present state of the arts; and, in their progress towards perfection, will become less and less. To estimate and obviate this, will be the artist's province. It is as nothing when compared with the sources of inaccuracy hitherto attending measures.

Before quitting the subject of the inconveniences, some of which attend the pendulum alone, others both the pendulum and rod, it must be added that the rod would have an accidental but very precious advantage over the pendulum in this country, in the event of our fixing the foot at the nearest aliquot part of either; for the difference between the common foot, and those so to be deduced, would be three times greater in the case of the pendulum than in that of the rod.

Let the standard of measure, then, be a uniform cylindrical rod of iron, of such length as, in latitude 45°, in the level of the ocean, and in a cellar, or other place, the temperature of which does not vary through the year, shall perform its vibrations in small and equal arcs, in one second of mean time.

A standard of invariable length being thus obtained, we may proceed to identify, by that, the measures, weights and coins of the United States; but here a doubt presents itself as to the extent of the reformation meditated by the House of Representatives. The experiment made by Congress in the year one thousand seven hundred and eighty-six, by declaring that there should be one money of account and payment through the United States, and that its parts and multiples should be in a decimal ratio, has obtained such general approbation, both at home and abroad, that nothing seems wanting but the actual coinage, to banish the discordant pounds, shillings, pence, and farthings of the different States, and to establish in their stead the new denominations. Is it in contemplation with the House of Representatives to extend a like improvement to our measures and weights, and to arrange them also in a decimal ratio? The facility which this would introduce into the vulgar arithmetic would, unquestionably, be soon and sensibly felt by the whole mass of the people, who would thereby be enabled to compute for themselves whatever they should have occasion to buy, to sell, or to measure, which the present complicated and difficult ratios place beyond their computation for the most part. Or, is it the opinion of the Representatives that the difficulty of changing the established habits of a whole nation opposes an insuperable bar to this improvement? Under this uncertainty, the Secretary of State thinks it his duty to submit alternative plans, that the House may, at their will, adopt either the one or the other, exclusively, or the one for the present and the other for a future time, when the public mind may be supposed to have become familiarized to it.

I. And first, on the supposition that the present measures and weights are to be retained but to be rendered uniform and invariable, by bringing them to the same invariable standard.

The first settlers of these States, having come chiefly from England, brought with them the measures and weights of that country. These alone are generally established among us, either by law or usage; and these, therefore, are alone to be retained and fixed. We must resort to that country for information of what they are, or ought to be.

This rests, principally, on the evidence of certain standard measures and weights, which have been preserved, of long time, in different deposits. But differences among these having been known to exist, the House of Commons, in the years 1757 and 1758, appointed committees to inquire into the original standards of their weights and measures. These committees, assisted by able mathematicians and artists, examined and compared with each other the several standard measures and weights, and made reports on them in the years 1758 and 1759. The circumstances under which these reports were made entitle them to be considered, as far as they go, as the best written testimony existing of the standard measures and weights of England; and as such, they will be relied on in the progress of this report.

MEASURES OF LENGTH.

The measures of length in use among us are:

The league of 3 miles,	The fathom of 2 yards,
The mile of 8 furlongs,	The ell of a yard and
The furlong of 40 poles or	quarter,
perches,	The yard of 3 feet,
The pole or perch of 5½	The foot of 12 inches, and
yards,	The inch of 10 lines.

On this branch of their subject, the committee of 1757–1758, says that the standard measures of length at the receipt of the exchequer, are a yard, supposed to be of the time of Henry VII., and a yard and ell supposed to have been made about the year 1601; that they are brass rods, very coarsely made, their divisions not exact, and the rods bent; and that in the year 1742, some members of the Royal Society had been at great pains in taking an exact measure of these standards, by very curious instruments, prepared by the ingenious Mr. Graham; that the Royal Society had had a brass rod made pursuant to their experiments, which was made so accurately, and by persons so skilful and exact, that it was thought not easy to obtain a more exact one; and the committee, in fact, found it to agree with the standards at the exchequer, as near as it was possible. They furnish no means, to persons at a distance, of knowing what this standard is. This, however, is supplied by the evidence of the second pendulum, which, according to the authority before quoted, is, at London, 39.1682 English inches, and, consequently, the second rod there is of 58.7523 of the same inches. When we shall have found, then, by actual trial, the second rod for 45° by adding the difference of their computed length, to wit: $^{287}/_{10000}$ of an inch, or rather $^{3}/_{10}$ of a line (which in practice will endanger less error than an attempt at so minute a fraction as the ten thousandth parts of an inch) we shall have the second rod of London, or a true measure of 58¾ English inches. Or, to shorten the operation, without varying the result,

Let the standard rod of 45° be divided into 587⅕ equal parts, and let each of these parts be declared a line.

10 lines an inch,	5½ yards a perch or pole,
12 inches a foot,	40 poles or perches a
3 feet a yard,	furlong,
3 feet 9 inches an ell,	8 furlongs a mile,
6 feet a fathom,	3 miles a league.

SUPERFICIAL MEASURES.

Our measures of surface are, the acre of 4 roods and the rood of 40 square poles; so established by a statute of 33 Edw. I. Let them remain the same.

MEASURES OF CAPACITY.

The measures of capacity in use among us are the following names and proportions:

The gill, four of which make a pint.

Two pints make a quart.

Two quarts a pottle.

Two pottles a gallon.

Two gallons a peck, dry measure.

Eight gallons make a measure called a firkin, in liquid substances, and a bushel, dry.

Two firkins, or bushels, make a measure called a rundlet or kilderkin, liquid, and a strike, dry.

Two kilderkins, or strikes, make a measure called a barrel, liquid, and a coomb, dry; this last term being ancient and little used.

Two barrels, or coombs, make a measure called a hogshead, liquid, or a quarter, dry; each being the quarter of a ton.

A hogshead and a third make a tierce, or third of a ton.

Two hogsheads make a pipe, butt, or puncheon; and

Two pipes make a ton.

But no one of these measures is of a determinate capacity. The report of the committee of 1757–8, shows that the gallon is of very various content; and that being the unit, all the others must vary with it.

The gallon and bushel contain—

224 and 1792 cubic inches, according to the standard wine gallon preserved at Guildhall.

231 and 1848, according to the statute of 5th of Anne.

264.8 and 2118.4, according to the ancient Rumford quart, of 1228, examined by the committee.

265.5 and 2124, according to three standard bushels preserved in the Exchequer, to wit: one of Henry VII., without a rim; one dated 1091, supposed for 1591, or 1601, and one dated 1601.

266.25 and 2130, according to the ancient Rumford gallon of 1228, examined by the committee.

268.75 and 2150, according to the Winchester bushel, as declared by statute 13, 14, William III., which has been the model for some of the grain States.

271, less 2 spoonfuls, and 2168, less 16 spoonfuls, according to a standard gallon of Henry VII., and another dated 1601, marked E. E., both in the Exchequer.

271 and 2168, according to a standard gallon in the Exchequer, dated 1601, marked E., and called the corn gallon.

272 and 2176, according to the three standard corn gallons last mentioned, as measured in 1688, by an artist for the Commissioners of the Excise, generally used in the seaport towns, and by mercantile people, and thence introduced into some of the grain States.

277.18 and 2217.44, as established for the measure of coal by the statute 12 Anne.

278 and 2224, according to the standard bushel of Henry VII., with a copper rim, in the Exchequer.

278.4 and 2227.2 according to two standard pints of 1601 and 1602, in the Exchequer.

280 and 2240, according to the standard quart of 1601, in the Exchequer.

282 and 2256, according to the standard gallon for beer and ale in the Treasury.

There are, moreover, varieties on these varieties, from the barrel to the ton, inclusive; for, if the barrel be of herrings, it must contain 28 gallons by the statute 13 Eliz. c. 11. If of wine, it must contain 31½ gallons by the statute 2 Henry VI. c. 11, and 1 Rich. III. c. 15. If of beer or ale, it must contain 34 gallons by the statute 1 William and Mary, c. 24, and the higher measures in proportion.

In those of the United States which have not adopted the statutes of William and Mary, and of Anne before cited, nor their substance, the wine gallon of 231 cubic inches rests on the authority of very long usage, before the 5th of Anne, the origin and foundation of which are unknown; the bushel is the Winchester bushel, by the 11 Henry VII. undefined; and the barrel of ale 32 gallons, and of beer 36 gallons, by the statute 23 Henry VIII. c. 4.

The Secretary of State is not informed whether there have been any, and what, alterations of these measures by the laws of the particular States.

It is proposed to retain this series of measures, but to fix the gallon to one determinate capacity, as the unit of measure, both wet and dry; for convenience is in favor of abolishing the distinction between wet and dry measures.

The wine gallon, whether of 224 or 231 cubic inches, may be altogether disregarded, as concerning, principally, the mercantile and the wealthy, the least numerous part of the society, and the most capable of reducing one measure to another by calculation. This gallon is little used among the mass of farmers, whose chief habits and interests are in the size of the corn bushel.

Of the standard measures before stated, two are principally distinguished in authority and practice. The statute bushel of 2150 cubic inches, which gives a gallon of 268.75 cubic inches, and the standard gallon of 1601, called the corn gallon of 271 or 272 cubic inches, which has introduced the mercantile bushel of 2276 inches. The former of these is most used in some of the grain States, the latter in others. The middle term of 270 cubic inches may be taken as a mutual compromise of convenience, and as offering this general advantage: that the bushel being of 2160 cubic inches, is exactly a cubic foot and a quarter, and so facilitates the conversion of wet and dry measures into solid contents and tonnage, and simplifies the

connection of measures and weights, as will be shown hereafter. It may be added, in favor of this, as a medium measure,
that eight of the standard, or statute measures before enumerated, are below this term, and nine above it.

The measures to be made for use, being four sided, with
   rectangular sides and bottom.

The pint will be 3 inches square, and 3¾ inches deep;

The quart 3 inches square, and 7½ inches deep;

The pottle 3 inches square, and 15 inches deep, or 4½, 5,
   and 6 inches.

The gallon 6 inches square, and 7½ inches deep, or 5, 6,
   and 9 inches;

The peck 6, 9, and 10 inches;

The half bushel 12 inches square, and 7½ inches deep; and

The bushel 12 inches square, and 15 inches deep, or 9, 15,
   and 16 inches.

Cylindrical measures have the advantage of superior
strength, but square ones have the greater advantage of enabling every one who has a rule in his pocket, to verify their
contents by measuring them. Moreover, till the circle can be
squared, the cylinder cannot be cubed, nor its contents exactly
expressed in figures.

Let the measures of capacity, then, for the United States
   be—

A gallon of 270 cubic inches;

The gallon to contain 2 pottles;

The pottle 2 quarts;

The quart 2 pints;

The pint 4 gills;

Two gallons to make a peck;

Eight gallons a bushel or firkin;

Two bushels, or firkin, a strike or kilderkin;

Two strikes, or kilderkins, a coomb or barrel;

Two coombs, or barrels, a quarter or hogshead;

A hogshead and a third one tierce;

Two hogsheads a pipe, butt, or puncheon; and

Two pipes a ton.

And let all measures of capacity of dry subjects be stricken
   with a straight strike.

Weights.

There are two series of weights in use among us; the one called avoirdupois, the other troy.

In the Avoirdupois series:

The pound is divided into 16 ounces;
The ounce into 16 drachms;
The drachm into 4 quarters.

In the Troy series:

The pound is divided into 12 ounces;
The ounce (according to the subdivision of the apothecaries) into 8 drachms;
The drachm into 3 scruples;
The scruple into 20 grains.

According to the subdivision for gold and silver, the ounce is divided into twenty pennyweights, and the pennyweight into twenty-four grains.

So that the pound troy contains 5760 grains, of which 7000 are requisite to make the pound avoirdupois; of course the weight of the pound troy is to that of the pound avoirdupois as 5760 to 7000, or as 144 to 175.

It is remarkable that this is exactly the proportion of the ancient liquid gallon of Guildhall of 224 cubic inches, to the corn gallon of 272; for 224 are to 272 as 144 to 175. (4.)

It is further remarkable still, that this is also the exact proportion between the specific weight of any measure of wheat, and of the same measure of water: for the statute bushel is of 64 pounds of wheat. Now as 144 to 175, so are 64 pounds to 77.7 pounds; but 77.7 pounds is known to be the weight of (5.) 2150.4 cubic inches of pure water, which is exactly the content of the Winchester bushel, as declared by the statute 13, 14, Will. 3. That statute determined the bushel to be a cylinder of 18½ inches diameter, and 8 inches depth. Such a cylinder, as nearly as it can be cubed, and expressed in figures, contains 2150.425 cubic inches; a result which reflects authority on the declaration of Parliament, and induces a favorable opinion of the care with which they investigated the contents of the ancient bushel, and also a belief that there might exist evidence of it at that day, unknown to the committees of 1758 and 1759.

We find, then, in a continued proportion 64 to 77.7 as 224 to 272, and as 144 to 175, that is to say, the specific weight of a measure of wheat, to that of the same measure of water, as the cubic contents of the wet gallon, to those of the dry; and as the weight of a pound troy to that of a pound avoirdupois.

This seems to have been so combined as to render it indifferent whether a thing were dealt out by weight or measure; for the dry gallon of wheat, and the liquid one of wine, were of the same weight; and the avoirdupois pound of wheat, and the troy pound of wine, were of the same measure. Water and the vinous liquors, which enter most into commerce, are so nearly of a weight, that the difference, in moderate quantities, would be neglected by both buyer and seller; some of the wines being a little heavier, and some a little lighter, than water.

Another remarkable correspondence is that between weights and measures. For 1000 ounces avoirdupois of pure water fill a cubic foot, with mathematical exactness.

What circumstances of the times, or purposes of barter or commerce, called for this combination of weights and measures, with the subjects to be exchanged or purchased, are not now to be ascertained. But a triple set of exact proportionals representing weights, measures, and the things to be weighed and measured, and a relation so integral between weights and solid measures, must have been the result of design and scientific calculation, and not a mere coincidence of hazard. It proves that the dry and wet measures, the heavy and light weights, must have been original parts of the system they compose—contrary to the opinion of the committee of 1757, 1758, who thought that the avoirdupois weight was not an ancient weight of the kingdom, nor ever even a legal weight, but during a single year of the reign of Henry VIII.; and, therefore, concluded, otherwise than will be here proposed, to suppress it altogether. Their opinion was founded chiefly on the silence of the laws as to this weight. But the harmony here developed in the system of weights and measures, of which the avoirdupois makes an essential member, corroborated by a general use, from very high antiquity, of that, or of a nearly similar weight under another (6.) name, seem stronger proofs that this is legal weight, than the mere silence of the written laws is of the contrary.

Be this as it may, it is in such general use with us, that, on the principle of popular convenience, its higher denominations, at least, must be preserved. It is by the avoirdupois pound and ounce that our citizens have been used to buy and sell. But the smaller subdivisions of drachms and quarters are not in use with them. On the other hand, they have been used to weigh their money and medicine with the pennyweights and grains troy weight, and are not in the habit of using the pounds and ounces of that series. It would be for their convenience, then, to suppress the pound and ounce troy, and the drachm and quarter avoirdupois; and to form into one series the avoirdupois pound and ounce, and the troy pennyweight and grain. The avoirdupois ounce contains 18 pennyweights 5½ grains troy weight. Divide it, then, into 18 pennyweights, and the pennyweight, as heretofore, into 24 grains, and the new pennyweight will contain between a third and a quarter of a grain more than the present troy pennyweight; or, more accurately, it will be to that as 875 to 864— a difference not to be noticed, either in money or medicine, below the denomination of an ounce.

But it will be necessary to refer these weights to a determinate mass of some substance, the specific gravity of which is invariable. Rain water is such a substance, and may be referred to everywhere, and through all time. It has been found by accurate experiments that a cubic foot of rain water weighs 1000 ounces avoirdupois, standard weights of the exchequer. It is true that among these standard weights the committee report small variations; but this experiment must decide in favor of those particular weights, between which, and an integral mass of water, so remarkable a coincidence has been found. To render this standard more exact, the water should be weighed always in the same temperature of air; as heat, by increasing its volume, lessens its specific gravity. The cellar of uniform temperature is best for this also.

Let it, then, be established that an ounce is of the weight of a cube of rain water, of one-tenth of a foot; or, rather, that it is the thousandth part of the weight of a cubic foot of rain water, weighed in the standard temperature; that the series of weights of the United States shall consist of pounds, ounces, pennyweights, and grains; whereof

24 grains shall be one pennyweight;

18 pennyweights one ounce;

16 ounces one pound.

COINS.

Congress, in 1786, established the money unit at 375.64 troy grains of pure silver. It is proposed to enlarge this by about the third of a grain in weight, or a mill in value; that is to say, to establish it at 376 (or, more exactly, 375.989343) instead of 375.64 grains; because it will be shown that this, as the unit of coin, will link in system with the units of length, surface, capacity, and weight, whenever it shall be thought proper to extend the decimal ratio through all these branches. It is to preserve the possibility of doing this, that this very minute alteration is proposed.

We have this proportion, then, 875 to 864, as 375.989343 grains troy to 371.2626277; the expression of the unit in the new grains.

Let it be declared, therefore, that the money unit, or dollar of the United States, shall contain 371.262 American grains of pure silver.

If nothing more, then, is proposed, than to render uniform and stable the system we already possess, this may be effected on the plan herein detailed; the sum of which is: 1st. That the present measures of length be retained, and fixed by an invariable standard. 2d. That the measures of surface remain as they are, and be invariable also as the measures of length to which they are to refer. 3d. That the unit of capacity, now so equivocal, be settled at a medium and convenient term, and defined by the same invariable measures of length. 4th. That the more known terms in the two kinds of weights be retained, and reduced to one series, and that they be referred to a definite mass of some substance, the specific gravity of which never changes. And 5th. That the quantity of pure silver in the money unit be expressed in parts of the weights so defined.

In the whole of this no change is proposed, except an insensible one in the troy grain and pennyweight, and the very minute one in the money unit.

II. But if it be thought that, either now, or at any future time, the citizens of the United States may be induced to undertake a thorough reformation of their whole system of measures, weights and coins, reducing every branch to the same decimal ratio already established in their coins, and thus bringing the calculation of the principal affairs of life within the arithmetic of every man who can multiply and divide plain numbers, greater changes will be necessary.

The unit of measure is still that which must give law through the whole system; and from whatever unit we set out, the coincidences between the old and new ratios will be rare. All that can be done, will be to choose such a unit as will produce the most of these. In this respect the second rod has been found, on trial, to be far preferable to the second pendulum.

MEASURES OF LENGTH.

Let the second rod, then, as before described, be the standard of measure; and let it be divided into five equal parts, each of which shall be called a foot; for, perhaps, it may be better generally to retain the name of the nearest present measure, where there is one tolerably near. It will be about one quarter of an inch shorter than the present foot.

Let the foot be divided into 10 inches;
Let 10 feet make a decad;

The inch into 10 lines;
10 decads one rood;

The line into 10 points;
10 roods a furlong;
10 furlongs a mile.

SUPERFICIAL MEASURES.

Superficial measures have been estimated, and so may continue to be, in squares of the measures of length, except in the case of lands, which have been estimated by squares, called roods and acres. Let the rood be equal to a square, every side of which is 100 feet. This will be 6.483 English feet less than the English (7.) rood every way, and 1311 square feet less in its whole contents; that is to say, about one-eighth; in which proportion, also, 4 roods will be less than the present acre.

MEASURES OF CAPACITY.

Let the unit of capacity be the cubic foot, to be called a bushel. It will contain 1620.05506862 cubic inches, English; be about one-fourth less than that before proposed to be adopted as a medium; one-tenth less than the bushel made from 8 of the Guildhall gallons; and one-fourteenth less than the bushel made from 8 Irish gallons of 217.6 cubic inches.

Let the bushel be divided into 10 pottles;

Each pottle into 10 demi-pints;

Each demi-pint into 10 metres, which will be of a cubic inch each.

Let 10 bushels be a quarter, and

10 quarters a last, or double ton.

The measures for use being four-sided, and the sides and bottoms rectangular, the bushel will be a foot cube.

The pottle 5 inches square and four inches deep;

The demi-pint 2 inches square, and 2½ inches deep;

The metre, an inch cube.

WEIGHTS.

Let the weight of a cubic inch of rain water, or the thousandth part of a cubic foot, be called an ounce; and let the ounce be divided into 10 double scruples:

The double scruple into 10 carats;

The carat into 10 minims or demi-grains;

The minim into 10 mites.

Let 10 ounces make a pound;

10 pounds a stone;

16 stones a kental;

10 kentals a hogshead.

COINS.

Let the money unit, or dollar, contain eleventh-twelfths of an ounce of pure silver. This will be 376 troy grains, (or more exactly, 375.989343 troy grains,) which will be about a third of a grain, (or more exactly, .349343 of a grain,) more than the present unit. This, with the twelfth of alloy already established, will make the dollar or unit, of the weight of an ounce, or of a cubic inch of rain water, exactly. The series of mills, cents, dimes, dollars, and eagles, to remain as already established. (8.)

The second rod, or the second pendulum, expressed in the measures of other countries, will give the proportion between their measures and those of the United States.

Measures, weights and coins, thus referred to standards unchangeable in their nature, (as is the length of a rod vibrating seconds, and the weight of a definite mass of rain water,) will themselves be unchangeable. These standards, too, are such as to be accessible to all persons, in all times and places. The measures and weights derived from them fall in so nearly with some of those now in use, as to facilitate their introduction; and being arranged in decimal ratio, they are within the calculation of every one who possesses the first elements of arithmetic, and of easy comparison, both for foreigners and citizens, with the measures, weights, and coins of other countries.

A gradual introduction would lessen the inconveniences which might attend too sudden a substitution, even of an easier for a more difficult system. After a given term, for instance, it might begin in the custom-houses, where the merchants would become familiarized to it. After a further term, it might be introduced into all legal proceedings, and merchants and traders in foreign commodities might be required to use it in their dealings with one another. After a still further term, all other descriptions of people might receive it into common use. Too long a postponement, on the other hand, would increase the difficulties of its reception with the increase of our population.

Appendix, containing illustrations and developments of some passages of the preceding report.

(1.) In the second pendulum with a spherical bob, call the distance between the centres of suspension and of the bob, 2×19.575, or 2d, and the radius of the bob $= r$; then 2d : $r :: r : r^2/2d$ and $\frac{2}{5}$ of this last proportional expresses the displacement of the centre of oscillation, to wit: $2r^2/5 \times 2d = r^2/5d$.

Two inches have been proposed as a proper diameter for such a bob. In that case r will be $= 1.$ inch, and $r/_{5d} = \frac{1}{9787}$ inches.

In the cylindrical second rod, call the length of the rod, 3×19.575. or 3d, and its radius $= r$ and $r/_2 \times 3d = r/_{6d}$ will express the displacement of the centre of oscillation. It is thought the rod will be sufficiently inflexible if it be ⅕ of an inch in diameter. Then r will be $= .1$ inch, and $r/_{6d} = \frac{1}{11745}$ inches, which is but the 120th part of the displacement in the case of the pendulum with a spherical bob, and but the 689,710th part of the whole length of the rod. If the rod be even of half an inch diameter, the displacement will be but $\frac{1}{1879}$ of an inch, or $\frac{1}{110356}$ of the length of the rod.

(2.) Sir Isaac Newton computes the pendulum for 45° to be 36 pouces 8.428 lignes. Picard made the English foot 11 pouces 2.6 lignes, and Dr. Maskelyne 11 pouces 3.11 lignes. D'Alembert states it at 11 pouces 3 lignes, which has been used in these calculations as a middle term, and gives us 36 pouces 8.428 lignes $= 39.1491$ inches. This length for the pendulum of 45° had been adopted in this report before the Bishop of Autun's proposition was known here. He relies on Mairan's ratio for the length of the pendulum in the latitude of Paris, to wit: 504 : 257 : : 72 pouces to a 4th proportional, which will be 36.71428 pouces $= 39.1619$ inches, the length of the pendulum for latitude 48° 50′. The difference between this and the pendulum for 45° is .0113 of an inch; so that the pendulum for 45° would be estimated, according to Mairan, at $39.1619 - .0113 = 39.1506$ inches, almost precisely the same with Newton's computation herein adopted.

(3.) Sir Isaac Newton's computations for the different degrees of latitude, from 30° to 45°, are as follows:

	Pieds.	Lignes.			Pieds.	Lignes.
30°	. 3	. 7.948		42°	. 3	. 8.327
35	. 3	. 8.099		43	. 3	. 8.361
40	. 3	. 8.261		44	. 3	. 8.394
41	. 3	. 8.294		45	. 3	. 8.428

(4.) Or, more exactly, 144 : 175 : : 224 : 272.2.

(5.) Or, more exactly, 62.5 : 1728 : : 77.7 : 2150.39.

(6.) The merchant's weight.

(7.) The Eng. rood contains 10,890 sq. feet $= 104.355$ feet sq.

(8.) *The Measures, Weights, and Coins of the Decimal System, estimated in those of England, now used in the United States.*

1. MEASURES OF LENGTH.

	Feet.	Equivalent in English measure.

The point, . .001   . .011 inch.

The line, . .01   . .117

The inch, . .1   . 1.174, about $\frac{1}{7}$ more than the Eng. inch.

The foot, . 1. $\Big\}$. 11.744736 $\Big\}$ about $\frac{1}{48}$ less than
              . .978728 feet, $\Big\}$ the English foot.

The decad, . 10.   . 9.787, about $\frac{1}{48}$ less than the 10 feet rod of the carpenters.

The rood, . 100.   . 97.872, about $\frac{1}{16}$ less than the side of an English square rood.

The furlong, 1000.   . 978.728, about $\frac{1}{3}$ more than the Eng. fur.

The mile, . 10000.   . 9787.28, about $1\frac{6}{7}$ English mile, nearly the Scotch and Irish mile, and $\frac{1}{2}$ the German mile.

2. SUPERFICIAL MEASURE.

	Roods.	

The hundredth,   . .01   . 95.69 square feet English.

The tenth,   . .1   . 957.9

The rood,   . 1.   . 9579.085

The double acre,   . 10.   . 2.199, or say 2.2 acres English.

The square furlong, . 100.   . 22.

3. MEASURE OF CAPACITY.

	Bushels.	Cub. Inches.

The metre,   . .001   . 1.62

The demi-pint,   . .01   . 16.2, about $\frac{1}{24}$ less than the English half-pint.

The pottle,   . .1   . 162.005, about $\frac{1}{6}$ more than the English pottle.

The bushel,   . 1. $\Big\{$ 1620.05506862 $\Big\}$
                    $\Big\{$ .93753186841488435 cub feet. $\Big\}$

about $\frac{1}{4}$ less than the middle sized English bushel.

The quarter,	. 10.	. 9.375, about 1/5 less than the Eng. qr.
The last,	. 100.	. 93.753, about 1/7 more than the Eng. last.

4. WEIGHTS.

	Pounds.	Avoirdupois.	Troy.
Mite,	.00001	. . . .	.041 grains, about 1/5 less than the English mite.
Minim, or demi-grain,	.0001	. . . .	.4101, about 1/5 less than half-grain troy.
Carat,	.001	. . . .	4.101, about 1/40 more than the carat troy.
Double scruple,	.01	. . . .	41.017, about 1/40 more than 2 scruples troy.
Ounce, .	.1	.937531868414884352 oz.	410.170192431.85452 oz. about 1/16 less than the ounce avoirdupois.
Pound, .	1.	9.375 .585957417759 lb.	.712101 lb., about 1/4 less than the pound troy.
Stone, .	10.	93.753 oz. 5.8595 lb.	7.121 about 1/4 less than the English stone of 8 lbs. avoirdupois.
Kental, .	100.	937.531 oz. 58.5957 lb.	71.21 about 4/10 less than the English kental of 100 lbs. avoirdupois.
Hogshead, .	1000.	9375.318 oz. 585.9574 lb.	712.101

5. COINS.

	Dollars.			Troy grains	
The mill, .	.001	Dollar, .	1.	375.98934306	pure silver.
The cent, .	.01			34.18084937	alloy.
The dime, .	.1			410.17019243	
		Eagle, .	10.		

Postscript.

January 10, 1791

It is scarcely necessary to observe that the measures, weights, and coins, proposed in the preceding report, will be derived altogether from mechanical operations, viz.: A rod, vibrating seconds, divided into five equal parts, one of these subdivided, and multiplied decimally, for every measure of length, surface, and capacity, and these last filled with water, to determine the weights and coins. The arithmetical estimates in the report were intended only to give an idea of what the new measures, weights, and coins, would be nearly, when compared with the old. The length of the standard or second rod, therefore, was assumed from that of the pendulum; and as there has been small differences in the estimates of the pendulum by different persons, that of Sir Isaac Newton was taken, the highest authority the world has yet known. But, if even he has erred, the measures, weights, and coins proposed, will not be an atom the more or less. In cubing the new foot, which was estimated at .978728 of an English foot, or 11.744736 English inches, an arithmetical error of an unit happened in the fourth column of decimals, and was repeated in another line in the sixth column, so as to make the result one ten thousandth and one millionth of a foot too much. The thousandth part of this error (about one ten millionth of a foot) consequently fell on the metre of measure, the ounce weight, and the unit of money. In the last it made a difference of about the twenty-fifth part of a grain Troy, in weight, or the ninety-third of a cent in value. As it happened, this error was on the favorable side, so that the detection of it approximates our estimate of the new unit exactly that much nearer to the old, and reduces the difference between them to 34, instead of 38 hundredths of a grain Troy; that is to say, the money unit instead of 375.64 Troy grains of pure silver, as established heretofore, will now be 375.98934306 grains, as far as our knowledge of the length of the second pendulum enables us to judge; and the current of authorities since Sir Isaac Newton's time, gives reason to believe that his estimate is more probably above than below the truth, consequently future corrections of it will bring the estimate of the new unit still nearer to the old.

The numbers in which the arithmetical error before mentioned showed itself in the table, at the end of the report, have been rectified, and the table re-printed.

The head of superficial measures in the last part of the report, is thought to be not sufficiently developed. It is proposed that the rood of land, being 100 feet square, (and nearly a quarter of the present acre,) shall be the unit of land measure. This will naturally be divided into tenths and hundredths, the latter of which will be a square decad. Its multiples will also, of course, be tens, which may be called double acres, and hundreds, which will be equal to a square furlong each. The surveyor's chain should be composed of 100 links of one foot each.

Opinion on the Constitutionality of a
National Bank

February 15, 1791

THE BILL for establishing a National Bank undertakes among other things:—

1. To form the subscribers into a corporation.

2. To enable them in their corporate capacities to receive grants of land; and so far is against the laws of *Mortmain*.[1]

3. To make alien subscribers capable of holding lands; and so far is against the laws of *Alienage*.

4. To transmit these lands, on the death of a proprietor, to a certain line of successors; and so far changes the course of *Descents*.

5. To put the lands out of the reach of forfeiture or escheat; and so far is against the laws of *Forfeiture and Escheat*.

6. To transmit personal chattels to successors in a certain line; and so far is against the laws of *Distribution*.

7. To give them the sole and exclusive right of banking under the national authority; and so far is against the laws of Monopoly.

8. To communicate to them a power to make laws paramount to the laws of the States: for so they must be construed, to protect the institution from the control of the State legislatures; and so, probably, they will be construed.

I consider the foundation of the Constitution as laid on this ground: That "all powers not delegated to the United States, by the Constitution, nor prohibited by it to the States, are reserved to the States or to the people." [XIIth amendment.] To take a single step beyond the boundaries thus specially drawn around the powers of Congress, is to take possession of a boundless field of power, no longer susceptible of any definition.

The incorporation of a bank, and the powers assumed by this bill, have not, in my opinion, been delegated to the United States, by the Constitution.

---

[1] Though the Constitution controls the laws of Mortmain so far as to permit Congress itself to hold land for certain purposes, yet not so far as to permit them to communicate a similar right to other corporate bodies.

I. They are not among the powers specially enumerated: for these are: 1st. A power to lay taxes for the purpose of paying the debts of the United States; but no debt is paid by this bill, nor any tax laid. Were it a bill to raise money, its origination in the Senate would condemn it by the Constitution.

2d. "To borrow money." But this bill neither borrows money nor ensures the borrowing it. The proprietors of the bank will be just as free as any other money holders, to lend or not to lend their money to the public. The operation proposed in the bill, first, to lend them two millions, and then to borrow them back again, cannot change the nature of the latter act, which will still be a payment, and not a loan, call it by what name you please.

3. To "regulate commerce with foreign nations, and among the States, and with the Indian tribes." To erect a bank, and to regulate commerce, are very different acts. He who erects a bank, creates a subject of commerce in its bills; so does he who makes a bushel of wheat, or digs a dollar out of the mines; yet neither of these persons regulates commerce thereby. To make a thing which may be bought and sold, is not to prescribe regulations for buying and selling. Besides, if this was an exercise of the power of regulating commerce, it would be void, as extending as much to the internal commerce of every State, as to its external. For the power given to Congress by the Constitution does not extend to the internal regulation of the commerce of a State, (that is to say of the commerce between citizen and citizen,) which remain exclusively with its own legislature; but to its external commerce only, that is to say, its commerce with another State, or with foreign nations, or with the Indian tribes. Accordingly the bill does not propose the measure as a regulation of trade, but as "productive of considerable advantages to trade." Still less are these powers covered by any other of the special enumerations.

II. Nor are they within either of the general phrases, which are the two following:—

1. To lay taxes to provide for the general welfare of the United States, that is to say, "to lay taxes for *the purpose* of providing for the general welfare." For the laying of taxes is

the *power*, and the general welfare the *purpose* for which the power is to be exercised. They are not to lay taxes *ad libitum for any purpose they please*; but only *to pay the debts or provide for the welfare of the Union*. In like manner, they are not *to do anything they please* to provide for the general welfare, but only to *lay taxes* for that purpose. To consider the latter phrase, not as describing the purpose of the first, but as giving a distinct and independent power to do any act they please, which might be for the good of the Union, would render all the preceding and subsequent enumerations of power completely useless.

It would reduce the whole instrument to a single phrase, that of instituting a Congress with power to do whatever would be for the good of the United States; and, as they would be the sole judges of the good or evil, it would be also a power to do whatever evil they please.

It is an established rule of construction where a phrase will bear either of two meanings, to give it that which will allow some meaning to the other parts of the instrument, and not that which would render all the others useless. Certainly no such universal power was meant to be given them. It was intended to lace them up straitly within the enumerated powers, and those without which, as means, these powers could not be carried into effect. It is known that the very power now proposed *as a means* was rejected as *an end* by the Convention which formed the Constitution. A proposition was made to them to authorize Congress to open canals, and an amendatory one to empower them to incorporate. But the whole was rejected, and one of the reasons for rejection urged in debate was, that then they would have a power to erect a bank, which would render the great cities, where there were prejudices and jealousies on the subject, adverse to the reception of the Constitution.

2. The second general phrase is, "to make all laws *necessary* and proper for carrying into execution the enumerated powers." But they can all be carried into execution without a bank. A bank therefore is not *necessary*, and consequently not authorized by this phrase.

It has been urged that a bank will give great facility or convenience in the collection of taxes. Suppose this were true:

yet the Constitution allows only the means which are "*necessary*," not those which are merely "convenient" for effecting the enumerated powers. If such a latitude of construction be allowed to this phrase as to give any non-enumerated power, it will go to every one, for there is not one which ingenuity may not torture into a *convenience* in some instance *or other*, to *some one* of so long a list of enumerated powers. It would swallow up all the delegated powers, and reduce the whole to one power, as before observed. Therefore it was that the Constitution restrained them to the *necessary* means, that is to say, to those means without which the grant of power would be nugatory.

But let us examine this convenience and see what it is. The report on this subject, page 3, states the only *general* convenience to be, the preventing the transportation and re-transportation of money between the States and the treasury, (for I pass over the increase of circulating medium, ascribed to it as a want, and which, according to my ideas of paper money, is clearly a demerit.) Every State will have to pay a sum of tax money into the treasury; and the treasury will have to pay, in every State, a part of the interest on the public debt, and salaries to the officers of government resident in that State. In most of the States there will still be a surplus of tax money to come up to the seat of government for the officers residing there. The payments of interest and salary in each State may be made by treasury orders on the State collector. This will take up the greater part of the money he has collected in his State, and consequently prevent the great mass of it from being drawn out of the State. If there be a balance of commerce in favor of that State against the one in which the government resides, the surplus of taxes will be remitted by the bills of exchange drawn for that commercial balance. And so it must be if there was a bank. But if there be no balance of commerce, either direct or circuitous, all the banks in the world could not bring up the surplus of taxes but in the form of money. Treasury orders then, and bills of exchange may prevent the displacement of the main mass of the money collected, without the aid of any bank; and where these fail, it cannot be prevented even with that aid.

Perhaps, indeed, bank bills may be a more *convenient* vehicle than treasury orders. But a little *difference* in the degree of *convenience*, cannot constitute the necessity which the constitution makes the ground for assuming any non-enumerated power.

Besides; the existing banks will, without a doubt, enter into arrangements for lending their agency, and the more favorable, as there will be a competition among them for it; whereas the bill delivers us up bound to the national bank, who are free to refuse all arrangement, but on their own terms, and the public not free, on such refusal, to employ any other bank. That of Philadelphia, I believe, now does this business, by their post-notes, which, by an arrangement with the treasury, are paid by any State collector to whom they are presented. This expedient alone suffices to prevent the existence of that *necessity* which may justify the assumption of a non-enumerated power as a means for carrying into effect an enumerated one. The thing may be done, and has been done, and well done, without this assumption; therefore, it does not stand on that degree of *necessity* which can honestly justify it.

It may be said that a bank whose bills would have a currency all over the States, would be more convenient than one whose currency is limited to a single State. So it would be still more convenient that there should be a bank, whose bills should have a currency all over the world. But it does not follow from this superior conveniency, that there exists anywhere a power to establish such a bank; or that the world may not go on very well without it.

Can it be thought that the Constitution intended that for a shade or two of *convenience*, more or less, Congress should be authorised to break down the most ancient and fundamental laws of the several States; such as those against Mortmain, the laws of Alienage, the rules of descent, the acts of distribution, the laws of escheat and forfeiture, the laws of monopoly? Nothing but a necessity invincible by any other means, can justify such a prostitution of laws, which constitute the pillars of our whole system of jurisprudence. Will Congress be too straight-laced to carry the constitution into honest effect, unless they may pass over the foundation-laws of the State government for the slightest convenience of theirs?

The negative of the President is the shield provided by the

constitution to protect against the invasions of the legislature:
1. The right of the Executive. 2. Of the Judiciary. 3. Of the
States and State legislatures. The present is the case of a right
remaining exclusively with the States, and consequently one
of those intended by the Constitution to be placed under its
protection.

It must be added, however, that unless the President's
mind on a view of everything which is urged for and against
this bill, is tolerably clear that it is unauthorised by the Constitution; if the pro and the con hang so even as to balance
his judgment, a just respect for the wisdom of the legislature
would naturally decide the balance in favor of their opinion.
It is chiefly for cases where they are clearly misled by error,
ambition, or interest, that the Constitution has placed a check
in the negative of the President.

Opinion on the French Treaties

I PROCEED, in compliance with the requisition of the President, to give an opinion in writing on the general Question, Whether the U S. have a right to renounce their treaties with France, or to hold them suspended till the government of that country shall be established?

In the Consultation at the President's on the 19th inst. the Secretary of the Treasury took the following positions & consequences. 'France was a monarchy when we entered into treaties with it: but it has now declared itself a Republic, & is preparing a Republican form of government. As it may issue in a Republic, or a Military despotism, or in something else which may possibly render our alliance with it dangerous to ourselves, we have a right of election to renounce the treaty altogether, or to declare it suspended till their government shall be settled in the form it is ultimately to take; and then we may judge whether we will call the treaties into operation again, or declare them forever null. Having that right of election now, if we receive their minister without any qualifications, it will amount to an act of election to continue the treaties; & if the change they are undergoing should issue in a form which should bring danger on us, we shall not be then free to renounce them. To elect to continue them is equivalent to the making a new treaty at this time in the same form, that is to say, with a clause of guarantee; but to make a treaty with a clause of guarantee, during a war, is a departure from neutrality, and would make us associates in the war. To renounce or suspend the treaties therefore is a necessary act of neutrality.'

If I do not subscribe to the soundness of this reasoning, I do most fully to its ingenuity.—I shall now lay down the principles which according to my understanding govern the case.

I consider the people who constitute a society or nation as the source of all authority in that nation, as free to transact their common concerns by any agents they think proper, to change these agents individually, or the organisation of them in form or function whenever they please: that all the acts done by those agents under the authority of the nation, are the acts of the nation, are obligatory on them, & enure to their use, & can in no wise be annulled or affected by any change in the form of the government, or of the persons administering it. Consequently the Treaties between the U S. and France, were not treaties between the U S. & Louis Capet, but between the two nations of America & France, and the nations remaining in existance, tho' both of them have since changed their forms of government, the treaties are not annulled by these changes.

The Law of nations, by which this question is to be determined, is composed of three branches. 1. The Moral law of our nature. 2. The Usages of nations. 3. Their special Conventions. The first of these only, concerns this question, that is to say the Moral law to which Man has been subjected by his creator, & of which his feelings, or Conscience as it is sometimes called, are the evidence with which his creator has furnished him. The Moral duties which exist between individual and individual in a state of nature, accompany them into a state of society & the aggregate of the duties of all the individuals composing the society constitutes the duties of that society towards any other; so that between society & society the same moral duties exist as did between the individuals composing them while in an unassociated state, their maker not having released them from those duties on their forming themselves into a nation. Compacts then between nation & nation are obligatory on them by the same moral law which obliges individuals to observe their compacts. There are circumstances however which sometimes excuse the non-performance of contracts between man & man: so are there also between nation & nation. When performance, for instance, becomes *impossible*, non-performance is not immoral. So if performance becomes *self-destructive* to the party, the law of self-preservation overrules the laws of obligation to others. For the reality of these principles I appeal to the true fountains of evidence, the head & heart of every rational & honest man. It is there Nature has written her moral laws, & where every man may read them for himself. He will never read there the permission to annul his obligations for a time, or for ever, whenever they become 'dangerous, useless, or disagreeable.' Certainly not when merely *useless* or *disagreeable*, as seems to be said in an authority which has been quoted, Vattel. 2. 197, and tho he may under certain degrees of *danger*, yet the danger must be imminent, & the degree great. Of these, it is true, that nations are to be judges for themselves, since no one nation has a right to sit in judgment over another. But the tribunal of our consciences remains, & that also of the opinion of the world. These will revise the sentence we pass in our own case, & as we respect these, we must see that in judging ourselves we have honestly done the part of impartial & vigorous judges.

But Reason, which gives this right of self-liberation from a contract in certain cases, has subjected it to certain just limitations.

I. The danger which absolves us must be great, inevitable & imminent. Is such the character of that now apprehended from our treaties with France? What is that danger? 1. Is it that if their government issues in a military despotism, an alliance with them may taint us with despotic principles? But their government, when we allied ourselves to it, was a perfect despotism, civil & military, yet the treaties were made in that very state of things, & therefore that danger can furnish no just cause. 2. Is it that their government may issue in a republic, and too much strengthen our republican principles? But this is the hope of the great mass of our constituents, & not their dread. They do not look with longing to the happy mean of a limited monarchy. 3. But says the doctrine I am combating, the change the French are undergoing may possibly end in something we know not what, and bring on us danger we know not whence. In short it may end in a Rawhead & bloody-bones in the dark. Very well. Let Rawhead & bloody bones come, & then we shall be justified in making our peace with him, by renouncing our antient friends & his enemies. For observe, it is not the *possibility of danger*, which absolves a party from his contract: for that possibility always exists, & in every case. It existed in the present one at the moment of making the contract. If *possibilities* would avoid contracts, there never could be a valid contract. For possibilities hang over everything. Obligation is not suspended, till the danger is become real, & the moment of it so imminent, that we can no longer avoid decision without forever losing the opportunity to do it. But can a danger which has not yet taken it's shape, which does not yet exist, & never may exist, which cannot therefore be defined, can such a danger I ask, be so imminent that if we fail to pronounce on it in this moment we can never have another opportunity of doing it?

4. The danger apprehended, is it that, the treaties remaining valid, the clause guarantying their West India islands will engage us in the war? But does the Guarantee engage us to enter into the war in any event?

Are we to enter into it before we are called on by our allies? Have we been called on by them?—shall we ever be called on? Is it their interest to call on us?

Can they call on us before their islands are invaded, or imminently threatened?

If they can save them themselves, have they a right to call on us?

Are we obliged to go to war at once, without trying peaceable negociations with their enemy?

If all these questions be against us, there are still others behind.

Are we in a condition to go to war?

Can we be expected to begin before we are in condition?

Will the islands be lost if we do not save them? Have we the means of saving them?

If we cannot save them are we bound to go to war for a desperate object?

Will not a 10. years forbearance in us to call them into the guarantee of our posts, entitle us to some indulgence?

Many, if not most of these questions offer grounds of doubt whether the clause of guarantee will draw us into the war. Consequently if this be the danger apprehended, it is not yet certain enough to authorize us in sound morality to declare, at this moment, the treaties null.

5. Is the danger apprehended from the 17th article of the treaty of Commerce, which admits French ships of war & privateers to come and go freely, with prizes made on their enemies, while their enemies are not to have the same privilege with prizes made on the French? But Holland & Prussia

have approved of this article in our treaty with France, by subscribing to an express Salvo of it in our treaties with them. [Dutch treaty 22. Convention 6. Prussian treaty 19.] And England in her last treaty with France [art. 40] has entered into the same stipulation verbatim, & placed us in her ports on the same footing on which she is in ours, in case of a war of either of us with France. If we are engaged in such a war, England must receive prizes made on us by the French, & exclude those made on the French by us. Nay further, in this very article of her treaty with France, is a salvo of any similar article in any anterior treaty of either party, and ours with France being anterior, this salvo confirms it expressly. Neither of these three powers then have a right to complain of this article in our treaty.

6. Is the danger apprehended from the 22^d Art. of our treaty of commerce, which prohibits the enemies of France from fitting out privateers in our ports, or selling their prizes here. But we are free to refuse the same thing to France, there being no stipulation to the contrary, and we ought to refuse it on principles of fair neutrality.

7. But the reception of a Minister from the Republic of France, without qualifications, it is thought will bring us into danger: because this, it is said, will determine the continuance of the treaty, and take from us the right of self-liberation when at any time hereafter our safety would require us to use it. The reception of the Minister at all (in favor of which Col? Hamilton has given his opinion, tho reluctantly as he confessed) is an acknolegement of the legitimacy of their government: and if the qualifications meditated are to deny that legitimacy, it will be a curious compound which is to admit & deny the same thing. But I deny that the reception of a Minister has any thing to do with the treaties. There is not a word, in either of them, about sending ministers. This has been done between us under the common usage of nations, & can have no effect either to continue or annul the treaties.

But how can any act of election have the effect to continue a treaty which is acknoleged to be going on still? For it was not pretended the treaty was void, but only voidable if we chuse to declare it so. To make it void would require an act of election, but to let it go on requires only that we should do nothing, and doing nothing can hardly be an infraction of peace or neutrality.

But I go further & deny that the most explicit declaration made at this moment that we acknolege the obligation of the treatys could take from us the right of non-compliance at any future time when compliance would involve us in great & inevitable danger.

I conclude then that few of these sources threaten any danger at all; and from none of them is it inevitable: & consequently none of them give us the right at this moment of releasing ourselves from our treaties.

II. A second limitation on our right of releasing ourselves is that we are to do it from so much of the treaties only as is bringing great & inevitable danger on us, & not from the residue, allowing to the other party a right at the same time to determine whether on our non-compliance with that part they will declare the whole void. This right they would have, but we should not. Vattel. 2. 202. The only part of the treaties which can really lead us into danger is the clause of guarantee. That clause is all then we could suspend in any case, and the residue will remain or not at the will of the other party.

III. A third limitation is that where a party from necessity or danger withholds compliance with part of a treaty, it is bound to make compensation where the nature of the case admits & does not dispense with it. 2. Vattel 324. Wolf. 270. 443. If actual circumstances excuse us from entering into the war under the clause of guarantee, it will be a question whether they excuse us from compensation. Our weight in the war admits of an estimate; & that estimate would form the measure of compensation.

If in withholding a compliance with any part of the treaties, we do it without just cause or compensation, we give to France a cause of war, and so become associated in it on the other side. An injured friend is the bitterest of foes, & France had not discovered either timidity, or over-much forbearance on the late occasions. Is this the position we wish to take for our constituents? It is certainly not the one they would take for themselves.

I will proceed now to examine the principal authority which has been relied on for establishing the right of self liberation; because tho' just in part, it would lead us far beyond justice, if taken in all the latitude of which his expressions would admit. Questions of natural right are triable by their conformity with the moral sense & reason of man. Those who write treatises of natural law, can only declare what their own moral sense & reason dictate in the several cases they state. Such of them as happen to have feelings & a reason coincident with those of the wise & honest part of mankind, are respected & quoted as witnesses of what is morally right or wrong in particular cases. Grotius, Puffendorf, Wolf, & Vattel are of this number. Where they agree their authority is strong. But where they differ, & they often differ, we must appeal to our own feelings and reason to decide between them.

The passages in question shall be traced through all these writers, that we may see wherein they concur, & where that concurrence is wanting. It shall be quoted from them in the order in which they wrote, that is to say, from Grotius first, as being the earliest writer, Puffendorf next, then Wolf, & lastly Vattel as latest in time.

The doctrine then of Grotius, Puffendorf & Wolf is that 'treaties remain obligatory notwithstanding any change in the form of government, except in the single case where the preservation of that form was the object of the treaty.' There the treaty extinguishes, not by the election or declaration of the party remaining in statu quo; but independantly of that, by the evanishment of the object. Vattel lays down, in fact, the same doctrine, that treaties continue obligatory, notwithstanding a change of government by the will of the other party, that to oppose that will would be a wrong, & that the ally remains an ally notwithstanding the change. So far he concurs with all the previous writers. But he then adds what they had not said, nor would say 'but if this change renders the alliance *useless*, dangerous, or *disagreeable* to it, it is free to renounce it.' It was unnecessary for him to have specified the exception of *danger* in this particular case, because that exception exists in all cases & it's extent has been considered. But when he adds that, because a contract is become merely *useless* or *disagreeable*, we are free to renounce it, he is in opposition to Grotius, Puffendorf, & Wolf, who admit no such licence against the obligation of treaties, & he is in opposition to the morality of every honest man, to whom we may safely appeal to decide whether he feels himself free to renounce a contract the moment it becomes merely *useless* or *disagreeable*, to him? We may appeal too to Vattel himself, in those parts of his book where he cannot be misunderstood, & to his known character, as one of the most zealous & constant advocates for the preservation of good faith in all our dealings. Let us hear him on other occasions; & first where he shews what degree of danger or injury will authorize self-liberation from a treaty. 'If simple lezion' (lezion means the loss sustained by selling a thing for less than half value, which degree of loss rendered the sale void by the Roman law), 'if simple lezion, says he, or some degree of disadvantage in a treaty does not suffice to render it invalid, it is not so as to inconveniences which would go to the *ruin* of the nation. As every treaty ought to be made by a sufficient power, a treaty pernicious to the state is null, & not at all obligatory; no governor of a nation having power to engage things capable of *destroying* the state, for the safety of which the empire is trusted to him. The nation itself, bound necessarily to whatever it's preservation & safety require, cannot enter into engagements contrary to it's indispensable obligations.' Here then we find that the degree of injury or danger which he deems sufficient to liberate us from a treaty, is that which would go to the absolute *ruin* or *destruction* of the state; not simply the lezion of the Roman law, not merely the being disadvantageous, or dangerous. For as he says himself § 158. 'lezion cannot render a treaty invalid. It is his duty, who enters into engagements, to weigh well all things before he concludes. He may do with his property what he pleases, he may relinquish his rights, renounce his advantages, as he judges proper: the acceptant is not obliged to inform himself of his motives, nor to weigh their just value. If we could free ourselves from a compact because we find ourselves injured by it, there would be nothing firm in the contracts of nations. Civil laws may set limits to lezion, & determine the degree capable of producing a nullity of the contract. But sovereigns acknolege no judge. How establish lezion among them? Who will determine the degree sufficient to invalidate a treaty? The happiness & peace

Grotius. 2. 16. 16.	Puffendorf. 8. 9. 6.	Wolf. 1146.	Vattel. 2. 197.
'Hither must be referred the common question, concerning personal & real treaties. If indeed it be with a free people, there can be no doubt but that the engagement is in it's nature real, because the subject is a permanent thing, and even tho the government of the state be changed into a Kingdom, the treaty remains, because the same body remains, tho' the head is changed, and, as we have before said, the government which is exercised by a King, does not cease to be the government of the people. There is an *exception*, when the object seems peculiar to the government as if free cities contract a league for the defence of their freedom.'	'It is certain that every alliance made with a republic, is real, & continues consequently to the term agreed on by the treaty, altho' the magistrates who concluded it be dead before, or that the form of government is changed, even from a democracy to a monarchy: for in this case the people does not cease to be the same, and the King, in the case supposed, being established by the consent of the people, who abolished the republican government, is understood to accept the crown with all the engagements which the people contracting it had contracted, as being free & governing themselves. There must nevertheless be an *Exception* of the alliances contracted with a	'The alliance which is made with a free people, or with a popular government, is a real alliance; and as when the form of government changes, the people remains the same, (for it is the association which forms the people, & not the manner of administering the government) this alliance subsists, tho' the form of government changes, *unless*, as is evident, the reason of the alliance was particular to the popular state.'	'The same question presents itself in real alliances, & in general on every alliance made with a state, & not in particular with a King for the defense of his person. We ought without doubt to defend our ally against all invasion, against all foreign violence, & even against rebel subjects. We ought in like manner to defend a republic against the enterprises of an oppressor of the public liberty. But we ought to recollect that we are the ally of the state, or of the nation, & not it's judge. If the nation has deposed it's King in form, if the people of a republic has driven away it's magistrates, & have established themselves free, or if they have acknoleged the authority of an

view to preserve the present government. As if two Republics league for neutral defence against those who would undertake to invade their liberty: for if one of these two people consent afterwards voluntarily to change the form of their government, the alliance ends of itself, because the reason on which it was founded no longer subsists.'

usurper, whether expressly or tacitly, to oppose these domestic arrangements, to contest their justice or validity, would be to meddle with the government of the nation, & to do it an injury. The ally remains the ally of the state, notwithstanding the change which has taken place. *But if this change renders the alliance useless, dangerous or disagreeable to it, it is free to renounce it. For it may say with truth, that it would not have allied itself with this nation, if it had been under the present form of it's government.'*

of nations require manifestly that their treaties should not depend on a means of nullity so vague & so dangerous.'

Let us hear him again on the general subject of the observance of treaties § 163. 'It is demonstrated in natural law that he who promises another confers on him a perfect right to require the thing promised, & that, consequently, not to observe a perfect promise, is to violate the right of another; it is as manifest injustice as to plunder any one of their right. All the tranquillity, the happiness & security of mankind rest on justice, on the obligation to respect the rights of others. The respect of others for our rights of domain & property is the security of our actual possessions; the faith of promises is our security for the things which cannot be delivered or executed on the spot. No more security, no more commerce among men, if they think themselves not obliged to preserve faith, to keep their word. This obligation then is as necessary as it is natural & indubitable, among nations who live together in a state of nature, & who acknolege no superior on earth, to maintain order & peace in their society. Nations & their governors then ought to observe inviolably their promises & their treaties. This great truth, altho' too often neglected in practice, is generally acknoleged by all nations: the reproach of perfidy is a bitter affront among sovereigns: now he who does not observe a treaty is assuredly perfidious, since he violates his faith. On the contrary nothing is so glorious to a prince & his nation, as the reputation of inviolable fidelity to his word.' Again § 219. 'Who will doubt that treaties are of the things sacred among nations? They decide matters the most important. They impose rules on the pretensions of sovereigns: they cause the rights of nations to be acknoleged, they assure their most precious interests. Among political bodies, sovereigns, who acknolege no superior on earth, treaties are the only means of adjusting their different pretensions, of establishing a rule, to know on what to count, on what to depend. But treaties are but vain words if nations do not consider them as respectable engagements, as rules, inviolable for sovereigns, & sacred through the whole earth. § 220. The faith of treaties, that firm & sincere will, that invariable constancy in fulfilling engagements, of which a declaration is made in a treaty, is there holy & sacred, among nations, whose safety & repose it ensures; & if nations will not be wanting to themselves, they will load with infamy whoever violates his faith.'

After evidence so copious & explicit of the respect of this author for the sanctity of treaties, we should hardly have expected that his authority would have been resorted to for a wanton invalidation of them whenever they should become merely *useless* or *disagreeable*. We should hardly have expected that, rejecting all the rest of his book, this scrap would have been culled, & made the hook whereon to hang such a chain of immoral consequences. Had the passage accidentally met our eye, we should have imagined it had fallen from the author's pen under some momentary view, not sufficiently developed to found a conjecture what he meant: and we may certainly affirm that a fragment like this cannot weigh against the authority of all other writers, against the uniform & systematic doctrine of every work from which it is torn, against the moral feelings & the reason of all honest men. If the terms of the fragment are not misunderstood, they are in full contradiction to all the written & unwritten evidences of morality: if they are misunderstood, they are no longer a foundation for the doctrines which have been built on them.

But even had this doctrine been as true as it is manifestly false, it would have been asked, to whom is it that the treaties with France have become *disagreeable*? How will it be proved that they are *useless*?

The conclusion of the sentence suggests a reflection too strong to be suppressed 'for the party may say with truth that it would not have allied itself with this nation, if it had been under the present form of it's government.' The Republic of the U.S. allied itself with France when under a despotic government. She changes her government, declares it shall be a Republic, prepares a form of Republic extremely free, and in the mean time is governing herself as such, and it is proposed that America shall declare the treaties void because 'it may say with truth that it would not have allied itself with that nation, if it had been under the present form of it's government!' Who is the American who can say with truth that he would not have allied himself to France if she had been a republic? or that a Republic of any form would be as *disagreeable* as her antient despotism?

Upon the whole I conclude

That the treaties are still binding, notwithstanding the change of government in France: that no part of them, but the clause of guarantee, holds up *danger*, even at a distance.

And consequently that a liberation from no other part could be proposed in any case: that if that clause may ever bring *danger*, it is neither extreme, nor imminent, nor even probable: that the authority for renouncing a treaty, when *useless* or *disagreeable*, is either misunderstood, or in opposition to itself, to all their writers, & to every moral feeling: that were it not so, these treaties are in fact neither useless nor disagreeable.

That the receiving a Minister from France at this time is an act of no significance with respect to the treaties, amounting neither to an admission nor a denial of them, forasmuch as he comes not under any stipulation in them:

That were it an explicit admission, or were an express declaration of this obligation now to be made, it would not take from us that right which exists at all times of liberating ourselves when an adherence to the treaties would be *ruinous* or *destructive* to the society: and that the not renouncing the treaties now is so far from being a breach of neutrality, that the doing it would be the breach, by giving just cause of war to France.

Report on the Privileges and Restrictions on the Commerce of the United States in Foreign Countries

December 16, 1793

The Secretary of State, to whom was referred by the House of Representatives, the report of a committee on the written message of the President of the United States, of the 14th of February, 1791, with instructions to report to Congress the nature and extent of the privileges and restrictions of the commercial intercourse of the United States with foreign nations, and the measures which he should think proper to be adopted for the improvement of the commerce and navigation of the same, has had the same under consideration, and thereupon makes the following Report:

THE COUNTRIES with which the United States have their chief commercial intercourse are Spain, Portugal, France, Great Britain, the United Netherlands, Denmark, and Sweden, and their American possessions; and the articles of export, which constitute the basis of that commerce, with their respective amounts, are,

Breadstuff, that is to say, bread grains, meals, and bread, to the annual amount of.	$7,649,887
Tobacco	4,349,567
Rice	1,753,796
Wood	1,263,534
Salted fish	941,696
Pot and pearl ash	839,093
Salted meats	599,130
Indigo	537,379
Horses and mules	339,753
Whale oil	252,591
Flax seed	236,072
Tar, pitch and turpentine	217,177
Live provisions	137,743
Ships	
Foreign goods	620,274

To descend to articles of smaller value than these, would lead into a minuteness of detail neither necessary nor useful to the present object.

The proportions of our exports, which go to the nations

before mentioned, and to their dominions, respectively, are as follows:

To Spain and its dominions	$2,005,907
Portugal and its dominions.	1,283,462
France and its dominions	4,698,735
Great Britain and its dominions	9,363,416
The United Netherlands and their dominions	1,963,880
Denmark and its dominions	224,415
Sweden and its dominions	47,240

Our imports from the same countries, are

Spain and its dominions	335,110
Portugal and its dominions.	595,763
France and its dominions	2,068,348
Great Britain and its dominions	15,285,428
United Netherlands and their dominions.	1,172,692
Denmark and its dominions	351,364
Sweden and its dominions	14,325

These imports consist mostly of articles on which industry has been exhausted.

Our *navigation*, depending on the same commerce, will appear by the following statement of the tonnage of our own vessels, entering in our ports, from those several nations and their possessions, in one year: that is to say, from October, 1789, to September, 1790, inclusive, as follows:

	Tons.
Spain	19,695
Portugal	23,576
France	116,410
Great Britain	43,580
United Netherlands	58,858
Denmark	14,655
Sweden	750

Of our commercial objects, Spain receives favorably our breadstuff, salted fish, wood, ships, tar, pitch, and turpentine. On our meals, however, as well as on those of other foreign countries, when re-exported to their colonies, they have lately imposed duties of from half-a-dollar to two dollars the barrel, the duties being so proportioned to the current price of their own flour, as that both together are to make the constant sum of nine dollars per barrel.

They do not discourage our rice, pot and pearl ash, salted provisions, or whale oil; but these articles, being in small demand at their markets, are carried thither but in a small degree. Their demand for rice, however, is increasing. Neither tobacco nor indigo are received there. Our commerce is permitted with their Canary islands under the same conditions.

Themselves, and their colonies, are the actual consumers of what they receive from us.

Our navigation is free with the kingdom of Spain; foreign goods being received there in our ships on the same conditions as if carried in their own, or in the vessels of the country of which such goods are the manufacture or produce.

Portugal receives favorably our grain and bread, salted fish, and other salted provisions, wood, tar, pitch and turpentine.

For flax-seed, pot and pearl ash, though not discouraged, there is little demand.

Our ships pay 20 per cent. on being sold to their subjects, and are then free-bottoms.

Foreign goods (except those of the East Indies) are received on the same footing in our vessels as in their own, or any others; that is to say, on general duties of from 20 to 28 per cent., and, consequently, our navigation is unobstructed by them. Tobacco, rice, and meals, are prohibited.

Themselves and their colonies consume what they receive from us.

These regulations extend to the Azores, Madeira, and the Cape de Verd islands, except that in these, meals and rice are received freely.

France receives favorably our bread-stuffs, rice, wood, pot and pearl ashes.

A duty of 5 sous the quintal, or nearly 4½ cents, is paid on our tar, pitch, and turpentine. Our whale oils pay 6 livres the quintal, and are the only foreign whale oils admitted. Our indigo pays 5 livres the quintal, their own 2½; but a difference of quality, still more than a difference of duty, prevents its seeking that market.

Salted beef is received freely for re-exportation; but if for home consumption, it pays five livres the quintal. Other salted provisions pay that duty in all cases, and salted fish is made lately to pay the prohibitory one of twenty livres the quintal.

Our ships are free to carry thither all foreign goods which may be carried in their own or any other vessels, except tobaccoes not of our own growth; and they participate with theirs, the exclusive carriage of our whale oils and tobaccoes.

During their former government, our tobacco was under a monopoly, but paid no duties; and our ships were freely sold in their ports and converted into national bottoms. The first national assembly took from our ships this privilege. They emancipated tobacco from its monopoly, but subjected it to duties of eighteen livres, fifteen sous the quintal, carried in their own vessels, and five livres carried in ours—a difference more than equal to the freight of the article.

They and their colonies consume what they receive from us.

Great Britain receives our pot and pearl ashes free, whilst those of other nations pay a duty of two shillings and three pence the quintal. There is an equal distinction in favor of our bar iron; of which article, however, we do not produce enough for our own use. Woods are free from us, whilst they pay some small duty from other countries. Indigo and flaxseed are free from all countries. Our tar and pitch pay eleven pence, sterling, the barrel. From other alien countries they pay about a penny and a third more.

Our tobacco, for their own consumption, pays one shilling and three pence, sterling, the pound, custom and excise, besides heavy expenses of collection; and rice, in the same case, pays seven shillings and four pence, sterling, the hundred weight; which rendering it too dear, as an article of common food, it is consequently used in very small quantity.

Our salted fish and other salted provisions, except bacon, are prohibited. Bacon and whale oils are under prohibitory duties, so are our grains, meals, and bread, as to internal consumption, unless in times of such scarcity as may raise the price of wheat to fifty shillings, sterling, the quarter, and other grains and meals in proportion.

Our ships, though purchased and navigated by their own

subjects, are not permitted to be used, even in their trade with us.

While the vessels of other nations are secured by standing laws, which cannot be altered but by the concurrent will of the three branches of the British legislature, in carrying thither any produce or manufacture of the country to which they belong, which may be lawfully carried in any vessels, ours, with the same prohibition of what is foreign, are further prohibited by a standing law (12 Car. 2, 18, sect. 3), from carrying thither all and any of our own domestic productions and manufactures. A subsequent act, indeed, has authorized their executive to permit the carriage of our own productions in our own bottoms, at its sole discretion; and the permission has been given from year to year by proclamation, but subject every moment to be withdrawn on that single will; in which event, our vessels having anything on board, stand interdicted from the entry of all British ports. The disadvantage of a tenure which may be so suddenly discontinued, was experienced by our merchants on a late occasion,* when an official notification that this law would be stricly enforced, gave them just apprehensions for the fate of their vessels and cargoes despatched or destined for the ports of Great Britain. The minister of that court, indeed, frankly expressed his personal convictions that the words of the order went farther than was intended, and so he afterwards officially informed us: but the embarrassments of the moment were real and great, and the possibility of their renewal lays our commerce to that country under the same species of discouragement as to other countries, where it is regulated by a single legislator; and the distinction is too remarkable not to be noticed, that our navigation is excluded from the security of fixed laws, while that security is given to the navigation of others.

Our vessels pay in their ports one shilling and nine pence, sterling, per ton, light and trinity dues, more than is paid by British ships, except in the port of London, where they pay the same as British.

The greater part of what they receive from us, is re-exported to other countries, under the useless charges of an

*April 12, 1792.

intermediate deposit, and double voyage. From tables published in England, and composed, as is said, from the books
of their customhouses, it appears, that of the indigo imported
there in the years 1773, '4, '5, one-third was re-exported; and
from a document of authority, we learn, that of the rice and
tobacco imported there before the war, four-fifths were re-
exported. We are assured, indeed, that the quantities sent
thither for re-exportation since the war, are considerably diminished, yet less so than reason and national interest would
dictate. The whole of our grain is re-exported when wheat
is below fifty shillings the quarter, and other grains in proportion.

The *United Netherlands* prohibit our pickled beef and pork,
meals and bread of all sorts, and lay a prohibitory duty on
spirits distilled from grain.

All other of our productions are received on varied duties,
which may be reckoned, on a medium, at about three per
cent.

They consume but a small proportion of what they receive.
The residue is partly forwarded for consumption in the inland
parts of Europe, and partly re-shipped to other maritime
countries. On the latter portion they intercept between us and
the consumer, so much of the value as is absorbed in the
charges attending and intermediate deposit.

Foreign goods, except some East India articles, are received
in vessels of any nation.

Our ships may be sold and neutralized there, with exceptions of one or two privileges, which somewhat lessen their
value.

Denmark lays considerable duties on our tobacco and rice,
carried in their own vessels, and half as much more, if carried
in ours; but the exact amount of these duties is not perfectly
known here. They lay such duties as amount to prohibitions
on our indigo and corn.

Sweden receives favorably our grains and meals, salted provisions, indigo, and whale oil.

They subject our rice to duties of sixteen mills the pound
weight, carried in their own vessels, and of forty per cent.
additional on that, or twenty-two and four-tenths mills, carried in ours or any others. Being thus rendered too dear as an

article of common food, little of it is consumed with them. They consume some of our tobaccoes, which they take circuitously through Great Britain, levying heavy duties on them also; their duties of entry, town duties, and excise, being 4 34 dollars the hundred weight, if carried in their own vessels, and of forty per cent. on that additional, if carried in our own or any other vessels.

They prohibit altogether our bread, fish, pot and pearl ashes, flax-seed, tar, pitch, and turpentine, wood (except oak timber and masts), and all foreign manufactures.

Under so many restrictions and prohibitions, our navigation with them is reduced to almost nothing.

With our neighbors, an order of things much harder presents itself.

Spain and *Portugal* refuse, to all those parts of America which they govern, all direct intercourse with any people but themselves. The commodities in mutual demand between them and their neighbors, must be carried to be exchanged in some port of the dominant country, and the transportation between that and the subject state, must be in a domestic bottom.

France, by a standing law, permits her West India possessions to receive directly our vegetables, live provisions, horses, wood, tar, pitch, turpentine, rice, and maize, and prohibits our other bread stuff; but a suspension of this prohibition having been left to the colonial legislatures, in times of scarcity, it was formerly suspended occasionally, but latterly without interruption.

Our fish and salted provisions (except pork) are received in their islands under a duty of three colonial livres the quintal, and our vessels are as free as their own to carry our commodities thither, and to bring away rum and molasses.

Great Britain admits in her islands our vegetables, live provisions, horses, wood, tar, pitch, and turpentine, rice and bread stuff, by a proclamation of her executive, limited always to the term of a year, but hitherto renewed from year to year. She prohibits our salted fish and other salted provisions. She does not permit our vessels to carry thither our own produce. Her vessels alone may take it from us, and bring in exchange rum, molasses, sugar, coffee, cocoa-nuts, ginger, and pimento. There are, indeed, some freedoms in the island of Dominica, but, under such circumstances, as to be little used by us. In the British continental colonies, and in Newfoundland, all our productions are prohibited, and our vessels forbidden to enter their ports. Their governors, however, in times of distress, have power to permit a temporary importation of certain articles in their own bottoms, but not in ours.

Our citizens cannot reside as merchants or factors within any of the British plantations, this being expressly prohibited by the same statute of 12 Car. 2, c. 18, commonly called the navigation act.

In the *Danish American* possessions a duty of 5 per cent. is levied on our corn, corn meal, rice, tobacco, wood, salted fish, indigo, horses, mules and live stock, and of 10 per cent. on our flour, salted pork and beef, tar, pitch and turpentine.

In the American islands of the *United Netherlands* and Sweden, our vessels and produce are received, subject to duties, not so heavy as to have been complained of; but they are heavier in the Dutch possessions on the continent.

To sum up these restrictions, so far as they are important:

FIRST. In Europe—

Our bread stuff is at most times under prohibitory duties in England, and considerably dutied on re-exportation from Spain to her colonies.

Our tobaccoes are heavily dutied in England, Sweden and France, and prohibited in Spain and Portugal.

Our rice is heavily dutied in England and Sweden, and prohibited in Portugal.

Our fish and salted provisions are prohibited in England, and under prohibitory duties in France.

Our whale oils are prohibited in England and Portugal.

And our vessels are denied naturalization in England, and of late in France.

SECOND. In the West Indies—

All intercourse is prohibited with the possessions of Spain and Portugal.

Our salted provisions and fish are prohibited by England.

Our salted pork and bread stuff (except maize) are received under temporary laws only, in the dominions of France, and our salted fish pays there a weighty duty.

THIRD. In the article of navigation—

Our own carriage of our own tobacco is heavily dutied in Sweden, and lately in France.

We can carry no article, not of our own production, to the British ports in Europe. Nor even our own produce to her American possessions.

Such being the restrictions on the commerce and navigation of the United States; the question is, in what way they may best be removed, modified or counteracted?

As to commerce, two methods occur. 1. By friendly arrangements with the several nations with whom these restrictions exist; Or, 2. By the separate act of our own legislatures for countervailing their effects.

There can be no doubt but that of these two, friendly arrangements is the most eligible. Instead of embarrassing commerce under piles of regulating laws, duties, and prohibitions, could it be relieved from all its shackles in all parts of the world, could every country be employed in producing that which nature has best fitted it to produce, and each be free to exchange with others mutual surpluses for mutual wants, the greatest mass possible would then be produced of those things which contribute to human life and human happiness; the numbers of mankind would be increased, and their condition bettered.

Would even a single nation begin with the United States this system of free commerce, it would be advisable to begin it with that nation; since it is one by one only that it can be extended to all. Where the circumstances of either party render it expedient to levy a revenue, by way of impost, on commerce, its freedom might be modified, in that particular, by mutual and equivalent measures, preserving it entire in all others.

Some nations, not yet ripe for free commerce in all its extent, might still be willing to mollify its restrictions and regulations for us, in proportion to the advantages which an intercourse with us might offer. Particularly they may concur with us in reciprocating the duties to be levied on each side, or in compensating any excess of duty by equivalent advantages of another nature. Our commerce is certainly of a character to entitle it to favor in most countries. The commodities

we offer are either necessaries of life, or materials for manufacture, or convenient subjects of revenue; and we take in exchange, either manufactures, when they have received the last
finish of art and industry, or mere luxuries. Such customers
may reasonably expect welcome and friendly treatment at
every market. Customers, too, whose demands, increasing
with their wealth and population, must very shortly give full
employment to the whole industry of any nation whatever, in
any line of supply they may get into the habit of calling for
from it.

But should any nation, contrary to our wishes, suppose it
may better find its advantage by continuing its system of prohibitions, duties and regulations, it behooves us to protect
our citizens, their commerce and navigation, by counter prohibitions, duties and regulations, also. Free commerce and
navigation are not to be given in exchange for restrictions and
vexations; nor are they likely to produce a relaxation of them.

Our navigation involves still higher considerations. As a
branch of industry, it is valuable, but as a resource of defence,
essential.

Its value, as a branch of industry, is enhanced by the dependence of so many other branches on it. In times of general
peace it multiplies competitors for employment in transportation, and so keeps that at its proper level; and in times of
war, that is to say, when those nations who may be our principal carriers, shall be at war with each other, if we have not
within ourselves the means of transportation, our produce
must be exported in belligerent vessels, at the increased expense of war-freight and insurance, and the articles which will
not bear that, must perish on our hands.

But it is as a resource of defence that our navigation will
admit neither negligence nor forbearance. The position and
circumstances of the United States leave them nothing to fear
on their land-board, and nothing to desire beyond their present rights. But on their seaboard, they are open to injury, and
they have there, too, a commerce which must be protected.
This can only be done by possessing a respectable body of
citizen-seamen, and of artists and establishments in readiness
for ship-building.

Were the ocean, which is the common property of all, open

to the industry of all, so that every person and vessel should be free to take employment wherever it could be found, the United States would certainly not set the example of appropriating to themselves, exclusively, any portion of the common stock of occupation. They would rely on the enterprise and activity of their citizens for a due participation of the benefits of the seafaring business, and for keeping the marine class of citizens equal to their object. But if particular nations grasp at undue shares, and, more especially, if they seize on the means of the United States, to convert them into aliment for their own strength, and withdraw them entirely from the support of those to whom they belong, defensive and protecting measures become necessary on the part of the nation whose marine resources are thus invaded; or it will be disarmed of its defence; its productions will lie at the mercy of the nation which has possessed itself exclusively of the means of carrying them, and its politics may be influenced by those who command its commerce. The carriage of our own commodities, if once established in another channel, cannot be resumed in the moment we may desire. If we lose the seamen and artists whom it now occupies, we lose the present means of marine defence, and time will be requisite to raise up others, when disgrace or losses shall bring home to our feelings the error of having abandoned them. The materials for maintaining our due share of navigation, are ours in abundance. And, as to the mode of using them, we have only to adopt the principles of those who put us on the defensive, or others equivalent and better fitted to our circumstances.

The following principles, being founded in reciprocity, appear perfectly just, and to offer no cause of complaint to any nation:

1. Where a nation imposes high duties on our productions, or prohibits them altogether, it may be proper for us to do the same by theirs; first burdening or excluding those productions which they bring here, in competition with our own of the same kind; selecting next, such manufactures as we take from them in greatest quantity, and which, at the same time, we could the soonest furnish to ourselves, or obtain from other countries; imposing on them duties lighter at first, but heavier and heavier afterwards, as other channels of supply

open. Such duties having the effect of indirect encouragement to domestic manufactures of the same kind, may induce the manufacturer to come himself into these States, where cheaper subsistence, equal laws, and a vent of his wares, free of duty, may ensure him the highest profits from his skill and industry. And here, it would be in the power of the State governments to co-operate essentially, by opening the resources of encouragement which are under their control, extending them liberally to artists in those particular branches of manufacture for which their soil, climate, population and other circumstances have matured them, and fostering the precious efforts and progress of *household* manufacture, by some patronage suited to the nature of its objects, guided by the local informations they possess, and guarded against abuse by their presence and attentions. The oppressions on our agriculture, in foreign ports, would thus be made the occasion of relieving it from a dependence on the councils and conduct of others, and of promoting arts, manufactures and population at home.

2. Where a nation refuses permission to our merchants and factors to reside within certain parts of their dominions, we may, if it should be thought expedient, refuse residence to theirs in any and every part of ours, or modify their transactions.

3. Where a nation refuses to receive in our vessels any productions but our own, we may refuse to receive, in theirs, any but their own productions. The first and second clauses of the bill reported by the committee, are well formed to effect this object.

4. Where a nation refuses to consider any vessel as ours which has not been built within our territories, we should refuse to consider as theirs, any vessel not built within their territories.

5. Where a nation refuses to our vessels the carriage even of our own productions, to certain countries under their domination, we might refuse to theirs of every description, the carriage of the same productions to the same countries. But as justice and good neighborhood would dictate that those who have no part in imposing the restriction on us, should not be the victims of measures adopted to defeat its effect, it

may be proper to confine the restrictions to vessels owned or navigated by any subjects of the same dominant power, other than the inhabitants of the country to which the said productions are to be carried. And to prevent all inconvenience to the said inhabitants, and to our own, by too sudden a check on the means of transportation, we may continue to admit the vessels marked for future exclusion, on an advanced tonnage, and for such length of time only, as may be supposed necessary to provide against that inconvenience.

The establishment of some of these principles by Great Britain, alone, has already lost to us in our commerce with that country and its possessions, between eight and nine hundred vessels of near 40,000 tons burden, according to statements from official materials, in which they have confidence. This involves a proportional loss of seamen, shipwrights, and ship-building, and is too serious a loss to admit forbearance of some effectual remedy.

It is true we must expect some inconvenience in practice from the establishment of discriminating duties. But in this, as in so many other cases, we are left to choose between two evils. These inconveniences are nothing when weighed against the loss of wealth and loss of force, which will follow our perseverance in the plan of indiscrimination. When once it shall be perceived that we are either in the system or in the habit of giving equal advantages to those who extinguish our commerce and navigation by duties and prohibitions, as to those who treat both with liberality and justice, liberality and justice will be converted by all into duties and prohibitions. It is not to the moderation and justice of others we are to trust for fair and equal access to market with our productions, or for our due share in the transportation of them; but to our own means of independence, and the firm will to use them. Nor do the inconveniences of discrimination merit consideration. Not one of the nations before mentioned, perhaps not a commercial nation on earth, is without them. In our case one distinction alone will suffice: that is to say, between nations who favor our productions and navigation, and those who do not favor them. One set of moderate duties, say the present duties, for the first, and a fixed advance on these as to some articles, and prohibitions as to others, for the last.

Still, it must be repeated that friendly arrangements are preferable with all who will come into them; and that we should carry into such arrangements all the liberality and spirit of accommodation which the nature of the case will admit.

France has, of her own accord, proposed negotiations for improving, by a new treaty on fair and equal principles, the commercial relations of the two countries. But her internal disturbances have hitherto prevented the prosecution of them to effect, though we have had repeated assurances of a continuance of the disposition.

Proposals of friendly arrangement have been made on our part, by the present government, to that of Great Britain, as the message states; but, being already on as good a footing in law, and a better in fact, than the most favored nation, they have not, as yet, discovered any disposition to have it meddled with.

We have no reason to conclude that friendly arrangements would be declined by the other nations, with whom we have such commercial intercourse as may render them important. In the meanwhile, it would rest with the wisdom of Congress to determine whether, as to those nations, they will not surcease *ex parte* regulations, on the reasonable presumption that they will concur in doing whatever justice and moderation dictate should be done.

Draft of the Kentucky Resolutions

October 1798

1. *Resolved*, That the several States composing the United States of America, are not united on the principle of unlimited submission to their General Government; but that, by a compact under the style and title of a Constitution for the United States, and of amendments thereto, they constituted a General Government for special purposes,—delegated to that government certain definite powers, reserving, each State to itself, the residuary mass of right to their own self-government; and that whensoever the General Government assumes undelegated powers, its acts are unauthoritative, void, and of no force; that to this compact each State acceded as a State, and is an integral party, its co-States forming, as to itself, the other party: that the government created by this compact was not made the exclusive or final judge of the extent of the powers delegated to itself; since that would have made its discretion, and not the Constitution, the measure of its powers; but that, as in all other cases of compact among powers having no common judge, each party has an equal right to judge for itself, as well of infractions as of the mode and measure of redress.

2. *Resolved*, That the Constitution of the United States, having delegated to Congress a power to punish treason, counterfeiting the securities and current coin of the United States, piracies, and felonies committed on the high seas, and offences against the law of nations, and no other crimes whatsoever; and it being true as a general principle, and one of the amendments to the Constitution having also declared, that "the powers not delegated to the United States by the Constitution, nor prohibited by it to the States, are reserved to the States respectively, or to the people," therefore the act of Congress, passed on the 14th day of July, 1798, and intituled "An Act in addition to the act intituled An Act for the punishment of certain crimes against the United States," as also the act passed by them on the — day of June, 1798, intituled "An Act to punish frauds committed on the bank of the United States," (and all their other acts which assume to

create, define, or punish crimes, other than those so enumerated in the Constitution,) are altogether void, and of no force;
and that the power to create, define, and punish such other
crimes is reserved, and, of right, appertains solely and exclusively to the respective States, each within its own territory.

3. *Resolved*, That it is true as a general principle, and is also
expressly declared by one of the amendments to the Constitution, that "the powers not delegated to the United States
by the Constitution, nor prohibited by it to the States, are
reserved to the States respectively, or to the people;" and that
no power over the freedom of religion, freedom of speech, or
freedom of the press being delegated to the United States by
the Constitution, nor prohibited by it to the States, all lawful
powers respecting the same did of right remain, and were
reserved to the States or the people: that thus was manifested
their determination to retain to themselves the right of judging how far the licentiousness of speech and of the press may
be abridged without lessening their useful freedom, and how
far those abuses which cannot be separated from their use
should be tolerated, rather than the use be destroyed. And
thus also they guarded against all abridgment by the United
States of the freedom of religious opinions and exercises, and
retained to themselves the right of protecting the same, as this
State, by a law passed on the general demand of its citizens,
had already protected them from all human restraint or inter-
ference. And that in addition to this general principle and
express declaration, another and more special provision has
been made by one of the amendments to the Constitution,
which expressly declares, that "Congress shall make no law
respecting an establishment of religion, or prohibiting the
free exercise thereof, or abridging the freedom of speech or
of the press:" thereby guarding in the same sentence, and under the same words, the freedom of religion, of speech, and
of the press: insomuch, that whatever violated either, throws
down the sanctuary which covers the others, and that libels,
falsehood, and defamation, equally with heresy and false religion, are withheld from the cognizance of federal tribunals.
That, therefore, the act of Congress of the United States,
passed on the 14th day of July, 1798, intituled "An Act in addition to the act intituled An Act for the punishment of cer-

tain crimes against the United States," which does abridge the freedom of the press, is not law, but is altogether void, and of no force.

4. *Resolved*, That alien friends are under the jurisdiction and protection of the laws of the State wherein they are: that no power over them has been delegated to the United States, nor prohibited to the individual States, distinct from their power over citizens. And it being true as a general principle, and one of the amendments to the Constitution having also declared, that "the powers not delegated to the United States by the Constitution, nor prohibited by it to the States, are reserved to the States respectively, or to the people," the act of the Congress of the United States, passed on the — day of July, 1798, intituled "An Act concerning aliens," which assumes powers over alien friends, not delegated by the Constitution, is not law, but is altogether void, and of no force.

5. *Resolved*, That in addition to the general principle, as well as the express declaration, that powers not delegated are reserved, another and more special provision, inserted in the Constitution from abundant caution, has declared that "the migration or importation of such persons as any of the States now existing shall think proper to admit, shall not be prohibited by the Congress prior to the year 1808;" that this commonwealth does admit the migration of alien friends, described as the subject of the said act concerning aliens: that a provision against prohibiting their migration, is a provision against all acts equivalent thereto, or it would be nugatory: that to remove them when migrated, is equivalent to a prohibition of their migration, and is, therefore, contrary to the said provision of the Constitution, and void.

6. *Resolved*, That the imprisonment of a person under the protection of the laws of this commonwealth, on his failure to obey the simple *order* of the President to depart out of the United States, as is undertaken by said act intituled "An Act concerning aliens," is contrary to the Constitution, one amendment to which has provided that "no person shall be deprived of liberty without due process of law;" and that another having provided that "in all criminal prosecutions the accused shall enjoy the right to public trial by an impartial jury, to be informed of the nature and cause of the accusation,

to be confronted with the witnesses against him, to have compulsory process for obtaining witnesses in his favor, and to have the assistance of counsel for his defence," the same act, undertaking to authorize the President to remove a person out of the United States, who is under the protection of the law, on his own suspicion, without accusation, without jury, without public trial, without confrontation of the witnesses against him, without hearing witnesses in his favor, without defence, without counsel, is contrary to the provision also of the Constitution, is therefore not law, but utterly void, and of no force: that transferring the power of judging any person, who is under the protection of the laws, from the courts to the President of the United States, as is undertaken by the same act concerning aliens, is against the article of the Constitution which provides that "the judicial power of the United States shall be vested in courts, the judges of which shall hold their offices during good behavior;" and that the said act is void for that reason also. And it is further to be noted, that this transfer of judiciary power is to that magistrate of the General Government who already possesses all the Executive, and a negative on all legislative powers.

7. *Resolved*, That the construction applied by the General Government (as is evidenced by sundry of their proceedings) to those parts of the Constitution of the United States which delegate to Congress a power "to lay and collect taxes, duties, imports, and excises, to pay the debts, and provide for the common defence and general welfare of the United States," and "to make all laws which shall be necessary and proper for carrying into execution the powers vested by the Constitution in the government of the United States, or in any department or officer thereof," goes to the destruction of all limits prescribed to their power by the Constitution: that words meant by the instrument to be subsidiary only to the execution of limited powers, ought not to be so construed as themselves to give unlimited powers, nor a part to be so taken as to destroy the whole residue of that instrument: that the proceedings of the General Government under color of these articles, will be a fit and necessary subject of revisal and correction, at a time of greater tranquillity, while those specified in the preceding resolutions call for immediate redress.

8th. *Resolved*, That a committee of conference and correspondence be appointed, who shall have in charge to communicate the preceding resolutions to the legislatures of the several States; to assure them that this commonwealth continues in the same esteem of their friendship and union which it has manifested from that moment at which a common danger first suggested a common union: that it considers union, for specified national purposes, and particularly to those specified in their late federal compact, to be friendly to the peace, happiness and prosperity of all the States: that faithful to that compact, according to the plain intent and meaning in which it was understood and acceded to by the several parties, it is sincerely anxious for its preservation: that it does also believe, that to take from the States all the powers of self-government and transfer them to a general and consolidated government, without regard to the special delegations and reservations solemnly agreed to in that compact, is not for the peace, happiness or prosperity of these States; and that therefore this commonwealth is determined, as it doubts not its co-States are, to submit to undelegated, and consequently unlimited powers in no man, or body of men on earth: that in cases of an abuse of the delegated powers, the members of the General Government, being chosen by the people, a change by the people would be the constitutional remedy; but, where powers are assumed which have not been delegated, a nullification of the act is the rightful remedy: that every State has a natural right in cases not within the compact, (casus non fœderis,) to nullify of their own authority all assumptions of power by others within their limits: that without this right, they would be under the dominion, absolute and unlimited, of whosoever might exercise this right of judgment for them: that nevertheless, this commonwealth, from motives of regard and respect for its co-States, has wished to communicate with them on the subject: that with them alone it is proper to communicate, they alone being parties to the compact, and solely authorized to judge in the last resort of the powers exercised under it, Congress being not a party, but merely the creature of the compact, and subject as to its assumptions of power to the final judgment of those by whom, and for whose use itself and its powers were all created and modified: that if the acts

before specified should stand, these conclusions would flow
from them; that the General Government may place any act
they think proper on the list of crimes, and punish it themselves whether enumerated or not enumerated by the Constitution as cognizable by them: that they may transfer its
cognizance to the President, or any other person, who may
himself be the accuser, counsel, judge and jury, whose *suspicions* may be the evidence, his *order* the sentence, his *officer* the
executioner, and his breast the sole record of the transaction:
that a very numerous and valuable description of the inhabitants of these States being, by this precedent, reduced, as out-
laws, to the absolute dominion of one man, and the barrier
of the Constitution thus swept away from us all, no rampart
now remains against the passions and the powers of a majority in Congress to protect from a like exportation, or other
more grievous punishment, the minority of the same body,
the legislatures, judges, governors, and counsellors of the
States, nor their other peaceable inhabitants, who may venture to reclaim the constitutional rights and liberties of the
States and people, or who for other causes, good or bad, may
be obnoxious to the views, or marked by the suspicions of
the President, or be thought dangerous to his or their election, or other interests, public or personal: that the friendless
alien has indeed been selected as the safest subject of a first
experiment; but the citizen will soon follow, or rather, has
already followed, for already has a sedition act marked him as
its prey: that these and successive acts of the same character,
unless arrested at the threshold, necessarily drive these States
into revolution and blood, and will furnish new calumnies
against republican government, and new pretexts for those
who wish it to be believed that man cannot be governed but
by a rod of iron: that it would be a dangerous delusion were a
confidence in the men of our choice to silence our fears for the
safety of our rights: that confidence is everywhere the parent
of despotism—free government is founded in jealousy, and
not in confidence; it is jealousy and not confidence which prescribes limited constitutions, to bind down those whom we
are obliged to trust with power: that our Constitution has accordingly fixed the limits to which, and no further, our confidence may go; and let the honest advocate of confidence read

the alien and sedition acts, and say if the Constitution has not been wise in fixing limits to the government it created, and whether we should be wise in destroying those limits. Let him say what the government is, if it be not a tyranny, which the men of our choice have conferred on our President, and the President of our choice has assented to, and accepted over the friendly strangers to whom the mild spirit of our country and its laws have pledged hospitality and protection: that the men of our choice have more respected the bare *suspicions* of the President, than the solid right of innocence, the claims of justification, the sacred force of truth, and the forms and substance of law and justice. In questions of power, then, let no more be heard of confidence in man, but bind him down from mischief by the chains of the Constitution. That this commonwealth does therefore call on its co-States for an expression of their sentiments on the acts concerning aliens, and for the punishment of certain crimes herein before specified, plainly declaring whether these acts are or are not authorized by the federal compact. And it doubts not that their sense will be so announced as to prove their attachment unaltered to limited government, whether general or particular. And that the rights and liberties of their co-States will be exposed to no dangers by remaining embarked in a common bottom with their own. That they will concur with this commonwealth in considering the said acts as so palpably against the Constitution as to amount to an undisguised declaration that that compact is not meant to be the measure of the powers of the General Government, but that it will proceed in the exercise over these States, of all powers whatsoever: that they will view this as seizing the rights of the States, and consolidating them in the hands of the General Government, with a power assumed to bind the States, not merely as the cases made federal, (casus fœderis,) but in all cases whatsoever, by laws made, not with their consent, but by others against their consent: that this would be to surrender the form of government we have chosen, and live under one deriving its powers from its own will, and not from our authority; and that the co-States, recurring to their natural right in cases not made federal, will concur in declaring these acts void, and of no force, and will each take measures of its own for providing that neither these acts, nor any others of the General Government not plainly and intentionally authorized by the Constitution, shall be exercised within their respective territories.

9th. *Resolved*, That the said committee be authorized to communicate by writing or personal conferences, at any times or places whatever, with any person or person who may be appointed by any one or more co-States to correspond or confer with them; and that they lay their proceedings before the next session of Assembly.

Report of the Commissioners for the University of Virginia

August 4, 1818

T HE COMMISSIONERS for the University of Virginia, having met, as by law required, at the tavern, in Rockfish Gap, on the Blue Ridge, on the first day of August, of this present year, 1818; and having formed a board, proceeded on that day to the discharge of the duties assigned to them by the act of the Legislature, entitled "An act, appropriating part of the revenue of the literary fund, and for other purposes;" and having continued their proceedings by adjournment, from day to day, to Tuesday, the 4th day of August, have agreed to a report on the several matters with which they were charged, which report they now respectfully address and submit to the Legislature of the State.

The first duty enjoined on them, was to enquire and report a site, in some convenient and proper part of the State, for an university, to be called the "University of Virginia." In this enquiry, they supposed that the governing considerations should be the healthiness of the site, the fertility of the neighboring country, and its centrality to the white population of the whole State. For, although the act authorized and required them to receive any voluntary contributions, whether conditional or absolute, which might be offered through them to the President and Directors of the Literary Fund, for the benefit of the University, yet they did not consider this as establishing an auction, or as pledging the location to the highest bidder.

Three places were proposed, to wit: Lexington, in the county of Rockbridge, Staunton, in the county of Augusta, and the Central College, in the county of Albemarle. Each of these was unexceptionable as to healthiness and fertility. It was the degree of centrality to the white population of the State which alone then constituted the important point of comparison between these places; and the Board, after full enquiry, and impartial and mature consideration, are of opinion, that the central point of the white population of the State is nearer to the Central College than to either Lexington or

Staunton, by great and important differences; and all other circumstances of the place in general being favorable to it, as a position for an university, they do report the Central College, in Albemarle, to be a convenient and proper part of the State for the University of Virginia.

2. The Board having thus agreed on a proper site for the University, to be reported to the Legislature, proceed to the second of the duties assigned to them—that of proposing a plan for its buildings—and they are of opinion that it should consist of distinct houses or pavilions, arranged at proper distances on each side of a lawn of a proper breadth, and of indefinite extent, in one direction, at least; in each of which should be a lecturing room, with from two to four apartments, for the accommodation of a professor and his family; that these pavilions should be united by a range of dormitories, sufficient each for the accommodation of two students only, this provision being deemed advantageous to morals, to order, and to uninterrupted study; and that a passage of some kind, under cover from the weather, should give a communication along the whole range. It is supposed that such pavilions, on an average of the larger and smaller, will cost each about $5,000; each dormitory about $350, and hotels of a single room, for a refectory, and two rooms for the tenant, necessary for dieting the students, will cost about $3500 each. The number of these pavilions will depend on the number of professors, and that of the dormitories and hotels on the number of students to be lodged and dieted. The advantages of this plan are: greater security against fire and infection; tranquillity and comfort to the professors and their families thus insulated; retirement to the students; and the admission of enlargement to any degree to which the institution may extend in future times. It is supposed probable, that a building of somewhat more size in the middle of the grounds may be called for in time, in which may be rooms for religious worship, under such impartial regulations as the Visitors shall prescribe, for public examinations, for a library, for the schools of music, drawing, and other associated purposes.

3, 4. In proceeding to the third and fourth duties prescribed by the Legislature, of reporting "the branches of learning, which should be taught in the University, and the number and description of the professorships they will require," the Commissioners were first to consider at what point it was understood that university education should commence? Certainly not with the alphabet, for reasons of expediency and impracticability, as well from the obvious sense of the Legislature, who, in the same act, make other provision for the primary instruction of the poor children, expecting, doubtless, that in other cases it would be provided by the parent, or become, perhaps, subject of future and further attention of the Legislature. The objects of this primary education determine its character and limits. These objects would be,

To give to every citizen the information he needs for the transaction of his own business;

To enable him to calculate for himself, and to express and preserve his ideas, his contracts and accounts, in writing;

To improve, by reading, his morals and faculties;

To understand his duties to his neighbors and country, and to discharge with competence the functions confided to him by either;

To know his rights; to exercise with order and justice those he retains; to choose with discretion the fiduciary of those he delegates; and to notice their conduct with diligence, with candor, and judgment;

And, in general, to observe with intelligence and faithfulness all the social relations under which he shall be placed.

To instruct the mass of our citizens in these, their rights, interests and duties, as men and citizens, being then the objects of education in the primary schools, whether private or public, in them should be taught reading, writing and numerical arithmetic, the elements of mensuration, (useful in so many callings,) and the outlines of geography and history. And this brings us to the point at which are to commence the higher branches of education, of which the Legislature require the development; those, for example, which are,

To form the statesmen, legislators and judges, on whom public prosperity and individual happiness are so much to depend;

To expound the principles and structure of government, the

laws which regulate the intercourse of nations, those formed municipally for our own government, and a sound spirit of legislation, which, banishing all arbitrary and unnecessary restraint on individual action, shall leave us free to do whatever does not violate the equal rights of another;

To harmonize and promote the interests of agriculture, manufactures and commerce, and by well informed views of political economy to give a free scope to the public industry;

To develop the reasoning faculties of our youth, enlarge their minds, cultivate their morals, and instill into them the precepts of virtue and order;

To enlighten them with mathematical and physical sciences, which advance the arts, and administer to the health, the subsistence, and comforts of human life;

And, generally, to form them to habits of reflection and correct action, rendering them examples of virtue to others, and of happiness within themselves.

These are the objects of that higher grade of education, the benefits and blessings of which the Legislature now propose to provide for the good and ornament of their country, the gratification and happiness of their fellow-citizens, of the parent especially, and his progeny, on which all his affections are concentrated.

In entering on this field, the Commissioners are aware that they have to encounter much difference of opinion as to the extent which it is expedient that this institution should occupy. Some good men, and even of respectable information, consider the learned sciences as useless acquirements; some think that they do not better the condition of man; and others that education, like private and individual concerns, should be left to private individual effort; not reflecting that an establishment embracing all the sciences which may be useful and even necessary in the various vocations of life, with the buildings and apparatus belonging to each, are far beyond the reach of individual means, and must either derive existence from public patronage, or not exist at all. This would leave us, then, without those callings which depend on education, or send us to other countries to seek the instruction they require. But the Commissioners are happy in considering the statute under which they are assembled as proof that the

Legislature is far from the abandonment of objects so interesting. They are sensible that the advantages of well-directed
education, moral, political and economical, are truly above all
estimate. Education generates habits of application, of order,
and the love of virtue; and controls, by the force of habit, any
innate obliquities in our moral organization. We should be
far, too, from the discouraging persuasion that man is fixed,
by the law of his nature, at a given point; that his improvement is a chimera, and the hope delusive of rendering ourselves wiser, happier or better than our forefathers were. As
well might it be urged that the wild and uncultivated tree,
hitherto yielding sour and bitter fruit only, can never be made
to yield better; yet we know that the grafting art implants a
new tree on the savage stock, producing what is most estima-
ble both in kind and degree. Education, in like manner, en-
grafts a new man on the native stock, and improves what in
his nature was vicious and perverse into qualities of virtue and
social worth. And it cannot be but that each generation succeeding to the knowledge acquired by all those who preceded
it, adding to it their own acquisitions and discoveries, and
handing the mass down for successive and constant accumulation, must advance the knowledge and well-being of mankind, not *infinitely*, as some have said, but *indefinitely*, and to
a term which no one can fix and foresee. Indeed, we need
look back half a century, to times which many now living
remember well, and see the wonderful advances in the sciences and arts which have been made within that period.
Some of these have rendered the elements themselves subser-
vient to the purposes of man, have harnessed them to the
yoke of his labors, and effected the great blessings of moder-
ating his own, of accomplishing what was beyond his feeble
force, and extending the comforts of life to a much enlarged
circle, to those who had before known its necessaries only.
That these are not the vain dreams of sanguine hope, we have
before our eyes real and living examples. What, but education, has advanced us beyond the condition of our indigenous
neighbors? And what chains them to their present state of
barbarism and wretchedness, but a bigotted veneration for
the supposed superlative wisdom of their fathers, and the preposterous idea that they are to look backward for better

things, and not forward, longing, as it should seem, to return to the days of eating acorns and roots, rather than indulge in the degeneracies of civilization? And how much more encouraging to the achievements of science and improvement is this, than the desponding view that the condition of man cannot be ameliorated, that what has been must ever be, and that to secure ourselves where we are, we must tread with awful reverence in the footsteps of our fathers. This doctrine is the genuine fruit of the alliance between Church and State; the tenants of which, finding themselves but too well in their present condition, oppose all advances which might unmask their usurpations, and monopolies of honors, wealth, and power, and fear every change, as endangering the comforts they now hold. Nor must we omit to mention, among the benefits of education, the incalculable advantage of training up able counsellors to administer the affairs of our country in all its departments, legislative, executive and judiciary, and to bear their proper share in the councils of our national government; nothing more than education advancing the prosperity, the power, and the happiness of a nation.

Encouraged, therefore, by the sentiments of the Legislature, manifested in this statute, we present the following tabular statement of the branches of learning which we think should be taught in the University, forming them into groups, each of which are within the powers of a single professor:

I. Languages, ancient:
   Latin,
   Greek,
   Hebrew.

II. Languages, modern:
   French,
   Spanish,
   Italian,
   German,
   Anglo-Saxon.

III. Mathematics, pure:
   Algebra,
   Fluxions,
   Geometry, Elementary, Transcendental.
   Architecture, Military, Naval.

IV. Physico-Mathematics:
    Mechanics,
    Statics,
    Dynamics,
    Pneumatics,
    Acoustics,
    Optics,
    Astronomy,
    Geography.

V. Physics, or Natural
    Philosophy:
    Chemistry,
    Mineralogy.

VI. Botany, Zoology.

VII. Anatomy, Medicine.

VIII. Government,
    Political Economy,
    Law of Nature and
      Nations,
    History, being inter-
      woven with Politics
      and Law.

IX. Law, municipal.

X. Ideology,
    General Grammar,
    Ethics, Rhetoric,
    Belles Lettres,
      and the fine arts.

Some of the terms used in this table being subject to a difference of acceptation, it is proper to define the meaning and comprehension intended to be given them here:

Geometry, Elementary, is that of straight lines and of the circle.
    Transcendental, is that of all other curves; it includes, of course, *Projectiles*, a leading branch of the military art.
Military Architecture includes Fortification, another branch of that art.
Statics respect matter generally, in a state of rest, and include Hydrostatics, or the laws of fluids particularly, at rest or in equilibrio.
Dynamics, used as a general term, include
    Dynamics proper, or the laws of *solids* in motion; and
    Hydrodynamics, or Hydraulics, those of *fluids* in motion.
Pneumatics teach the theory of air, its weight, motion, condensation, rarefaction, &c.
Acoustics, or Phonics, the theory of sound.
Optics, the laws of light and vision.
Physics, or Physiology, in a general sense, mean the doctrine of the physical objects of our senses.

Chemistry is meant, with its other usual branches, to comprehend the theory of agriculture.

Mineralogy, in addition to its peculiar subjects, is here understood to embrace what is real in geology.

Ideology is the doctrine of thought.

General Grammar explains the construction of language.

Some articles in this distribution of sciences will need observation. A professor is proposed for ancient languages, the
Latin, Greek, and Hebrew, particularly; but these languages
being the foundation common to all the sciences, it is difficult
to foresee what may be the extent of this school. At the same
time, no greater obstruction to industrious study could be
proposed than the presence, the intrusions and the noisy tur-
bulence of a multitude of small boys; and if they are to be
placed here for the rudiments of the languages, they may be
so numerous that its character and value as an University will
be merged in those of a Grammar school. It is, therefore,
greatly to be wished, that preliminary schools, either on private or public establishment, could be distributed in districts
through the State, as preparatory to the entrance of students
into the University. The tender age at which this part of education commences, generally about the tenth year, would
weigh heavily with parents in sending their sons to a school
so distant as the central establishment would be from most of
them. Districts of such extent as that every parent should be
within a day's journey of his son at school, would be desirable in cases of sickness, and convenient for supplying their
ordinary wants, and might be made to lessen sensibly the expense of this part of their education. And where a sparse population would not, within such a compass, furnish subjects
sufficient to maintain a school, a competent enlargement of
district must, of necessity, there be submitted to. At these
district schools or colleges, boys should be rendered able to
read the easier authors, Latin and Greek. This would be useful and sufficient for many not intended for an University education. At these, too, might be taught English grammar, the
higher branches of numerical arithmetic, the geometry of
straight lines and of the circle, the elements of navigation, and
geography to a sufficient degree, and thus afford to greater
numbers the means of being qualified for the various voca-

tions of life, needing more instruction than merely menial or prædial labor, and the same advantages to youths whose education may have been neglected until too late to lay a foundation in the learned languages. These institutions, intermediate between the primary schools and University, might then be the passage of entrance for youths into the University, where their classical learning might be critically completed, by a study of the authors of highest degree; and it is at this stage only that they should be received at the University. Giving then a portion of their time to a finished knowledge of the Latin and Greek, the rest might be appropriated to the modern languages, or to the commencement of the course of science for which they should be destined. This would generally be about the fifteenth year of their age, when they might go with more safety and contentment to that distance from their parents. Until this preparatory provision shall be made, either the University will be overwhelmed with the grammar school, or a separate establishment, under one or more ushers, for its lower classes, will be advisable, at a mile or two distant from the general one; where, too, may be exercised the stricter government necessary for young boys, but unsuitable for youths arrived at years of discretion.

The considerations which have governed the specification of languages to be taught by the professor of modern languages were, that the French is the language of general intercourse among nations, and as a depository of human science, is unsurpassed by any other language, living or dead; that the Spanish is highly interesting to us, as the language spoken by so great a portion of the inhabitants of our continents, with whom we shall probably have great intercourse ere long, and is that also in which is written the greater part of the earlier history of America. The Italian abounds with works of very superior order, valuable for their matter, and still more distinguished as models of the finest taste in style and composition. And the German now stands in a line with that of the most learned nations in richness of erudition and advance in the sciences. It is too of common descent with the language of our own country, a branch of the same original Gothic stock, and furnishes valuable illustrations for us. But in this point of view, the Anglo-Saxon is of peculiar value. We have placed it among the modern languages, because it is in fact that which we speak, in the earliest form in which we have knowledge of it. It has been undergoing, with time, those gradual changes which all languages, ancient and modern, have experienced; and even now needs only to be printed in the modern character and orthography to be intelligible, in a considerable degree, to an English reader. It has this value, too, above the Greek and Latin, that while it gives the radix of the mass of our language, they explain its innovations only. Obvious proofs of this have been presented to the modern reader in the disquisitions of Horn Tooke; and Fortescue Aland has well explained the great instruction which may be derived from it to a full understanding of our ancient common law, on which, as a stock, our whole system of law is engrafted. It will form the first link in the chain of an historical review of our language through all its successive changes to the present day, will constitute the foundation of that critical instruction in it which ought to be found in a seminary of general learning, and thus reward amply the few weeks of attention which would alone be requisite for its attainment; a language already fraught with all the eminent science of our parent country, the future vehicle of whatever we may ourselves achieve, and destined to occupy so much space on the globe, claims distinguished attention in American education.

Medicine, where fully taught, is usually subdivided into several professorships, but this cannot well be without the accessory of an hospital, where the student can have the benefit of attending clinical lectures, and of assisting at operations of surgery. With this accessory, the seat of our University is not yet prepared, either by its population or by the numbers of poor who would leave their own houses, and accept of the charities of an hospital. For the present, therefore, we propose but a single professor for both medicine and anatomy. By him the medical science may be taught, with a history and explanations of all its successive theories from Hippocrates to the present day; and anatomy may be fully treated. Vegetable pharmacy will make a part of the botanical course, and mineral and chemical pharmacy of those of mineralogy and chemistry. This degree of medical information is such as the mass of scientific students would wish to possess, as enabling them in their course through life, to estimate with satisfaction the extent and limits of the aid to human life and health, which they may understandingly expect from that art; and it constitutes such a foundation for those intended for the profession, that the finishing course of practice at the bed-sides of the sick, and at the operations of surgery in a hospital, can neither be long nor expensive. To seek this finishing elsewhere, must therefore be submitted to for a while.

In conformity with the principles of our Constitution, which places all sects of religion on an equal footing, with the jealousies of the different sects in guarding that equality from encroachment and surprise, and with the sentiments of the Legislature in favor of freedom of religion, manifested on former occasions, we have proposed no professor of divinity; and the rather as the proofs of the being of a God, the creator, preserver, and supreme ruler of the universe, the author of all the relations of morality, and of the laws and obligations these infer, will be within the province of the professor of ethics; to which adding the developments of these moral obligations, of those in which all sects agree, with a knowledge of the languages, Hebrew, Greek, and Latin, a basis will be formed common to all sects. Proceeding thus far without offence to the Constitution, we have thought it proper at this point to leave every sect to provide, as they think fittest, the means of further instruction in their own peculiar tenets.

We are further of opinion, that after declaring by law that certain sciences shall be taught in the University, fixing the number of professors they require, which we think should, at present, be ten, limiting (except as to the professors who shall be first engaged in each branch,) a maximum for their salaries, (which should be a certain but moderate subsistence, to be made up by liberal tuition fees, as an excitement to assiduity,) it will be best to leave to the discretion of the visitors, the grouping of these sciences together, according to the accidental qualifications of the professors; and the introduction also of other branches of science, when enabled by private donations, or by public provision, and called for by the increase of population, or other change of circumstances; to establish beginnings, in short, to be developed by time, as those who come after us shall find expedient. They will be more advanced than we are in science and in useful arts, and will know best what will suit the circumstances of their day.

We have proposed no formal provision for the gymnastics of the school, although a proper object of attention for every institution of youth. These exercises with ancient nations, constituted the principal part of the education of their youth. Their arms and mode of warfare rendered them severe in the extreme; ours, on the same correct principle, should be adapted to our arms and warfare; and the manual exercise, military manœuvres, and tactics generally, should be the frequent exercises of the students, in their hours of recreation. It is at that age of aptness, docility, and emulation of the practices of manhood, that such things are soonest learnt and longest remembered. The use of tools too in the manual arts is worthy of encouragement, by facilitating to such as choose it, an admission into the neighboring workshops. To these should be added the arts which embellish life, dancing, music, and drawing; the last more especially, as an important part of military education. These innocent arts furnish amusement and happiness to those who, having time on their hands, might less inoffensively employ it. Needing, at the same time, no regular incorporation with the institution, they may be left to accessory teachers, who will be paid by the individuals employing them, the University only providing proper apartments for their exercise.

The fifth duty prescribed to the Commissioners, is to propose such general provisions as may be properly enacted by the Legislature, for the better organizing and governing the University.

In the education of youth, provision is to be made for, 1, tuition; 2, diet; 3, lodging; 4, government; and 5, honorary excitements. The first of these constitutes the proper functions of the professors; 2, the dieting of the students should be left to private boarding houses of their own choice, and at their own expense; to be regulated by the Visitors from time to time, the house only being provided by the University within its own precincts, and thereby of course subjected to the general regimen, moral or sumptuary, which they shall prescribe. 3. They should be lodged in dormitories, making a part of the general system of buildings. 4. The best mode of government for youth, in large collections, is certainly a desideratum not yet attained with us. It may be well questioned whether *fear* after a certain age, is a motive to which we should have ordinary recourse. The human character is susceptible of other incitements to correct conduct, more worthy of employ, and of better effect. Pride of character, laudable ambition, and moral dispositions are innate correctives of the indiscretions of that lively age; and when strengthened by habitual appeal and exercise, have a happier effect on future character than the degrading motive of fear. Hardening them to disgrace, to corporal punishments, and servile humiliations cannot be the best process for producing erect character. The affectionate deportment between father and son, offers in truth the best example for that of tutor and pupil; and the experience and practice of other* countries, in this respect, may be worthy of enquiry and consideration with us. It will then be for the wisdom and discretion of the Visitors to devise and perfect a proper system of government, which, if it be founded in reason and comity, will be more likely to nourish in the minds of our youth the combined spirit of order and self-respect, so congenial with our political institutions, and so important to be woven into the American character.

5. What qualifications shall be required to entitle to entrance into the University, the arrangement of the days and hours of lecturing for the different schools, so as to facilitate to the students the circle of attendance on them; the establishment of periodical and public examinations, the premiums to be given for distinguished merit; whether honorary degrees shall be conferred, and by what appellations; whether the title to these shall depend on the time the candidate has been at the University, or, where nature has given a greater share of understanding, attention, and application; whether he shall not be allowed the advantages resulting from these endowments, with other minor items of government, we are of opinion should be entrusted to the Visitors; and the statute under which we act having provided for the appointment of these, we think they should moreover be charged with

*A police exercised by the students themselves, under proper discretion, has been tried with success in some countries, and the rather as forming them for initiation into the duties and practices of civil life.

The erection, preservation, and repair of the buildings, the care of the grounds and appurtenances, and of the interest of the University generally.

That they should have power to appoint a bursar, employ a proctor, and all other necessary agents.

To appoint and remove professors, two-thirds of the whole number of Visitors voting for the removal.

To prescribe their duties and the course of education, in conformity with the law.

To establish rules for the government and discipline of the students, not contrary to the laws of the land.

To regulate the tuition fees, and the rent of the dormitories they occupy.

To prescribe and control the duties and proceedings of all officers, servants, and others, with respect to the buildings, lands, appurtenances, and other property and interests of the University.

To draw from the literary fund such moneys as are by law charged on it for this institution; and in general

To direct and do all matters and things which, not being inconsistent with the laws of the land, to them shall seem most expedient for promoting the purposes of the said institution; which several functions they should be free to exercise in the form of by-laws, rules, resolutions, orders, instructions, or otherwise, as they should deem proper.

That they should have two stated meetings in the year, and occasional meetings at such times as they should appoint, or on a special call with such notice as themselves shall prescribe by a general rule; which meetings should be at the University, a majority of them constituting a quorum for business; and that on the death or resignation of a member, or on his removal by the President and Directors of the Literary Fund, or the Executive, or such other authority as the Legislature shall think best, such President and Directors, or the Executive, or other authority, shall appoint a successor.

That the said Visitors should appoint one of their own body to be Rector, and with him be a body corporate, under the style and title of the Rector and Visitors of the University of Virginia, with the right, as such, to use a common seal; that they should have capacity to plead and be impleaded in all courts of justice, and in all cases interesting to the University, which may be the subjects of legal cognizance and jurisdiction; which pleas should not abate by the determination of their office, but should stand revived in the name of their successors, and they should be capable in law and in trust for the University, of receiving subscriptions and donations, real and personal, as well from bodies corporate, or persons associated, as from private individuals.

And that the said Rector and Visitors should, at all times, conform to such laws as the Legislature may, from time to time, think proper to enact for their government; and the said University should, in all things, and at all times, be subject to the control of the Legislature.

And lastly, the Commissioners report to the Legislature the following conditional offers to the President and Directors of the Literary Fund, for the benefit of the University:

On the condition that Lexington, or its vicinity, shall be selected as the site of the University, and that the same be permanently established there within two years from the date, John Robinson, of Rockbridge county, has executed a deed to the President and Directors of the Literary Fund, to take effect at his death, for the following tracts of land, to wit:

400 acres on the North fork of James river, known by the name of Hart's bottom, purchased of the late Gen. Bowyer.

171 acres adjoining the same, purchased of James Griggsby.

203 acres joining the last mentioned tract, purchased of William Paxton.

112 acres lying on the North river, above the lands of Arthur Glasgow, conveyed to him by William Paxton's heirs.

500 acres adjoining the lands of Arthur Glasgow, Benjamin Camden and David Edmonson.

545 acres lying in Pryor's gap, conveyed to him by the heirs of William Paxton, deceased.

260 acres lying in Childer's gap, purchased of Wm. Mitchell.

300 acres lying, also, in Childer's gap, purchased of Nicholas Jones.

500 acres lying on Buffalo, joining the lands of Jas. Johnston.

340 acres on the Cowpasture river, conveyed to him by

General James Breckenridge—reserving the right of selling the two last mentioned tracts, and converting them into other lands contiguous to Hart's bottom, for the benefit of the University; also the whole of his slaves, amounting to 57 in number; one lot of 22 acres, joining the town of Lexington, to pass immediately on the establishment of the University, together with all the personal estate of every kind, subject only to the payment of his debts and fulfillment of his contracts.

It has not escaped the attention of the Commissioners, that the deed referred to is insufficient to pass the estate in the lands intended to be conveyed, and may be otherwise defective; but if necessary, this defect may be remedied before the meeting of the Legislature, which the Commissioners are advised will be done.

The Board of Trustees of Washington College have also proposed to transfer the whole of their funds, viz: 100 shares in the funds of the James River Company, 31 acres of land upon which their buildings stand, their philosophical apparatus, their expected interest in the funds of the Cincinnati Society, the libraries of the Graham and Washington Societies, and $3,000 in cash, on condition that a reasonable provision be made for the present professors. A subscription has also been offered by the people of Lexington and its vicinity, amounting to $17,878, all which will appear from the deed and other documents, reference thereto being had.

In this case, also, it has not escaped the attention of the Commissioners, that questions may arise as to the power of the trustees to make the above transfers.

On the condition that the Central College shall be made the site of the University, its whole property, real and personal, in possession or in action, is offered. This consists of a parcel of land of 47 acres, whereon the buildings of the college are begun, one pavilion and its appendix of dormitories being already far advanced, and with one other pavilion, and equal annexation of dormitories, being expected to be completed during the present season—of another parcel of 153 acres, near the former, and including a considerable eminence very favorable for the erection of a future observatory; of the proceeds of the sales of two glebes, amounting to $3,280 86 cents; and of a subscription of $41,248, on papers in hand, besides what is on outstanding papers of unknown amount, not yet returned—out of these sums are to be taken, however, the cost of the lands, of the buildings, and other works done, and for existing contracts. For the conditional transfer to these to the President and Directors of the Literary Fund, a regular power, signed by the subscribers and founders of the Central College generally, has been given to its Visitors and Proctor, and a deed conveying the said property accordingly to the President and Directors of the Literary Fund, has been duly executed by the said Proctor, and acknowledged for record in the office of the clerk of the county court of Albemarle.

Signed and certified by the members present, each in his proper hand-writing, this 4th day of August, 1818.

TH: JEFFERSON,
CREED TAYLOR,
PETER RANDOLPH,
WM. BROCKENBROUGH,
ARCH'D RUTHERFORD,
ARDH'D STUART,
JAMES BRECKENRIDGE,
HENRY E. WATKINS,
JAMES MADISON,
A. T. MASON,
HUGH HOLMES,

PHIL. C. PENDLETON,
SPENCER ROANE,
JOHN M. C. TAYLOR,
J. G. JACKSON,
PHIL. SLAUGHTER,
WM. H. CABELL,
NAT. H. CLAIBORNE,
WM. A. C. DADE,
WILLIAM JONES,
THOMAS WILSON.

Memorial on the Book Duty

November 30, 1821

To the Senate and House of Representatives of the United States of America in Congress assembled:

THE PETITION of the rector and visiters of the University of Virginia, on behalf of those for whom they are in the office of preparing the means of instruction, as well as of others seeking it elsewhere, respectfully representeth:

That the Commonwealth of Virginia has thought proper lately to establish a university for instruction, generally, in all the useful branches of science, of which your petitioners are appointed rector and visiters, and, as such, are charged with attention to the interests of those who shall be committed to their care.

That they observe, by the tariff of duties imposed by the laws of Congress on importations into the United States, an article peculiarly inauspicious to the objects of their own, and of all other literary institutions throughout the United States.

That at an early period of the present Government, when our country was burdened with a heavy debt, contracted in the war of Independence, and its resources for revenue were untried and uncertain, the National Legislature thought it as yet inexpedient to indulge in scruples as to the subjects of taxation, and, among others, imposed a duty on books imported from abroad, which has been continued, and now is, of fifteen per cent., on their prime cost, raised by ordinary custom-house charges to eighteen per cent., and by the importer's profits to perhaps twenty-five per cent., and more.

That, after many years' experience, it is certainly found that the reprinting of books in the United States is confined chiefly to those in our native language, and of popular characters, and to cheap editions of a few of the classics for the use of schools; while the valuable editions of the classical authors, even learned works in the English language, and books in all foreign living languages, (vehicles of the important discoveries and improvements in science and the arts, which are daily advancing the interest and happiness of other nations,) are unprinted here, and unobtainable from abroad but under the burden of a heavy duty.

That of many important books, in different branches of science, it is believed that there is not a single copy in the United States; of others, but a few; and these too distant and difficult of access for students and writers generally.

That the difficulty resulting from this mode of procuring books of the first order in the sciences, and in foreign languages, ancient and modern, is an unfair impediment to the American student, who, for want of these aids, already possessed or easily procurable in all countries except our own, enters on his course with very unequal means, with wants unknown to his foreign competitors, and often with that imperfect result which subjects us to reproaches not unfelt by minds alive to the honor and mortified sensibilities of their country.

That, to obstruct the acquisition of books from abroad, as an encouragement of the progress of literature at home, is burying the fountain to increase the flow of its waters.

That books, and especially those of the rare and valuable character, thus burdened, are not articles of consumption, but of permanent preservation and value, lasting often as many centuries as the houses we live in, of which examples are to be found in every library of note.

That books, therefore, are capital, often the only capital of professional men on their outset in life, and of students destined for professions, (as most of our scholars are,) and barely able, too, for the most part, to meet the expenses of tuition, and less to pay as extra tax on the books necessary for their instruction, that they are consequently less instructed than they would be; and that our citizens at large do not derive from their employment all the benefits which higher qualifications would procure them.

That this is the only form of capital on which a tax of from 18 to 25 per cent. is first levied on the gross, and the proprietor then subject to all other taxes in detail, as those holding capitals in other forms, on which no such extra tax has been previously levied.

That it is true that no duty is required on books imported for seminaries of learning; but these, locked up in libraries, can be of no avail to the practical man, when he wishes a recurrence to them for the uses of life.

That more than thirty years' experience of the resources of our country prove them equal to all its debts and wants, and permit its Legislature now to favor such objects as the public interests recommend to favor.

That the value of science to a republican people; the security it gives to liberty, by enlightening the minds of its citizens; the protection it affords against foreign power; the virtues it inculcates; the just emulation of the distinction it confers on nations foremost in it; in short, its identification with power, morals, order, and happiness, (which merits to it premiums of encouragement rather than repressive taxes,) are topics, which your petitioners do not permit themselves to urge on the wisdom of Congress, before whose minds these considerations are always present, and bearing with their just weight.

And they conclude, therefore, with praying that Congress will be pleased to bestow on this important subject the attention it merits, and give the proper relief to the candidates of science among ourselves, devoting themselves to the laudable object of qualifying themselves to become the instructors and benefactors of their fellow-citizens.

And your petitioners, as in duty bound, shall ever pray, &c.

From the Minutes of the Board of Visitors, University of Virginia, 1822–1825

Report to the President and Directors of the Literary Fund (extract)

October 7, 1822

IN THE SAME REPORT of the commissioners of 1818 it was stated by them that "in conformity with the principles of our constitution, which places all sects of religion on an equal footing, with the jealousies of the different sects in guarding that equality from encroachment or surprise, and with the sentiments of the legislature in freedom of religion, manifested on former occasions, they had not proposed that any professorship of divinity should be established in the University; that provision, however, was made for giving instruction in the Hebrew, Greek and Latin languages, the depositories of the originals, and of the earliest and most respected authorities of the faith of every sect, and for courses of ethical lectures, developing those moral obligations in which all sects agree. That, proceeding thus far, without offence to the constitution, they had left, at this point, to every sect to take into their own hands the office of further instruction in the peculiar tenet of each."

It was not, however, to be understood that instruction in religious opinion and duties was meant to be precluded by the public authorities, as indifferent to the interests of society. On the contrary, the relations which exist between man and his Maker, and the duties resulting from those relations, are the most interesting and important to every human being, and the most incumbent on his study and investigation. The want of instruction in the various creeds of religious faith existing among our citizens presents, therefore, a chasm in a general institution of the useful sciences. But it was thought that this want, and the entrustment to each society of instruction in its own doctrine, were evils of less danger than a permission to the public authorities to dictate modes or principles of religious instruction, or than opportunities furnished them by giving countenance or ascendancy to any one sect over another. A remedy, however, has been suggested of promising aspect, which, while it excludes the public authorities from the domain of religious freedom, will give to the sectarian schools of divinity the full benefit the public provisions made for instruction in the other branches of science. These branches are equally necessary to the divine as to the other professional or civil characters, to enable them to fulfill the duties of their calling with understanding and usefulness. It has, therefore, been in contemplation, and suggested by some pious individuals, who perceive the advantages of associating other studies with those of religion, to establish their religious schools on the confines of the University, so as to give to their students ready and convenient access and attendance on the scientific lectures of the University; and to maintain, by that means, those destined for the religious professions on as high a standing of science, and of personal weight and respectability, as may be obtained by others from the benefits of the University. Such establishments would offer the further and greater advantage of enabling the students of the University to attend religious exercises with the professor of their particular sect, either in the rooms of the building still to be erected, and destined to that purpose under impartial regulations, as proposed in the same report of the commissioners, or in the lecturing room of such professor. To such propositions the Visitors are disposed to lend a willing ear, and would think it their duty to give every encouragement, by assuring to those who might choose such a location for their schools, that the regulations of the University should be so modified and accommodated as to give every facility of access and attendance to their students, with such regulated use also as may be permitted to the other students, of the library which may hereafter be acquired, either by public or private munificence. But always understanding that these schools shall be independent of the University and of each other. Such an arrangement would complete the circle of the useful sciences embraced by this institution, and would fill the chasm now existing, on principles which would leave inviolate the constitutional freedom of religion, the most inalienable and sacred of all human rights, over which the people and authorities of this state, individually and publicly, have ever manifested the most watchful jealousy: and could this jealousy be now alarmed, in the opinion of the legislature, by what is here suggested, the idea will be relinquished on any surmise of disapprobation which they might think proper to express.

March 4, 1825

A resolution was moved and agreed to in the following words:

Whereas, it is the duty of this Board to the government under which it lives, and especially to that of which this University is the immediate creation, to pay especial attention to the principles of government which shall be inculcated therein, and to provide that none shall be inculcated which are incompatible with those on which the Constitutions of this State, and of the United States were genuinely based, in the common opinion; and for this purpose it may be necessary to point out specially where these principles are to be found legitimately developed:

Resolved, that it is the opinion of this Board that as to the general principles of liberty and the rights of man, in nature and in society, the doctrines of Locke, in his "Essay concerning the true original extent and end of civil government," and of Sidney in his "Discourses on government," may be considered as those generally approved by our fellow citizens of this, and the United States, and that on the distinctive principles of the government of our State, and of that of the United States, the best guides are to be found in, 1. The Declaration of Independence, as the fundamental act of union of these States. 2. The book known by the title of "The Federalist," being an authority to which appeal is habitually made by all, and rarely declined or denied by any as evidence of the general opinion of those who framed, and of those who accepted the Constitution of the United States, on questions as to its genuine meaning. 3. The Resolutions of the General Assembly of Virginia in 1799 on the subject of the alien and sedition laws, which appeared to accord with the predominant sense of the people of the United States. 4. The valedictory address of President Washington, as conveying political lessons of peculiar value. And that in the branch of the school of law, which is to treat on the subject of civil polity, these shall be used as the text and documents of the school.

Resolved, that it be communicated to the Faculty of the professors of the University, as the earnest request and recommendation of the rector and Visitors, that so far as can be effected by their exertions, they cause the statutes and rules enacted for the government of the University, to be exactly and strictly observed; that the roll of each school particularly be punctually called at the hour at which its students should attend; that the absent and the tardy, without reasonable cause, be noted, and a copy of these notations be communicated by mail or otherwise to the parent or guardian of each student respectively, on the first days of every month during the term (instead of the days prescribed in a former statute for such communications).

That it is requested of them to make known to the students that it is with great regret that some breaches of order, committed by the unworthy few who lurk among them unknown, render necessary the extension to all of processes afflicting to the feelings of those who are conscious of their own correctness, and who are above all participation in these vicious irregularities. While the offenders continue unknown the tarnish of their faults spreads itself over the worthy also, and confounds all in a common censure. But that it is in their power to relieve themselves from the imputations and painful proceedings to which they are thereby subjected, by lending their aid to the faculty, on all occasions towards detecting the real guilty. The Visitors are aware that a prejudice prevails too extensively among the young that it is dishonorable to bear witness one against another. While this prevails, and under the form of a matter of conscience, they have been unwilling to authorize constraint, and have therefore, in their regulations on this subject, indulged the error, however unfounded in reason or morality. But this loose principle in the ethics of school-boy combinations, is unworthy of mature and regulated minds, and is accordingly condemned by the laws of their country, which, in offences within their cognisance, compel those who have knowledge of a fact, to declare it for the purposes of justice, and of the general good and safety of society. And certainly, where wrong has been done, he who knows and conceals the doer of it, makes himself an accomplice, and justly censurable as such. It becomes then but an act of justice to themselves, that the innocent and the worthy should throw off with disdain all communion of character with such offenders, should determine no longer to screen the irregular and the vicious under the respect of their cloak, and to notify them, even by a solemn association for the purpose, that they will co-operate with the faculty in future, for preservation of order, the vindication of their own character, and the reputation and usefulness of an institution which their country has so liberally established for their improvement, and to place within their reach those acquirements in knowledge on which their future happiness and fortunes depend. Let the good and the virtuous of the alumni of the University do this, and the disorderly will then be singled out for observation, and deterred by punishment, or disabled by expulsion, from infecting with their inconsideration the institution itself, and the sound mass of those which it is preparing for virtue and usefulness.

Draft Declaration and Protest of the Commonwealth of Virginia, on the Principles of the Constitution of the United States of America, and on the Violations of them

December 1825

W E, the General Assembly of Virginia, on behalf, and in the name of the people thereof, do declare as follows:

The States in North America which confederated to establish their independence of the government of Great Britain, of which Virginia was one, became, on that acquisition, free and independent States, and as such, authorized to constitute governments, each for itself, in such form as it thought best.

They entered into a compact, (which is called the Constitution of the United States of America,) by which they agreed to unite in a single government as to their relations with each other, and with foreign nations, and as to certain other articles particularly specified. They retained at the same time, each to itself, the other rights of independent government, comprehending mainly their domestic interests.

For the administration of their federal branch, they agreed to appoint, in conjunction, a distinct set of functionaries, legislative, executive, and judiciary, in the manner settled in that compact: while to each, severally, and of course, remained its original right of appointing, each for itself, a separate set of functionaries, legislative, executive, and judiciary, also, for administering the domestic branch of their respective governments.

These two sets of officers, each independent of the other, constitute thus a *whole* of government, for each State separately; the powers ascribed to the one, as specifically made federal, exercised over the whole, the residuary powers, retained to the other, exercisable exclusively over its particular State, foreign herein, each to the others, as they were before the original compact.

To this construction of government and distribution of its powers, the Commonwealth of Virginia does religiously and affectionately adhere, opposing, with equal fidelity and firmness, the usurpation of either set of functionaries on the rightful powers of the other.

But the federal branch has assumed in some cases, and claimed in others, a right of enlarging its own powers by constructions, inferences, and indefinite deductions from those directly given, which this assembly does declare to be usurpations of the powers retained to the independent branches, mere interpolations into the compact, and direct infractions of it.

They claim, for example, and have commenced the exercise of a right to construct roads, open canals, and effect other internal improvements within the territories and jurisdictions exclusively belonging to the several States, which this assembly does declare has not been given to that branch by the constitutional compact, but remains to each State among its domestic and unalienated powers, exercisable within itself and by its domestic authorities alone.

This assembly does further disavow and declare to be most false and unfounded, the doctrine that the compact, in authorizing its federal branch to lay and collect taxes, duties, imposts and excises to pay the debts and provide for the common defence and general welfare of the United States, has given them thereby a power to do whatever *they* may think, or pretend, would promote the general welfare, which construction would make that, of itself, a complete government, without limitation of powers; but that the plain sense and obvious meaning were, that they might levy the taxes necessary to provide for the general welfare, by the various acts of power therein specified and delegated to them, and by no others.

Nor is it admitted, as has been said, that the people of these States, by not investing their federal branch with all the means of bettering their condition, have denied to themselves any which may effect that purpose; since, in the distribution of these means they have given to that branch those which belong to its department, and to the States have reserved separately the residue which belong to them separately. And thus by the organization of the two branches taken together, have completely secured the first object of human association, the full improvement of their condition, and reserved to themselves all the faculties of multiplying their own blessings.

Whilst the General Assembly thus declares the rights retained by the States, rights which they have never yielded, and which this State will never voluntarily yield, they do not mean to raise the banner of disaffection, or of separation from their sister States, co-parties with themselves to this compact. They know and value too highly the blessings of their Union as to foreign nations and questions arising among themselves, to consider every infraction as to be met by actual resistance. They respect too affectionately the opinions of those possessing the same rights under the same instrument, to make every difference of construction a ground of immediate rupture. They would, indeed, consider such a rupture as among the greatest calamities which could befall them; but not the greatest. There is yet one greater, submission to a government of unlimited powers. It is only when the hope of avoiding this shall become absolutely desperate, that further forebearance could not be indulged. Should a majority of the co-parties, therefore, contrary to the expectation and hope of this assembly, prefer, at this time, acquiescence in these assumptions of power by the federal member of the government, we will be patient and suffer much, under the confidence that time, ere it be too late, will prove to them also the bitter consequences in which that usurpation will involve us all. In the meanwhile, we will breast with them, rather than separate from them, every misfortune, save that only of living under a government of unlimited powers. We owe every other sacrifice to ourselves, to our federal brethren, and to the world at large, to pursue with temper and perseverance the great experiment which shall prove that man is capable of living in society, governing itself by laws self-imposed, and securing to its members the enjoyment of life, liberty, property, and peace; and further to show, that even when the government of its choice shall manifest a tendency to degeneracy, we are not at once to despair but that the will and the watchfulness of its sounder parts will reform its aberrations, recall it to original and legitimate principles, and restrain it within the rightful limits of self-government. And these are the objects of this Declaration and Protest.

Supposing then, that it might be for the good of the whole, as some of its co-States seem to think, that the power of making roads and canals should be added to those directly given to the federal branch, as more likely to be systematically and beneficially directed, than by the independent action of the several States, this commonwealth, from respect to these opinions, and a desire of conciliation with its co-States, will consent, in concurrence with them, to make this addition, provided it be done regularly by an amendment of the compact, in the way established by that instrument, and provided also, it be sufficiently guarded against abuses, compromises, and corrupt practices, not only of possible, but of probable occurrence.

And as a further pledge of the sincere and cordial attachment of this commonwealth to the union of the whole, so far as has been consented to by the compact called "The Constitution of the United States of America," (constructed according to the plain and ordinary meaning of its language, to the common intendment of the time, and of those who framed it;) to give also to all parties and authorities, time for reflection and for consideration, whether, under a temperate view of the possible consequences, and especially of the constant obstructions which an equivocal majority must ever expect to meet, they will still prefer the assumption of this power rather than its acceptance from the free will of their constituents; and to preserve peace in the meanwhile, we proceed to make it the duty of our citizens, until the legislature shall otherwise and ultimately decide, to acquiesce under those acts of the federal branch of our government which we have declared to be usurpations, and against which, in point of right, we do protest as null and void, and never to be quoted as precedents of right.

We therefore do enact, and be it enacted by the General Assembly of Virginia, that all citizens of this commonwealth, and persons and authorities within the same, shall pay full obedience at all times to the acts which may be passed by the Congress of the United States, the object of which shall be the construction of post roads, making canals of navigation, and maintaining the same in any part of the United States, in like manner as if said acts were, *totidem verbis*, passed by the legislature of this commonwealth.

Addresses, Messages,
and Replies

Contents

INDIAN ADDRESSES

Response to the Citizens of Albemarle

February 12, 1790

GENTLEMEN,

The testimony of esteem with which you are pleased to honour my return to my native country fills me with gratitude and pleasure. While it shews that my absence has not lost me your friendly recollection, it holds out the comfortable hope that when the hour of retirement shall come, I shall again find myself amidst those with whom I have long lived, with whom I wish to live, and whose affection is the source of my purest happiness. Their favor was the door thro' which I was ushered on the stage of public life; and while I have been led on thro' it's varying scenes, I could not be unmindful of those who assigned me my first part.

My feeble and obscure exertions in their service, and in the holy cause of freedom, have had no other merit than that they were my best. We have all the same. We have been fellow-labourers and fellow-sufferers, and heaven has rewarded us with a happy issue from our struggles. It rests now with ourselves alone to enjoy in peace and concord the blessings of self-government, so long denied to mankind: to shew by example the sufficiency of human reason for the care of human affairs and that the will of the majority, the Natural law of every society, is the only sure guardian of the rights of man. Perhaps even this may sometimes err. But it's errors are honest, solitary and short-lived.—Let us then, my dear friends, for ever bow down to the general reason of the society. We are safe with that, even in it's deviations, for it soon returns again to the right way. These are lessons we have learnt together. We have prospered in their practice, and the liberality with which you are pleased to approve my attachment to the general rights of mankind assures me we are still together in these it's kindred sentiments.

Wherever I may be stationed, by the will of my country, it will be my delight to see, in the general tide of happiness, that yours too flows on in just place and measure. That it may flow thro' all times, gathering strength as it goes, and spreading the happy influence of reason and liberty over the face of the earth, is my fervent prayer to heaven.

First Inaugural Address

March 4, 1801

FRIENDS AND FELLOW-CITIZENS,

Called upon to undertake the duties of the first executive office of our country, I avail myself of the presence of that portion of my fellow-citizens which is here assembled to express my grateful thanks for the favor with which they have been pleased to look toward me, to declare a sincere consciousness that the task is above my talents, and that I approach it with those anxious and awful presentiments which the greatness of the charge and the weakness of my powers so justly inspire. A rising nation, spread over a wide and fruitful land, traversing all the seas with the rich productions of their industry, engaged in commerce with nations who feel power and forget right, advancing rapidly to destinies beyond the reach of mortal eye—when I contemplate these transcendent objects, and see the honor, the happiness, and the hopes of this beloved country committed to the issue and the auspices of this day, I shrink from the contemplation, and humble myself before the magnitude of the undertaking. Utterly, indeed, should I despair did not the presence of many whom I here see remind me that in the other high authorities provided by our Constitution I shall find resources of wisdom, of virtue, and of zeal on which to rely under all difficulties. To you, then, gentlemen, who are charged with the sovereign functions of legislation, and to those associated with you, I look with encouragement for that guidance and support which may enable us to steer with safety the vessel in which we are all embarked amidst the conflicting elements of a troubled world.

During the contest of opinion through which we have passed the animation of discussions and of exertions has sometimes worn an aspect which might impose on strangers unused to think freely and to speak and to write what they think; but this being now decided by the voice of the nation, announced according to the rules of the Constitution, all will, of course, arrange themselves under the will of the law, and unite in common efforts for the common good. All, too, will bear in mind this sacred principle, that though the will of the majority is in all cases to prevail, that will to be rightful must be reasonable; that the minority possess their equal rights, which equal law must protect, and to violate would be oppression. Let us, then, fellow-citizens, unite with one heart and one mind. Let us restore to social intercourse that harmony and affection without which liberty and even life itself are but dreary things. And let us reflect that, having banished from our land that religious intolerance under which mankind so long bled and suffered, we have yet gained little if we countenance a political intolerance as despotic, as wicked, and capable of as bitter and bloody persecutions. During the throes and convulsions of the ancient world, during the agonizing spasms of infuriated man, seeking through blood and slaughter his long-lost liberty, it was not wonderful that the agitation of the billows should reach even this distant and peaceful shore; that this should be more felt and feared by some and less by others, and should divide opinions as to measures of safety. But every difference of opinion is not a difference of principle. We have called by different names brethren of the same principle. We are all Republicans, we are all Federalists. If there be any among us who would wish to dissolve this Union or to change its republican form, let them stand undisturbed as monuments of the safety with which error of opinion may be tolerated where reason is left free to combat it. I know, indeed, that some honest men fear that a republican government can not be strong, that this Government is not strong enough; but would the honest patriot, in the full tide of successful experiment, abandon a government which has so far kept us free and firm on the theoretic and visionary fear that this Government, the world's best hope, may by possibility want energy to preserve itself? I trust not. I believe this, on the contrary, the strongest Government on earth. I believe it the only one where every man, at the call of the law, would fly to the standard of the law, and would meet invasions of the public order as his own personal concern. Sometimes it is said that man can not be trusted with the government of himself. Can he, then, be trusted with the government of others? Or have we found angels in the forms of kings to govern him? Let history answer this question.

Let us, then, with courage and confidence pursue our own

Federal and Republican principles, our attachment to union and representative government. Kindly separated by nature and a wide ocean from the exterminating havoc of one quarter of the globe; too high-minded to endure the degradations of the others; possessing a chosen country, with room enough for our descendants to the thousandth and thousandth generation; entertaining a due sense of our equal right to the use of our own faculties, to the acquisitions of our own industry, to honor and confidence from our fellow-citizens, resulting not from birth, but from our actions and their sense of them; enlightened by a benign religion, professed, indeed, and practiced in various forms, yet all of them inculcating honesty, truth, temperance, gratitude, and the love of man; acknowledging and adoring an overruling Providence, which by all its dispensations proves that it delights in the happiness of man here and his greater happiness hereafter—with all these blessings, what more is necessary to make us a happy and a prosperous people? Still one thing more, fellow-citizens—a wise and frugal Government, which shall restrain men from injuring one another, shall leave them otherwise free to regulate their own pursuits of industry and improvement, and shall not take from the mouth of labor the bread it has earned. This is the sum of good government, and this is necessary to close the circle of our felicities.

About to enter, fellow-citizens, on the exercise of duties which comprehend everything dear and valuable to you, it is proper you should understand what I deem the essential principles of our Government, and consequently those which ought to shape its Administration. I will compress them within the narrowest compass they will bear, stating the general principle, but not all its limitations. Equal and exact justice to all men, of whatever state or persuasion, religious or political; peace, commerce, and honest friendship with all nations, entangling alliances with none; the support of the State governments in all their rights, as the most competent administrations for our domestic concerns and the surest bulwarks against antirepublican tendencies; the preservation of the General Government in its whole constitutional vigor, as the sheet anchor of our peace at home and safety abroad; a jealous care of the right of election by the people—a mild and safe corrective of abuses which are lopped by the sword of revolution where peaceable remedies are unprovided; absolute acquiescence in the decisions of the majority, the vital principle of republics, from which is no appeal but to force, the vital principle and immediate parent of despotism; a well-disciplined militia, our best reliance in peace and for the first moments of war till regulars may relieve them; the supremacy of the civil over the military authority; economy in the public expense, that labor may be lightly burthened; the honest payment of our debts and sacred preservation of the public faith; encouragement of agriculture, and of commerce as its handmaid; the diffusion of information and arraignment of all abuses at the bar of the public reason; freedom of religion; freedom of the press, and freedom of person under the protection of the habeas corpus, and trial by juries impartially selected. These principles form the bright constellation which has gone before us and guided our steps through an age of revolution and reformation. The wisdom of our sages and blood of our heroes have been devoted to their attainment. They should be the creed of our political faith, the text of civic instruction, the touchstone by which to try the services of those we trust; and should we wander from them in moments of error or of alarm, let us hasten to retrace our steps and to regain the road which alone leads to peace, liberty, and safety.

I repair, then, fellow-citizens, to the post you have assigned me. With experience enough in subordinate offices to have seen the difficulties of this the greatest of all, I have learnt to expect that it will rarely fall to the lot of imperfect man to retire from this station with the reputation and the favor which bring him into it. Without pretensions to that high confidence you reposed in our first and greatest revolutionary character, whose preeminent services had entitled him to the first place in his country's love and destined for him the fairest page in the volume of faithful history, I ask so much confidence only as may give firmness and effect to the legal administration of your affairs. I shall often go wrong through defect of judgment. When right, I shall often be thought wrong by those whose positions will not command a view of the whole ground. I ask your indulgence for my own errors, which will never be intentional, and your support against the errors of others, who may condemn what they would not if seen in all its parts. The approbation implied by your suffrage is a great consolation to me for the past, and my future solicitude will be to retain the good opinion of those who have bestowed it in advance, to conciliate that of others by doing them all the good in my power, and to be instrumental to the happiness and freedom of all.

Relying, then, on the patronage of your good will, I advance with obedience to the work, ready to retire from it whenever you become sensible how much better choice it is in your power to make. And may that Infinite Power which rules the destinies of the universe lead our councils to what is best, and give them a favorable issue for your peace and prosperity.

To Elias Shipman and Others, a Committee of the Merchants of New Haven

Washington, July 12, 1801

GENTLEMEN,

I have received the remonstrance you were pleased to address to me, on the appointment of Samuel Bishop to the office of collector of New Haven, lately vacated by the death of David Austin. The right of our fellow citizens to represent to the public functionaries their opinion on proceedings interesting to them, is unquestionably a constitutional right, often useful, sometimes necessary, and will always be respectfully acknoleged by me.

Of the various executive duties, no one excites more anxious concern than that of placing the interests of our fellow citizens in the hands of honest men, with understandings sufficient for their station. No duty, at the same time, is more difficult to fulfil. The knolege of characters possessed by a single individual is, of necessity, limited. To seek out the best through the whole Union, we must resort to other information, which, from the best of men, acting disinterestedly and with the purest motives, is sometimes incorrect. In the case of Samuel Bishop, however, the subject of your remonstrance, time was taken, information was sought, & such obtained as could leave no room for doubt of his fitness. From private sources it was learnt that his understanding was sound, his integrity pure, his character unstained. And the offices confided to him within his own State, are public evidences of the estimation in which he is held by the State in general, and the city & township particularly in which he lives. He is said to be the town clerk, a justice of the peace, mayor of the city of New Haven, an office held at the will of the legislature, chief judge of the court of common pleas for New Haven county, a court of high criminal and civil jurisdiction wherein most causes are decided without the right of appeal or review, and sole judge of the court of probates, wherein he singly decides all questions of wills, settlement of estates, testate and intestate, appoints guardians, settles their accounts, and in fact has under his jurisdiction and care all the property real and personal of persons dying. The two last offices, in the annual gift of the legislature, were given to him in May last. Is it possible that the man to whom the legislature of Connecticut has so recently committed trusts of such difficulty & magnitude, is 'unfit to be the collector of the district of New Haven,' tho' acknoleged in the same writing, to have obtained all this confidence 'by a long life of usefulness?' It is objected, indeed, in the remonstrance, that he is 77. years of age; but at a much more advanced age, our Franklin was the ornament of human nature. He may not be able to perform in person, all the details of his office; but if he gives us the benefit of his understanding, his integrity, his watchfulness, and takes care that all the details are well performed by himself or his necessary assistants, all public purposes will be answered. The remonstrance, indeed, does not allege that the office *has been* illy conducted, but only apprehends that it *will be* so. Should this happen in event, be assured I will do in it what shall be just and necessary for the public service. In the meantime, he should be tried without being prejudged.

The removal, as it is called, of Mr. Goodrich, forms another subject of complaint. Declarations by myself in favor of *political tolerance*, exhortations to *harmony* and affection in social intercourse, and to respect for the *equal rights* of the minority, have, on certain occasions, been quoted & misconstrued into assurances that the tenure of offices was to be undisturbed. But could candor apply such a construction? It is not indeed in the remonstrance that we find it; but it leads to the explanations which that calls for. When it is considered, that during the late administration, those who were not of a particular sect of politics were excluded from all office; when, by a steady pursuit of this measure, nearly the whole offices of the U S were monopolized by that sect; when the public sentiment at length declared itself, and burst open the doors of honor and confidence to those whose opinions they more approved, was it to be imagined that this monopoly of office was still to be continued in the hands of the minority? Does it violate their *equal rights*, to assert some rights in the majority also? Is it *political intolerance* to claim a proportionate share in the direction of the public affairs? Can they not *harmonize* in society unless they have everything in their own hands? If the will of the nation, manifested by their various elections, calls for an administration of government according with the opinions of those elected; if, for the fulfilment of that will, displacements are necessary, with whom can they so justly begin as with persons appointed in the last moments of an administration, not for its own aid, but to begin a career at the same time with their successors, by whom they had never been approved, and who could scarcely expect from them a cordial cooperation? Mr. Goodrich was one of these. Was it proper for him to place himself in office, without knowing whether those whose agent he was to be would have confidence in his agency? Can the preference of another, as the successor to Mr. Austin, be candidly called a removal of Mr. Goodrich? If a due participation of office is a matter of right, how are vacancies to be obtained? Those by death are few; by resignation, none. Can any other mode than that of removal be proposed? This is a painful office; but it is made my duty, and I meet it as such. I proceed in the operation with deliberation & inquiry, that it may injure the best men least, and effect the purposes of justice & public utility with the least private distress; that it may be thrown, as much as possible, on delinquency, on oppression, on intolerance, on incompetence, on ante-revolutionary adherence to our enemies.

The remonstrance laments "that a change in the administration must produce a change in the subordinate officers;" in other words, that it should be deemed necessary for all officers to think with their principal. But on whom does this imputation bear? On those who have excluded from office every shade of opinion which was not theirs? Or on those who have been so excluded? I lament sincerely that unessential differences of political opinion should ever have been deemed sufficient to interdict half the society from the rights and the blessings of self-government, to proscribe them as characters unworthy of every trust. It would have been to me a circumstance of great relief, had I found a moderate participation of office in the hands of the majority. I would gladly have left to time and accident to raise them to their just share. But their total exclusion calls for prompter correctives. I shall correct the procedure; but that done, disdain to follow it, shall return with joy to that state of things, when the only questions concerning a candidate shall be, is he honest? Is he capable? Is he faithful to the Constitution?

I tender you the homage of my high respect.

First Annual Message

December 8, 1801

FELLOW CITIZENS OF THE SENATE AND HOUSE OF REPRE-
SENTATIVES:

It is a circumstance of sincere gratification to me that on meeting the great council of our nation, I am able to announce to them, on the grounds of reasonable certainty, that the wars and troubles which have for so many years afflicted our sister nations have at length come to an end, and that the communications of peace and commerce are once more opening among them. While we devoutly return thanks to the beneficent Being who has been pleased to breathe into them the spirit of conciliation and forgiveness, we are bound with peculiar gratitude to be thankful to him that our own peace has been preserved through so perilous a season, and ourselves permitted quietly to cultivate the earth and to practice and improve those arts which tend to increase our comforts. The assurances, indeed, of friendly disposition, received from all the powers with whom we have principal relations, had inspired a confidence that our peace with them would not have been disturbed. But a cessation of the irregularities which had effected the commerce of neutral nations, and of the irritations and injuries produced by them, cannot but add to this confidence; and strengthens, at the same time, the hope, that wrongs committed on offending friends, under a pressure of circumstances, will now be reviewed with candor, and will be considered as founding just claims of retribution for the past and new assurances for the future.

Among our Indian neighbors, also, a spirit of peace and friendship generally prevailing and I am happy to inform you that the continued efforts to introduce among them the implements and the practice of husbandry, and of the household arts, have not been without success; that they are becoming more and more sensible of the superiority of this dependence for clothing and subsistence over the precarious resources of hunting and fishing; and already we are able to announce, that instead of that constant diminution of their numbers, produced by their wars and their wants, some of them begin to experience an increase of population.

To this state of general peace with which we have been blessed, one only exception exists. Tripoli, the least considerable of the Barbary States, had come forward with demands unfounded either in right or in compact, and had permitted itself to denounce war, on our failure to comply before a given day. The style of the demand admitted but one answer. I sent a small squadron of frigates into the Mediterranean, with assurances to that power of our sincere desire to remain in peace, but with orders to protect our commerce against the threatened attack. The measure was seasonable and salutary. The bey had already declared war in form. His cruisers were out. Two had arrived at Gibraltar. Our commerce in the Mediterranean was blockaded, and that of the Atlantic in peril. The arrival of our squadron dispelled the danger. One of the Tripolitan cruisers having fallen in with, and engaged the small schooner Enterprise, commanded by Lieutenant Sterret, which had gone as a tender to our larger vessels, was captured, after a heavy slaughter of her men, without the loss of a single one on our part. The bravery exhibited by our citizens on that element, will, I trust, be a testimony to the world that it is not the want of that virtue which makes us seek their peace, but a conscientious desire to direct the energies of our nation to the multiplication of the human race, and not to its destruction. Unauthorized by the constitution, without the sanction of Congress, to go out beyond the line of defence, the vessel being disabled from committing further hostilities, was liberated with its crew. The legislature will doubtless consider whether, by authorizing measures of offence, also, they will place our force on an equal footing with that of its adversaries. I communicate all material information on this subject, that in the exercise of the important function considered by the constitution to the legislature exclusively, their judgment may form itself on a knowledge and consideration of every circumstance of weight.

I wish I could say that our situation with all the other Barbary states was entirely satisfactory. Discovering that some delays had taken place in the performance of certain articles stipulated by us, I thought it my duty, by immediate measures for fulfilling them, to vindicate to ourselves the right of considering the effect of departure from stipulation on their side. From the papers which will be laid before you, you will be enabled to judge whether our treaties are regarded by them as fixing at all the measure of their demands, or as guarding from the exercise of force our vessels within their power; and to consider how far it will be safe and expedient to leave our affairs with them in their present posture.

I lay before you the result of the census lately taken of our inhabitants, to a conformity with which we are to reduce the ensuing rates of representation and taxation. You will perceive that the increase of numbers during the last ten years, proceeding in geometrical ratio, promises a duplication in little more than twenty-two years. We contemplate this rapid growth, and the prospect it holds up to us, not with a view to the injuries it may enable us to do to others in some future day, but to the settlement of the extensive country still remaining vacant within our limits, to the multiplications of men susceptible of happiness, educated in the love of order, habituated to self-government, and value its blessings above all price.

Other circumstances, combined with the increase of numbers, have produced an augmentation of revenue arising from consumption, in a ratio far beyond that of population alone, and though the changes of foreign relations now taking place so desirably for the world, may for a season affect this branch of revenue, yet, weighing all probabilities of expense, as well as of income, there is reasonable ground of confidence that we may now safely dispense with all the internal taxes, comprehending excises, stamps, auctions, licenses, carriages, and refined sugars, to which the postage on newspapers may be added, to facilitate the progress of information, and that the remaining sources of revenue will be sufficient to provide for the support of government to pay the interest on the public debts, and to discharge the principals in shorter periods than the laws or the general expectations had contemplated. War, indeed, and untoward events, may change this prospect of things, and call for expenses which the imposts could not meet; but sound principles will not justify our taxing the industry of our fellow citizens to accumulate treasure for wars to happen we know not when, and which might not perhaps happen but from the temptations offered by that treasure.

These views, however, of reducing our burdens, are formed

on the expectation that a sensible, and at the same time a salutary reduction, may take place in our habitual expenditures. For this purpose, those of the civil government, the army, and navy, will need revisal.

When we consider that this government is charged with the external and mutual relations only of these states; that the states themselves have principal care of our persons, our property, and our reputation, constituting the great field of human concerns, we may well doubt whether our organization is not too complicated, too expensive; whether offices or officers have not been multiplied unnecessarily, and sometimes injuriously to the service they were meant to promote. I will cause to be laid before you an essay toward a statement of those who, under public employment of various kinds, draw money from the treasury or from our citizens. Time has not permitted a perfect enumeration, the ramifications of office being too multipled and remote to be completely traced in a first trial. Among those who are dependent on executive discretion, I have begun the reduction of what was deemed necessary. The expenses of diplomatic agency have been considerably diminished. The inspectors of internal revenue who were found to obstruct the accountability of the institution, have been discontinued. Several agencies created by executive authority, on salaries fixed by that also, have been suppressed, and should suggest the expediency of regulating that power by law, so as to subject its exercises to legislative inspection and sanction. Other reformations of the same kind will be pursued with that caution which is requisite in removing useless things, not to injure what is retained. But the great mass of public offices is established by law, and, therefore, by law alone can be abolished. Should the legislature think it expedient to pass this roll in review, and try all its parts by the test of public utility, they may be assured of every aid and light which executive information can yield. Considering the general tendency to multiply offices and dependencies, and to increase expense to the ultimate term of burden which the citizen can bear, it behooves us to avail ourselves of every occasion which presents itself for taking off the surcharge; that it may never be seen here that, after leaving to labor the smallest portion of its earnings on which it can subsist, government shall itself consume the residue of what it was instituted to guard.

In our care, too, of the public contributions intrusted to our direction, it would be prudent to multiply barriers against their dissipation, by appropriating specific sums to every specific purpose susceptible of definition; by disallowing applications of money varying from the appropriation in object, or transcending it in amount; by reducing the undefined field of contingencies, and thereby circumscribing discretionary powers over money; and by bringing back to a single department all accountabilities for money where the examination may be prompt, efficacious, and uniform.

An account of the receipts and expenditures of the last year, as prepared by the secretary of the treasury, will as usual be laid before you. The success which has attended the late sales of the public lands, shows that with attention they may be made an important source of receipt. Among the payments, those made in discharge of the principal and interest of the national debt, will show that the public faith has been exactly maintained. To these will be added an estimate of appropriations necessary for the ensuing year. This last will of course be effected by such modifications of the systems of expense, as you shall think proper to adopt.

A statement has been formed by the secretary of war, on mature consideration, of all the posts and stations where garrisons will be expedient, and of the number of men requisite for each garrison. The whole amount is considerably short of the present military establishment. For the surplus no particular use can be pointed out. For defence against invasion, their number is as nothing; nor is it conceived needful or safe that a standing army should be kept up in time of peace for that purpose. Uncertain as we must ever be of the particular point in our circumference where an enemy may choose to invade us, the only force which can be ready at every point and competent to oppose them, is the body of neighboring citizens as formed into a militia. On these, collected from the parts most convenient, in numbers proportioned to the invading foe, it is best to rely, not only to meet the first attack, but if it threatens to be permanent, to maintain the defence until regulars may be engaged to relieve them. These considerations render it important that we should at every session continue to amend the defects which from time to time show themselves in the laws for regulating the militia, until they are sufficiently perfect. Nor should we now or at any time separate, until we can say we have done everything for the militia which we could do were an enemy at our door.

The provisions of military stores on hand will be laid before you, that you may judge of the additions still requisite.

With respect to the extent to which our naval preparations should be carried, some difference of opinion may be expected to appear; but just attention to the circumstances of every part of the Union will doubtless reconcile all. A small force will probably continue to be wanted for actual service in the Mediterranean. Whatever annual sum beyond that you may think proper to appropriate to naval preparations, would perhaps be better employed in providing those articles which may be kept without waste or consumption, and be in readiness when any exigence calls them into use. Progress has been made, as will appear by papers now communicated, in providing materials for seventy-four gun ships as directed by law.

How far the authority given by the legislature for procuring and establishing sites for naval purposes has been perfectly understood and pursued in the execution, admits of some doubt. A statement of the expenses already incurred on that subject, shall be laid before you. I have in certain cases suspended or slackened these expenditures, that the legislature might determine whether so many yards are necessary as have been contemplated. The works at this place are among those permitted to go on; and five of the seven frigates directed to be laid up, have been brought and laid up here, where, besides the safety of their position, they are under the eye of the executive administration, as well as of its agents and where yourselves also will be guided by your own view in the legislative provisions respecting them which may from time to time be necessary. They are preserved in such condition, as well the vessels as whatever belongs to them, as to be at all times ready for sea on a short warning. Two others are yet to be laid up so soon as they shall have reserved the repairs requisite to put them also into sound condition. As a superintending officer will be necessary at each yard, his duties and emoluments, hitherto fixed by the executive, will be a more proper subject for legislation. A communication will also be made of our progress in the execution of the law respecting the vessels directed to be sold.

The fortifications of our harbors, more or less advanced, present considerations of great difficulty. While some of them are on a scale sufficiently proportioned to the advantages of their position, to the efficacy of their protection, and the importance of the points within it, others are so extensive, will cost so much in their first erection, so much in their maintenance, and require such a force to garrison them, as to make it questionable what is best now to be done. A statement of those commenced or projected, of the expenses already incurred, and estimates of their future cost, so far as can be foreseen, shall be laid before you, that you may be enabled to judge whether any attention is necessary in the laws respecting this subject.

Agriculture, manufactures, commerce, and navigation, the four pillars of our prosperity, are the most thriving when left most free to individual enterprise. Protection from casual embarrassments, however, may sometimes be seasonably interposed. If in the course of your observations or inquiries they should appear to need any aid within the limits of our constitutional powers, your sense of their importance is a sufficient assurance they will occupy your attention. We cannot, indeed, but all feel an anxious solicitude for the difficulties under which our carrying trade will soon be placed. How far it can be relieved, otherwise than by time, is a subject of important consideration.

The judiciary system of the United States, and especially that portion of it recently erected, will of course present itself to the contemplation of Congress: and that they may be able to judge of the proportion which the institution bears to the business it has to perform, I have caused to be procured from the several States, and now lay before Congress, an exact statement of all the causes decided since the first establishment of the courts, and of those which were depending when additional courts and judges were brought in to their aid.

And while on the judiciary organization, it will be worthy your consideration, whether the protection of the inestimable institution of juries has been extended to all the cases involving the security of our persons and property. Their impartial selection also being essential to their value, we ought further to consider whether that is sufficiently secured in those States where they are named by a marshal depending on executive will, or designated by the court or by officers dependent on them.

I cannot omit recommending a revisal of the laws on the subject of naturalization. Considering the ordinary chances of human life, a denial of citizenship under a residence of fourteen years is a denial to a great proportion of those who ask it, and controls a policy pursued from their first settlement by many of these States, and still believed of consequence to their prosperity. And shall we refuse the unhappy fugitives from distress that hospitality which the savages of the wilderness extended to our fathers arriving in this land? Shall oppressed humanity find no asylum on this globe? The constitution, indeed, has wisely provided that, for admission to certain offices of important trust, a residence shall be required sufficient to develop character and design. But might not the general character and capabilities of a citizen be safely communicated to every one manifesting a *bona fide* purpose of embarking his life and fortunes permanently with us? with restrictions, perhaps, to guard against the fraudulent usurpation of our flag; an abuse which brings so much embarrassment and loss on the genuine citizen, and so much danger to the nation of being involved in war, that no endeavor should be spared to detect and suppress it.

These, fellow citizens, are the matters respecting the state of the nation, which I have thought of importance to be submitted to your consideration at this time. Some others of less moment, or not yet ready for communication, will be the subject of separate messages. I am happy in this opportunity of committing the arduous affairs of our government to the collected wisdom of the Union. Nothing shall be wanting on my part to inform, as far as in my power, the legislative judgment, nor to carry that judgment into faithful execution. The prudence and temperance of your discussions will promote, within your own walls, that conciliation which so much befriends national conclusion; and by its example will encourage among our constituents that progress of opinion which is tending to unite them in object and in will. That all should be satisfied with any one order of things is not to be expected, but I indulge the pleasing persuasion that the great body of our citizens will cordially concur in honest and disinterested efforts, which have for their object to preserve the general and State governments in their constitutional form and equilibrium; to maintain peace abroad, and order and obedience to the laws at home; to establish principles and practices of administration favorable to the security of liberty and prosperity, and to reduce expenses to what is necessary for the useful purposes of government.

To Messrs. Nehemiah Dodge and Others, a Committee of the Danbury Baptist Association, in the State of Connecticut

January 1, 1802

GENTLEMEN,

The affectionate sentiments of esteem and approbation which you are so good as to express towards me, on behalf of the Danbury Baptist Association, give me the highest satisfaction. My duties dictate a faithful and zealous pursuit of the interests of my constituents, and in proportion as they are persuaded of my fidelity to those duties, the discharge of them becomes more and more pleasing.

Believing with you that religion is a matter which lies solely between man and his God, that he owes account to none other for his faith or his worship, that the legislative powers of government reach actions only, and not opinions, I contemplate with sovereign reverence that act of the whole American people which declared that their legislature should "make no law respecting an establishment of religion, or prohibiting the free exercise thereof," thus building a wall of separation between church and State. Adhering to this expression of the supreme will of the nation in behalf of the rights of conscience, I shall see with sincere satisfaction the progress of those sentiments which tend to restore to man all his natural rights, convinced he has no natural right in opposition to his social duties.

I reciprocate your kind prayers for the protection and blessing of the common Father and Creator of man, and tender you for yourselves and your religious association, assurances of my high respect and esteem.

Third Annual Message

To the Senate and House of Representatives of the
United States:

In calling you together, fellow citizens, at an earlier day
than was contemplated by the act of the last session of Congress, I have not been insensible to the personal inconveniences necessarily resulting from an unexpected change in
your arrangements. But matters of great public concernment
have rendered this call necessary, and the interest you feel in
these will supersede in your minds all private considerations.

Congress witnessed, at their last session, the extraordinary
agitation produced in the public mind by the suspension of our
right of deposit at the port of New Orleans, no assignment of
another place having been made according to treaty. They
were sensible that the continuance of that privation would be
more injurious to our nation than any consequences which
could flow from any mode of redress, but reposing just confidence in the good faith of the government whose officer had
committed the wrong, friendly and reasonable representations
were resorted to, and the right of deposit was restored.

Previous, however, to this period, we had not been unaware of the danger to which our peace would be perpetually
exposed while so important a key to the commerce of the
western country remained under foreign power. Difficulties,
too, were presenting themselves as to the navigation of other
streams, which, arising within our territories, pass through
those adjacent. Propositions had, therefore, been authorized
for obtaining, on fair conditions, the sovereignty of New Orleans, and of other possessions in that quarter interesting to
our quiet, to such extent as was deemed practicable; and the
provisional appropriation of two millions of dollars, to be applied and accounted for by the president of the United States,
intended as part of the price, was considered as conveying the
sanction of Congress to the acquisition proposed. The enlightened government of France saw, with just discernment,
the importance to both nations of such liberal arrangements
as might best and permanently promote the peace, friendship,
and interests of both; and the property and sovereignty of all

Louisiana, which had been restored to them, have on certain conditions been transferred to the United States by instruments bearing date the 30th of April last. When these shall have received the constitutional sanction of the senate, they will without delay be communicated to the representatives also, for the exercise of their functions, as to those conditions which are within the powers vested by the constitution in Congress. While the property and sovereignty of the Mississippi and its waters secure an independent outlet for the produce of the western States, and an uncontrolled navigation through their whole course, free from collision with other powers and the dangers to our peace from that source, the fertility of the country, its climate and extent, promise in due season important aids to our treasury, an ample provision for our posterity, and a wide-spread field for the blessings of freedom and equal laws.

With the wisdom of Congress it will rest to take those ulterior measures which may be necessary for the immediate occupation and temporary government of the country; for its incorporation into our Union; for rendering the change of government a blessing to our newly-adopted brethren; for securing to them the rights of conscience and of property: for confirming to the Indian inhabitants their occupancy and self-government, establishing friendly and commercial relations with them, and for ascertaining the geography of the country acquired. Such materials for your information, relative to its affairs in general, as the short space of time has permitted me to collect, will be laid before you when the subject shall be in a state for your consideration.

Another important acquisition of territory has also been made since the last session of Congress. The friendly tribe of Kaskaskia Indians with which we have never had a difference, reduced by the wars and wants of savage life to a few individuals unable to defend themselves against the neighboring tribes, has transferred its country to the United States, reserving only for its members what is sufficient to maintain them in an agricultural way. The considerations stipulated are, that we shall extend to them our patronage and protection, and give them certain annual aids in money, in implements of agriculture, and other articles of their choice. This country, among the most fertile within our limits, extending along the Mississippi from the mouth of the Illinois to and up the Ohio, though not so necessary as a barrier since the acquisition of the other bank, may yet be well worthy of being laid open to immediate settlement, as its inhabitants may descend with rapidity in support of the lower country should future circumstances expose that to foreign enterprise. As the stipulations in this treaty also involve matters within the competence of both houses only, it will be laid before Congress as soon as the senate shall have advised its ratification.

With many other Indian tribes, improvements in agriculture and household manufacture are advancing, and with all our peace and friendship are established on grounds much firmer than heretofore. The measure adopted of establishing trading houses among them, and of furnishing them necessaries in exchange for their commodities, at such moderated prices as leave no gain, but cover us from loss, has the most conciliatory and useful effect upon them, and is that which will best secure their peace and good will.

The small vessels authorized by Congress with a view to the Mediterranean service, have been sent into that sea, and will be able more effectually to confine the Tripoline cruisers within their harbors, and supersede the necessity of convoy to our commerce in that quarter. They will sensibly lessen the expenses of that service the ensuing year.

A further knowledge of the ground in the north-eastern and north-western angles of the United States has evinced that the boundaries established by the treaty of Paris, between the British territories and ours in those parts, were too imperfectly described to be susceptible of execution. It has therefore been thought worthy of attention, for preserving and cherishing the harmony and useful intercourse subsisting between the two nations, to remove by timely arrangements what unfavorable incidents might otherwise render a ground of future misunderstanding. A convention has therefore been entered into, which provides for a practicable demarkation of those limits to the satisfaction of both parties.

An account of the receipts and expenditures of the year ending 30th September last, with the estimates for the service of the ensuing year, will be laid before you by the secretary of the treasury so soon as the receipts of the last quarter shall be returned from the more distant States. It is already ascertained that the amount paid into the treasury for that year has been between eleven and twelve millions of dollars, and that the revenue accrued during the same term exceeds the sum counted on as sufficient for our current expenses, and to extinguish the public debt within the period heretofore proposed.

The amount of debt paid for the same year is about three millions one hundred thousand dollars, exclusive of interest, and making, with the payment of the preceding year, a discharge of more than eight millions and a half of dollars of the principal of that debt, besides the accruing interest; and there remain in the treasury nearly six millions of dollars. Of these, eight hundred and eighty thousand have been reserved for payment of the first instalment due under the British convention of January 8th, 1802, and two millions are what have been before mentioned as placed by Congress under the power and accountability of the president, toward the price of New Orleans and other territories acquired, which, remaining untouched, are still applicable to that object, and go in diminution of the sum to be funded for it.

Should the acquisition of Louisiana be constitutionally confirmed and carried into effect, a sum of nearly thirteen millions of dollars will then be added to our public debt, most of which is payable after fifteen years; before which term the present existing debts will all be discharged by the established operation of the sinking fund. When we contemplate the ordinary annual augmentation of imposts from increasing population and wealth, the augmentation of the same revenue by its extension to the new acquisition, and the economies which may still be introduced into our public expenditures, I cannot but hope that Congress in reviewing their resources will find means to meet the intermediate interests of this additional debt without recurring to new taxes, and applying to this object only the ordinary progression of our revenue. Its extraordinary increase in times of foreign war will be the proper and sufficient fund for any measures of safety or precaution which that state of things may render necessary in our neutral position.

Remittances for the instalments of our foreign debt having been found impracticable without loss, it has not been thought expedient to use the power given by a former act of Congress of continuing them by reloans, and of redeeming instead thereof equal sums of domestic debt, although no difficulty was found in obtaining that accommodation.

The sum of fifty thousand dollars appropriated by Congress for providing gun-boats, remains unexpended. The favorable and peaceful turn of affairs on the Mississippi rendered an immediate execution of that law unnecessary, and time was desirable in order that the institution of that branch of our force might begin on models the most approved by experience. The same issue of events dispensed with a resort to the appropriation of a million and a half of dollars contemplated for purposes which were effected by happier means.

We have seen with sincere concern the flames of war lighted up again in Europe, and nations with which we have the most friendly and useful relations engaged in mutual destruction. While we regret the miseries in which we see others involved let us bow with gratitude to that kind Providence which, inspiring with wisdom and moderation our late legislative councils while placed under the urgency of the greatest wrongs, guarded us from hastily entering into the sanguinary contest, and left us only to look on and to pity its ravages. These will be heaviest on those immediately engaged. Yet the nations pursuing peace will not be exempt from all evil. In the course of this conflict, let it be our endeavor, as it is our interest and desire, to cultivate the friendship of the belligerent nations by every act of justice and of incessant kindness; to receive their armed vessels with hospitality from the distresses of the sea, but to administer the means of annoyance to none; to establish in our harbors such a police as may maintain law and order; to restrain our citizens from embarking individually in a war in which their country takes no part; to punish severely those persons, citizen or alien, who shall usurp the cover of our flag for vessels not entitled to it, infecting thereby with suspicion those of real Americans, and committing us into controversies for the redress of wrongs not our own; to exact from every nation the observance, toward our vessels and citizens, of those principles and practices which all civilized people acknowledge; to merit the character of a just nation, and maintain that of an independent one, preferring every consequence to insult and habitual wrong. Congress will consider whether the existing laws enable us efficaciously to maintain this course with our citizens in all places, and with others while within the limits of our jurisdiction, and will give them the new modifications necessary for these objects. Some contraventions of right have already taken place, both within our jurisdictional limits and on the high seas. The friendly disposition of the governments from whose agents they have proceeded, as well as their wisdom and regard for justice, leave us in reasonable expectation that they will be rectified and prevented in future; and that no act will be countenanced by them which threatens to disturb our friendly intercourse. Separated by a wide ocean from the nations of Europe, and from the political interests which entangle them together, with productions and wants which render our commerce and friendship useful to them and theirs to us, it cannot be the interest of any to assail us, nor ours to disturb them. We should be most unwise, indeed, were we to cast away the singular blessings of the position in which nature has placed us, the opportunity she has endowed us with of pursuing, at a distance from foreign contentions, the paths of industry, peace, and happiness; of cultivating general friendship, and of bringing collisions of interest to the umpirage of reason rather than of force. How desirable then must it be, in a government like ours, to see its citizens adopt individually the views, the interests, and the conduct which their country should pursue, divesting themselves of those passions and partialities which tend to lessen useful friendships, and to embarrass and embroil us in the calamitous scenes of Europe. Confident, fellow citizens, that you will duly estimate the importance of neutral dispositions toward the observance of neutral conduct, that you will be sensible how much it is our duty to look on the bloody arena spread before us with commiseration indeed, but with no other wish than to see it closed, I am persuaded you will cordially cherish these dispositions in all discussions among yourselves, and in all communications with your constituents; and I anticipate

with satisfaction the measures of wisdom which the great interests now committed to *you* will give you an opportunity of
providing, and *myself* that of approving and carrying into execution with the fidelity I owe to my country.

Second Inaugural Address

March 4, 1805

Proceeding, fellow citizens, to that qualification which the constitution requires, before my entrance on the charge again conferred upon me, it is my duty to express the deep sense I entertain of this new proof of confidence from my fellow citizens at large, and the zeal with which it inspires me, so to conduct myself as may best satisfy their just expectations.

On taking this station on a former occasion, I declared the principles on which I believed it my duty to administer the affairs of our commonwealth. My conscience tells me that I have, on every occasion, acted up to that declaration, according to its obvious import, and to the understanding of every candid mind.

In the transaction of your foreign affairs, we have endeavored to cultivate the friendship of all nations, and especially of those with which we have the most important relations. We have done them justice on all occasions, favored where favor was lawful, and cherished mutual interests and intercourse on fair and equal terms. We are firmly convinced, and we act on that conviction, that with nations, as with individuals, our interests soundly calculated, will ever be found inseparable from our moral duties; and history bears witness to the fact, that a just nation is taken on its word, when recourse is had to armaments and wars to bridle others.

At home, fellow citizens, you best know whether we have done well or ill. The suppression of unnecessary offices, of useless establishments and expenses, enabled us to discontinue our internal taxes. These covering our land with officers, and opening our doors to their intrusions, had already begun that process of domiciliary vexation which, once entered, is scarcely to be restrained from reaching successively every article of produce and property. If among these taxes some minor ones fell which had not been inconvenient, it was because their amount would not have paid the officers who collected them, and because, if they had any merit, the state authorities might adopt them, instead of others less approved.

The remaining revenue on the consumption of foreign articles, is paid cheerfully by those who can afford to add foreign luxuries to domestic comforts, being collected on our seaboards and frontiers only, and incorporated with the transactions of our mercantile citizens, it may be the pleasure and pride of an American to ask, what farmer, what mechanic, what laborer, ever sees a tax-gatherer of the United States? These contributions enable us to support the current expenses of the government, to fulfil contracts with foreign nations, to extinguish the native right of soil within our limits, to extend those limits, and to apply such a surplus to our public debts, as places at a short day their final redemption, and that redemption once effected, the revenue thereby liberated may, by a just repartition among the states, and a corresponding amendment of the constitution, be applied, *in time of peace*, to rivers, canals, roads, arts, manufactures, education, and other great objects within each state. *In time of war*, if injustice, by ourselves or others, must sometimes produce war, increased as the same revenue will be increased by population and consumption, and aided by other resources reserved for that crisis, it may meet within the year all the expenses of the year, without encroaching on the rights of future generations, by burdening them with the debts of the past. War will then be but a suspension of useful works, and a return to a state of peace, a return to the progress of improvement.

I have said, fellow citizens, that the income reserved had enabled us to extend our limits; but that extension may possibly pay for itself before we are called on, and in the meantime, may keep down the accruing interest; in all events, it will repay the advances we have made. I know that the acquisition of Louisiana has been disapproved by some, from a candid apprehension that the enlargement of our territory would endanger its union. But who can limit the extent to which the federative principle may operate effectively? The larger our association, the less will it be shaken by local passions; and in any view, is it not better that the opposite bank of the Mississippi should be settled by our own brethren and children, than by strangers of another family? With which shall we be most likely to live in harmony and friendly intercourse?

In matters of religion, I have considered that its free exercise is placed by the constitution independent of the powers of the general government. I have therefore undertaken, on no occasion, to prescribe the religious exercises suited to it; but have left them, as the constitution found them, under the direction and discipline of state or church authorities acknowledged by the several religious societies.

The aboriginal inhabitants of these countries I have regarded with the commiseration their history inspires. Endowed with the faculties and the rights of men, breathing an ardent love of liberty and independence, and occupying a country which left them no desire but to be undisturbed, the stream of overflowing population from other regions directed itself on these shores; without power to divert, or habits to contend against, they have been overwhelmed by the current, or driven before it; now reduced within limits too narrow for the hunter's state, humanity enjoins us to teach them agriculture and the domestic arts; to encourage them to that industry which alone can enable them to maintain their place in existence, and to prepare them in time for that state of society, which to bodily comforts adds the improvement of the mind and morals. We have therefore liberally furnished them with the implements of husbandry and household use; we have placed among them instructors in the arts of first necessity; and they are covered with the ægis of the law against aggressors from among ourselves.

But the endeavors to enlighten them on the fate which awaits their present course of life, to induce them to exercise their reason, follow its dictates, and change their pursuits with the change of circumstances, have powerful obstacles to encounter; they are combated by the habits of their bodies, prejudice of their minds, ignorance, pride, and the influence of interested and crafty individuals among them, who feel themselves something in the present order of things, and fear to become nothing in any other. These persons inculcate a sanctimonious reverence for the customs of their ancestors; that whatsoever they did, must be done through all time; that reason is a false guide, and to advance under its counsel, in their physical, moral, or political condition, is perilous innovation; that their duty is to remain as their Creator made them, ignorance being safety, and knowledge full of danger; in short, my friends, among them is seen the action and counteraction of good sense and bigotry; they, too, have their anti-philosophers, who find an interest in keeping things in their present state, who dread reformation, and exert all their faculties to maintain the ascendency of habit over the duty of improving our reason, and obeying its mandates.

In giving these outlines, I do not mean, fellow citizens, to arrogate to myself the merit of the measures; that is due, in the first place, to the reflecting character of our citizens at large, who, by the weight of public opinion, influence and strengthen the public measures; it is due to the sound discretion with which they select from among themselves those to whom they confide the legislative duties; it is due to the zeal and wisdom of the characters thus selected, who lay the foundations of public happiness in wholesome laws, the execution of which alone remains for others; and it is due to the able and faithful auxiliaries, whose patriotism has associated with me in the executive functions.

During this course of administration, and in order to disturb it, the artillery of the press has been levelled against us, charged with whatsoever its licentiousness could devise or dare. These abuses of an institution so important to freedom and science, are deeply to be regretted, inasmuch as they tend to lessen its usefulness, and to sap its safety; they might, indeed, have been corrected by the wholesome punishments reserved and provided by the laws of the several States against falsehood and defamation; but public duties more urgent press on the time of public servants, and the offenders have therefore been left to find their punishment in the public indignation.

Nor was it uninteresting to the world, that an experiment should be fairly and fully made, whether freedom of discussion, unaided by power, is not sufficient for the propagation and protection of truth—whether a government, conducting itself in the true spirit of its constitution, with zeal and purity, and doing no act which it would be unwilling the whole world should witness, can be written down by falsehood and defamation. The experiment has been tried; you have witnessed the scene; our fellow citizens have looked on, cool and collected; they saw the latent source from which these outrages proceeded; they gathered around their public functionaries, and when the constitution called them to the decision by suffrage, they pronounced their verdict, honorable to those who had served them, and consolatory to the friend of man, who believes he may be intrusted with his own affairs.

No inference is here intended, that the laws, provided by the State against false and defamatory publications, should not be enforced; he who has time, renders a service to public morals and public tranquillity, in reforming these abuses by the salutary coercions of the law; but the experiment is noted, to prove that, since truth and reason have maintained their ground against false opinions in league with false facts, the press, confined to truth, needs no other legal restraint; the public judgment will correct false reasonings and opinions, on a full hearing of all parties; and no other definite line can be drawn between the inestimable liberty of the press and its demoralizing licentiousness. If there be still improprieties which this rule would not restrain, its supplement must be sought in the censorship of public opinion.

Contemplating the union of sentiment now manifested so generally, as auguring harmony and happiness to our future course, I offer to our country sincere congratulations. With those, too, not yet rallied to the same point, the disposition to do so is gaining strength; facts are piercing through the veil drawn over them; and our doubting brethren will at length see, that the mass of their fellow citizens, with whom they cannot yet resolve to act, as to principles and measures, think as they think, and desire what they desire; that our wish, as well as theirs, is, that the public efforts may be directed honestly to the public good, that peace be cultivated, civil and religious liberty unassailed, law and order preserved; equality of rights maintained, and that state of property, equal or unequal, which results to every man from his own industry, or that of his fathers. When satisfied of these views, it is not in human nature that they should not approve and support them; in the meantime, let us cherish them with patient affection; let us do them justice, and more than justice, in all competitions of interest; and we need not doubt that truth, reason, and their own interests, will at length prevail, will gather them into the fold of their country, and will complete their entire union of opinion, which gives to a nation the blessing of harmony, and the benefit of all its strength.

I shall now enter on the duties to which my fellow citizens have again called me, and shall proceed in the spirit of those principles which they have approved. I fear not that any motives of interest may lead me astray; I am sensible of no passion which could seduce me knowingly from the path of justice; but the weakness of human nature, and the limits of my own understanding, will produce errors of judgment sometimes injurious to your interests. I shall need, therefore, all the indulgence I have heretofore experienced—the want of it will certainly not lessen with increasing years. I shall need, too, the favor of that Being in whose hands we are, who led our forefathers, as Israel of old, from their native land, and planted them in a country flowing with all the necessaries and comforts of life; who has covered our infancy with his providence, and our riper years with his wisdom and power; and to whose goodness I ask you to join with me in supplications, that he will so enlighten the minds of your servants, guide their councils, and prosper their measures, that whatsoever they do, shall result in your good, and shall secure to you the peace, friendship, and approbation of all nations.

Sixth Annual Message

December 2, 1806

To the Senate and House of Representatives of the
United States in Congress assembled:

It would have given me, fellow citizens, great satisfaction
to announce in the moment of your meeting that the difficulties in our foreign relations, existing at the time of your last
separation, had been amicably and justly terminated. I lost no
time in taking those measures which were most likely to bring
them to such a termination, by special missions charged with
such powers and instructions as in the event of failure could
leave no imputation on either our moderation or forbearance.
The delays which have since taken place in our negotiations
with the British government appears to have proceeded from
causes which do not forbid the expectation that during the
course of the session I may be enabled to lay before you their
final issue. What will be that of the negotiations for settling
our differences with Spain, nothing which had taken place at
the date of the last despatches enables us to pronounce. On
the western side of the Mississippi she advanced in considerable force, and took post at the settlement of Bayou Pierre,
on the Red river. This village was originally settled by France,
was held by her as long as she held Louisiana, and was delivered to Spain only as a part of Louisiana. Being small, insu-
lated, and distant, it was not observed, at the moment of
redelivery to France and the United States, that she continued
a guard of half a dozen men which had been stationed there.
A proposition, however, having been lately made by our com-
mander-in-chief, to assume the Sabine river as a temporary
line of separation between the troops of the two nations until
the issue of our negotiations shall be known; this has been
referred by the Spanish commandant to his superior, and in
the meantime, he has withdrawn his force to the western side
of the Sabine river. The correspondence on this subject, now
communicated, will exhibit more particularly the present state
of things in that quarter.

The nature of that country requires indispensably that an
unusual proportion of the force employed there should be
cavalry or mounted infantry. In order, therefore, that the

commanding officer might be enabled to act with effect, I had authorized him to call on the governors of Orleans and Mississippi for a corps of five hundred volunteer cavalry. The temporary arrangement he has proposed may perhaps render this unnecessary. But I inform you with great pleasure of the promptitude with which the inhabitants of those territories have tendered their services in defence of their country. It has done honor to themselves, entitled them to the confidence of their fellow-citizens in every part of the Union, and must strengthen the general determination to protect them efficaciously under all circumstances which may occur.

Having received information that in another part of the United States a great number of private individuals were combining together, arming and organizing themselves contrary to law, to carry on military expeditions against the territories of Spain, I thought it necessary, by proclamations as well as by special orders, to take measures for preventing and suppressing this enterprise, for seizing the vessels, arms, and other means provided for it, and for arresting and bringing to justice its authors and abettors. It was due to that good faith which ought ever to be the rule of action in public as well as in private transactions; it was due to good order and regular government, that while the public force was acting strictly on the defensive and merely to protect our citizens from aggression, the criminal attempts of private individuals to decide for their country the question of peace or war, by commencing active and unauthorized hostilities, should be promptly and efficaciously suppressed.

Whether it will be necessary to enlarge our regular force will depend on the result of our negotiation with Spain; but as it is uncertain when that result will be known, the provisional measures requisite for that, and to meet any pressure intervening in that quarter, will be a subject for your early consideration.

The possession of both banks of the Mississippi reducing to a single point the defence of that river, its waters, and the country adjacent, it becomes highly necessary to provide for that point a more adequate security. Some position above its mouth, commanding the passage of the river, should be rendered sufficiently strong to cover the armed vessels which may be stationed there for defence, and in conjunction with them to present an insuperable obstacle to any force attempting to pass. The approaches to the city of New Orleans, from the eastern quarter also, will require to be examined, and more effectually guarded. For the internal support of the country, the encouragement of a strong settlement on the western side of the Mississippi, within reach of New Orleans, will be worthy the consideration of the legislature.

The gun-boats authorized by an act of the last session are so advanced that they will be ready for service in the ensuing spring. Circumstances permitted us to allow the time necessary for their more solid construction. As a much larger number will still be wanting to place our seaport towns and waters in that state of defence to which we are competent and they entitled, a similar appropriation for a further provision for them is recommended for the ensuing year.

A further appropriation will also be necessary for repairing fortifications already established, and the erection of such works as may have real effect in obstructing the approach of an enemy to our seaport towns, or their remaining before them.

In a country whose constitution is derived from the will of the people, directly expressed by their free suffrages; where the principal executive functionaries, and those of the legislature, are renewed by them at short periods; where under the characters of jurors, they exercise in person the greatest portion of the judiciary powers; where the laws are consequently so formed and administered as to bear with equal weight and favor on all, restraining no man in the pursuits of honest industry, and securing to every one the property which that acquires, it would not be supposed that any safeguards could be needed against insurrection or enterprise on the public peace or authority. The laws, however, aware that these should not be trusted to moral restraints only, have wisely provided punishments for these crimes when committed. But would it not be salutary to give also the means of preventing their commission? Where an enterprise is meditated by private individuals against a foreign nation in amity with the United States, powers of prevention to a certain extent are given by the laws; would they not be as reasonable and useful were the enterprise preparing against the United States? While adverting to this branch of the law, it is proper to observe, that in enterprises meditated against foreign nations, the ordinary process of binding to the observance of the peace and good behavior, could it be extended to acts to be done out of the jurisdiction of the United States, would be effectual in some cases where the offender is able to keep out of sight every indication of his purpose which could draw on him the exercise of the powers now given by law.

The states on the coast of Barbary seem generally disposed at present to respect our peace and friendship; with Tunis alone some uncertainty remains. Persuaded that it is our interest to maintain our peace with them on equal terms, or not at all, I propose to send in due time a reinforcement into the Mediterranean, unless previous information shall show it to be unnecessary.

We continue to receive proofs of the growing attachment of our Indian neighbors, and of their disposition to place all their interests under the patronage of the United States. These dispositions are inspired by their confidence in our justice, and in the sincere concern we feel for their welfare; and as long as we discharge these high and honorable functions with the integrity and good faith which alone can entitle us to their continuance, we may expect to reap the just reward in their peace and friendship.

The expedition of Messrs. Lewis and Clarke, for exploring the river Missouri, and the best communication from that to the Pacific ocean, has had all the success which could have been expected. They have traced the Missouri nearly to its source, descended the Columbia to the Pacific ocean, ascertained with accuracy the geography of that interesting communication across our continent, learned the character of the country, of its commerce, and inhabitants; and it is but justice to say that Messrs. Lewis and Clarke, and their brave companions, have by this arduous service deserved well of their country.

The attempt to explore the Red river, under the direction of Mr. Freeman, though conducted with a zeal and prudence meriting entire approbation, has not been equally successful. After proceeding up it about six hundred miles, nearly as far as the French settlements had extended while the country was in their possession, our geographers were obliged to return without completing their work.

Very useful additions have also been made to our knowledge of the Mississippi by Lieutenant Pike, who has ascended to its source, and whose journal and map, giving the details of the journey, will shortly be ready for communication to both houses of Congress. Those of Messrs. Lewis and Clarke, and Freeman, will require further time to be digested and prepared. These important surveys, in addition to those before possessed, furnish materials for commencing an accurate map of the Mississippi, and its western waters. Some principal rivers, however, remain still to be explored, toward which the authorization of Congress, by moderate appropriations, will be requisite.

I congratulate you, fellow-citizens, on the approach of the period at which you may interpose your authority constitutionally, to withdraw the citizens of the United States from all further participation in those violations of human rights which have been so long continued on the unoffending inhabitants of Africa, and which the morality, the reputation, and the best interests of our country, have long been eager to proscribe. Although no law you may pass can take prohibitory effect till the first day of the year one thousand eight hundred and eight, yet the intervening period is not too long to prevent, by timely notice, expeditions which cannot be completed before that day.

The receipts at the treasury during the year ending on the 30th of September last, have amounted to near fifteen millions of dollars, which have enabled us, after meeting the current demands, to pay two millions seven hundred thousand dollars of the American claims, in part of the price of Louisiana; to pay of the funded debt upward of three millions of principal, and nearly four of interest; and in addition, to reimburse, in the course of the present month, near two millions of five and a half per cent. stock. These payments and reimbursements of the funded debt, with those which have been made in the four years and a half preceding, will, at the close of the present year, have extinguished upwards of twenty-three millions of principal.

The duties composing the Mediterranean fund will cease by law at the end of the present season. Considering, however, that they are levied chiefly on luxuries, and that we have an impost on salt, a necessary of life, the free use of which otherwise is so important, I recommend to your consideration the suppression of the duties on salt, and the continuation of the Mediterranean fund, instead thereof, for a short time, after which that also will become unnecessary for any purpose now within contemplation.

When both of these branches of revenue shall in this way be relinquished, there will still ere long be an accumulation of moneys in the treasury beyond the instalments of public debt which we are permitted by contract to pay. They cannot, then, without a modification assented to by the public creditors, be applied to the extinguishment of this debt, and the complete liberation of our revenues—the most desirable of all objects; nor, if our peace continues, will they be wanting for any other existing purpose. The question, therefore, now comes forward,—to what other objects shall these surpluses be appropriated, and the whole surplus of impost, after the entire discharge of the public debt, and during those intervals when the purposes of war shall not call for them? Shall we suppress the impost and give that advantage to foreign over domestic manufactures? On a few articles of more general and necessary use, the suppression in due season will doubtless be right, but the great mass of the articles on which impost is paid is foreign luxuries, purchased by those only who are rich enough to afford themselves the use of them. Their patriotism would certainly prefer its continuance and application to the great purposes of the public education, roads, rivers, canals, and such other objects of public improvement as it may be thought proper to add to the constitutional enumeration of federal powers. By these operations new channels of communication will be opened between the States; the lines of separation will disappear, their interests will be identified, and their union cemented by new and indissoluble ties. Education is here placed among the articles of public care, not that it would be proposed to take its ordinary branches out of the hands of private enterprise, which manages so much better all the concerns to which it is equal; but a public institution can alone supply those sciences which, though rarely called for, are yet necessary to complete the circle, all the parts of which contribute to the improvement of the country, and some of them to its preservation. The subject is now proposed for the consideration of Congress, because, if approved by the time the State legislatures shall have deliberated on this extension of the federal trusts, and the laws shall be passed, and other arrangements made for their execution, the necessary funds will be on hand and without employment. I suppose an amendment to the constitution, by consent of the States, necessary, because the objects now recommended are not among those enumerated in the constitution, and to which it permits the public moneys to be applied.

The present consideration of a national establishment for education, particularly, is rendered proper by this circumstance also, that if Congress, approving the proposition, shall yet think it more eligible to found it on a donation of lands, they have it now in their power to endow it with those which will be among the earliest to produce the necessary income. This foundation would have the advantage of being independent on war, which may suspend other improvements by requiring for its own purposes the resources destined for them.

This, fellow citizens, is the state of the public interest at the present moment, and according to the information now possessed. But such is the situation of the nations of Europe, and such too the predicament in which we stand with some of them, that we cannot rely with certainty on the present aspect of our affairs that may change from moment to moment, during the course of your session or after you shall have separated. Our duty is, therefore, to act upon things as they are, and to make a reasonable provision for whatever they may be. Were armies to be raised whenever a speck of war is visible in our horizon, we never should have been without them. Our resources would have been exhausted on dangers which have never happened, instead of being reserved for what is really to take place. A steady, perhaps a quickened pace in preparations for the defence of our seaport towns and waters; an early settlement of the most exposed and vulnerable parts of our country; a militia so organized that its effective portions can be called to any point in the Union, or volunteers instead of them to serve a sufficient time, are means which may always be ready yet never preying on our resources until actually called into use. They will maintain the public interests while a more permanent force shall be in course of preparation. But much will depend on the promptitude with which these means can be brought into activity. If war be forced upon us in spite of our long and vain appeals to the justice of nations, rapid and vigorous movements in its outset will go far toward securing us in its course and issue, and toward throwing its burdens on those who render necessary the resort from reason to force.

The result of our negotiations, or such incidents in their course as may enable us to infer their probable issue; such further movements also on our western frontiers as may show whether war is to be pressed there while negotiation is protracted elsewhere, shall be communicated to you from time to time as they become known to me, with whatever other information I possess or may receive, which may aid your deliberations on the great national interests committed to your charge.

Special Message on the Burr Conspiracy

January 22, 1807

To the Senate and House of Representatives of the United States:

Agreeably to the request of the House of Representatives, communicated in their resolution of the sixteenth instant, I proceed to state under the reserve therein expressed, information received touching an illegal combination of private individuals against the peace and safety of the Union, and a military expedition planned by them against the territories of a power in amity with the United States, with the measures I have pursued for suppressing the same.

I had for some time been in the constant expectation of receiving such further information as would have enabled me to lay before the legislature the termination as well as the beginning and progress of this scene of depravity, so far it has been acted on the Ohio and its waters. From this the state and safety of the lower country might have been estimated on probable grounds, and the delay was indulged the rather, because no circumstance had yet made it necessary to call in the aid of the legislative functions. Information now recently communicated has brought us nearly to the period contemplated. The mass of what I have received, in the course of these transactions, is voluminous, but little has been given under the sanction of an oath, so as to constitute formal and legal evidence. It is chiefly in the form of letters, often containing such a mixture of rumors, conjectures, and suspicions, as render it difficult to sift out the real facts, and unadvisable to hazard more than general outlines, strengthened by concurrent information, or the particular credibility of the relater. In this state of the evidence, delivered sometimes too under the restriction of private confidence, neither safety nor justice will permit the exposing names, except that of the principal actor, whose guilt is placed beyond question.

Some time in the latter part of September, I received intimations that designs were in agitation in the western country, unlawful and unfriendly to the peace of the Union; and that the prime mover in these was Aaron Burr, heretofore distinguished by the favor of his country. The grounds of these intimations being inconclusive, the objects uncertain, and the fidelity of that country known to be firm, the only measure taken was to urge the informants to use their best endeavors to get further insight into the designs and proceedings of the suspected persons, and to communicate them to me.

It was not until the latter part of October, that the objects of the conspiracy began to be perceived, but still so blended and involved in mystery that nothing distinct could be singled out for pursuit. In this state of uncertainty as to the crime contemplated, the acts done, and the legal course to be pursued, I thought it best to send to the scene where these things were principally in transaction, a person, in whose integrity, understanding, and discretion, entire confidence could be reposed, with instructions to investigate the plots going on, to enter into conference (for which he had sufficient credentials) with the governors and all other officers, civil and military, and with their aid to do on the spot whatever should be necessary to discover the designs of the conspirators, arrest their means, bring their persons to punishment, and to call out the force of the country to suppress any unlawful enterprise in which it should be found they were engaged. By this time it was known that many boats were under preparation, stores of provisions collecting, and an unusual number of suspicious characters in motion on the Ohio and its waters. Besides despatching the confidential agent to that quarter, orders were at the same time sent to the governors of the Orleans and Mississippi territories, and to the commanders of the land and naval forces there, to be on their guard against surprise, and in constant readiness to resist any enterprise which might be attempted on the vessels, posts, or other objects under their care; and on the 8th of November, instructions were forwarded to General Wilkinson to hasten an accommodation with the Spanish commander on the Sabine, and as soon as that was effected, to fall back with his principal force to the hither bank of the Mississippi, for the defence of the intersecting points on that river. By a letter received from that officer on the 25th of November, but dated October 21st, we learn that a confidential agent of Aaron Burr had been deputed to him, with communications partly written in cipher and partly oral, explaining his designs, exaggerating his resources, and making such offers of emolument and command, to engage him and the army in his unlawful enterprise, as he had flattered himself would be successful. The general, with the honor of a soldier and fidelity of a good citizen, immediately despatched a trusty officer to me with information of what had passed, proceeding to establish such an understanding with the Spanish commandant on the Sabine as permitted him to withdraw his force across the Mississippi, and to enter on measures for opposing the projected enterprise.

The general's letter, which came to hand on the 25th of November, as has been mentioned, and some other information received a few days earlier, when brought together, developed Burr's general designs, different parts of which only had been revealed to different informants. It appeared that he contemplated two distinct objects, which might be carried on either jointly or separately, and either the one or the other first, as circumstances should direct. One of these was the severance of the Union of these States by the Alleghany mountains; the other, an attack on Mexico. A third object was provided, merely ostensible, to wit: the settlement of a pretended purchase of a tract of country on the Washita, claimed by a Baron Bastrop. This was to serve as the pretext for all his preparations, an allurement for such followers as really wished to acquire settlements in that country, and a cover under which to retreat in the event of final discomfiture of both branches of his real design.

He found at once that the attachment of the western country to the present Union was not to be shaken; that its dissolution could not be effected with the consent of its inhabitants, and that his resources were inadequate, as yet, to effect it by force. He took his course then at once, determined to seize on New Orleans, plunder the bank there, possess himself of the military and naval stores, and proceed on his expedition to Mexico; and to this object all his means and preparations were now directed. He collected from all the quarters where himself or his agents possessed influence, all the ardent, restless, desperate, and disaffected persons who were ready for any enterprise analogous to their characters. He seduced good and well-meaning citizens, some by assurances that he possessed the confidence of the government and was acting under its secret patronage, a pretence which obtained some credit from the state of our differences with Spain; and others by offers of land in Bastrop's claim on the Washita.

This was the state of my information of his proceedings about the last of November, at which time, therefore, it was first possible to take specific measures to meet them. The proclamation of November 27th, two days after the receipt of General Wilkinson's information, was now issued. Orders were despatched to every intersecting point on the Ohio and Mississippi, from Pittsburg to New Orleans, for the employment of such force either of the regulars or of the militia, and of such proceedings also of the civil authorities, as might enable them to seize on all the boats and stores provided for the enterprise, to arrest the persons concerned, and to suppress effectually the further progress of the enterprise. A little before the receipt of these orders in the State of Ohio, our confidential agent, who had been diligently employed in investigating the conspiracy, had acquired sufficient information to open himself to the governor of that State, and apply for the immediate exertion of the authority and power of the State to crush the combination. Governor Tiffin and the legislature, with a promptitude, an energy, and patriotic zeal, which entitle them to a distinguished place in the affection of their sister States, effected the seizure of all the boats, provisions, and other preparations within their reach, and thus gave a first blow, materially disabling the enterprise in its outset.

In Kentucky, a premature attempt to bring Burr to justice, without sufficient evidence for his conviction, had produced a popular impression in his favor, and a general disbelief of his guilt. This gave him an unfortunate opportunity of hastening his equipments. The arrival of the proclamation and orders, and the application and information of our confidential agent, at length awakened the authorities of that State to the truth, and then produced the same promptitude and energy of which the neighboring State had set the example. Under an act of their legislature of December 23d, militia was instantly ordered to different important points, and measures taken for doing whatever could yet be done. Some boats (accounts vary from five to double or treble that number) and persons (differently estimated from one to three hundred) had in the meantime passed the falls of the Ohio, to rendezvous at the mouth of the Cumberland, with others expected down that river.

Not apprized, till very late, that any boats were building on Cumberland, the effect of the proclamation had been trusted to for some time in the State of Tennessee; but on the 19th of December, similar communications and instructions with those of the neighboring States were despatched by express to the governor, and a general officer of the western division of the State, and on the 23d of December our confidential agent left Frankfort for Nashville, to put into activity the means of that State also. But by information received yesterday I learn that on the 22d of December, Mr. Burr descended the Cumberland with two boats merely of accommodation, carrying with him from that State no quota toward his unlawful enterprise. Whether after the arrival of the proclamation, of the orders, or of our agent, any exertion which could be made by that State, or the orders of the governor of Kentucky for calling out the militia at the mouth of Cumberland, would be in time to arrest these boats, and those from the falls of the Ohio, is still doubtful.

On the whole, the fugitives from Ohio, with their associates from Cumberland, or any other place in that quarter, cannot threaten serious danger to the city of New Orleans.

By the same express of December nineteenth, orders were sent to the governors of New Orleans and Mississippi, supplementary to those which had been given on the twenty-fifth of November, to hold the militia of their territories in readiness to co-operate for their defence, with the regular troops and armed vessels then under command of General Wilkinson. Great alarm, indeed, was excited at New Orleans by the exaggerated accounts of Mr. Burr, disseminated through his emissaries, of the armies and navies he was to assemble there. General Wilkinson had arrived there himself on the 24th of November and had immediately put into activity the resources of the place for the purpose of its defence; and on the tenth of December he was joined by his troops from the Sabine. Great zeal was shown by the inhabitants generally, the merchants of the place readily agreeing to the most laudable exertions and sacrifices for manning the armed vessels with their seamen, and the other citizens manifesting unequivocal fidelity to the Union, and a spirit of determined resistance to their expected assailants.

Surmises have been hazarded that this enterprise is to receive aid from certain foreign powers. But these surmises are without proof or probability. The wisdom of the measures sanctioned by Congress at its last session had placed us in the paths of peace and justice with the only powers with whom we had any differences, and nothing has happened since which makes it either their interest or ours to pursue another course. No change of measures has taken place on our part; none ought to take place at this time. With the one, friendly arrangement was then proposed, and the law deemed necessary on the failure of that was suspended to give time for a fair trial of the issue. With the same power, negotiation is still preferred and provisional measures only are necessary to meet the event of rupture. While, therefore, we do not deflect in the slightest degree from the course we then assumed, and are still pursuing, with mutual consent, to restore a good understanding, we are not to impute to them practices as irreconcilable to interest as to good faith, and changing necessarily the relations of peace and justice between us to those of war. These surmises are, therefore, to be imputed to the vauntings of the author of this enterprise, to multiply his partisans by magnifying the belief of his prospects and support.

By letters from General Wilkinson, of the 14th and 18th of September, which came to hand two days after date of the resolution of the House of Representatives, that is to say, on the morning of the 18th instant, I received the important affidavit, a copy of which I now communicate, with extracts of so much of the letters as come within the scope of the resolution. By these it will be seen that of three of the principal emissaries of Mr. Burr, whom the general had caused to be apprehended, one had been liberated by *habeas corpus*, and the two others, being those particularly employed in the endeavor to corrupt the general and army of the United States, have been embarked by him for our ports in the Atlantic States, probably on the consideration that an impartial trial could not be expected during the present agitations of New Orleans, and that that city was not as yet a safe place of confinement. As soon as these persons shall arrive, they will be delivered to the custody of the law, and left to such course of trial, both as to place and process, as its functionaries may direct. The presence of the highest judicial authorities, to be assembled at this place within a few days, the means of pursuing a sounder course of proceedings here than elsewhere, and the aid of the executive means, should the judges have occasion to use them, render it equally desirable for the criminals as for the public, that being already removed from the place where they were first apprehended, the first regular arrest should take place here, and the course of proceedings receive here its proper direction.

Special Message on Gun-Boats

February 10, 1807

To the Senate and House of Representatives of the United States:

In compliance with the request of the House of Representatives, expressed in their resolution of the 5th instant, I proceed to give such information as is possessed, of the effect of gun-boats in the protection and defense of harbors, of the numbers thought necessary, and of the proposed distribution of them among the ports and harbors of the United States.

Under the present circumstances, and governed by the intentions of the legislature, as manifested by their annual appropriations of money for the purposes of defence, it has been concluded to combine—1st, land batteries, furnished with heavy cannon and mortars, and established on all the points around the place favorable for preventing vessels from lying before it; 2d, movable artillery which may be carried, as an occasion may require, to points unprovided with fixed batteries; 3d, floating batteries; and 4th, gun-boats, which may oppose an enemy at its entrance and co-operate with the batteries for his expulsion.

On this subject professional men were consulted as far as we had opportunity. General Wilkinson, and the late General Gates, gave their opinions in writing, in favor of the system, as will be seen by their letters now communicated. The higher officers of the navy gave the same opinions in separate conferences, as their presence at the seat of government offered occasions of consulting them, and no difference of judgment appeared on the subjects. Those of Commodore Barron and Captain Tingey, now here, are recently furnished in writing, and transmitted herewith to the legislature.

The efficacy of gun-boats for the defence of harbors, and of other smooth and enclosed waters, may be estimated in part from that of galleys, formerly much used, but less powerful, more costly in their construction and maintenance, and requiring more men. But the gun-boat itself is believed to be in use with every modern maritime nation for the purpose of defence. In the Mediterranean, on which are several small powers, whose system like ours is peace and defence, few harbors are without this article of protection. Our own experience there of the effect of gun-boats for harbor service, is recent. Algiers is particularly known to have owed to a great provision of these vessels the safety of its city, since the epoch of their construction. Before that it had been repeatedly insulted and injured. The effect of gun-boats at present in the neighborhood of Gibraltar, is well known, and how much they were used both in the attack and defence of that place during a former war. The extensive resort to them by the two greatest naval powers in the world, on an enterprise of invasion not long since in prospect, shows their confidence in their efficacy for the purposes for which they are suited. By the northern powers of Europe, whose seas are particularly adapted to them, they are still more used. The remarkable action between the Russian flotilla of gun-boats and galleys, and a Turkish fleet of ships-of-the-line and frigates, in the Liman sea, 1788, will be readily recollected. The latter, commanded by their most celebrated admiral, were completely defeated, and several of their ships-of-the-line destroyed.

From the opinions given as to the number of gun-boats necessary for some of the principal seaports, and from a view of all the towns and ports from Orleans to Maine inclusive, entitled to protection, in proportion to their situation and circumstances, it is concluded, that to give them a due measure of protection in time of war, about two hundred gun-boats will be requisite. According to first ideas, the following would be their general distribution, liable to be varied on more mature examination, and as circumstances shall vary, that is to say:—

To the Mississippi and its neighboring waters, forty gun-boats.

To Savannah and Charleston, and the harbors on each side, from St. Mary's to Currituck, twenty-five.

To the Chesapeake and its waters, twenty.

To Delaware bay and river, fifteen.

To New York, the Sound, and waters as far as Cape Cod, fifty.

To Boston and the harbors north of Cape Cod, fifty.

The flotilla assigned to these several stations, might each be under the care of a particular commandant, and the vessels composing them would, in ordinary, be distributed among the harbors within the station in proportion to their importance.

Of these boats a proper proportion would be of the larger size, such as those heretofore built, capable of navigating any seas, and of reinforcing occasionally the strength of even the most distant port when menaced with danger. The residue would be confined to their own or the neighboring harbors, would be smaller, less furnished for accommodation, and consequently less costly. Of the number supposed necessary, seventy-three are built or building, and the hundred and twenty-seven still to be provided, would cost from five to six hundred thousand dollars. Having regard to the convenience of the treasury, as well as to the resources of building, it has been thought that one half of these might be built in the present year, and the other half the next. With the legislature, however, it will rest to stop where we are, or at any further point, when they shall be of opinion that the number provided shall be sufficient for the object.

At times when Europe as well as the United States shall be at peace, it would not be proposed that more than six or eight of these vessels should be kept afloat. When Europe is in war, treble that number might be necessary to be distributed among those particular harbors which foreign vessels of war are in the habit of frequenting, for the purpose of preserving order therein.

But they would be manned, in ordinary, with only their complement for navigation, relying on the seamen and militia of the port if called into action on sudden emergency. It would be only when the United States should themselves be at war, that the whole number would be brought into actual service, and would be ready in the first moments of the war to co-operate with other means for covering at once the line of our seaports. At all times, those unemployed would be withdrawn into places not exposed to sudden enterprise, hauled up under sheds from the sun and weather, and kept in preservation with little expense for repairs or maintenance.

It must be superfluous to observe, that this species of naval armament is proposed merely for defensive operation; that it can have but little effect toward protecting our commerce in the open seas even on our coast; and still less can it become an excitement to engage in offensive maritime war, toward which it would furnish no means.

Eighth Annual Message

November 8, 1808

TO THE SENATE AND HOUSE OF REPRESENTATIVES OF THE UNITED STATES:

It would have been a source, fellow citizens, of much gratification, if our last communications from Europe had enabled me to inform you that the belligerent nations, whose disregard of neutral rights has been so destructive to our commerce, had become awakened to the duty and true policy of revoking their unrighteous edicts. That no means might be omitted to produce this salutary effect, I lost no time in availing myself of the act authorizing a suspension, in whole or in part, of the several embargo laws. Our ministers at London and Paris were instructed to explain to the respective governments there, our disposition to exercise the authority in such manner as would withdraw the pretext on which the aggressions were originally founded, and open a way for a renewal of that commercial intercourse which it was alleged on all sides had been reluctantly obstructed. As each of those governments had pledged its readiness to concur in renouncing a measure which reached its adversary through the incontestable rights of neutrals only, and as the measure had been assumed by each as a retaliation for an asserted acquiescence in the aggressions of the other, it was reasonably expected that the occasion would have been seized by both for evincing the sincerity of their profession, and for restoring to the commerce of the United States its legitimate freedom. The instructions to our ministers with respect to the different belligerents were necessarily modified with reference to their different circumstances, and to the condition annexed by law to the executive power of suspension, requiring a degree of security to our commerce which would not result from a repeal of the decrees of France. Instead of a pledge, therefore, of a suspension of the embargo as to her in case of such a repeal, it was presumed that a sufficient inducement might be found in other considerations, and particularly in the change produced by a compliance with our just demands by one belligerent, and a refusal by the other, in the relations between the other and the United States. To Great Britain, whose power on the ocean is so ascendant, it was deemed not inconsistent with that condition to state explicitly, that on her rescinding her orders in relation to the United States their trade would be opened with her, and remain shut to her enemy, in case of his failure to rescind his decrees also. From France no answer has been received, nor any indication that the requisite change in her decrees is contemplated. The favorable reception of the proposition to Great Britain was the less to be doubted, as her orders of council had not only been referred for their vindication to an acquiescence on the part of the United States no longer to be pretended, but as the arrangement proposed, while it resisted the illegal decrees of France, involved, moreover, substantially, the precise advantages professedly aimed at by the British orders. The arrangement has nevertheless been rejected.

This candid and liberal experiment having thus failed, and no other event having occurred on which a suspension of the embargo by the executive was authorized, it necessarily remains in the extent originally given to it. We have the satisfaction, however, to reflect, that in return for the privations by the measure, and which our fellow citizens in general have borne with patriotism, it has had the important effects of saving our mariners and our vast mercantile property, as well as of affording time for prosecuting the defensive and provisional measures called for by the occasion. It has demonstrated to foreign nations the moderation and firmness which govern our councils, and to our citizens the necessity of uniting in support of the laws and the rights of their country, and has thus long frustrated those usurpations and spoliations which, if resisted, involve war; if submitted to, sacrificed a vital principle of our national independence.

Under a continuance of the belligerent measures which, in defiance of laws which consecrate the rights of neutrals, overspread the ocean with danger, it will rest with the wisdom of Congress to decide on the course best adapted to such a state of things; and bringing with them, as they do, from every part of the Union, the sentiments of our constituents, my confidence is strengthened, that in forming this decision they will, with an unerring regard to the essential rights and interests of the nation, weigh and compare the painful alternatives out of which a choice is to be made. Nor should I do justice to the virtues which on other occasions have marked the character of our fellow citizens, if I did not cherish an equal confidence that the alternative chosen, whatever it may be, will be maintained with all the fortitude and patriotism which the crisis ought to inspire.

The documents containing the correspondences on the subject of the foreign edicts against our commerce, with the instructions given to our ministers at London and Paris, are now laid before you.

The communications made to Congress at their last session explained the posture in which the close of the discussion relating to the attack by a British ship of war on the frigate Chesapeake left a subject on which the nation had manifested so honorable a sensibility. Every view of what had passed authorized a belief that immediate steps would be taken by the British government for redressing a wrong, which, the more it was investigated, appeared the more clearly to require what had not been provided for in the special mission. It is found that no steps have been taken for the purpose. On the contrary, it will be seen, in the documents laid before you, that the inadmissible preliminary which obstructed the adjustment is still adhered to; and, moreover, that it is now brought into connection with the distinct and irrelative case of the orders in council. The instructions which had been given to our ministers at London with a view to facilitate, if necessary, the reparation claimed by the United States, are included in the documents communicated.

Our relations with the other powers of Europe have undergone no material changes since your last session. The important negotiations with Spain, which had been alternately suspended and resumed, necessarily experience a pause under the extraordinary and interesting crisis which distinguished her internal situation.

With the Barbary powers we continue in harmony, with the exception of an unjustifiable proceeding of the dey of Algiers toward our consul to that regency. Its character and circumstances are now laid before you, and will enable you to decide how far it may, either now or hereafter, call for any measures not within the limits of the executive authority.

With our Indian neighbors the public peace has been steadily maintained. Some instances of individual wrong have, as at other times, taken place, but in nowise implicating the will of the nation. Beyond the Mississippi, the Iowas, the Sacs, and the Alabamas, have delivered up for trial and punishment individuals from among themselves accused of murdering citizens of the United States. On this side of the Mississippi, the Creeks are exerting themselves to arrest offenders of the same kind; and the Choctaws have manifested their readiness and desire for amicable and just arrangements respecting depredations committed by disorderly persons of their tribe. And, generally, from a conviction that we consider them as part of ourselves, and cherish with sincerity their rights and interests, the attachment of the Indian tribes is gaining strength daily— is extending from the nearer to the more remote, and will amply requite us for the justice and friendship practised towards them. Husbandry and household manufacture are advancing among them, more rapidly with the southern than the northern tribes, from circumstances of soil and climate; and one of the two great divisions of the Cherokee nation have now under consideration to solicit the citizenship of the United States, and to be identified with us in laws and government, in such progressive manner as we shall think best.

In consequence of the appropriations of the last session of Congress for the security of our seaport towns and harbors, such works of defence have been erected as seemed to be called for by the situation of the several places, their relative importance, and the scale of expense indicated by the amount of the appropriation. These works will chiefly be finished in the course of the present season, except at New York and New Orleans, where most was to be done; and although a great proportion of the last appropriation has been expended on the former place, yet some further views will be submitted by Congress for rendering its security entirely adequate against naval enterprise. A view of what has been done at the several places, and of what is proposed to be done, shall be communicated as soon as the several reports are received.

Of the gun-boats authorized by the act of December last, it has been thought necessary to build only one hundred and three in the present year. These, with those before possessed, are sufficient for the harbors and waters exposed, and the residue will require little time for their construction when it is deemed necessary.

Under the act of the last session for raising an additional military force, so many officers were immediately appointed as were necessary for carrying on the business of recruiting, and in proportion as it advanced, others have been added. We have reason to believe their success has been satisfactory, although such returns have not yet been received as enable me to present to you a statement of the numbers engaged.

I have not thought it necessary in the course of the last season to call for any general detachments of militia or volunteers under the law passed for that purpose. For the ensuing season, however, they will require to be in readiness should their services be wanted. Some small and special detachments have been necessary to maintain the laws of embargo on that portion of our northern frontier which offered peculiar facilities for evasion, but these were replaced as soon as it could be done by bodies of new recruits. By the aid of these, and of the armed vessels called into actual service in other quarters, the spirit of disobedience and abuse which manifested itself early, and with sensible effect while we were unprepared to meet it, has been considerably repressed.

Considering the extraordinary character of the times in which we live, our attention should unremittingly be fixed on the safety of our country. For a people who are free, and who mean to remain so, a well-organized and armed militia is their best security. It is, therefore, incumbent on us, at every meeting, to revise the condition of the militia, and to ask ourselves if it is prepared to repel a powerful enemy at every point of our territories exposed to invasion. Some of the States have paid a laudable attention to this object; but every degree of neglect is to be found among others. Congress alone have power to produce a uniform state of preparation in this great organ of defence; the interests which they so deeply feel in their own and their country's security will present this as among the most important objects of their deliberation.

Under the acts of March 11th and April 23d, respecting arms, the difficulty of procuring them from abroad, during the present situation and dispositions of Europe, induced us to direct our whole efforts to the means of internal supply. The public factories have, therefore, been enlarged, additional machineries erected, and in proportion as artificers can be found or formed, their effect, already more than doubled, may be increased so as to keep pace with the yearly increase of the militia. The annual sums appropriated by the latter act, have been directed to the encouragement of private factories of arms, and contracts have been entered into with individual undertakers to nearly the amount of the first year's appropriation.

The suspension of our foreign commerce, produced by the injustice of the belligerent powers, and the consequent losses and sacrifices of our citizens, are subjects of just concern. The situation into which we have thus been forced, has impelled us to apply a portion of our industry and capital to internal manufactures and improvements. The extent of this conversion is daily increasing, and little doubt remains that the establishments formed and forming will—under the auspices of cheaper materials and subsistence, the freedom of labor from taxation with us, and of protecting duties and prohibitions—become permanent. The commerce with the Indians, too, within our own boundaries, is likely to receive abundant aliment from the same internal source, and will secure to them peace and the progress of civilization, undisturbed by practices hostile to both.

The accounts of the receipts and expenditures during the year ending on the 30th day of September last, being not yet made up, a correct statement will hereafter be transmitted from the Treasury. In the meantime, it is ascertained that the receipts have amounted to near eighteen millions of dollars, which, with the eight millions and a half in the treasury at the beginning of the year, have enabled us, after meeting the current demands and interest incurred, to pay two millions three hundred thousand dollars of the principal of our funded debt, and left us in the treasury, on that day, near fourteen millions of dollars. Of these, five millions three hundred and fifty thousand dollars will be necessary to pay what will be due on the first day of January next, which will complete the reimbursement of the eight per cent. stock. These payments, with those made in the six years and a half preceding, will have extinguished thirty-three millions five hundred and eighty thousand dollars of the principal of the funded debt, being the whole which could be paid or purchased within the limits of the law and our contracts; and the amount of principal thus discharged will have liberated the revenue from about two millions of dollars of interest, and added that sum annually to the disposable surplus. The probable accumulation of the surpluses of revenue beyond what can be applied to the payment of the public debt, whenever the freedom and safety of our commerce shall be restored, merits the consideration of Congress. Shall it lie unproductive in the public vaults? Shall the revenue be reduced? Or shall it rather be appropriated to the improvements of roads, canals, rivers, education, and other great foundations of prosperity and union, under the powers which Congress may already possess, or such amendment of the constitution as may be approved by the States? While uncertain of the course of things, the time may be advantageously employed in obtaining the powers necessary for a system of improvement, should that be thought best.

Availing myself of this the last occasion which will occur of addressing the two houses of the legislature at their meeting, I cannot omit the expression of my sincere gratitude for the repeated proofs of confidence manifested to me by themselves and their predecessors since my call to the administration, and the many indulgences experienced at their hands. The same grateful acknowledgments are due to my fellow citizens generally, whose support has been my great encouragement under all embarrassments. In the transaction of their business I cannot have escaped error. It is incident to our imperfect nature. But I may say with truth, my errors have been of the understanding, not of intention; and that the advancement of their rights and interests has been the constant motive for every measure. On these considerations I solicit their indulgence. Looking forward with anxiety to their future destinies, I trust that, in their steady character unshaken by difficulties, in their love of liberty, obedience to law, and support of the public authorities, I see a sure guaranty of the permanence of our republic; and retiring from the charge of their affairs, I carry with me the consolation of a firm persuasion that Heaven has in store for our beloved country long ages to come of prosperity and happiness.

To the Inhabitants of Albemarle County, in Virginia

April 3, 1809

Returning to the scenes of my birth and early life, to the society of those with whom I was raised, and who have been ever dear to me, I receive, fellow citizens and neighbors, with inexpressible pleasure, the cordial welcome you are so good as to give me. Long absent on duties which the history of a wonderful era made incumbent on those called to them, the pomp, the turmoil, the bustle and splendor of office, have drawn but deeper sighs for the tranquil and irresponsible occupations of private life, for the enjoyment of an affectionate intercourse with you, my neighbors and friends, and the endearments of family love, which nature has given us all, as the sweetener of every hour. For these I gladly lay down the distressing burthen of power, and seek, with my fellow citizens, repose and safety under the watchful cares, the labors, and perplexities of younger and abler minds. The anxieties you express to administer to my happiness, do, of themselves, confer that happiness; and the measure will be complete, if my endeavors to fulfil my duties in the several public stations to which I have been called, have obtained for me the approbation of my country. The part which I have acted on the theatre of public life, has been before them; and to their sentence I submit it; but the testimony of my native country, of the individuals who have known me in private life, to my conduct in its various duties and relations, is the more grateful, as proceeding from eye witnesses and observers, from triers of the vicinage. Of you, then, my neighbors, I may ask, in the face of the world, "whose ox have I taken, or whom have I defrauded? Whom have I oppressed, or of whose hand have I received a bribe to blind mine eyes therewith?" On your verdict I rest with conscious security. Your wishes for my happiness are received with just sensibility, and I offer sincere prayers for your own welfare and prosperity.

To Brother John Baptist de Coigne

Charlottesville, June 1781

BROTHER JOHN BAPTIST DE COIGNE,—I am very much pleased with the visit you have made us, and particularly that it has happened when the wise men from all parts of our country were assembled together in council, and had an opportunity of hearing the friendly discourse you held to me. We are all sensible of your friendship, and of the services you have rendered, and I now, for my countrymen, return you thanks, and, most particularly, for your assistance to the garrison which was besieged by the hostile Indians. I hope it will please the great being above to continue you long in life, in health and in friendship to us; and that your son will afterwards succeed you in wisdom, in good disposition, and in power over your people. I consider the name you have given as particularly honorable to me, but I value it the more as it proves your attachment to my country. We, like you, are Americans, born in the same land, and having the same interests. I have carefully attended to the figures represented on the skins, and to their explanation, and shall always keep them hanging on the walls in remembrance of you and your nation. I have joined with you sincerely in smoking the pipe of peace; it is a good old custom handed down by your ancestors, and as such I respect and join in it with reverence. I hope we shall long continue to smoke in friendship together. You find us, brother, engaged in war with a powerful nation. Our forefathers were Englishmen, inhabitants of a little island beyond the great water, and, being distressed for land, they came and settled here. As long as we were young and weak, the English whom we had left behind, made us carry all our wealth to their country, to enrich them; and, not satisfied with this, they at length began to say we were their slaves, and should do whatever they ordered us. We were now grown up and felt ourselves strong, we knew we were free as they were, that we came here of our own accord and not at their biddance, and were determined to be free as long as we should exist. For this reason they made war on us. They have now waged that war six years, and have not yet won more land from us than will serve to bury the warriors they have lost. Your old father, the king of France, has joined us in the war, and done many good things for us. We are bound forever to love him, and wish you to love him, brother, because he is a good and true friend to us. The Spaniards have also joined us, and other powerful nations are now entering into the war to punish the robberies and violences the English have committed on them. The English stand alone, without a friend to support them, hated by all mankind because they are proud and unjust. This quarrel, when it first began, was a family quarrel between us and the English, who were then our brothers. We, therefore, did not wish you to engage in it at all. We are strong enough of ourselves without wasting your blood in fighting our battles. The English, knowing this, have been always suing to the Indians to help them fight. We do not wish you to take up the hatchet. We love and esteem you. We wish you to multiply and be strong. The English, on the other hand, wish to set you and us to cutting one another's throats, that when we are dead they may take all our land. It is better for you not to join in this quarrel, unless the English have killed any of your warriors or done you any other injury. If they have, you have a right to go to war with them, and revenge the injury, and we have none to restrain you. Any free nation has a right to punish those who have done them an injury. I say the same, brother, as to the Indians who treat you ill. While I advise you, like an affectionate friend, to avoid unnecessary war, I do not assume the right of restraining you from punishing your enemies. If the English have injured you, as they have injured the French and Spaniards, do like them and join us in the war. General Clarke will receive you and show you the way to their towns. But if they have not injured you, it is better for you to lie still and be quiet. This is the advice which has been always given by the great council of the Americans. We must give the same, because we are but one of thirteen nations, who have agreed to act and speak together. These nations keep a council of wise men always sitting together, and each of us separately follow their advice. They have the care of all the people and the lands between the Ohio and Mississippi, and will see that no wrong be committed on them. The French settled at Kaskaskias, St. Vincennes, and the Cohos, are subject to that council, and they will punish them if they do you any injury. If you will make known to me any just cause of complaint against them, I will represent it to the great council at Philadelphia, and have justice done you.

Our good friend, your father, the King of France, does not lay any claim to them. Their misconduct should not be imputed to him. He gave them up to the English the last war, and we have taken them from the English. The Americans alone have a right to maintain justice in all the lands on this side the Mississippi,—on the other side the Spaniards rule. You complain, brother, of the want of goods for the use of your people. We know that your wants are great, notwithstanding we have done everything in our power to supply them, and have often grieved for you. The path from hence to Kaskaskias is long and dangerous; goods cannot be carried to you in that way. New Orleans has been the only place from which we could get goods for you. We have bought a great deal there; but I am afraid not so much of them have come to you as we intended. Some of them have been sold of necessity to buy provisions for our posts. Some have been embezzled by our own drunken and roguish people. Some have been taken by the Indians and many by the English.

The Spaniards, having now taken all the English posts on the Mississippi, have opened that channel free for our commerce, and we are in hopes of getting goods for you from them. I will not boast to you, brother, as the English do, nor promise more than we shall be able to fulfil. I will tell you honestly, what indeed your own good sense will tell you, that a nation at war cannot buy so many goods as when in peace. We do not make so many things to send over the great waters to buy goods, as we made and shall make again in time of peace. When we buy those goods, the English take many of them, as they are coming to us over the great water. What we get in safe, are to be divided among many, because we have a great many soldiers, whom we must clothe. The remainder we send to our brothers the Indians, and in going, a great deal of it is stolen or lost. These are the plain reasons why you cannot get so much from us in war as in peace. But peace is not far off. The English cannot hold out long, because all the world is against them. When that takes place, brother, there will not be an Englishman left on this side the great water. What will those foolish nations then do, who have made us their enemies, sided with the English, and laughed at you for not being as wicked as themselves? They are clothed for a day, and will be naked forever after; while you, who have submitted to short inconvenience, will be well supplied through the rest of your lives. Their friends will be gone and their enemies left behind; but your friends will be here, and will make you strong against all your enemies. For the present you shall have a share of what little goods we can get. We will order some immediately up the Mississippi for you and for us. If they be little, you will submit to suffer a little as your brothers do for a short time. And when we shall have beaten our enemies and forced them to make peace, we will share more plentifully. General Clarke will furnish you with ammunition to serve till we can get some from New Orleans. I must recommend to you particular attention to him. He is our great, good, and trusty warrior; and we have put everything under his care beyond the Alleghanies. He will advise you in all difficulties, and redress your wrongs. Do what he tells you, and you will be sure to do right. You ask us to send schoolmasters to educate your son and the sons of your people. We desire above all things, brother, to instruct you in whatever we know ourselves. We wish to learn you all our arts and to make you wise and wealthy. As soon as there is peace we shall be able to send you the best of schoolmasters; but while the war is raging, I am afraid it will not be practicable. It shall be done, however, before your son is of an age to receive instruction.

This, brother, is what I had to say to you. Repeat it from me to all your people, and to our friends, the Kickapous, Piorias, Piankeshaws and Wyattanons. I will give you a commission to show them how much we esteem you. Hold fast the chain of friendship which binds us together, keep it bright as the sun, and let them, you and us, live together in perpetual love.

To Brother Handsome Lake

To Brother Handsome Lake:—

I have received the message in writing which you sent me through Captain Irvine, our confidential agent, placed near you for the purpose of communicating and transacting between us, whatever may be useful for both nations. I am happy to learn you have been so far favored by the Divine spirit as to be made sensible of those things which are for your good and that of your people, and of those which are hurtful to you; and particularly that you and they see the ruinous effects which the abuse of spirituous liquors have produced upon them. It has weakened their bodies, enervated their minds, exposed them to hunger, cold, nakedness, and poverty, kept them in perpetual broils, and reduced their population. I do not wonder then, brother, at your censures, not only on your own people, who have voluntarily gone into these fatal habits, but on all the nations of white people who have supplied their calls for this article. But these nations have done to you only what they do among themselves. They have sold what individuals wish to buy, leaving to every one to be the guardian of his own health and happiness. Spirituous liquors are not in themselves bad, they are often found to be an excellent medicine for the sick; it is the improper and intemperate use of them, by those in health, which makes them injurious. But as you find that your people cannot refrain from an ill use of them, I greatly applaud your resolution not to use them at all. We have too affectionate a concern for your happiness to place the paltry gain on the sale of these articles in competition with the injury they do you. And as it is the desire of your nation, that no spirits should be sent among them, I am authorized by the great council of the United States to prohibit them. I will sincerely coöperate with your wise men in any proper measures for this purpose, which shall be agreeable to them.

You remind me, brother, of what I said to you, when you visited me the last winter, that the lands you then held would remain yours, and shall never go from you but when you should be disposed to sell. This I now repeat, and will ever abide by. We, indeed, are always ready to buy land; but we will never ask but when you wish to sell; and our laws, in order to protect you against imposition, have forbidden individuals to purchase lands from you; and have rendered it necessary, when you desire to sell, even to a State, that an agent from the United States should attend the sale, see that your consent is freely given, a satisfactory price paid, and report to us what has been done, for our approbation. This was done in the late case of which you complain. The deputies of your nation came forward, in all the forms which we have been used to consider as evidence of the will of your nation. They proposed to sell to the State of New York certain parcels of land, of small extent, and detached from the body of your other lands; the State of New York was desirous to buy. I sent an agent, in whom we could trust, to see that your consent was free, and the sale fair. All was reported to be free and fair. The lands were your property. The right to sell is one of the rights of property. To forbid you the exercise of that right would be a wrong to your nation. Nor do I think, brother, that the sale of lands is, under all circumstances, injurious to your people. While they depended on hunting, the more extensive the forest around them, the more game they would yield. But going into a state of agriculture, it may be as advantageous to a society, as it is to an individual, who has more land than he can improve, to sell a part, and lay out the money in stocks and implements of agriculture, for the better improvement of the residue. A little land well stocked and improved, will yield more than a great deal without stock or improvement. I hope, therefore, that on further reflection, you will see this transaction in a more favorable light, both as it concerns the interest of your nation, and the exercise of that superintending care which I am sincerely anxious to employ for their subsistence and happiness. Go on then, brother, in the great reformation you have undertaken. Persuade our red brethren then to be sober, and to cultivate their lands; and their women to spin and weave for their families. You will soon see your women and children well fed and clothed, your men living happily in peace and plenty, and your numbers increasing from year to year. It will be a great glory to you to have been the instrument of so happy a change, and your children's children, from generation to generation, will repeat your name with love and gratitude forever. In all your enterprises for the good of your people, you may count with confidence on the aid and protection of the United States, and on the sincerity and zeal with which I am myself animated in the furthering of this humane work. You are our brethren of the same land; we wish your prosperity as brethren should do. Farewell.

To the Brothers of the Choctaw Nation

December 17, 1803

BROTHERS OF THE CHOCTAW NATION:—

We have long heard of your nation as a numerous, peaceable, and friendly people; but this is the first visit we have had from its great men at the seat of our government. I welcome you here; am glad to take you by the hand, and to assure you, for your nation, that we are their friends. Born in the same land, we ought to live as brothers, doing to each other all the good we can, and not listening to wicked men, who may endeavor to make us enemies. By living in peace, we can help and prosper one another; by waging war, we can kill and destroy many on both sides; but those who survive will not be the happier for that. Then, brothers, let it forever be peace and good neighborhood between us. Our seventeen States compose a great and growing nation. Their children are as the leaves of the trees, which the winds are spreading over the forest. But we are just also. We take from no nation what belongs to it. Our growing numbers make us always willing to buy lands from our red brethren, when they are willing to sell. But be assured we never mean to disturb them in their possessions. On the contrary, the lines established between us by mutual consent, shall be sacredly preserved, and will protect your lands from all encroachments by our own people or any others. We will give you a copy of the law, made by our great Council, for punishing our people, who may encroach on your lands, or injure you otherwise. Carry it with you to your homes, and preserve it, as the shield which we spread over you, to protect your land, your property and persons.

It is at the request which you sent me in September, signed by Puckshanublee and other chiefs, and which you now repeat, that I listen to your proposition to sell us lands. You say you owe a great debt to your merchants, that you have nothing to pay it with but lands, and you pray us to take lands, and pay your debt. The sum you have occasion for, brothers, is a very great one. We have never yet paid as much to any of our red brethren for the purchase of lands. You propose to us some on the Tombigbee, and some on the Mississippi. Those on the Mississippi suit us well. We wish to have establishments on that river, as resting places for our boats, to furnish them provisions, and to receive our people who fall sick on the way to or from New Orleans, which is now ours. In that quarter, therefore, we are willing to purchase as much as you will spare. But as to the manner in which the line shall be run, we are not judges of it here, nor qualified to make any bargain. But we will appoint persons hereafter to treat with you on the spot, who, knowing the country and quality of the lands, will be better able to agree with you on a line which will give us a just equivalent for the sum of money you want paid.

You have spoken, brothers, of the lands which your fathers formerly sold and marked off to the English, and which they ceded to us with the rest of the country they held here; and you say that, though you do not know whether your fathers were paid for them, you have marked the line over again for us, and do not ask repayment. It has always been the custom, brothers, when lands were bought of the red men, to pay for them immediately, and none of us have ever seen an example of such a debt remaining unpaid. It is to satisfy their immediate wants that the red men have usually sold lands; and in such a case, they would not let the debt be unpaid. The presumption from custom then is strong; so it is also from the great length of time since your fathers sold these lands. But we have, moreover, been informed by persons now living, and who assisted the English in making the purchase, that the price was paid at the time. Were it otherwise, as it was their contract, it would be their debt, not ours.

I rejoice, brothers, to hear you propose to become cultivators of the earth for the maintenance of your families. Be assured you will support them better and with less labor, by raising stock and bread, and by spinning and weaving clothes, than by hunting. A little land cultivated, and a little labor, will procure more provisions than the most successful hunt; and a woman will clothe more by spinning and weaving, than a man by hunting. Compared with you, we are but as of yesterday in this land. Yet see how much more we have multiplied by industry, and the exercise of that reason which you possess in common with us. Follow then our example, brethren, and we will aid you with great pleasure.

The clothes and other necessaries which we sent you the last year, were, as you supposed, a present from us. We never meant to ask land or any other payment for them; and the store which we sent on, was at your request also; and to accommodate you with necessaries at a reasonable price, you wished of course to have it on your land; but the land would continue yours, not ours.

As to the removal of the store, the interpreter, and the agent, and any other matters you may wish to speak about, the Secretary at War will enter into explanations with you, and whatever he says, you may consider as said by myself, and what he promises you will be faithfully performed.

I am glad, brothers, you are willing to go and visit some other parts of our country. Carriages shall be ready to convey you, and you shall be taken care of on your journey; and when you shall have returned here and rested yourselves to your own mind, you shall be sent home by land. We had provided for your coming by land, and were sorry for the mistake which carried you to Savannah instead of Augusta, and exposed you to the risks of a voyage by sea. Had any accident happened to you, though we could not help it, it would have been a cause of great mourning to us. But we thank the Great Spirit who took care of you on the ocean, and brought you safe and in good health to the seat of our great Council; and we hope His care will accompany and protect you, on your journey and return home; and that He will preserve and prosper your nation in all its just pursuits.

To the Chiefs of the Cherokee Nation

Washington, January 10, 1806

MY FRIENDS AND CHILDREN, CHIEFLY OF THE CHERO-
KEE NATION,—Having now finished our business and finished it I hope to mutual satisfaction, I cannot take leave of
you without expressing the satisfaction I have received from
your visit. I see with my own eyes that the endeavors we have
been making to encourage and lead you in the way of improving your situation have not been unsuccessful; it has been
like grain sown in good ground, producing abundantly. You
are becoming farmers, learning the use of the plough and
the hoe, enclosing your grounds and employing that labor
in their cultivation which you formerly employed in hunting
and in war; and I see handsome specimens of cotton cloth
raised, spun and wove by yourselves. You are also raising
cattle and hogs for your food, and horses to assist your labors.
Go on, my children, in the same way and be assured the further you advance in it the happier and more respectable you
will be.

Our brethren, whom you have happened to meet here from
the West and Northwest, have enabled you to compare your
situation now with what it was formerly. They also make the
comparison, and they see how far you are ahead of them, and
seeing what you are they are encouraged to do as you have
done. You will find your next want to be mills to grind your
corn, which by relieving your women from the loss of time
in beating it into meal, will enable them to spin and weave
more. When a man has enclosed and improved his farm,
builds a good house on it and raised plentiful stocks of animals, he will wish when he dies that these things shall go to
his wife and children, whom he loves more than he does his
other relations, and for whom he will work with pleasure during his life. You will, therefore, find it necessary to establish
laws for this. When a man has property, earned by his own
labor, he will not like to see another come and take it from
him because he happens to be stronger, or else to defend it
by spilling blood. You will find it necessary then to appoint
good men, as judges, to decide contests between man and
man, according to reason and to the rules you shall establish.

If you wish to be aided by our counsel and experience in these things we shall always be ready to assist you with our advice.

My children, it is unnecessary for me to advise you against spending all your time and labor in warring with and destroying your fellow-men, and wasting your own members. You already see the folly and iniquity of it. Your young men, however, are not yet sufficiently sensible of it. Some of them cross the Mississippi to go and destroy people who have never done them an injury. My children, this is wrong and must not be; if we permit them to cross the Mississippi to war with the Indians on the other side of that river, we must let those Indians cross the river to take revenge on you. I say again, this must not be. The Mississippi now belongs to us. It must not be a river of blood. It is now the water-path along which all our people of Natchez, St. Louis, Indiana, Ohio, Tennessee, Kentucky and the western parts of Pennsylvania and Virginia are constantly passing with their property, to and from New Orleans. Young men going to war are not easily restrained. Finding our people on the river they will rob them, perhaps kill them. This would bring on a war between us and you. It is better to stop this in time by forbidding your young men to go across the river to make war. If they go to visit or to live with the Cherokees on the other side of the river we shall not object to that. That country is ours. We will permit them to live in it.

My children, this is what I wished to say to you. To go on in learning to cultivate the earth and to avoid war. If any of your neighbors injure you, our beloved men whom we place with you will endeavor to obtain justice for you and we will support them in it. If any of your bad people injure your neighbors, be ready to acknowledge it and to do them justice. It is more honorable to repair a wrong than to persist in it. Tell all your chiefs, your men, women and children, that I take them by the hand and hold it fast. That I am their father, wish their happiness and well-being, and am always ready to promote their good.

My children, I thank you for your visit and pray to the Great Spirit who made us all and planted us all in this land to live together like brothers that He will conduct you safely to your homes, and grant you to find your families and your friends in good health.

To the Wolf and People of the Mandan Nation

Washington, December 30, 1806

MY CHILDREN, THE WOLF AND PEOPLE OF THE MANDAN NATION:—I take you by the hand of friendship and give you a hearty welcome to the seat of the government of the United States. The journey which you have taken to visit your fathers on this side of our island is a long one, and your having undertaken it is a proof that you desired to become acquainted with us. I thank the Great Spirit that he has protected you through the journey and brought you safely to the residence of your friends, and I hope He will have you constantly in his safe keeping, and restore you in good health to your nations and families.

My friends and children, we are descended from the old nations which live beyond the great water, but we and our forefathers have been so long here that we seem like you to have grown out of this land. We consider ourselves no longer of the old nations beyond the great water, but as united in one family with our red brethren here. The French, the English, the Spaniards, have now agreed with us to retire from all the country which you and we hold between Canada and Mexico, and never more to return to it. And remember the words I now speak to you, my children, they are never to return again. We are now your fathers; and you shall not lose by the change. As soon as Spain had agreed to withdraw from all the waters of the Missouri and Mississippi, I felt the desire of becoming acquainted with all my red children beyond the Mississippi, and of uniting them with us as we have those on this side of that river, in the bonds of peace and friendship. I wished to learn what we could do to benefit them by furnishing them the necessaries they want in exchange for their furs and peltries. I therefore sent our beloved man, Captain Lewis, one of my own family, to go up the Missouri river to get acquainted with all the Indian nations in its neighborhood, to take them by the hand, deliver my talks to them, and to inform us in what way we could be useful to them. Your nation received him kindly, you have taken him by the hand and been friendly to him. My children, I thank you for the services you rendered him, and for your attention to his words.

He will now tell us where we should establish trading houses to be convenient to you all, and what we must send to them.

My friends and children, I have now an important advice to give you. I have already told you that you and all the red men are my children, and I wish you to live in peace and friendship with one another as brethren of the same family ought to do. How much better is it for neighbors to help than to hurt one another; how much happier must it make them. If you will cease to make war on one another, if you will live in friendship with all mankind, you can employ all your time in providing food and clothing for yourselves and your families. Your men will not be destroyed in war, and your women and children will lie down to sleep in their cabins without fear of being surprised by their enemies and killed or carried away. Your numbers will be increased instead of diminishing, and you will live in plenty and in quiet. My children, I have given this advice to all your red brethren on this side of the Mississippi; they are following it, they are increasing in their numbers, are learning to clothe and provide for their families as we do. Remember then my advice, my children, carry it home to your people, and tell them that from the day that they have become all of the same family, from the day that we became father to them all, we wish, as a true father should do, that we may all live together as one household, and that before they strike one another, they should go to their father and let him endeavor to make up the quarrel.

My children, you are come from the other side of our great island, from where the sun sets, to see your new friends at the sun rising. You have now arrived where the waters are constantly rising and falling every day, but you are still distant from the sea. I very much desire that you should not stop here, but go and see your brethren as far as the edge of the great water. I am persuaded you have so far seen that every man by the way has received you as his brothers, and has been ready to do you all the kindness in his power. You will see the same thing quite to the sea shore; and I wish you, therefore, to go and visit our great cities in that quarter, and see how many friends and brothers you have here. You will then have travelled a long line from west to east, and if you had time to go from north to south, from Canada to Florida, you would find it as long in that direction, and all the people as sincerely your friends. I wish you, my children, to see all you can, and to tell your people all you see; because I am sure the more they know of us, the more they will be our hearty friends. I invite you, therefore, to pay a visit to Baltimore, Philadelphia, New York, and the cities still beyond that, if you are willing to go further. We will provide carriages to convey you and a person to go with you to see that you want for nothing. By the time you come back the snows will be melted on the mountains, the ice in the rivers broken up, and you will be wishing to set out on your return home.

My children, I have long desired to see you; I have now opened my heart to you, let my words sink into your hearts and never be forgotten. If ever lying people or bad spirits should raise up clouds between us, call to mind what I have said, and what you have seen yourselves. Be sure there are some lying spirits between us; let us come together as friends and explain to each other what is misrepresented or misunderstood, the clouds will fly away like morning fog, and the sun of friendship appear and shine forever bright and clear between us.

My children, it may happen that while you are here occasion may arise to talk about many things which I do not now particularly mention. The Secretary at War will always be ready to talk with you, and you are to consider whatever he says as said by myself. He will also take care of you and see that you are furnished with all comforts here.

Miscellany

Contents

Reply to the Representations of Affairs in America by British Newspapers

[before November 20, 1784]

I AM an officer lately returned from service & residence in the U.S. of America. I have fought & bled for that country because I thought it's cause just. From the moment of peace to that in which I left it, I have seen it enjoying all the happiness which easy government, order & industry are capable of giving to a people. On my return to my native country what has been my astonishment to find all the public papers of Europe filled with accounts of the anarchy & destractions supposed to exist in that country. I have received serious condolances from all my friends on the bitter fruits of so prosperous a war. These friends I know to be so well disposed towards America that they wished the reverse of what they repeated from the public papers. I have enquired into the source of all this misinformation & have found it not difficult to be traced. The printers on the Continent have not yet got into the habit of taking the American newspapers. Whatever they retail therefore on the subject of America, they take from the English. If your readers will reflect a moment they will recollect that every unfavourable account they have seen of the transactions in America has been taken from the English papers only. Nothing is known in Europe of the situation of the U.S. since the acknowlegement of their independance but thro' the channel of these papers.

But these papers have been under the influence of two ruling motives 1. deep-rooted hatred springing from an unsuccesful attempt to injure 2. a fear that their island will be depopulated by the emigration of it's inhabitants to America. Hence no paper comes out without a due charge of paragraphs manufactured by persons employed for that purpose. According to these America is a scene of continued riot & anarchy. Wearied out with contention, it is on the verge of falling again into the lap of Gr. Br. for repose. It's citizens are groaning under the oppression of heavy taxes. They are flying for refuge to the frozen regions which still remain subject to Gr. Br. Their assemblies and congresses are become odious, in one paragraph represented as tyrranising over their constituents, & in another as possessing no power or influence at all, &c. &c. The truth is as follows without aggravation or diminution. There was a mutiny of 300 souldiers in Philadelphia soon after the peace; & Congress thinking the executive of that state did not act with proper energy to suppress & punish it they left that city in disgust. Yet in this mutiny there neither was blood shed nor a blow struck. There has lately been a riot in Charlestown, occasioned by the feuds between the whigs who had been driven from their country by the British while they possessed it, and the tories who were permitted to remain by the Americans when they recovered it. There were a few instances in other states where individuals disgusted with some articles in the peace undertook to call town meetings, published the resolves of the few citizens whom they could prevail upon to meet as if they had been the resolves of the whole town, and endeavored unsuccesfully to engage the people in the execution of their private views. It is beleived that these attempts have not been more than ten or a dozen thro' the whole 13 states & not one of them has been succesful: on the contrary where any illegal act has been committed by the demagogues they have been put under a due course of legal prosecution. The British when they evacuated New York having carried off, contrary to the express articles of the treaty of peace, a great deal of property belonging to the citizens of the U.S. & particularly to those of the state of Virginia, amounting as has been said to half a million of pounds sterling, the assembly of that state lately resolved that till satisfaction was made for this, the article respecting British debts ought not to be carried into full execution, submitting nevertheless this their opinion to Congress and declaring that if they thought otherwise, all laws obstructing the recovery of debts should be immediately repealed. Yet even this was opposed by a respectable minority in their senate who entered a protest against it in strong terms. The protest as it stands in the records follows immediately the resolutions protested against & therefore does not recite them. The English papers publish the protest without the resolutions and thus lead Europe to beleive that the resolutions had definitively decided against the paiment of Brit-

ish debts. Yet nothing is less true. This is a faithful history of
the high sounded disturbances of America. Those who have
visited that country since the peace will vouch that it is impossible for any governments to be more tranquil & orderly
than they are. What were the mutiny of 300 souldiers in Philada, the riot of whigs & tories in Charlestown to the riots of
London under L.ᵈ G. Gordon, and of London & the country
in general in the late elections? Where is there any country of
equal extent with the U.S. in which fewer disturbances have
happened in the same space of time? Where has there been an
instance of an army disbanded as was that of America without
receiving a shilling of the long arrearages due them or even
having their accounts settled & yet disbanded peaceably? Instead of resorting as is too often the case with disbanded armies to beggary or robbery for a livelihood they returned
every man to his home & resumed his axe & spade; & it is a
fact as true as it is singular that on the disbanding of an army
of 30,000 men in America there have been but two or three
instances of any of those who composed it being brought to
the bar of justice as criminals: and that you may travel from
one end to the other of the continent without seeing a beg-
gar. With respect to the people their confidence in their rulers
in general is what common sense will tell us it must be, where
they are of their own choice annually, unbribed by money,
undebauched by feasting, & drunkenness. It would be difficult to find one man among them who would not consider a
return under the dominion of Gr. Br. as the greatest of all
possible miseries. Their taxes are light, as they should be with
a people so lately wasted in the most cruel manner by war.
They pay in proportion to their property from one half to
one & a half per cent annually on it's whole value as estimated by their neighbors, the different states requiring more
or less as they have been less or more ravaged by their enemies. Where any taxes are imposed they are very trifling &
are calculated cheifly to bring merchants into contribution
with the farmers. Against their emigration to the remaining
British dominions the superior rigor of their climate, the in-
feriority of their soil, the nature of their governments and
their being actually inhabited by their most mortal enemies
the tory refugees, will be an eternal security. During the

course of the war the English papers were constantly filled with accounts of their great victories, their armies were daily gaining. Yet Europe saw that they were daily losing ground in America, & formed it's idea of the truth not from what it heard but from what it saw. They wisely considered an enlargement of territory on the one side & contraction of it on the other as the best indication on which side victory really was. It is hoped that Europe will be as wise & as just now: that they will not consider the fabricated papers of England as any evidence of truth; but that they will continue to judge of causes from effects. If the distractions of America were what these papers pretend, some great facts would burst out & lay their miseries open to the eyes of all the world: no such effects appear, therefore no such causes exist. If any such existed they would appear in the American newspapers which are as free as any on earth. But none such can be found in them. These are the testimonials to which I appeal for beleif. To bring more home to every reader the reliance which may be put on the English papers let him examine, if a Frenchman, what account they give of the affairs of France, if a Dutchman, what of the United Netherl^ds, if an Irishman, what of Ireland &c. If he finds that those of his own country with which he happens to be acquainted are wickedly misrepresented, let him consider how much more likely to be so are those of a nation so hated as America. America was the great pillar on which British glory was raised: America has been the instrument for levelling that glory with the dust. A little ill humour therefore might have found excuse in our commiseration: but an apostasy from truth, under whatever misfortunes, calls up feelings of a very different order.

Answers and Observations for Démeunier's Article on the United States in the Encyclopédie Methodique, *1786*

I. From *Answers to Démeunier's First Queries*

January 24, 1786

11. The Confederation is a wonderfully perfect instrument, considering the circumstances under which it was formed. There are however some alterations which experience proves to be wanting. These are principally three. 1. To establish a general rule for the admission of new states into the Union. By the Confederation no new state, except Canada, can be permitted to have a vote in Congress without first obtaining the consent of all the thirteen legislatures. It becomes necessary to agree what districts may be established into separate states, and at what period of their population they may come into Congress. The act of Congress of April 23, 1784, has pointed out what ought to be agreed on, to say also what number of votes must concur when the number of voters shall be thus enlarged. 2. The Confederation in it's eighth article, decides that the quota of money to be contributed by the several states shall be proportioned to the value of landed property in the state. Experience has shown it impracticable to come at this value. Congress have therefore recommended to the states to agree that their quotas shall be in proportion to the number of their inhabitants, counting 5 slaves however but as equal to 3 free inhabitants. I believe all the states have agreed to this alteration except Rhode island. 3. The Confederation forbids the states individually to enter into treaties of commerce, or of any other nature, with foreign nations: and it authorizes Congress to establish such treaties, with two reservations however, viz., that they shall agree to no treaty which would 1. restrain the legislatures from imposing such duties on foreigners, as natives are subjected to; or 2. from prohibiting the exportation or importation of any species of commodities. Congress may therefore be said to have a power to regulate commerce, so far as it can be effected by conventions with other nations, & by conventions which do not infringe the two fundamental reservations before mentioned.

But this is too imperfect. Because till a convention be made with any particular nation, the commerce of any one of our states with that nation may be regulated by the State itself, and even when a convention is made, the regulation of the commerce is taken out of the hands of the several states only so far as it is covered or provided for by that convention or treaty. But treaties are made in such general terms, that the greater part of the regulations would still result to the legislatures. Let us illustrate these observations by observing how far the commerce of France & of England can be affected by the state legislatures. As to England, any one of the legislatures may impose on her goods double the duties which are paid other nations; may prohibit their goods altogether; may refuse them the usual facilities for recovering their debts or withdrawing their property, may refuse to receive their Consuls or to give those Consuls any jurisdiction. But with France, whose commerce is protected by a treaty, no state can give any molestation to that commerce which is defended by the treaty. Thus, tho' a state may exclude the importation of all wines (because one of the reservations aforesaid is that they may prohibit the importation of any species of commodities) yet they cannot prohibit the importation of *French* wines particularly while they allow wines to be brought in from other countries. They cannot impose heavier duties on French commodities than on those of other nations. They cannot throw peculiar obstacles in the way of their recovery of debts due to them &c. &c. because those things are provided for by treaty. Treaties however are very imperfect machines for regulating commerce in the detail. The principal objects in the regulation of our commerce would be: 1. to lay such duties, restrictions, or prohibitions on the goods of any particular nation as might oblige that nation to concur in just & equal arrangements of commerce. 2. To lay such uniform duties on the articles of commerce throughout all the states, as may avail them of that fund for assisting to bear the burthen of public expenses. Now this cannot be done by the states separately; because they will not separately pursue the same plan. New Hampshire cannot lay a given duty on a particular article, unless Massachusetts will do the same; because it will turn the importation of that article from her ports into those of Massachusetts, from whence they will be smuggled into New Hampshire by land. But tho Massachusetts were willing to concur with N Hampshire in laying the same duty, yet she cannot do it, for the same reason, unless Rhode island will also, nor can Rhode island without Connecticut, nor Connecticut without N York, nor N York without N Jersey, & so on quite to Georgia. It is visible therefore that the commerce of the states cannot be regulated to the best advantage but by a single body, and no body so proper as Congress. Many of the states have agreed to add an article to the Confederation for allowing to Congress the regulation of their commerce, only providing that the revenues to be raised on it, shall belong to the state in which they are levied. Yet it is believed that Rhode island will prevent this also. An everlasting recurrence to this same obstacle will occasion a question to be asked. How happens it that Rhode island is opposed to every useful proposition? Her geography accounts for it, with the aid of one or two observations. The cultivators of the earth are the most virtuous citizens, and possess most of the amor patriæ. Merchants are the least virtuous, and possess the least of the amor patriæ. The latter reside principally in the seaport towns, the former in the interior country. Now it happened that of the territory constituting Rhode island & Connecticut, the part containing the seaports was erected into a state by itself & called Rhode island, & that containing the interior country was erected into another state called Connecticut. For tho it has a little seacoast, there are no good ports in it. Hence it happens that there is scarcely one merchant in the whole state of Connecticut, while there is not a single man in Rhode island who is not a merchant of some sort. Their whole territory is but a thousand square miles, and what of that is in use is laid out in grass farms almost entirely. Hence they have scarcely any body employed in agriculture. All exercise some species of commerce. This circumstance has decided the characters of these two states. The remedies to this evil are hazardous. One would be to consolidate the two states into one. Another would be to banish Rhode island from the union. A third to compel her submission to the will of the other twelve. A fourth for the other twelve to govern themselves according to the new propositions and to let

Rhode island go on by herself according to the antient articles. But the dangers & difficulties attending all these remedies are obvious.

These are the only alterations proposed to the confederation, and the last of them is the only additional power which Congress is thought to need.

21. Broils among the states may happen in the following ways: 1. A state may be embroiled with the other twelve by not complying with the lawful requisitions of Congress. 2. Two states may differ about their boundaries. But the method of settling these is fixed by the Confederation, and most of the states which have any differences of this kind are submitting them to this mode of determination; and there is no danger of opposition to the decree by any state. The individuals interested may complain, but this can produce no difficulty. 3. Other contestations may arise between two states, such as pecuniary demands, affrays among their citizens, & whatever else may arise between any two nations. With respect to these, there are two opinions. One that they are to be decided according to the 9th article of the Confederation, which says that "Congress shall be the last resort in all differences between two or more states, concerning boundary jurisdiction, *or any other cause whatever*"; and prescribes the mode of decision, and the weight of reason is undoubtedly in favor of this opinion, yet there are some who question it.

It has been often said that the decisions of Congress are impotent because the Confederation provides no compulsory power. But when two or more nations enter into compact, it is not usual for them to say what shall be done to the party who infringes it. Decency forbids this, and it is unnecessary as indecent, because the right of compulsion naturally results to the party injured by the breach. When any one state in the American Union refuses obedience to the Confederation by which they have bound themselves, the rest have a natural right to compel them to obedience. Congress would probably exercise long patience before they would recur to force; but if the case ultimately required it, they would use that recurrence. Should this case ever arise, they will probably coerce by a naval force, as being more easy, less dangerous to liberty, & less likely to produce much bloodshed.

It has been said too that our governments both federal and particular want energy; that it is difficult to restrain both individuals & states from committing wrong. This is true, & it is an inconvenience. On the other hand that energy which absolute governments derive from an armed force, which is the effect of the bayonet constantly held at the breast of every citizen, and which resembles very much the stillness of the grave, must be admitted also to have it's inconveniences. We weigh the two together, and like best to submit to the former. Compare the number of wrongs committed with impunity by citizens among us, with those committed by the sovereign in other countries, and the last will be found most numerous, most oppressive on the mind, and most degrading of the dignity of man.

2. From *Observations on Démeunier's Manuscript*

OBSERVATIONS ON THE ARTICLE ETATS-UNIS
PREPARED FOR THE ENCYCLOPEDIE.

June 22, 1786

1. II. 17. 29. Pa 8. The Malefactors sent to America were not sufficient in number to merit enumeration as one class out of three which peopled America. It was at a late period of their history that this practice began. I have no book by me which enables me to point out the date of it's commencement. But I do not think the whole number sent would amount to 2000 & being principally men, eaten up with disease, they married seldom & propagated little. I do not suppose that themselves & their descendants are at present 4000, which is little more than one thousandth part of the whole inhabitants.

Indented servants formed a considerable supply. These were poor Europeans who went to America to settle themselves. If they could pay their passage it was well. If not, they must find means of paying it. They were at liberty therefore to make an agreement with any person they chose, to serve him such a length of time as they agreed on, on condition that he would repay to the master of the vessel the expenses of their passage. If being foreigners unable to speak the lan-

guage, they did not know how to make a bargain for themselves the captain of the vessel contracted for them with such
persons as he could. This contract was by deed indented,
which occasioned them to be called indented servants. Sometimes they were called Redemptioners, because by their agreement with the master of the vessel they could *redeem*
themselves from his power by paying their passage, which
they frequently effected by hiring themselves on their arrival
as is before mentioned. In some states I know that these people had a right of marrying themselves without their master's
leave, & I did suppose they had that right everywhere. I did
not know that in any of the states they demanded so much as
a week for every day's absence without leave. I suspect this
must have been at a very early period while the governments
were in the hands of the first emigrants, who being mostly
labourers, were narrow-minded and severe. I know that in
Virginia the laws allowed their servitude to be protracted
only two days for every one they were absent without leave.
So mild was this kind of servitude, that it was very frequent
for foreigners who carried to America money enough, not
only to pay their passage, but to buy themselves a farm, it
was common I say for them to indent themselves to a master
for three years, for a certain sum of money, with a view to
learn the husbandry of the country. I will here make a general
observation. So desirous are the poor of Europe to get to
America, where they may better their condition, that, being
unable to pay their passage, they will agree to serve two or
three years on their arrival there, rather than not go. During
the time of that service they are better fed, better clothed, and
have lighter labour than while in Europe. Continuing to work
for hire a few years longer, they buy a farm, marry, and enjoy
all the sweets of a domestic society of their own. The American governments are censured for permitting this species of
servitude which lays the foundation of the happiness of these
people. But what should these governments do? Pay the passage of all those who chuse to go into their country? They
are not able; nor, were they able, do they think the purchase
worth the price? Should they exclude these people from their
shores? Those who know their situations in Europe & America, would not say that this is the alternative which humanity

dictates. It is said that these people are deceived by those who carry them over. But this is done in Europe. How can the American governments prevent it? Should they punish the deceiver? It seems more incumbent on the European government, where the act is done, and where a public injury is sustained from it. However it is only in Europe that this deception is heard of. The individuals are generally satisfied in America with their adventure, and very few of them wish not to have made it. I must add that the Congress have nothing to do with this matter. It belongs to the legislatures of the several states.

Ib. l. 12. "Mal-aisé d' indiquer la nuance precise &c." In forming a scale of crimes & punishments, two considerations have principal weight. 1. The atrocity of the crime. 2. The peculiar circumstances of a country which furnish greater temptations to commit it, or greater facilities for escaping detection. The punishment must be heavier to counterbalance this. Was the first the only consideration, all nations would form the same scale. But as the circumstances of a country have influence on the punishment, and no two countries exist precisely under the same circumstances, no two countries will form the same scale of crimes & punishments. For example in America, the inhabitants let their horses go at large in the uninclosed lands which are so extensive as to maintain them altogether. It is easy therefore to steal them & easy to escape. Therefore the laws are obliged to oppose these temptations with a heavier degree of punishment. For this reason the stealing of a horse in America is punished more severely than stealing the same value in any other form. In Europe where horses are confined so securely that it is impossible to steal them, that species of theft need not be punished more severely than any other. In some countries of Europe, stealing fruit from trees is punished capitally. The reason is that it being impossible to lock fruit trees up in coffers, as we do our money, it is impossible to oppose physical bars to this species of theft. Moral ones are therefore opposed by the laws. This to an unreflecting American, appears the most enormous of all the abuses of power; because he has been used to see fruits hanging in such quantities that if not taken by men they would rot: he has been used to consider it therefore as of no value, as not furnishing materials for the commission of a crime. This must serve as an apology for the arrangements of crimes & punishments in the scale under our consideration. A different one would be formed here; & still different ones in Italy, Turkey, China, &c.

Pa. 240. "Les officiers Americains &c." to pa 264. "qui le meritoient." I would propose to new-model this Section in the following manner. 1. Give a succinct history of the origin & establishment of the Cincinnati. 2. Examine whether in its present form it threatens any dangers to the state. 3. Propose the most practicable method of preventing them.

Having been in America during the period in which this institution was formed, and being then in a situation which gave me opportunities of seeing it in all it's stages, I may venture to give M. de Meusnier materials for the 1st branch of the preceding distribution of the subject. The 2d and 3d he will best execute himself. I should write it's history in the following form.

When, on the close of that war which established the independance of America, it's army was about to be disbanded, the officers, who during the course of it had gone thro the most trying scenes together, who by mutual aids & good offices had become dear to one another, felt with great oppression of mind the approach of that moment which was to separate them never perhaps to meet again. They were from different states & from distant parts of the same state. Hazard alone could therefore give them but rare & partial occasions of seeing each other. They were of course to abandon altogether the hope of ever meeting again, or to devise some occasion which might bring them together. And why not come together on purpose at stated times? Would not the trouble of such a journey be greatly overpaid by the pleasure of seeing each other again, by the sweetest of all consolations, the talking over the scenes of difficulty & of endearment they had gone through? This too would enable them to know who of them should succeed in the world, who should be unsuccessful, and to open the purses of all to every labouring brother. This idea was too soothing not to be cherished in conversation. It was improved into that of a regular association with an organized administration, with periodical meetings general & particular, fixed contributions for those who should be in distress, & a badge by which not only those who had not had occasion to become personally known should be able to recognize one another, but which should be worn by their descendants to perpetuate among them the friendships which had bound their ancestors together. Genl. Washington was at that moment oppressed with the operation of disbanding an army which was not paid, and the difficulty of this operation was increased by some two or three of the states having expressed sentiments which did not indicate a sufficient attention to their paiment. He was sometimes present when his officers were fashioning in their conversations their newly proposed society. He saw the innocence of it's origin, & foresaw no effects less innocent. He was at that time writing his valedictory letter to the states, which has been so deservedly applauded by the world. Far from thinking it a moment to multiply the causes of irritation, by thwarting a proposition which had absolutely no other basis but of benevolence & friendship, he was rather satisfied to find himself aided in his difficulties by this new incident, which occupied, &, at the same time soothed the minds of the officers. He thought too that this institution would be one instrument the more for strengthening the federal bond, & for promoting federal ideas. The institution was formed. They incorporated into it the officers of the French army & navy by whose sides they had fought, and with whose aid they had finally prevailed, extending it to such grades as they were told might be permitted to enter into it. They sent an officer to France to make the proposition to them & to procure the badges which they had devised for their order. The moment of disbanding the army having come on before they could have a full meeting to appoint their president, the General was prayed to act in that office till their first general meeting which was to be held at Philadelphia in the month of May following. The laws of the society were published. Men who read them in their closets, unwarmed by those sentiments of friendship which had produced them, inattentive to those pains which an approaching separation had excited in the minds of the institutors, Politicians, who see in everything only the dangers with which it threatens civil society, in fine the labouring people, who, shielded by equal laws, had never seen any difference between man and man, but had read of terrible oppressions which people of their description experience in other countries from those who are distinguished by titles & badges, began to be alarmed at this new institution. A remarkable silence however was observed. Their sollicitudes were long confined within the circles of private conversation. At length however a Mr. Burke, chief justice of South Carolina, broke that silence. He wrote against the new institution; foreboding it's dangers very imperfectly indeed, because he had nothing but his imagination to aid him. An American could do no more: for to detail the real evils of aristocracy they must be seen in Europe. Burke's fears were thought exaggerations in America; while in Europe it is known that even Mirabeau has but faintly sketched the curses of hereditary aristocracy as they are experienced here, and as they would have followed in America had this institution remained. The epigraph of Burke's pamphlet was "Blow ye the trumpet in Zion." It's effect corresponded with it's epigraph. This institution became first the subject of general conversation. Next it was made the subject of deliberation in the legislative assemblies of some of the States. The governor of South Carolina censured it in an address to his Assembly. The assemblies of Massachusetts, Rhode island and Pennsylvania condemned it's principles. No circumstance indeed brought the consideration of it expressly before Congress, yet it had sunk deep into their minds. An offer having been made to them on the part of the Polish order of divine providence to receive some of their distinguished citizens into that order, they made that an occasion to declare that these distinctions were contrary to the principles of their confederation. The uneasiness excited by this institution had very early caught the notice of General Washington. Still recollecting all the purity of the motives which gave it birth, he became sensible that it might produce political evils which the warmth of these motives had masked. Add to this that it was disapproved by the mass of citizens of the Union. This alone was reason strong enough in a country where the will of the majority is the law, & ought to be the

law. He saw that the objects of the institution were too light
to be opposed to considerations as serious as these; and that
it was become necessary to annihilate it absolutely. On this
therefore he was decided. The first annual meeting at Philadelphia was now at hand. He went to that, determined to
exert all his influence for it's suppression. He proposed it to
his fellow officers, and urged it with all his powers. It met an
opposition which was observed to cloud his face with an anxiety that the most distressful scenes of the war had scarcely
ever produced. It was canvassed for several days, & at length
it was no more a doubt what would be it's ultimate fate. The
order was on the point of receiving it's annihilation by the
vote of a very great majority of it's members. In this moment
their envoy arrived from France, charged with letters from the
French officers accepting with cordiality the proposed badges
of union, with sollicitations from others to be received into
the order, & with notice that their respectable sovereign had
been pleased to recognize it, & permit his officers to wear it's
badges. The prospect now changed. The question assumed a
new form. After the offer made by them, & accepted by their
friends, in what words could they clothe a proposition to re-
tract it which would not cover themselves with the reproaches
of levity & ingratitude? which would not appear an insult to
those whom they loved? Federal principles, popular discontent, were considerations whose weight was known & felt by
themselves. But would foreigners know & feel them equally?
Would they so far acknowledge their cogency as to permit
without any indignation the eagle & ribbon to be torn from
their breasts by the very hands which had placed them there?
The idea revolted the whole society. They found it necessary
then to preserve so much of their institution as might continue to support this foreign branch, while they should prune
off every other which would give offence to their fellow citizens; thus sacrificing on each hand to their friends & to their
country. The society was to retain it's existence, it's name,
it's meetings, & it's charitable funds: but these last were to
be deposited with their respective legislatures; the order was
to be no longer hereditary; a reformation which had been
pressed even from this side of the Atlantic; it was to be communicated to no new members; the general meetings instead

of annual were to be triennial only. The eagle & ribbon indeed were retained; because they were worn, & they wished them to be worn, by their friends who were in a country where they would not be objects of offence; but themselves never wore them. They laid them up in their bureaus with the medals of American Independance, with those of the trophies they had taken & the battles they had won. But through all the United States no officer is seen to offend the public eye with the display of this badge. These changes have tranquillized the American states. Their citizens do justice to the circumstances which prevented a total annihilation of the order. They feel too much interest in the reputation of their officers, and value too much whatever may serve to recall to the memory of their allies the moments wherein they formed but one people. Tho they are obliged by a prudent foresight to keep out everything from among themselves which might pretend to divide them into orders, and to degrade one description of men below another, yet they hear with pleasure that their allies whom circumstances have already placed under these distinctions, are willing to consider it as one to have aided them in the establishment of their liberties & to wear a badge which may recall to their remembrance; and it would be an extreme affliction to them if the domestic reformation which has been found necessary, if the censures of individual writers, or if any other circumstance should discourage the wearing their badge, or lessen it's reputation.

This short but true history of the order of the Cincinnati, taken from the mouths of persons on the spot who were privy to it's origin & progress, & who knew it's present state, is the best apology which can be made for an institution which appeared to be, & was really, so heterogeneous to the governments in which it was erected.

It should be further considered that, in America, no other distinction between man & man had ever been known, but that of persons in office exercising powers by authority of the laws, and private individuals. Among these last the poorest labourer stood on equal ground with the wealthiest millionnaire, & generally on a more favoured one whenever their rights seem to jar. It has been seen that a shoemaker, or other artisan, removed by the voice of his country from his work bench into a chair of office, has instantly commanded all the respect and obedience which the laws ascribe to his office. But of distinction by birth or badge they had no more idea than they had of the mode of existence in the moon or planets. They had heard only that there were such, & knew that they must be wrong. A due horror of the evils which flow from these distinctions could be excited in Europe only, where the dignity of man is lost in arbitrary distinctions, where the human species is classed into several stages of degradation, where the many are crushed under the weight of the few, & where the order established can present to the contemplation of a thinking being no other picture than that of God almighty & his angels trampling under foot the hosts of the damned. No wonder then that the institution of the Cincinnati should be innocently conceived by one order of American citizens, could raise in the other orders only a slow, temperate, & rational opposition, and could be viewed in Europe as a detestable parricide.

The 2d & 3d branches of this subject, no body can better execute than M. de. Meusnier. Perhaps it may be curious to him to see how they strike an American mind at present. He shall therefore have the ideas of one who was an enemy to the institution from the first moment of it's conception, but who was always sensible that the officers neither foresaw, nor intended the injury they were doing to their country.

As to the question then, whether any evil can proceed from the institution as it stands at present, I am of opinion there may. 1. From the meetings. These will keep the officers formed into a body; will continue a distinction between the civil & military which it would be for the good of the whole to obliterate as soon as possible; & the military assemblies will not only keep alive the jealousies & the fears of the civil government, but give ground for these fears & jealousies. For when men meet together, they will make business if they have none; they will collate their grievances, some real, some imaginary, all highly painted; they will communicate to each other the sparks of discontent; & this may engender a flame which will consume their particular, as well as the general, happiness. 2. The charitable part of the institution is still more likely to do mischief, as it perpetuates the dangers apprehended in the preceding clause. For here is a fund provided of permanent existence. To whom will it belong? To the descendants of American officers of a certain description. These descendants then will form a body, having sufficient interest to keep up an attention to their description, to continue meetings, & perhaps, in some moment, when the political eye shall be slumbering, or the firmness of their fellow-citizens realized, to replace the insignia of the order & revive all its pretensions. What good can the officers propose which may weigh against these possible evils? The securing their descendants against want? Why afraid to trust them to the same fertile soil, & the same genial climate which will secure from want the descendants of their other fellow citizens? Are they afraid they will be reduced to labour the earth for their sustenance? They will be rendered thereby both honester and happier. An industrious farmer occupies a more dignified place in the scale of beings, whether moral or political, than a lazy lounger, valuing himself on his family, too proud to work, & drawing out a miserable existence by eating on that surplus of other men's labour which is the sacred fund of the helpless poor. A pitiful annuity will only prevent them from exerting that industry & those talents which would soon lead them to better fortune.

How are these evils to be prevented? 1. At their first general meeting let them distribute the funds on hand to the existing objects of their destination, & discontinue all further contributions. 2. Let them declare at the same time that their meetings general & particular shall henceforth cease. 3. Let them melt up their eagles & add the mass to the distributable fund that their descendants may have no temptation to hang them in their button holes.

These reflections are not proposed as worthy the notice of M. de Meusnier. He will be so good as to treat the subject in his own way, & no body has a better. I will only pray him to avail us of his forcible manner to evince that there is evil to be apprehended even from the ashes of this institution, & to exhort the society in America to make their reformation complete; bearing in mind that we must keep the passions of men on our side even when we are persuading them to do what they ought to do.

Pa. 272. "Comportera peut etre une population de thirty millions."

The territories of the United States contain about a million of square miles, English. There is in them a greater proportion of fertile lands than in the British dominions in Europe. Suppose the territory of the U.S. then to attain an equal degree of population with the British European dominions, they will have an hundred millions of inhabitants. Let us extend our views to what may be the population of the two continents of North & South America supposing them divided at the narrowest part of the isthmus of Panama. Between this line and that of 50° of north latitude the northern continent contains about 5 millions of square miles, and South of this line of division the Southern continent contains about 7 millions of square miles. I do not pass the 50th degree of northern latitude in my reckoning, because we must draw a line somewhere, & considering the soil & climate beyond that, I would only avail my calculation of it, as a make weight, to make good what the colder regions within that line may be supposed to fall short in their future population. Here are 12 millions of square miles then, which at the rate of population before assumed, will nourish 1200 millions of inhabitants, a number greater than the present population of the whole globe is supposed to amount to. If those who propose medals for the resolution of questions, about which nobody makes any question, those who have invited discussions on the pretended problem Whether the discovery of America was for the good of mankind? if they, I say, would have viewed it only as doubling the numbers of mankind, & of course the quantum of existence & happiness, they might have saved the money & the reputation which their proposition has cost them. The present population of the inhabited parts of the U.S. is of about 10. to the square mile; & experience has shown us, that wherever we reach that the inhabitants become uneasy, as too much compressed, and go off in great numbers to search for vacant country. Within 40 years the whole territory will be peopled at that rate. We may fix that then as the term beyond which the people of those states will not be restrained within their present limits; we may fix it too as the term of population, which they will not exceed till the whole of those two continents are filled up to that mark, that is to say, till they shall contain 120 millions of inhabitants. The soil of the country on the western side of the Mississippi, it's climate, & it's vicinity to the U.S. point it out as the first which will receive population from that nest. The present occupiers will just have force enough to repress & restrain the emigrations to a certain degree of consistence. We have seen lately a single person go & decide on a settlement in Kentucky, many hundred miles from any white inhabitant, remove thither with his family and a few neighbors, & though perpetually harassed by the Indians, that settlement in the course of 10 years has acquired 30.000 inhabitants, it's numbers are increasing while we are writing, and the state of which it formerly made a part has offered it independance.

3. To Jean Nicolas Démeunier

June 26, 1786

Mr. Jefferson presents his compliments to M. de Meusnier & sends him copies of the 13th, 23d, & 24th articles of the treaty between the K. of Prussia & the United States.

In the negociation with the Minister of Portugal at London, the latter objected to the 13th article. The observations which were made in answer to his objections Mr. Jefferson incloses. They are a commentary on the 13th article. Mr. de Meusnier will be so good as to return the sheet on which these observations are as Mr. Jefferson does not retain a copy of it.

If M. de Meusnier proposes to mention the facts of cruelty of which he & Mr. Jefferson spoke yesterday, the 24th article will introduce them properly, because they produced a sense of the necessity of that article. These facts are 1. The death of upwards of 11,000 Americans in one prison ship (the Jersey) and in the space of 3. years. 2. General Howe's permitting our prisoners taken at the battle of Germantown and placed under a guard in the yard of the Statehouse of Philadelphia to be so long without any food furnished them that many perished with hunger. Where the bodies laid, it was seen that they had eaten all the grass round them within their reach, after they had lost the power of rising, or moving from their place. 3. The 2d fact was the act of a commandg officer; the 1st of several commanding officers, & for so long a time as must suppose the approbation of government. But the following was the act of government itself. During the periods that our affairs seemed unfavourable & theirs successful, that is to say, after the evacuation of New York, and again after the taking of Charlestown in South Carolina, they regularly sent our prisoners taken on the seas & carried to England to the E. Indies. This is so certain, that in the month of Novemb. or Decemb. 1785, Mr. Adams having officially demanded a delivery of the American prisoners sent to the East Indies, Ld. Cærmarthen answered officially "that orders were issued immediately for their discharge." M. de Meusnier is at liberty to quote this fact. 4. A fact not only of the government, but of the parliament, who passed an act for that purpose in the beginning of the war, was the obliging our prisoners taken at sea to join them and fight against their countrymen. This they effected by starving & whipping them. The insult on Capt. Stanhope, which happened at Boston last year, was a consequence of this. Two persons, Dunbar & Lorthrope, whom Stanhope had treated in this manner (having particularly inflicted 24 lashes on Dunbar), meeting him at Boston, attempted to beat him. But the people interposed & saved him. The fact is referred to in that paragraph of the declaration of independance which sais "he has constrained our fellow citizens taken captive on the high seas, to bear arms against their country, to become the executioners of their friends & brethren, or to fall themselves by their hands." This was the most afflicting to our prisoners of all the cruelties exercised on them. The others affected the body only, but this the mind—they were haunted by the horror of having perhaps themselves shot the ball by which a father or a brother fell. Some of them had constancy enough to hold out against half allowance of food & repeated whippings. These were generally sent to England & from thence to the East Indies. One of these escaped from the East Indies and got back to Paris, where he gave an account of his sufferings to Mr. Adams, who happened to be then at Paris.

M. de Meusnier, where he mentions that the slave-law has been passed in Virginia, without the clause of emancipation, is pleased to mention that neither Mr. Wythe nor Mr. Jeffer-

son were present to make the proposition they had meditated; from which people, who do not give themselves the
trouble to reflect or enquire, might conclude hastily that their
absence was the cause why the proposition was not made; &
of course that there were not in the assembly persons of virtue & firmness enough to propose the clause for emancipation. This supposition would not be true. There were persons
there who wanted neither the virtue to propose, nor talents
to enforce the proposition had they seen that the disposition
of the legislature was ripe for it. These worthy characters
would feel themselves wounded, degraded, & discouraged by
this idea. Mr. Jefferson would therefore be obliged to M. de
Meusnier to mention it in some such manner as this. "Of the
two commissioners who had concerted the amendatory clause
for the gradual emancipation of slaves Mr. Wythe could not
be present as being a member of the judiciary department,
and Mr. Jefferson was absent on the legation to France. But
there wanted not in that assembly men of virtue enough to
propose, & talents to vindicate this clause. But they saw that
the moment of doing it with success was not yet arrived, and
that an unsuccessful effort, as too often happens, would only
rivet still closer the chains of bondage, and retard the moment
of delivery to this oppressed description of men. What a stu-
pendous, what an incomprehensible machine is man! who can
endure toil, famine, stripes, imprisonment & death itself in
vindication of his own liberty, and the next moment be deaf
to all those motives whose power supported him thro' his
trial, and inflict on his fellow men a bondage, one hour of
which is fraught with more misery than ages of that which he
rose in rebellion to oppose. But we must await with patience
the workings of an overruling providence, & hope that that
is preparing the deliverance of these, our suffering brethren.
When the measure of their tears shall be full, when their
groans shall have involved heaven itself in darkness, doubtless
a god of justice will awaken to their distress, and by diffusing
light & liberality among their oppressors, or at length by his
exterminating thunder, manifest his attention to the things of
this world, and that they are not left to the guidance of a
blind fatality."

Thoughts on English Prosody

TO CHASTELLUX

October 1786

Among the topics of conversation which stole off like so many minutes the few hours I had the happiness of possessing you at Monticello, the measures of English verse was one. I thought it depended like Greek and Latin verse, on long and short syllables arranged into regular feet. You were of a different opinion. I did not pursue this subject after your departure, because it always presented itself with the painful recollection of a pleasure which in all human probability I was never to enjoy again. This probability like other human calculations has been set aside by events; and we have again discussed on this side the Atlantic a subject which had occupied us during some pleasing moments on the other. A daily habit of walking in the Bois de Boulogne gave me an opportunity of turning this subject in my mind and I determined to present you my thoughts on it in the form of a letter. I for some time parried the difficulties which assailed me, but at length I found they were not to be opposed, and their triumph was complete. Error is the stuff of which the web of life is woven and he who lives longest and wisest is only able to weave out the more of it. I began with the design of converting you to my opinion that the arrangement of long and short syllables into regular feet constituted the harmony of English verse. I ended by discovering that you were right in denying that proposition. The next object was to find out the real circumstance which gives harmony to English poetry and laws to those who make it. I present you with the result. It is a tribute due to your friendship. It is due you also as having recalled me from an error in my native tongue and that, too, in a point the most difficult of all others to a foreigner, the law of its poetical numbers.

Thoughts on English Prosody

Every one knows the difference between verse and prose in his native language; nor does he need the aid of prosody to enable him to read or to repeat verse according to its just rhythm. It is the business of the poet so to arrange his words as that, repeated in their accustomed measures they shall strike the ear with that regular rhythm which constitutes verse.

It is for foreigners principally that Prosody is necessary; not knowing the accustomed measures of words, they require the aid of rules to teach them those measures and to enable them to read verse so as to make themselves or others sensible of its music. I suppose that the system of rules or exceptions which constitutes Greek and Latin prosody, as shown with us, was unknown to those nations, and that it has been invented by the moderns to whom those languages were foreign. I do not mean to affirm this, however, because you have not searched into the history of this art, nor am I at present in a situation which admits of that search. By industrious examination of the Greek and Latin verse it has been found that pronouncing certain combinations of vowels and consonants long, and certain others short, the actual arrangement of those long and short syllables, as found in their verse, constitutes a rhythm which is regular and pleasing to the ear, and that pronouncing them with any other measures, the run is unpleasing, and ceases to produce the effect of the verse. Hence it is concluded and rationally enough that the Greeks and Romans pronounced those syllables long or short in reading their verse; and as we observe in modern languages that the syllables of words have the same measures both in verse and prose, we ought to conclude that they had the same also in those ancient languages, and that we must lengthen or shorten in their prose the same syllables which we lengthen or shorten in their verse. Thus, if I meet with the word *præteritos* in Latin prose and want to know how the Romans pronounced it, I search for it in some poet and find it in the line of Virgil, *"O mihi præteritos referat si Jupiter annos!"* where it is evident that *præ* is long and *te* short in direct opposition to the pronunciation which we often hear. The length allowed to a syllable is called its quantity, and hence we say that the Greek and Latin languages are to be pronounced according to quantity.

Those who have undertaken to frame a prosody for the English language have taken quantity for their basis and have mounted the English poetry on Greek and Latin feet. If this foundation admits of no question, the prosody of Doctor Johnson, built upon it, is perhaps the best. He comprehends under three different feet every combination of long and short syllables which he supposes can be found in English verse, to wit: 1. a long and a short, which is the trochee of the Greeks and Romans; 2. a short and a long, which is their iambus; and 3. two short and a long, which is their anapest. And he thinks that all English verse may be resolved into these feet.

It is true that in the English language some one syllable of a word is always sensibly distinguished from the others by an emphasis of pronunciation or by an accent as we call it. But I am not satisfied whether this accented syllable be pronounced longer, louder, or harder, and the others shorter, lower, or softer. I have found the nicest ears divided on the question. Thus in the word *calenture*, nobody will deny that the first syllable is pronounced more emphatically than the others; but many will deny that it is longer in pronunciation. In the second of the following verses of Pope, I think there are but two short syllables.

> Oh! be thou bless'd with all that Heav'n can send
> Long health, long youth, long pleasure, and a friend.

Innumerable instances like this might be produced. It seems, therefore, too much to take for the basis of a system a postulatum which one-half of mankind will deny. But the superstructure of Doctor Johnson's prosody may still be supported by substituting for its basis accent instead of quantity; and nobody will deny us the existence of accent.

In every word of more than one syllable there is some one syllable strongly distinguishable in pronunciation by its emphasis or accent.

If a word has more than two syllables it generally admits of a subordinate emphasis or accent on the alternate syllables counting backwards and forwards from the principal one, as in this verse of Milton:

> Well if thrown out as supernumerary,

where the principal accent is on *nu*, but there is a lighter one on *su* and *ra* also. There are some few instances indeed wherein the subordinate accent is differently arranged, as *parisyllabic, Constantinople*. It is difficult, therefore, to introduce words of this kind into verse.

That the accent shall never be displaced from the syllable whereon usage hath established it is the fundamental law of English verse.

There are but three arrangements into which these accents can be thrown in the English language which entitled the composition to be distinguished by the name of verse. That is, 1. Where the accent falls on all the odd syllables; 2. Where it falls on all the even syllables; 3. When it falls on every third syllable. If the reason of this be asked, no other can be assigned but that it results from the nature of the sounds which compose the English language and from the construction of the human ear. So, in the infinite gradations of sounds from the lowest to the highest in the musical scale, those only give pleasure to the ear which are at the intervals we call whole tones and semitones. The reason is that it has pleased God to make us so. The English poet then must so arrange his words that their established accents shall fall regularly in one of these three orders. To aid him in this he has at his command the whole army of monosyllables which in the English language is a very numerous one. These he may accent or not, as he pleases. Thus is this verse:

> 'Tis júst resentment and becómes the brave.
> —POPE

the monosyllable *and* standing between two unaccented syllables catches the accent and supports the measure. The same monosyllable serves to fill the interval between two accents in the following instance:

> From úse obscúre and súbtle, bút to knów.
> —Milton

The monosyllables *with* and *in* receive the accent in one of the following instances and suffer it to pass over them in the other.

> The témpted *with* dishónor fóul, suppósed.
> —Milton
> Attémpt *with* cónfidénce, the wórk is dóne.
> —Hopkins
> Which múst be mútual *ín* propórtion dúe.
> —Milton
> Too múch of órnamént *in* oútward shéw.
> —Milton

The following lines afford other proofs of this license.

> Yet, yét, I lóve—from Abelard it came.
> —Pope

> Flow, flow, my stream this devious way.
> —Shenstone

The Greeks and Romans in like manner had a number of syllables which might in any situation be pronounced long or short without offending the ear. They had others which they could make long or short by changing their position. These were of great avail to the poets. The following is an example:

> Πολλάκις ὢ πολυφάμε, τὰ | μη καλὰ | καλὰ πε | φανλαι.
> —Theocritus
> ᾿Αγες, ᾿Αγες βροτολοιγὲ, μιαι φόνε τει χεσιπλητα.
> —Hom. Il.
> Μετσα δε τεμ' χε θεοισι, το | νᵟ μετρον | εστιν ἀγίσον.
> —Phocyl.

where the word Ages, being used twice, the first syllable is long in the first and short in the second instance, and the second is short in the first and long in the second instance.

But though the poets have great authority over the monosyllables, yet it is not altogether absolute. The following is a proof of this:

Through the dárk póstern óf time lóng eláps'd.
—Young

It is impossible to read this without throwing the accent on the monosyllable *of* and yet the ear is shocked and revolts at this.

That species of our verse wherein the accent falls on all the odd syllables, I shall call, from that circumstance, odd or imparisyllabic verse. It is what has been heretofore called trochaic verse. To the foot which composes it, it will still be convenient and most intelligible to retain the ancient name of Trochee, only remembering that by that term we do not mean a long and a short syllable, but an accented and unaccented one.

That verse wherein the accent is on the even syllables may be called even or parisyllabic verse, and corresponds with what has been called iambic verse; retaining the term iambus for the name of the foot we shall thereby mean an unaccented and an accented syllable.

That verse wherein the accent falls on every third syllable, may be called trisyllabic verse; it is equivalent to what has been called anapestic; and we will still use the term anapest to express two unaccented and one accented syllable.

Accent then is, I think, the basis of English verse; and it leads us to the same threefold distribution of it to which the hypothesis of *quantity* had led Dr. Johnson. While it preserves to us the simplicity of his classification it relieves us from the doubtfulness, if not the error, on which it was founded.

Observations on the Three Measures.

Wherever a verse should regularly begin or end with an accented syllable, that unaccented syllable may be suppressed.

Bréd on pláins, or bórn in válleys,
  Whó would bid those scénes adiéu?
Stránger tó the arts of málice,
  Whó would éver coúrts pursúe?
                                        —SHENSTONE

Rúin séize thee, rúthléss king!
  Confúsion on thy bánners wáit;
Though, fanned by Cónquest's crímson wing,
  They mock the air with ídle state.
Helm, nor haúlberk's twisted mail,
Nor év'n thy vírtues, Týrant, shall aváil
To sáve thy sécret soúl from nightly féars.
From Cámbria's cúrse, from Cámbria's téars!
                                        —GRAY

Ye Shép | herds! give eár | to my láy,
  And take no more heéd of my shéep;
They have nóthing to dó but to stray;
  I have nóthing to dó but to wéep.
                                        —SHENSTONE

In the first example the unaccented syllable with which the imparisyllabic (odd) verse should end is omitted in the second and fourth lines. In the second example the unaccented syllable with which the parisyllabic (even) verse should begin is omitted in the first and fifth lines. In the third instance one of the unaccented syllables with which the trisyllabic (triple) verse should begin, is omitted in the first and second lines and in the first of the following line both are omitted:

Under this márble, or under this síll
Or under this túrf, or é'en what you will
Lies one who ne'er car'd, and still cares not a pin
What they said, or may say, of the mortal within;
But who, living or dying, serene still and free,
Trusts in God that as well as he was he shall be.
                                        —POPE

An accented syllable may be prefixed to a verse which should regularly begin with an accent and added to one which should end with an accent, thus:

    1. Daúntless ón his nátive sánds
       <u>The</u> drágon-són of Móna stánds;
       <u>In</u> glittering árms and glóry drést,
       Hígh he réars his rúby crést.
       Thére the thúndering strókes begín,
       Thére the préss, and thére the dín;
       Talymalfra's rocky shore
               —GRAY

Again:

       Thére Confúsion, Térror's chíld,
       Cónflict fiérce, and Rúin wíld,
       Ágoný, that pánts for bréath,
       Despaír, and hónoráble death.
               —GRAY

    2. Whát is this wórld? thy schóol Oh! mísery!
       Our ónly lésson iś to leárn to súffer;
       And hé who knóws not thát, was bórn for nóthing.
       My comfort iś each móment tákes awáy
       A gráin at léast fróm the dead lóad that's ón <u>me</u>
       And gíves a neárer próspect óf the gráve.
               —YOUNG

    3. Says Ríchard to Thómas (and seém'd half afráid),
       "I'm thinkíng to márry thy místress's máid;
       Now, becaúse Mrs. Lucý to theé is well knówn,
       I will dó't if thou bidst me, or lét it alóne."
       Said Thomás to Ríchard, "To speák my opí<u>nion</u>,
       There is nót such a bitch in King Géorge's domí<u>nion</u>;
       And I firmly beliéve, if thou knéw'st her as Í <u>do</u>,
       Thou wouldst choóse out a whipping-post fírst to be
           tied <u>to</u>.
       She's peévish, she's thiévish, she's úgly, shé's old,
       And a liár, and a foól, and a slút, and a scóld."

Next dáy Richard hásten'd to chúrch and was wéd,
And ere níght had infórm'd her what Thómas had sáid.
—SHENSTONE

An accented syllable can never be either omitted or added without changing the character of the verse. In fact it is the number of accented syllables which determines the length of the verse. That is to say, the number of feet of which it consists.

Imparisyllabic verse being made up of Trochees should regularly end with an unaccented syllable; and in that case if it be in rhyme both syllables of the foot must be rhymed. But most frequently the unaccented syllable is omitted according to the license before mentioned and then it suffices to rhyme the accented one. The following is given as a specimen of this kind of verse.

> Shépherd, woúldst thou hére obtaín
> Pléasure uńalloý'd with páin?
> Joý that súits the rúral sphére?
> Geńtle shépherd, leńd an eár.
>
> Leárn to rélish cálm delíght
> Vérdant váles and foúntains bríght;
> Treés that nód o'er slóping hílls,
> Cavés that écho tińkling rílls.
>
> Íf thou cánst no chárm disclóse
> Iń the símplest búd that blóws;
> Gó, forsake thy pláin aṇd fóld;
> Joiń the crowd, and toiḷ for góld.
>
> Tránquil pleásures néver clóy;
> Bánish eách tumúltuous jóy;
> All but lóve—for loṿe inspíres
> Fónder wisḥes, wármer fíres
>
> Seé, to sweeten thy repose,
> The blóssom buds, the fountain flows;

Ló! to crown thy healthful board,
Áll that milk and fruits afford.

Séek no more—the rest is vain;
Pléasure ending soon in pain:
Ańguish lightly gilded o'er;
Close thy wish, and seek no more.
                    —SHENSTONE

Parisyllabic verse should regularly be composed of all iam-
buses; that is to say, all its even syllables should be accented.
Yet it is very common for the first foot of the line to be a
trochee as in this verse:

Yé who e'er lóst an ańgel, píty me!

Sometimes a trochee is found in the midst of this verse. But
this is extremely rare indeed. The following, however, are instances of it taken from Milton.

To dó ought góod *néver* will bé our tásk
Behésts obéy, *wórthiest* to bé obéyed.

Than sélf-esteém, *groúnded* on júst and ríght
Leans the huge elephant the *wisest* of brutes!

In these instances it has not a good effect, but in the following it has:

This hánd is míne—*óh! what* a hánd is hére!
So soft, souls sink into it and are lost.

When this trochee is placed at the beginning of a verse, if it
be not too often repeated it produces a variety in the measure
which is pleasing. The following is a specimen of the parisyllabic verse, wherein the instances of this trochee beginning
the verse are noted:

Píty the sórrows óf a poór old mán,
    Whose trembling límbs have bórne him tó your doór.

Whose days are dwindled tó the shórtest span;
  Oh! give relief, and Heáven will bless your stóre.

These táttered clóthes my póverty bespeák,
  These hoáry locks proclaim my léngthen'd yéars
And mány a fúrrow in my grief-worn chéek
  Has beén the chánnel to a flóod of teárs.

Yon house, erécted on the rising ground,
  With témpting aspect, dréw me fróm my road;
For plénty there a résidénce has found,
  And grandeur á magnificent abóde.

Hard is the fáte of thé infirm and póor!
  Here, as I craved a mórsel of their bréad,
A pámper'd ménial drove me from the dóor,
  To seék a shélter in an húmbler shed.

Oh! take me tó your hospitáble dóme;
  Keén blows the wind, and piércing is the cóld;
Short is my pássage tó the friéndly tómb,
  For I am poór, and miserábly óld.

Heáven sends misfórtunes; why should we repíne!
  Tis Heáven has brought me tó the státe you seé;
And your condítion máy be soón like mine,
  The child of sórrow and of misery.

—Moss

Trisyllabic verse consists altogether of anapests, that is, of feet made up of two unaccented and one accented syllable; and it does not admit a mixture of any other feet. The following is a specimen of this kind of verse:

  I have found out a gift for my fair;
    I have found where the wood-pigeons bréed;
  But lét me that plunder forbeár,
    She will sáy 'twas a bárbarous déed:

  For he né'er could be trúe, she averr'd,
    Who could rób a poor bird of its young;

> And I lovéd her the móre when I héard
> Such ténderness fall from her tońgue.
> —SHENSTONE

The following are instances of an iambus in an anapestic verse:

> Or únder this túrf, or ev'ń what they wíll.
> —POPE
> It néver was knówn that círcular létters.
> —SWIFT

They are extremely rare and are deformities, which cannot be admitted to belong to the verse, notwithstanding the authority of the writers from whom they are quoted. Indeed, the pieces from which they are taken are merely pieces of sport on which they did not mean to rest their poetical merit.

But to what class shall we give the following species of verse? "God save great Washington." It is triple verse, but the accent is on the first syllable of the foot instead of the third. Is this an attempt at dactylian verse? or shall we consider it still as anapestic, wherein either the two unaccented syllables which should begin the verse are omitted; or else the two which should end it are, in reciting, transposed to the next verse to complete the first anapest of that, as in Virgil in the following instance, the last syllable of the line belongs to the next, being amalgamated with that into one.

I am not able to recollect another instance of this kind of verse and a single example cannot form a class. It is not worth while, therefore, to provide a foreigner with a critical investigation of its character.

OF ELISION.

The vowels only suffer elision except that "v" is also omitted in the word over and "w" in will, "h" in have. This is actually made in most cases, as it was with the Greeks. Sometimes, however, it is neglected to be done, and in those cases the reader must make it for himself, as in the following examples:

Thou yet *mightest* act the friendly part
And lass *unnoticed* from malignant right
And *fallen* to save his injur'd land
Impatient for *it is* past the promis'd hour.

He *also against* the house of God was bold
Anguish and doubt and fear and sorr*ow and* pain
Of Phlegma with *the h*eroic race was joined
Damasco, or Maro*cco, or* Trebisond
All her *original* brightness, nor appear'd
Open or understood must be resolv'd.

OF SYNECPHONESIS.

Diphthongs are considered as forming one syllable. But vowels belonging to different syllables are sometimes forced to coalesce into a diphthong if the measure requires it. Nor is this coalescence prevented by the intervention of an "h," a " w " or a liquid. In this case the two syllables are run into one another with such rapidity as to take but the time of one.

The following are examples:

And wish th*e a*venging fight
B*e it* so, for I submit, his doom is fair.
When wint'ry winds deform the plent*eo*us year
Droop'd their fair leaves, nor knew th*e u*nfriendly soil
The rad*ia*nt morn resumed her orient pride
While born to bring the Muse's happ*ie*r days
A patr*io*t's hand protects a poet's lays
Ye midnight lamps, ye cur*iou*s homes
That eagle gen*iu*s! had he let fall—

Fair fancy wept; and ech*oi*ng sighs confest
The sounding forest fluct*ua*tes in the storm
Thy greatest infl*ue*nce own
Iss*uei*ng from out the portals of the morn
What groves nor streams bestow a virt*uou*s mind
With many *a* proof of recollected love.
With kind concern our pit*yi*ng eyes o'erflow
Lies yet a little embr*yo* unperceiv'd—

Now Marg*aret*'s curse is fall'n upon our heads
And ev*en a* Shakespeare to her fame be born
When min*eral* fountains vainly bear
O how self-fettered was my grov*eli*ng soul!
To ev*ery* sod which wraps the dead
And beam protection on a wand*eri*ng maid
Him or his children, ev*il he* may be sure
Love unlibid*inou*s resigned, nor jealousy
And left *to he*rself, if evil thence ensue.
Big swell'd my heart and own'd the p*ow*erful maid
Proceeding, runs low bell*owi*ng round the hills
Thy cherishing, thy hon*ouri*ng, and thy love
With all its shad*owy* shapes is shown
The shepherd's so civil *you ha*ve nothing to fear.

The elision of a vowel is often actually made where the coalescence before noted be more musical. Perhaps a vowel should never suffer elision when it is followed by a vowel or where only an "h," a " w" or a liquid intervenes between that and a next vowel, or in other words there should never be an elision where synecphonesis may take place. Consider the following instances:

Full of the dear ecstatic pow'r, and sick
Dare not th' infectious sigh; thy pleading look
While ev'ning draws her crimson curtains round
And fright the tim'rous game
Fills ev'ry nerve, and pants in ev'ry vein.

Full of the dear ecstatic power, and sick
Dare not the infectious sigh; thy pleading look
While evening draws her crimson curtains round
And fright the timorous game
Fills every nerve, and pants in every vein.

The pronunciation in these instances with the actual elision is less agreeable to my ear than by synecphonesis.

Of Rules for the Accent.

Accent deciding the measure of English verse as quantity does that of the Latin, and rules having been formed for teaching the quantity of the Latins it would be expected that rules should also be offered for indicating to foreigners the accented syllable of every word in English. Such rules have been attempted. Were they to be so completely formed as that the rules and their necessary exceptions would reach every word in the language, they would be too great a charge on the memory and too complicated for use either in reading or conversation. In the imperfect manner in which they have been hitherto proposed they would lead into infinite errors. It is usage which has established the accent of every word, or rather I might say it has been caprice or chance, for nothing can be more arbitrary or less consistent. I am of opinion it is easier for a foreigner to learn the accent of every word individually, than the rules which would teach it. This his dictionary will teach him, if, when he recurs to it for the meaning of a word, he will recollect that he should notice also on which syllable is its accent. Or he may learn the accent by reading poetry, which differs our language from Greek and Latin, wherein you must learn their prosody in order to read their poetry. Knowing that with us the accent is on every odd syllable or on every even one or on every third, he has only to examine of which of these measures the verse is to be able to read it correctly. But how shall he distinguish the measure to which the verse belongs?

If he can find in the piece any one word the accent of which he already knows, that word will enable him to distinguish if it be parisyllabic or imparisyllabic. Let us suppose, for example, he would read the following piece:

> How sleep the brave, who sink to rest,
> By all their country's wishes blest!
> When Spring, with dewy fingers cold,
> Returns to deck their hallowed mould,
> She there shall dress a *sweeter* sod
> Than Fancy's feet have ever trod.
>
> By fairy hands their knell is rung;
> By forms unseen their dirge is sung;
> There Honor comes, a pilgrim gray,
> To bless the turf that wraps their clay;

And Freedom shall a while repair,
To dwell a weeping hermit there!
                              —COLLINS

He finds the word *sweeter*, the accent of which he has already
learned to be on the first syllable, sweet. He observes that that
is an even syllable, being the sixth of the line. He knows then
that it is parisyllabic verse and from that he can accent the
whole piece. If he does not already know the accent of a single word he must look in his dictionary for some one, and
that will be a key to the whole piece. He should take care not
to rely on the first foot of any line, because, as has been before observed, that is often a trochee even in the parisyllabic
verse. Without consulting his dictionary at all, or knowing a
single accent, the following observation will enable him to
distinguish between these two species of verse when they are
in rhyme. An odd number of syllables with a single rhyme, or
an even number with a double rhyme, prove the verse to be
imparisyllabic. An even number of syllables with a single
rhyme, or an odd number with a double one, prove it to be
parisyllabic, *e. g.*:

        Learn by this unguarded lover
            When your secret sighs prevail
        Not to let your tongue discover
            Raptures that you should conceal.
                              —CUNNINGHAM

        He sung and hell consented
            To hear the poet's prayer
        Stern Proserpine relented
            And gave him back the fair.
                              —POPE

If in thus examining the seat of the accent he finds it is
alternately on an odd and an even syllable, that is to say, on
the third, sixth, ninth, twelfth syllables, the verse is trisyllabic.

With her how I stray'd amid fóuntains and bowers!
Or loiter'd behínd, and collected the flowérś!

Then breathless with ardor my fair one pursued,
And to think with what kindness my garland she view'd!
But be still, my fond heart! this emotion give o'er;
Fain wouldst thou forget thou must love her no more.
—SHENSTONE

It must be stated that in this kind of verse we should count backward from the last syllable, if it be a single rhyme, or the last but one if it be double; because one of the unaccented syllables which should begin the verse is so often omitted. This last syllable in the preceding example should be the twelfth. When the line is full it is accented of course. Consulting the dictionary, therefore, we find in the first line the ninth syllable accented; in the second, the sixth; in the third line the accented syllables there being alternately odd and even, to wit, the third, sixth, ninth and twelfth, we know the verse must be trisyllabic.

The foreigner then first determining the measure of the verse, may read it boldly. He will commit a few errors, indeed; let us see what they are likely to be. In imparisyllabic verse none, because that consists of trochees invariably; if an unaccented syllable happens to be prefixed to the verse, he will discover it by the number of syllables. In parisyllabic verse, when a trochee begins the verse, he will pronounce that foot wrong. This will perhaps happen once in ten lines; in some authors more, in others less. In like manner he will pronounce wrong the trochee in the middle of the line. But this he will encounter once in some hundreds of times. In the trisyllabic verse he can never commit an error if he counts from the end of the line. These imperfections are as few as a foreigner can possibly expect in the beginning; and he will reduce their number in proportion as he acquires by practice a knowledge of the accents.

The subject of accent cannot be quitted till we apprise him of another imperfection which will show itself in his reading, and which will be longer removing. Though there be accents on the first, the second or the third syllables of the foot, as has been before explained, yet is there subordination among these accents, a modulation in their tone of which it is impossible to give a precise idea in writing. This is intimately connected with the sense; and though a foreigner will readily find to what words that would give distinguished emphasis, yet nothing but habit can enable him to give actually the different shades of emphasis which his judgment would dictate to him. Even natives have very different powers as to this article. This difference exists both in the organ and the judgment. Foote is known to have read Milton so exquisitely that he received great sums of money for reading him to audiences who attended him regularly for that purpose. This difference, too, enters deeply into the merit of theatrical actors. The foreigner, therefore, must acquiesce under a want of perfection which is the lot of natives in common with himself.

We will proceed to give examples which may explain what is here meant, distinguishing the accents into four shades by these marks `""" "" " '` the greater number of marks denoting the strongest accents.

> Oh when the growling winds contend and all
> The sounding forest fluctuates in the storm
> To sink in warm repose, and hear the din
> Howl o'er the steady battlements, delights
> Above the luxury of vulgar sleep.
>
> —ARMSTRONG

> Life's cares are comforts; such by heav'n design'd
> He that has none, must make them or be wretched
> Cares are employments; and without employ
> The soul is on a rack, the rack of rest.
>
> —YOUNG

> O! lost to virtue, lost to manly thought,
> Lost to the noble sallies of the soul!
> Who think it solitude, to be alone.
> Communion sweet! communion large and high!
> Our reason, guardian angel, and our God!
> Then nearest these, when others most remote;
> And all, ere long, shall be remote, but these.
>
> —YOUNG

By nature's law, what may be, may be now;
There's no prerogative in human hours.
In human hearts what bolder thought can rise,
Than man's presumption on to-morrow's dawn?
Where is to-morrow? In another world.
For numbers this is certain; the reverse
Is sure to none; and yet on this perhaps,
This peradventure, infamous for lies,
As on a rock of adamant, we build
Our mountain hopes; spin out eternal schemes.
As we the fatal sisters could outspin,
And, big with life's futurities, expire.

—YOUNG

Cowards die many times before their deaths:
The valiant never taste of death but once.
Of all the wonders that I yet have heard,
It seems to me most strange that men should fear,
Seeing that death, a necessary end,
Will come when it will come.

I cannot tell what you and other men
Think of this life, but for my single self,
I had as lief not be as live to be
In awe of such a thing as I myself.
I was born free as Cæsar, so were you;
We both have fed as well, and we can both
Endure the winter's cold as well as he.

The cloud-capp'd towers, the gorgeous palaces,
The solemn temples, the great globe itself,
Yea, all which it inherit, shall dissolve,
And, like this insubstantial pageant faded,
Leave not a rack behind.

I am far from presuming to give this accentuation as perfect. No two persons will accent the same passage alike. No
person but a real adept would accent it twice alike. Perhaps
two real adepts who should utter the same passage with infinite perfection yet by throwing the energy into different

words might produce very different effects. I suppose that in those passages of Shakespeare, for example, no man but Garrick ever drew their full tone out of them, if I may borrow an expression from music. Let those who are disposed to criticise, therefore, try a few experiments themselves. I have essayed these short passages to let the foreigner see that the accent is not equal; that they are not to be read monotonously. I chose, too, the most pregnant passages, those wherein every word teems with latent meaning, that he might form an idea of the degrees of excellence of which this art is capable. He must not apprehend that all poets present the same difficulty. It is only the most brilliant passages. The great mass, even of good poetry, is easily enough read. Take the following examples, wherein little differences in the enunciation will not change the meaning sensibly.

> Here, in cool grot and mossy cell,
> We rural fays and faeries dwell;
> Though rarely seen by mortal eye,
> When the pale Moon, ascending high,
> Darts through yon lines her quivering beams,
> We frisk it near these crystal streams.
>
> Her beams, reflected from the wave,
> Afford the light our revels crave;
> The turf, with daisies broider'd o'er,
> Exceeds, we wot, the Parian floor;
> Nor yet for artful strains we call,
> But listen to the water's fall.
>
> Would you then taste our tranquil scene,
> Be sure your bosoms be serene:
> Devoid of hate, devoid of strife,
> Devoid of all that poisons life:
> And much it 'vails you, in their place
> To graft the love of human race.
>
> And tread with awe these favor'd bowers,
> Nor wound the shrubs, nor bruise the flowers;
> So may your path with sweets abound;

So may your couch with rest be crown'd!
But harm betide the wayward swain,
Who dares our hallow'd haunts profane!
        —SHENSTONE

To fair Fidele's grassy tomb
    Soft maids and village hinds shall bring
Each opening sweet, of earliest bloom,
    And rifle all the breathing Spring.

No wailing ghost shall dare appear
    To vex with shrieks this quiet grove,
But shepherd lads assemble here,
    And melting virgins own their love.

No wither'd witch shall here be seen,
    No goblins lead their nightly crew;
The female fays shall haunt the green,
    And dress thy grave with pearly dew;

The red-breast oft at evening hours
    Shall kindly lend his little aid,
With hoary moss, and gather'd flowers,
    To deck the ground where thou art laid.

When howling winds, and beating rain,
    In tempests shake thy sylvan cell;
Or 'midst the chase on every plain,
    The tender thought on thee shall dwell.

Each lonely scene shall thee restore,
    For thee the tear be duly shed;
Belov'd, till life can charm no more
    And mourn'd, till Pity's self be dead.
        —COLLINS

OF THE LENGTH OF VERSE.

Having spoken of feet which are only the constituent part
of verse, it becomes necessary to say something of its larger
divisions, and even of the verse itself. For what is a verse?
This question naturally occurs, and it is not sufficiently an-

swered by saying it is a whole line. Should the printer think proper to print the following passage in this manner:

Ὡς εἰπὼν οὗ παιδὸς ὀρέξατο φαίδιμος Ἕκτωρ. ἂψ δ' ὁ πάϊς πρὸς κόλπον ἐϋζώνοιο τιθήνης ἐκλίνθη ἰάχων, πατρὸς φίλου ὄψιν ἀτυχθείς, ταρβήσας χαλκόν τε ἰδὲ λόφον ἱππιοχαίτην, δεινὸν ἀπ' ἀκροτάτης κόρυθος νεύοντα νοήσας ἐκ δ' ἐγέλασσε πατήρ τε φίλος καὶ πότνια μήτηρ. αὐτίκ' ἀπὸ κρατὸς κόρυθ' εἵλετο φαίδιμος Ἕκτωρ, καὶ τὴν μὲν κατέθηκεν ἐπὶ χθονὶ παμφανόωσαν· αὐτὰρ ὅ γ' ὃν φίλον υἱὸν ἐπεὶ κύσε πηλέ τε χερσίν, εἶπεν ἐπευξάμενος Διΐ τ' ἄλλοισίν τε θεοῖσι· Ζεῦ ἄλλοι τε θεοί, δότε δὴ καὶ τόνδε γενέσθαι παῖδ' ἐμόν, ὡς καὶ ἐγώ περ, ἀριπρεπέα Τρώεσσιν, ὧδε βίην τ' ἀγαθὸν καὶ Ἰλίου ἶφι ἀνάσσειν· καὶ ποτέ τις εἴποι, 'πατρός γ' ὅδε πολλὸν ἀμείνων' ἐκ πολέμου ἀνιόντα· φέροι δ' ἔναρα βροτόεντα κτείνας δήϊον ἄνδρα, χαρείη δὲ φρένα μήτηρ. Ὡς εἰπὼν ἀλόχοιο φίλης ἐν χερσὶν ἔθηκε παῖδ' ἑόν· ἡ δ' ἄρα μιν κηώδεϊ δέξατο κόλπῳ δακρυόεν γελάσασα· πόσις δ' ἐλέησε νοήσας, χειρί τέ μιν κατέρεξεν ἔπος τ' ἔφατ' ἔκ τ' ὀνόμαζε·

it would still be verse; it would still immortalize its author were every other syllable of his compositions lost. The poet then does not depend on the printer to give a character to his work. He has studied the human ear. He has discovered that in any rhythmical composition the ear is pleased to find at certain regular intervals a pause where it may rest, by which it may divide the composition into parts, as a piece of music is divided into bars. He contrives to mark this division by a pause in the sense or at least by an emphatical word which may force the pause so that the ear may feel the regular return of the pause. The interval then between these regular pauses constitutes a verse. In the morsel before cited this interval comprehends six feet, and though it is written in the manner of prose, yet he who can read it without pausing at every sixth foot, like him who is insensible to the charm of music, who is insensible of love or of gratitude, is an unfavored son of nature to whom she has given a faculty fewer than to others of her children, one source of pleasure the less in a world where there are none to spare. A well-organized ear makes the pause regularly whether it be printed as verse or as prose.

But not only the organization of the ear but the character of the language have influence in determining the length of the verse. Otherwise the constitution of the ear being the same with all nations the verse would be of the same length in all languages, which is not the case. But the difference in language occasions the ear to be pleased with a difference of interval in the pause. The language of Homer enabled him to compose in verse of six feet; the English language cannot bear this. They may be of one, two, three, four, or five feet, as in the following examples:

One foot.

Turning
Burning
Changing
Ranging
I mourn
I sigh
I burn
I die
Let us part—
Let us part
Will you break
My poor heart?

Two feet.

Flow'ry mountains
Mossy fountains
Shady woods
Crystal floods
To me the rose
No longer glows
Ev'ry plant
Has lost its scent.

Prithee Cupid no more
Hurl thy darts at threescore
To thy girls and thy boys
Give thy pains and thy joys.

Three feet.

> Farewell fear and sorrow
> Pleasure till to-morrow.

> Yes, ev'ry flow'r that blows
>   I passed unheeded by
> Till this enchanting rose
>   Had fix'd my wand'ring eye.
>   —CUNNINGHAM

> The rose though a beautiful red
>   Looks faded to Phyllis's bloom;
> And the breeze from the bean-flower bed
>   To her breath's but a feeble perfume;
> A lily I plucked in full pride
>   Its freshness with hers to compare,
> And foolishly thought till I try'd
>   The flow'ret was equally fair.
>   —CUNNINGHAM

Four feet.

> From the dark tremendous cell
> Where the fiends of magic dwell
> Now the sun hath left the skies
> Daughters of Enchantment, rise!
>   —CUNNINGHAM

> Come Hope, and to my pensive eye
> Thy far foreseeing tube apply
> Whose kind deception steals us o'er
> The gloomy waste that lies before.
>   —LANGHORNE

> 'Mongst lords and fine ladies we shepherds are told
> The dearest affections are barter'd for gold
> That discord in wedlock is often their lot
> While Cupid and Hymen shake hands in a cot.
>   —CUNNINGHAM

Here the parisyllabic alone bears one foot more.

Oh liberty! thou goddess heav'nly bright
Profuse of bliss, and pregnant with delight,
Eternal pleasures in thy presence reign,
And smiling Plenty leads thy wanton train;
Eas'd of her load subjection grows more light,
And Poverty looks cheerful in thy sight;
Thou mak'st the gloomy face of nature gay
Giv'st beauty to the sun, and pleasure to the day.
                              —ADDISON

The last line furnishes an instance of six feet, usually called an
Alexandrian; but no piece is ever wholly in that measure. A
single line only is tolerated now and then, and is never a
beauty. Formerly it was thought that the language bore lines
of seven feet in length, as in the following:

'Tis he whose ev'ry thought and deed by rules of virtue
     moves;
Whose gen'rous tongue disdains to speak the thing his heart
     disproves
Who never did a slander forge his neighbor's fame to
     wound;
Nor listen to a false report by malice whisper'd round.
                              —PSALM 15

But a little attention shows that there is as regular a pause at
the fourth foot as at the seventh, and as verse takes its denomination from the shortest regular intervals, this is no more
than an alternate verse of four and of three feet. It is, therefore, usually written as in the following stanzas of the same
piece:

          Who to his plighted vows and trust
               Has ever firmly stood
          And, though he promise to his loss,
               He makes his promise good.

          The man who by this steady course
               Has happiness ensur'd
          When earth's foundations shake, will stand
               By Providence secur'd.

We may justly consider, therefore, verses of five feet as the longest the language sustains, and it is remarkable that not only this length, though the extreme, is generally the most esteemed, but that it is the only one which has dignity enough to support blank verse, that is, verse without rhyme. This is attempted in no other measure. It constitutes, therefore, the most precious part of our poetry. The poet, unfettered by rhyme, is at liberty to prune his diction of those tautologies, those feeble nothings necessary to introtrude the rhyming word. With no other trammel than that of measure he is able to condense his thoughts and images and to leave nothing but what is truly poetical. When enveloped in all the pomp and majesty of his subject he sometimes even throws off the restraint of the regular pause:

> Of Man's first disobedience, and the fruit
> Of that forbidden tree, whose mortal taste
> Brought death into the world, and all our woe,
> With loss of Eden, till one greater Man
> Restore us, and regain the blissful seat,
> Sing, heavenly Muse! that on the sacred top
> Of Oreb, or of Sinai, didst inspire
> That shepherd, who first taught the chosen seed,
> In the beginning, how the Heavens and Earth
> Rose out of Chaos.
>
> Then stay'd the fervid wheels, and in his hand
> He took the golden compasses, prepared
> In God's eternal store, to circumscribe
> This universe, and all created things
> One foot he centred, and the other turn'd
> Round, through the vast profundity obscure
> And said, "Thus far extend."

There are but two regular pauses in this whole passage of seven verses. They are constantly drowned by the majesty of the rhythm and sense. But nothing less than this can authorize such a license. Take the following proof from the same author:

> Again, God said, "Let there be firmament
> Amid the waters, and let it divide
> The waters from the waters;" and God made
> The firmament.   —MILTON 7: 261

And God said, Let there be a firmament in the midst of the waters, and let it divide the waters from the waters.
And God made the firmament.   —GENESIS I: 6

I have here placed Moses and Milton side by side, that he who can may distinguish which verse belongs to the poet. To do this he will not have the aid either of the sentiment, diction or measure of poetry. The original is so servilely copied that though it be cut into pieces of ten syllables, no pause is marked between these portions.

What proves the excellence of blank verse is that the taste lasts longer than that for rhyme. The fondness for the jingle leaves us with that for the rattles and baubles of childhood, and if we continue to read rhymed verse at a later period of life it is such only where the poet has had force enough to bring great beauties of thought and diction into this form. When young any composition pleases which unites a little sense, some imagination, and some rhythm, in doses however small. But as we advance in life these things fall off one by one, and I suspect we are left at last with only Homer and Virgil, perhaps with Homer alone. He like

> Hope travels on nor quits us when we die.

Having noted the different lengths of line which the English poet may give to his verse it must be further observed that he may intermingle these in the same verse according to his fancy.

The following are selected as examples:

> A tear bedews my Delia's eye,
> To think yon playful kid must die;
> From crystal spring, and flowery mead,
> Must, in his prime of life, recede!

She tells with what delight he stood,
To trace his features in the flood;
Then skipp'd aloof with quaint amaze,
And then drew near again to gaze.
—SHENSTONE

Full many a gem of purest ray serene
  The dark unfathomed caves of ocean bear;
Full many a flower is born to blush unseen,
  And waste its sweetness on the desert air.

Some village Hampden, that, with dauntless breast,
  The little tyrant of his fields withstood,
Some mute inglorious Milton here may rest,
  Some Cromwell, guiltless of his country's blood.
—GRAY

There shall my plaintive song recount
    Dark themes of hopeless woe,
And faster than the drooping fount
    I'll teach mine eyes to flow.

There leaves, in spite of Autumn green
    Shall shade the hallow'd ground,
And Spring will there again be seen
    To call forth flowers around.
—SHENSTONE

O Health! capricious maid!
    Why dost thou shun my peaceful bower,
    Where I had hope to share thy power,
And bless thy lasting aid?
—SHENSTONE

The man whose mind, on virtue bent
Pursues some greatly good intent
    With undivided aim
Serene beholds the angry crowd
Nor can their clamors fierce and loud
    His stubborn purpose tame.

Ye gentle Bards! give ear,
  Who talk of amorous rage,
Who spoil the lily, rob the rose,
Come learn of me to weep your woes:
  "O sweet! O sweet Anne Page!"
                —SHENSTONE

Too long a stranger to repose,
At length from Pain's abhorred couch I rose
  And wander'd forth alone,
To court once more the balmy breeze,
And catch the verdure of the trees,
  Ere yet their charms were flown.
                —SHENSTONE

O thou, by Nature taught
To breathe her genuine thought,
In numbers warmly pure, and sweetly strong;
Who first, on mountains wild,
In Fancy, loveliest child,
Thy babe, and Pleasure's, nursed the powers of song!
                —COLLINS

'Twas in a land of learning,
The Muse's favorite city,
Such pranks of late
Were play'd by a rat,
As—tempt one to be witty.
            —SHENSTONE

Yet stay, O stay! celestial Pow'rs!
  And with a hand of kind regard
Dispel the boisterous storm that low'rs
  Destruction on the fav'rite bard;
O watch with me his last expiring breath
And snatch him from the arms of dark oblivious death.
                —GRAY

What is grandeur, what is power?
Heavier toil, superior pain.

What the bright reward we gain?
The grateful memory of the good.
Sweet is the breath of vernal shower,
The bee's collected treasures sweet,
Sweet music's melting fall, but sweeter yet
The still small voice of gratitude.

Methinks I hear, in accents low,
The sportive, kind reply:
Poor moralist! and what art thou?
A solitary fly!
Thy joys no glittering female meets,
No hive hast thou of hoarded sweets,
No painted plumage to display;
On hasty wings thy youth is flown;
Thy sun is set, thy spring is gone—
We frolic while 'tis May.

—GRAY

Then let me rove some wild and heathy scene;
Or find some ruin, 'midst its dreary dells,
    Whose walls more awful nod
    By thy religious gleams.

Or, if chill blustering winds, or driving rain,
Prevent my willing feet, be mine the hut,
    That, from the mountain's side,
    Views wilds, and swelling floods.

—COLLINS

Though the license to intermingle the different measures
admits an infinitude of combinations, yet this becomes less
and less pleasing in proportion as they depart from that simplicity and regularity of which the ear is most sensible. When
these are wholly or nearly neglected, as in the lyric pieces, the
poet renounces one of the most fascinating charms of his art.
He must then look well to his matter and supply in sublimity
or other beauties the loss of regular measure. In effect these
pieces are seldom read twice.

A Tour to some of the Gardens of England

[*Memorandums made on a tour to some of the gardens in England, described by Whateley in his book on gardening.*] While his descriptions, in point of style, are models of perfect elegance and classical correctness, they are as remarkable for their exactness. I always walked over the gardens with his book in my hand, examined with attention the particular spots he described, found them so justly characterized by him as to be easily recognized, and saw with wonder, that his fine imagination had never been able to seduce him from the truth. My inquiries were directed chiefly to such practical things as might enable me to estimate the expense of making and maintaining a garden in that style. My journey was in the months of March and April, 1786.

Chiswick.—Belongs to Duke of Devonshire. A garden about six acres;—the octagonal dome has an ill effect, both within and without: the garden shows still too much of art. An obelisk of very ill effect; another in the middle of a pond useless.

Hampton-Court.—Old fashioned. Clipt yews grown wild.

Twickenham.—Pope's original garden, three and a half acres. Sir Wm. Stanhope added one and a half acre. This is a long narrow slip, grass and trees in the middle, walk all round. Now Sir Wellbore Ellis's. Obelisk at bottom of Pope's garden, as monument to his mother. Inscription, "Ah! Editha, matrum optima, mulierum amantissima, Vale." The house about thirty yards from the Thames: the ground shelves gently to the water side; on the back of the house passes the street, and beyond that the garden. The grotto is under the street, and goes out level to the water. In the centre of the garden a mound with a spiral walk round it. A rookery.

Esher-Place.—The house in a bottom near the river; on the other side the ground rises pretty much. The road by which we come to the house forms a dividing line in the middle of the front; on the right are heights, rising one beyond and above another, with clumps of trees; on the farthest a temple.

A hollow filled up with a clump of trees, the tallest in the bottom, so that the top is quite flat. On the left the ground descends. Clumps of trees, the clumps on each hand balance finely—a most lovely mixture of concave and convex. The garden is of about forty-five acres, besides the park which joins. Belongs to Lady Frances Pelham.

Claremont.—Lord Clive's. Nothing remarkable.

Paynshill.—Mr. Hopkins. Three hundred and twenty-three acres, garden and park all in one. Well described by Whateley. Grotto said to have cost £7,000. Whateley says one of the bridges is of stone, but both now are of wood, the lower sixty feet high: there is too much evergreen. The dwelling-house built by Hopkins, ill-situated: he has not been there in five years. He lived there four years while building the present house. It is not finished; its architecture is incorrect. A Doric temple, beautiful.

Woburn.—Belongs to Lord Peters. Lord Loughborough is the present tenant for two lives. Four people to the farm, four to the pleasure garden, four to the kitchen garden. All are intermixed, the pleasure garden being merely a highly-ornamented walk through and round the divisions of the farm and kitchen garden.

Caversham.—Sold by Lord Cadogan to Major Marsac. Twenty-five acres of garden, four hundred acres of park, six acres of kitchen garden. A large lawn, separated by a sunk fence from the garden, appears to be part of it. A straight, broad gravel walk passes before the front and parallel to it, terminated on the right by a Doric temple, and opening at the other end on a fine prospect. This straight walk has an ill effect. The lawn in front, which is pasture, well disposed with clumps of trees.

Wotton.—Now belongs to the Marquis of Buckingham, son of George Grenville. The lake covers fifty acres, the river five acres, the basin fifteen acres, the little river two acres—equal to seventy-two acres of water. The lake and great river are on a level, they fall into the basin five feet below, and that again into the little river five feet lower. These waters lie in form of an L: the house is in middle of open side, fronting the angle. A walk goes round the whole, three miles in circumference, and containing within it about three hundred acres: sometimes it passes close to the water, sometimes so far off as to leave large pasture grounds between it and the water. But two hands to keep the pleasure grounds in order; much neglected. The water affords two thousand brace of carp a year. There is a Palladian bridge, of which, I think, Whateley does not speak.

Stowe.—Belongs to the Marquis of Buckingham, son of George Grenville, and who takes it from Lord Temple. Fifteen men and eighteen boys employed in keeping pleasure grounds. Within the walk are considerable portions separated by inclosures and used for pasture. The Egyptian pyramid is almost entirely taken down by the late Lord Temple, to erect a building there, in commemoration of Mr. Pitt, but he died before beginning it, and nothing is done to it yet. The grotto and two rotundas are taken away. There are four levels of water, receiving it one from the other. The basin contains seven acres, the lake below that ten acres. Kent's building is called the temple of Venus. The inclosure is entirely by ha-ha. At each end of the front line there is a recess like the bastion of a fort. In one of these is the temple of Friendship, in the other the temple of Venus. They are seen the one from the other, the line of sight passing, not through the garden, but through the country parallel to the line of the garden. This has a good effect. In the approach to Stowe, you are brought a mile through a straight avenue, pointing to the Corinthian arch and to the house, till you get to the arch, then you turn short to the right. The straight approach is very ill. The Corinthian arch has a very useless appearance, inasmuch as it has no pretension to any destination. Instead of being an object from the house, it is an obstacle to a very pleasing distant prospect. The Grecian valley being clear of trees, while the hill on each side is covered with them, is much deepened to appearance.

Leasowes, in Shropshire.—Now the property of Mr. Horne by purchase. One hundred and fifty acres within the walk. The waters small. This is not even an ornamented farm—it is only a grazing farm with a path round it, here and there a seat of board, rarely anything better. Architecture has contributed nothing. The obelisk is of brick. Shenstone had but three hundred pounds a year, and ruined himself by what he did to this farm. It is said that he died of the heart-aches which his debts occasioned him. The part next the road is of red earth, that on the further part gray. The first and second cascades are beautiful. The landscape at number eighteen, and prospect at thirty-two, are fine. The walk through the wood is umbrageous and pleasing. The whole arch of prospect may be of ninety degrees. Many of the inscriptions are lost.

Hagley, now Lord Wescot's.—One thousand acres: no distinction between park and garden—both blended, but more of the character of garden. Eight or nine laborers keep it in order. Between two and three hundred deer in it, some few of them red deer. They breed sometimes with the fallow. This garden occupying a descending hollow between the Clent and Witchbury hills, with the spurs from those hills, there is no level in it for a spacious water. There are, therefore, only some small ponds. From one of these there is a fine cascade; but it can only be occasionally, by opening the sluice. This is in a small, dark, deep hollow, with recesses of stone in the banks on every side. In one of these is a Venus predique, turned half round as if inviting you with her into the recess. There is another cascade seen from the portico on the bridge. The castle is triangular, with a round tower at each angle, one only entire; it seems to be between forty and fifty feet high. The ponds yield a great deal of trout. The walks are scarcely gravelled.

Blenheim.—Twenty-five hundred acres, of which two hundred is garden, one hundred and fifty water, twelve kitchen garden, and the rest park. Two hundred people employed to keep it in order, and to make alterations and additions. About fifty of these employed in pleasure grounds. The turf is mowed once in ten days. In summer, about two thousand fallow deer in the park, and two or three thousand sheep. The palace of Henry II. was remaining till taken down by Sarah, widow of the first Duke of Marlborough. It was on a round spot levelled by art, near what is now water, and but a little above it. The island was a part of the high road leading to the palace. Rosamond's bower was near where is now a little grove, about two hundred yards from the palace. The well is near where the bower was. The water here is very beautiful, and very grand. The cascade from the lake, a fine one; except this the garden has no great beauties. It is not

laid out in fine lawns and woods, but the trees are scattered
thinly over the ground, and every here and there small thick-
ets of shrubs, in oval raised beds, cultivated, and flowers
among the shrubs. The gravelled walks are broad—art appears too much. There are but a few seats in it, and nothing
of architecture more dignified. There is no one striking position in it. There has been a great addition to the length of the
river since Whateley wrote.

Enfield Chase.—One of the four lodges. Garden about sixty
acres. Originally by Lord Chatham, now in the tenure of Dr.
Beaver, who married the daughter of Mr. Sharpe. The lease
lately renewed—not in good repair. The water very fine;
would admit of great improvement by extending walks, &c.,
to the principal water at the bottom of the lawn.

Moor Park.—The lawn about thirty acres. A piece of
ground up the hill of six acres. A small lake. Clumps of spruce
firs. Surrounded by walk—separately inclosed—destroys
unity. The property of Mr. Rous, who bought of Sir Thomas
Dundas. The building superb; the principal front a Corinthian portico of four columns; in front of the wings a colon-
nade, Ionic, subordinate. Back front a terrace, four Corinthian pilasters. Pulling down wings of building; removing
deer; wants water.

Kew.—Archimedes' screw for raising water. A horizontal
shaft made to turn the oblique one of the screw by a patent
machinery of this form:

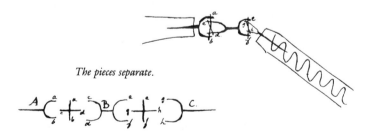

The pieces separate.

A is driven by its shank into the horizontal axis of the
wheel which turns the machine.

B is an intermediate iron to connect the motion of A and C.

C is driven by its shank into the axis of the screw.

D is a cross axis, the ends, *a* and *b*, going into the corresponding holes *a* and *b* of the iron A, and the ends, *c* and *d*, going into the corresponding holes *c* and *d* of the iron B.

E is another cross axis, the ends, *e* and *f*, going into the corresponding holes *e* and *f* of the iron B, and the ends, *g* and *h*, going into the corresponding holes *g* and *h* of the iron C.

Memorandums on a Tour from Paris to Amsterdam, Strasburg, and back to Paris

---

Amsterdam.—Joists of houses placed, not with their sides horizontally and perpendicularly, but diamond wise, thus: ◇ first, for greater strength; second, to arch between with brick, thus: 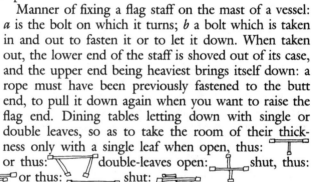 Windows opening so that they admit air and not rain. The upper sash opens on a horizontal axis, or pins in the centre of the sides, the lower sash slides up.

Manner of fixing a flag staff on the mast of a vessel: *a* is the bolt on which it turns; *b* a bolt which is taken in and out to fasten it or to let it down. When taken out, the lower end of the staff is shoved out of its case, and the upper end being heaviest brings itself down: a rope must have been previously fastened to the butt end, to pull it down again when you want to raise the flag end. Dining tables letting down with single or double leaves, so as to take the room of their thickness only with a single leaf when open, thus: or thus: double-leaves open: shut, thus: or thus: shut:

Peat costs about one doit each, or twelve and a half stivers the hundred. One hundred make seven cubic feet, and to keep a tolerably comfortable fire for a study or chamber, takes about six every hour and a half.

A machine for drawing light *empty* boats over a dam at Amsterdam. It is an axis in peritrochio fixed on the dam. From the dam each way is a sloping stage, the boat is presented to this, the rope of the axis made fast to it, and it is drawn up. The water on one side of the dam is about four feet higher than on the other.

The camels used for lightening ships over the Pampus will raise the ships eight feet. There are beams passing through the ship's sides, projecting to the off side of the camel and resting on it; of course that alone would keep the camel close to the ship. Besides this, there are a great number of wind-lasses on the camels, the ropes of which are made fast to the gunwale of the ship. The camel is shaped to the ship on the near side, and straight on the off one. When placed along side, water is let into it so as nearly to sink it; in this state it receives the beams, &c., of the ship, and then the water is pumped out.

Wind saw mills. See the plans detailed in the moolen book which I bought. A circular foundation of brick is raised about three or four feet high, and covered with a curb or sill of wood, and has little rollers under its sill which make it turn easily on the curb. A hanging bridge projects at each end about fifteen or twenty feet beyond the circular area, thus:

horizontally, and thus: in the profile

to increase the play of the timbers on the frame. The wings are at one side, as at *a*; there is a shelter over the hanging bridges, but of plank with scarce any frame, very light.

A bridge across a canal formed by two scows, which open each to the opposite shore and let boats pass.

A lanthern over the street door, which gives light equally into the antechamber and the street. It is a hexagon, and occupies the place of the middle pane of glass in the circular top of the street door.

A bridge on a canal, turning on a swivel, by which means it is arranged along the side of the canal so as not to be in the way of boats when not in use. When used, it is turned across the canal. It is, of course, a little more than double the width of the canal.

Hedges of beach, which, not losing the old leaf till the new bud pushes it off, has the effect of an evergreen as to cover.

Mr. Ameshoff, merchant at Amsterdam. The distribution of his aviary is worthy of notice. Each kind of the large birds has its coop eight feet wide and four feet deep; the middle of the front is occupied by a broad glass window, on one side of which is a door for the keeper to enter at, and on the other a little trap-door for the birds to pass in and out. The floor strewed with clean hay. Before each coop is a court of eight by sixteen feet, with wire in front and netting above, if the fowls be able to fly. For such as require it, there are bushes of evergreen growing in their court for them to lay their eggs under. The coops are frequently divided into two stories: the upper for those birds which perch, such as pigeons, &c., the lower for those which feed on the ground, as pheasants, partridges, &c. The court is in common for both stories, because the birds do no injury to each other. For the water-fowl there is a pond of water passing through the courts, with a movable separation. While they are breeding they must be separate, afterwards they may come together. The small birds are some of them in a common aviary, and some in cages.

The Dutch wheel-barrow is in this form: which is very convenient for loading and unloading.

Mr. Hermen Hend Damen, merchant-broker of Amsterdam, tells me that the emigrants to America come from the Palatinate down the Rhine, and take shipping from Amsterdam. Their passage is ten guineas if paid here, and eleven if paid in America. He says they might be had in any number to go to America, and settle lands as tenants on half stocks or metairies. Perhaps they would serve their employer one year as an indemnification for the passage, and then be bound to remain on his lands seven years. They would come to Amsterdam at their own expense. He thinks they would employ more than fifty acres each; but *quære*, especially if they have fifty acres for their wife also?

Hodson.—The best house. Stadhonderian, his son, in the government. Friendly, but old and very infirm.

Hope.—The first house in Amsterdam. His first object England; but it is supposed he would like to have the American business also, yet he would probably make our affairs subordinate to those of England.

Vollenhoven.—An excellent old house; connected with no party.

Sapportus.—A broker, very honest and ingenuous, well-disposed; acts for Hope, but will say with truth what he can do for us. The best person to consult with as to the best house to undertake a piece of business. He has brothers in London in business. Jacob Van Staphorst tells me there are about fourteen millions of florins, new money, placed in loans in Holland every year, being the savings of individuals out of their annual revenue, &c. Besides this, there are every year reimbursements of old loans from some quarter or other to be replaced at interest in some new loan.

1788. March 16th. Baron Steuben has been generally suspected of having suggested the first idea of the self-styled Order of Cincinnati. But Mr. Adams tells me, that in the year 1776 he had called at a tavern in the State of New York to dine, just at the moment when the British army was landing at Frog's Neck. Generals Washington, Lee, Knox and Parsons, came to the same tavern. He got into conversation with Knox. They talked of ancient history—of Fabius, who used to raise the Romans from the dust; of the present contest, &c.; and General Knox, in the course of the conversation, said he should wish for some ribbon to wear in his hat, or in his button hole, to be transmitted to his descendants as a badge and a proof that he had fought in defence of their liberties. He spoke of it in such precise terms, as showed he had revolved it in his mind before. Mr. Adams says he and Knox were standing together in the door of the tavern, and does not recollect whether General Washington and the others were near enough to hear the conversation, or were even in the room at that moment. Baron Steuben did not arrive in America till above a year after that. Mr. Adams is now fifty-three years old, *i.e.* nine years more than I am.

It is said this house will cost four tons of silver, or forty

HOPE'S HOUSE, NEAR HARLAEM.

thousand pounds sterling. The separation between the middle building and wings in the upper story has a capricious appearance, yet a pleasing one. The right wing of the house (which is the left in the plan) extends back to a great length, so as to make the ground plan in the form of an L. The parapet has a pannel of wall, and a pannel of ballusters alternately, which lighten it. There is no portico, the columns being backed against the wall of the front.

March 30th, 31st. *Amsterdam. Utrecht. Nimeguen.* The lower parts of the low countries seem partly to have been gained from the sea, and partly to be made up of the plains of the Yssel, the Rhine, the Maese and the Schelde united. To Utrecht nothing but plains are seen, a rich black mould, wet, lower than the level of the waters which intersect it; almost entirely in grass; few or no farm-houses, as the business of grazing requires few laborers. The canal is lined with country houses, which bespeak the wealth and cleanliness of the country; but generally in an uncouth state, and exhibiting no regular architecture. After passing Utrecht, the hills north-east of the Rhine come into view, and gather in towards the river, till at Wyck Dursted they are within three or four miles, and at Amelengen they join the river. The plains, after passing Utrecht, become more sandy; the hills are very poor and sandy, generally waste in broom, sometimes a little corn. The plains are in corn, grass, and willow. The plantations of the latter are immense, and give it the air of an uncultivated country. There are now few châteaux; farm-houses abound, built generally of brick, and covered with tile or thatch. There are some apple-trees, but no forest; a few inclosures of willow wattling. In the gardens are hedges of beach, one foot apart, which, not losing its old leaves till they are pushed off in the spring by the young ones, gives the shelter of evergreens. The Rhine is here about three hundred yards wide, and the road to Nimeguen passing it a little below Wattelingen, leaves Hetern in sight on the left. On this side, the plains of the Rhine, the Ling, and the Waal unite. The Rhine and Waal are crossed on vibrating boats, the rope supported by a line of seven little barks. The platform by which you go on to the ferry-boat is supported by boats. The view from the hill at Cress is sublime. It commands the Waal, and extends far up the Rhine. That also up and down the Waal from the Bellevue of Nimeguen, is very fine. The château here is pretended to have lodged Julius Cæsar. This is giving it an antiquity of at least eighteen centuries, which must be apocryphal. Some few sheep to-day, which were feeding in turnip patches.

April 1st. *Cranenburg. Cleves. Santen. Reynberg. Hoogstraat.* The transition from ease and opulence to extreme poverty is remarkable on crossing the line between the Dutch and Prussian territories. The soil and climate are the same; the governments alone differ. With the poverty, the fear also of slaves is visible in the faces of the Prussian subjects. There is an improvement, however, in the physiognomy, especially could it be a little brightened up. The road leads generally over the hills, but sometimes through skirts of the plains of the Rhine. These are always extensive and good. They want manure, being visibly worn down. The hills are almost always sandy, barren, uncultivated, and insusceptible of culture, covered with broom and moss; here and there a little indifferent forest, which is sometimes of beach. The plains are principally in corn; some grass and willow. There are no châteaux, nor houses that bespeak the existence even of a middle class. Universal and equal poverty overspreads the whole. In the villages, too, which seem to be falling down, the over-proportion of women is evident. The cultivators seem to live on their farms. The farm-houses are of mud, the better sort of brick; all covered over with thatch. Cleves is little more than a village. If there are shops or magazines of merchandise in it, they show little. Here and there at a window some small articles are hung up within the glass. The goose-berry beginning to leaf.

April 2d. Passed the Rhine at *Essenberg*. It is there about a quarter of a mile wide, or five hundred yards. It is crossed in a scow with sails. The wind being on the quarter, we were eight or ten minutes only in the passage. Duysberg is but a village in fact, walled in; the buildings mostly of brick. No new ones, which indicate a thriving state. I had understood that near that were remains of the encampment of Varus, in which he and his legions fell by the arms of Arminius (in the time of Tiberius I think it was), but there was not a person to be found in Duysberg who could understand either English, French, Italian, or Latin. So I could make no inquiry.

From *Duysberg* to *Dusseldorf* the road leads sometimes over the hills, sometimes through the plains of the Rhine, the quality of which are as before described. On the hills, however, are considerable groves of oak, of spontaneous growth, which seem to be of more than a century; but the soil being barren, the trees, though high, are crooked and knotty. The undergrowth is broom and moss. In the plains is corn entirely. As they are become rather sandy for grass, there are no inclosures on the Rhine at all. The houses are poor and ruinous, mostly of brick, and scantling mixed. A good deal of grape cultivated.

Dusseldorf. The gallery of paintings is sublime, particularly the room of Vanderwerff. The plains from Dusseldorf to Cologne are much more extensive, and go off in barren downs at some distance from the river. These downs extend far, according to appearance. They are manuring the plains with lime. A gate at the Elector's château on this road in this form. We cross at Cologne on a pendulum boat. I observe the hog of this country (Westphalia), of which the celebrated ham is made, is tall, gaunt, and with heavy lop ears. Fatted at a year old, would weigh one hundred or one hundred and twenty pounds. At two years old, two hundred pounds. Their principal food is acorns. The pork, fresh, sells at two and a half pence sterling the pound. The hams, ready made, at eight and a half pence sterling the pound. One hundred and six pounds of this country is equal to one hundred pounds of Holland. About four pounds of fine Holland salt is put on one hundred pounds of pork. It is smoked in a room which has no chimney. Well-informed people here tell me there is no other part of the world where the bacon is smoked. They do not know that we do it. Cologne is the principal market of exportation. They find that the small hog makes the sweetest meat.

Cologne is a sovereign city, having no territory out of its walls. It contains about sixty thousand inhabitants; appears to have much commerce, and to abound with poor. Its commerce is principally in the hands of Protestants, of whom there are about sixty houses in the city. They are extremely restricted in their operations, and otherwise oppressed in every form by the government, which is Catholic, and excessively intolerant. Their Senate, some time ago, by a majority of twenty-two to eighteen, allowed them to have a church;

but it is believed this privilege will be revoked. There are about two hundred and fifty Catholic churches in the city. The Rhine is here about four hundred yards wide. This city is in 51° latitude, wanting about 6'. Here the vines begin, and it is the most northern spot on the earth on which wine is made. Their first grapes came from Orleans, since that from Alsace, Champagne, &c. It is thirty-two years only since the first vines were sent from Cassel, near Mayence, to the Cape of Good Hope, of which the Cape wine is now made. Afterwards new supplies were sent from the same quarter. That I suppose is the most southern spot on the globe where wine is made, and it is singular that the same vine should have furnished two wines as much opposed to each other in quality as in situation. I was addressed here by Mr. Damen, of Amsterdam, to Mr. Jean Jaques Peuchen, of this place, Merchant.

April 4th. *Cologne. Bonne. Andernach. Coblentz.* I saw many walnut trees to-day in the open fields. It would seem as if this tree and wine required the same climate. The soil begins now to be reddish, both on the hills and in the plains. Those from Cologne to Bonne extend about three miles from the river on each side; but a little above Bonne they become contracted, and continue from thence to be from one mile to nothing, comprehending both sides of the river. They are in corn, some clover and rape, and many vines. These are planted in rows three feet apart both ways. The vine is left about six or eight feet high, and stuck with poles ten or twelve feet high. To these poles they are tied in two places, at the height of about two and four feet. They are now performing this operation. The hills are generally excessively steep, a great proportion of them barren; the rest in vines principally, sometimes small patches of corn. In the plains, though rich, I observed they dung their vines plentifully; and it is observed here, as elsewhere, that the plains yield much wine, but bad. The good is furnished from the hills. The walnut, willow, and apple tree beginning to leaf.

Andernach is the port on the Rhine to which the famous millstones of Cologne are brought; the quarry, as some say, being at Mendich, three or four leagues from thence. I suppose they have been called Cologne millstones, because the merchants of that place having the most extensive correspondence, have usually sent them to all parts of the world. I observed great collections of them at Cologne. This is one account.

April 5. *Coblentz. Nassau.* Another account is, that these stones are cut at Triers and brought down the Moselle. I could not learn the price of them at the quarry; but I was shown a grindstone of the same stone, five feet diameter, which cost at Triers six florins. It was of but half the thickness of a millstone. I supposed, therefore, that two millstones would cost about as much as three of these grindstones, *i. e.* about a guinea and a half. This country abounds with slate.

The best Moselle wines are made about fifteen leagues from hence, in an excessively mountainous country. The first quality (without any comparison) is that made on the mountain of Brownberg, adjoining to the village of Dusmond; and the best crops is that of the Baron Breidbach Burrhesheim, grand chambellan et grand Baillif de Coblentz. His Receveur, of the name of Mayer, lives at Dusmond. The last fine year was 1783, which sells now at fifty louis the foudre, which contains six aumes of one hundred and seventy bottles each, equal about one thousand one hundred and ten bottles. This is about twenty-two sous Tournois the bottle. In general, the Baron Burresheim's crops will sell as soon as made, say at the vintage, for one hundred and thirty, one hundred and forty, and one hundred and fifty ecus the foudre (the ecu is one and a half florin of Holland), say two hundred. 2. Vialen is the second quality, and sells new at one hundred and twenty ecus the foudre. 3. Crach-Bispost is the third, and sells for about one hundred and five ecus. I compared Crach of 1783 with Baron Burrhesheim's of the same year. The latter is quite clear of acid, stronger, and very sensibly the best. 4. Selting, which sells at one hundred ecus. 5. Kous-Berncastle, the fifth quality, sells at eighty or ninety. After this there is a gradation of qualities down to thirty ecus. These wines must be five or six years old before they are quite ripe for drinking. One thousand plants yield a foudre of wine a year in the most plentiful vineyards. In other vineyards, it will take two thousand or two thousand and five hundred plants to yield a foudre. The culture of one thousand plants costs about one louis a year. A day's labor of a man is paid in winter twenty kreitzers (*i. e.* one-third of a florin), in summer twenty-six; a woman's is half that. The red wines of this country are very indifferent, and will not keep. The Moselle is here from one hundred to two hundred yards wide; the Rhine three hundred to four hundred. A jessamine in the Count de Moustier's garden in leaf.

In the Elector of Treves' palace at *Coblentz*, are large rooms very well warmed by warm air conveyed from an oven below, through tubes which open into the rooms. An oil and vinegar cruet in this form: At Coblentz we pass the river on a pendulum boat, and the road to Nassau is over tremendous hills, on which is here and there a little corn, more vines, but mostly barren. In some of these barrens are forests of beach and oak, tolerably large, but crooked and knotty; the undergrowth beach brush, broom, and moss. The soil of the plains, and of the hills where they are cultivable, is reddish. Nassau is a village the whole rents of which should not amount to more than a hundred or two guineas. Yet it gives the title of Prince to the house of Orange to which it belongs.

April 6th. *Nassau. Schwelbach. Wisbaden. Hocheim. Frankfort.* The road from Nassau to Schwelbach is over hills, or rather mountains, both high and steep; always poor, and above half of them barren in beach and oak. At Schwelbach there is some chesnut. The other parts are either in winter grain, or preparing for that of the spring. Between Schwelbach and Wisbaden we come in sight of the plains of the Rhine, which are very extensive. From hence the lands, both high and low, are very fine, in corn, vines, and fruit trees. The country has the appearance of wealth, especially in the approach to Frankfort.

April 7th. *Frankfort.* Among the poultry, I have seen no turkies in Germany till I arrive at this place. The Stork, or Crane, is very commonly tame here. It is a miserable, dirty, ill-looking bird. The Lutheran is the reigning religion here, and is equally intolerant to the Catholic and Calvinist, excluding them from the free corps.

April 8th. *Frankfort. Hanau.* The road goes through the plains of the Maine, which are mulatto, and very fine. They are well cultivated till you pass the line between the republic and the landgraviate of Hesse, when you immediately see the effect of the difference of government, notwithstanding the tendency which the neighborhood of such a commercial town as Frankfort has to counteract the effects of tyranny in its vicinities, and to animate them in spite of oppression. In Frankfort all is life, bustle, and motion; in Hanau the silence and quiet of the mansions of the dead. Nobody is seen moving in the streets; every door is shut; no sound of the saw, the hammer, or other utensil of industry. The drum and fife is all that is heard. The streets are cleaner than a German floor, because nobody passes them. At Williamsbath, near Hanau, is a country seat of the Landgrave. There is a ruin which is clever. It presents the remains of an old castle.

The ground plan is in this form: ⊏⊐ The upper story in this: ◯ A circular room of thirty-one and a half feet diameter within. The four little square towers at the corners finish at the floor of the upper story, so as to be only platforms to walk out on. Over the circular room is a platform also, which is covered by the broken parapet which once crowned the top, but is now fallen off some parts, whilst the other parts remain. I like better, however, the form of the ruin at Hagley, in England, which was thus. There is a centry box here, covered over with bark, so as to look exactly like the trunk of an old tree. This is a good idea; and may be of much avail in a garden. There is a hermitage in which is a good figure of a hermit in plaster, colored to the life, with a table and book before him, in the attitude of reading and contemplation. In a little cell is his bed; in another his books, some tools, &c.; in another his little provision of firewood, &c. There is a monument erected to the son of the present landgrave, in the form of a pyramid, the base of which is eighteen and a half feet. The side declines from the perpendicular about twenty-two and a half degrees. An arch is carried through it both ways so as to present a door in each side. In the middle of this, at the crossing of the two arches, is a marble monument with this inscription: "ante tempus." He died at twelve years of age. Between Hanau and Frankfort, in sight of the road, is the village of

Bergen, where was fought the battle of Bergen in the war before last. Things worth noting here are: 1. A folding ladder. 2. Manner of packing china cups and saucers, the former in a circle within the latter. 3. The marks of different manufactures of china, to wit: Dresden with two swords. Hecks with a wheel with w , Frankendaal with 🜹 (for Charles Theodore), and a ⚶ over it. Berlin with   4. The top rail of a wagon supported by the washers on the ends of the axle-trees.

April 10th. *Frankfort. Hocheim. Mayence.* The little tyrants round about having disarmed their people, and made it very criminal to kill game, one knows when they quit the territory of Frankfort by the quantity of game which is seen. In the Republic, everybody being allowed to be armed, and to hunt on their own lands, there is very little game left in its territory. The hog hereabouts resembles extremely the little hog of Virginia. Round like that, a small head, and short upright ears. This makes the ham of Mayence so much esteemed at Paris.

We cross the Rhine at Mayence on a bridge one thousand eight hundred and forty feet long, supported by forty-seven boats. It is not in a direct line, but curved up against the stream; which may strengthen it if the difference between the upper and lower curve be sensible, if the planks of the floor be thick, well jointed together, and forming sectors of circles, so as to act on the whole as the stones of an arch. But it has by no means this appearance. Near one end, one of the boats has an axis in peritrochio, and a chain, by which it may be let drop down stream some distance, with the portion of the floor belonging to it, so as to let a vessel through. Then it is wound up again into place, and to consolidate it the more with the adjoining parts, the loose section is a little higher, and has at each end a folding stage, which folds back on it when it moves down, and when brought up again into place, these stages are folded over on the bridge. This whole operation takes but four or five minutes. In the winter the bridge is taken away entirely, on account of the ice. And then everything passes on the ice, through the whole winter.

April 11th. *Mayence. Rudesheim. Johansberg. Markebrom.* The women do everything here. They dig the earth, plough, saw, cut and split wood, row, tow the batteaux, &c. In a small but dull kind of batteau, with two hands rowing with a kind of large paddle, and a square sail, but scarcely a breath of wind, we went down the river at the rate of five miles an hour, making it three and a half hours to Rudesheim. The floats of wood which go with the current only, go one mile and a half an hour. They go night and day. There are five boat-mills abreast here. Their floats seem to be about eight feet broad. The Rhine yields salmon, carp, pike, and perch, and the little rivers running into it yield speckled trout. The plains from Maintz to Rudesheim are good and in corn; the hills mostly in vines. The banks of the river are so low that, standing up in the batteau, I could generally see what was in the plains. Yet they are seldom overflowed.

Though they begin to make wine, as has been said, at Cologne, and continue it up the river indefinitely, yet it is only from Rudesheim to Hocheim that wines of the very first quality are made. The river happens there to run due east and west, so as to give its hills on that side a southern aspect. And even in this canton, it is only Hocheim, Johansberg, and Rudesheim, that are considered as of the very first quality. Johansberg is a little mountain (berg signifies mountain), whereon is a religious house, about fifteen miles below Mayence, and near the village of Vingel. It has a southern aspect, the soil a barren mulatto clay, mixed with a good deal of stone, and some slate. This wine used to be but on a par with Hocheim and Rudesheim; but

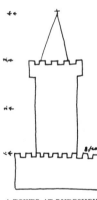

A TOWER AT RUDESHEIM.

the place having come to the Bishop of Fulda, he improved its culture so as to render it stronger; and since the year 1775, it sells at double the price of the other two. It has none of the acid of the Hocheim and other Rhenish wines. There are about sixty tons made in a good year, which sell, as soon as of a drinkable age, at one thousand franks each. The tun here contains seven and a-half aumes of one hundred and seventy bottles each. Rudesheim is a village of about eighteen or twenty miles below Mayence. Its fine wines are made on the hills about a mile

below the village, which look to the south, and on the middle
and lower parts of them. They are terraced. The soil is gray,
about one-half of slate and rotten stone, the other half of barren clay, excessively steep. Just behind the village also is a
little spot, called Hinder House, belonging to the Counts of
Sicken and Oschstein, whereon each makes about a ton of
wine of the very first quality. This spot extends from the bottom to the top of the hill. The vignerons of Rudesheim dung
their wines about once in five or six years, putting a one-horse
tumbrel load of dung on every twelve feet square. One thousand plants yield about four aumes in a good year. The best
crops are,

The Chanoines of Mayence, who make . . .	15	pieces of 7½ aumes.	
Le Comte de Sicken	6	"	"
Le Comte d'Oschstein	9	"	"
L'Electeur de Mayence	6	"	"
Le Comte de Meternisch	6	"	"
Monsieur de Boze	5	"	"
M. Ackerman, baliff et aubergiste des 3 couronnes	8	"	"
M. Ackerman le fils, aubergiste à la couronne .	5	"	"
M. Lynn, aubergiste de l'ange	5	"	"
Baron de Wetzel	7	"	"
Convent de Mariahousen, des religieuses Benedictines	7	"	"
M. Johan Yung	8	"	"
M. de Rieden	5	"	"
	92		

These wines begin to be drinkable at about five years old.
The proprietors sell them old or young, according to the
prices offered, and according to their own want of money.
There is always a little difference between different casks, and
therefore when you choose and buy a single cask, you pay
three, four, five or six hundred florins for it. They are not at
all acid, and to my taste much preferable to Hocheim, though
but of the same price. Hocheim is a village about three miles
above Mayence, on the Maine, where it empties into the
Rhine. The spot whereon the good wine is made is the hill
side from the church down to the plain, a gentle slope of
about a quarter of a mile wide, and extending half a mile
towards Mayence. It is of south-western aspect, very poor,

sometimes gray, sometimes mulatto, with a moderate mixture of small broken stone. The wines are planted three feet apart, and stuck with sticks about six feet high. The wine, too, is cut at that height. They are dunged once in three or four years. One thousand plants yield from one to two aumes a year: they begin to yield a little at three years old, and continue to one hundred years, unless sooner killed by a cold winter. Dick, keeper of the Rothen-house tavern at Frankfort, a great wine merchant, who has between three and four hundred tons of wine in his cellars, tells me that Hocheim of the year 1783, sold, as soon as it was made, at ninety florins the aume, Rudesheim of the same year, as soon as made, at one hundred and fifteen florins, and Markebronn seventy florins. But a peasant of Hocheim tells me that the best crops of Hocheim in the good years, when sold new, sell but for about thirty-two or thirty-three florins the aume; but that it is only the poorer proprietors who sell new. The fine crops are,

Count Ingleheim about . . . 10 tuns.		
Baron d'Alberg . . . . 8 "		All of these keep till about fifteen years old, before they sell, unless they are offered a very good price sooner.
Count Schimbon . . . . 14 "		
The Chanoines of Mayence . 18 "		
Counsellor Schik de Vetsler . 15 "		
Convent of Jacobsberg . . 8 "		
The Chanoine of Fechbach . 10 "		
The Carmelites of Frankfort. 8 "		Who only sell by the bottle in their own tavern in Frankfort.
The Bailiff of Hocheim . . 11 "		Who sells at three or four years old.
Zimmerman, a bourgeois. . 4 "		These being poor, sell new.
Feldman, a carpenter. . . 2 "		

Markebronn (bronn signifies a spring, and is probably of affinity with the Scotch word, burn) is a little canton in the same range of hills, adjoining to the village of Hagenheim, about three miles above Johansberg, subject to the elector of Mayence. It is a sloping hill side of southern aspect, mulatto, poor, and mixed with some stone. This yields wine of the second quality.

April 12th. *Mayence. Oppenheim. Dorms. Manheim.* On the road between Mayence and Oppenheim are three cantons, which are also esteemed as yielding wines of the second quality. These are Laudenheim, Bodenheim, and Nierstein. Laudenheim is a village about four or five miles from Mayence. Its wines are made on a steep hill side, the soil of which is gray, poor and mixed with some stone. The river there happens to make a short turn to the south-west, so as to present its hills to the south-east. Bodenheim is a village nine miles, and Nierstein another about ten or eleven miles from Mayence. Here, too, the river is north-east and south-west, so as to give the hills between these villages a south-east aspect; and at Thierstein, a valley making off, brings the face of the hill round to the south. The hills between these villages are almost perpendicular, of a vermilion red, very poor, and having as much rotten stone as earth. It is to be observed that these are the only cantons on the south side of the river which yield good wine, the hills on this side being generally exposed to the cold winds, and turned from the sun. The annexed bill of prices current, will give an idea of the estimation of these wines respectively.

With respect to the grapes in this country, there are three kinds in use for making white wine, (for I take no notice of the red wines, as being absolutely worthless.) 1. The Klemperien, of which the inferior qualities of Rhenish wines are made, and is cultivated because of its hardness. The wines of this grape descend as low as one hundred florins the tun of eight aumes. 2. The Rhysslin grape, which grows only from Hocheim down to Rudesheim. This is small and delicate, and therefore succeeds only in this chosen spot. Even at Rudesheim it yields a fine wine only in the little spot called Hinder House, before mentioned; the mass of good wines made at Rudesheim, below the village, being of the third kind of grape, which is called the Orleans grape.

To Oppenheim the plains of the Rhine and Maine are united. From that place we see the commencement of the Berg-strasse, or mountains which separate at first the plains of the Rhine and Maine, then cross the Neckar at Heidelberg, and from thence forms the separation between the plains of the Neckar and Rhine, leaving those of the Rhine about ten or twelve miles wide. These plains are sometimes black, sometimes mulatto, always rich. They are in corn, potatoes, and some willow. On the other side again, that is, on the west side, the hills keep at first close to the river. They are about one hundred and fifty, or two hundred feet high, sloping, red, good, and mostly in vines. Above Oppenheim, they begin to go off till they join the mountains of Lorraine and Alsace, which separate the waters of the Moselle and Rhine, leaving to the whole valley of the Rhine about twenty or twenty-five miles breadth. About Worms these plains are sandy, poor, and often covered only with small pine.

April 13th. *Manheim*. There is a bridge over the Rhine here, supported on thirty-nine boats, and one over the Neckar on eleven boats. The bridge over the Rhine is twenty-one and a half feet wide from rail to rail. The boats are four feet deep, fifty-two feet long, and nine feet eight inches broad. The space between boat and boat is eighteen feet ten inches. From these data the length of the bridge should be 9ft. 8in. + 18ft. 10in. × 40 = 1140 feet. In order to let vessels pass through, two boats well framed together, with their flooring, are made to fall down stream together. Here, too, they make good ham. It is fattened on round potatoes and Indian corn. The farmers smoke what is for their own use in their chimneys. When it is made for sale, and in greater quantities than the chimney will hold, they make the smoke of the chimney pass into an adjoining loft, or apartment, from which it has no issue; and here they hang their hams.

An economical curtain bedstead. The bedstead is seven feet by four feet two inches. From each leg there goes up an iron rod three-eighths of an inch in diameter. Those from the legs at the foot of the bed meeting at top as in the margin, and

those from the head meeting in like manner, so that the two at the foot form one point, and the two at the head another. On these points lays an oval iron rod, whose long diameter is five feet, and short one three feet one inch. There is a hole through this rod at each end, by which it goes on firm on the point of the upright rods. Then a nut screws it down firmly. Ten breadths of stuff two feet ten inches wide, and eight feet six inches long, form the curtains. There is no top nor vallons. The rings are fastened within two and a half or three inches of the top on the inside, which two and a half or three inches stand up, and are an ornament somewhat like a ruffle.

I have observed all along the Rhine that they make the oxen draw by the horns. A pair of very handsome chariot horses, large, bay, and seven years old, sell for fifty louis. One pound of beef sells for eight kreitzers, (*i. e.* eight sixtieths of a florin;) one pound of mutton or veal, six kreitzers; one pound of pork, seven and a half kreitzers; one pound of ham, twelve kreitzers; one pound of fine wheat bread, two kreitzers; one pound of butter, twenty kreitzers; one hundred and sixty pounds of wheat, six francs; one hundred and sixty pounds of maize, five francs; one hundred and sixty pounds of potatoes, one franc; one hundred pounds of hay, one franc; a cord of wood (which is 4 4 and 6 feet), seven francs; a laborer by the day receives twenty-four kreitzers, and feeds himself. A journee or arpent of land (which is eight by two hundred steps), such as the middling plains of the Rhine, will sell for two hundred francs. There are more soldiers here than other inhabitants, to wit: six thousand soldiers and four thousand males of full age of the citizens, the whole number of whom is reckoned at twenty thousand.

April 14th. *Manheim. Dossenheim. Heidelberg. Schwetzingen. Manheim.* The elector placed, in 1768, two males and five females of the Angora goat at Dossenheim, which is at the foot of the Bergstrasse mountains. He sold twenty-five last year, and has now seventy. They are removed into the mountains four leagues beyond Dossenheim. Heidelberg is on the Neckar just where it issues from the Bergstrasse mountains, occupying the first skirt of plain which it forms. The château is up the hill a considerable height. The gardens lie above the château, climbing up the mountain in terraces. This château is the most noble ruin I have ever seen, having been reduced to that state by the French in the time of Louis XIV., 1693. Nothing remains under cover but the chapel. The situation is romantic and pleasing beyond expression. It is on a great scale much like the situation of Petrarch's château, at Vaucluse, on a small one. The climate, too, is like that of Italy. The apple, the pear, cherry, peach, apricot, and almond, are

all in bloom. There is a station in the garden to which the
château re-echoes distinctly four syllables. The famous ton of
Heidelberg was new built in 1751, and made to contain thirty
foudres more than the ancient one. It is said to contain two
hundred and thirty-six foudres of one thousand two hundred
bottles each. I measured it, and found its length external to
be twenty-eight feet ten inches; its diameter at the end twenty
feet three inches; the thickness of the staves seven and a half
inches; thickness of the hoops seven and a half inches; besides
a great deal of external framing. There is no wine in it now.
The gardens at Schwetzingen show how much money may be
laid out to make an ugly thing. What is called the English
quarter, however, relieves the eye from the straight rows of
trees, round and square basins, which constitute the great
mass of the garden. There are some tolerable morsels of Grecian architecture, and a good ruin. The Aviary, too, is clever.
It consists of cells of about eight feet wide, arranged round,
and looking into a circular area of about forty or fifty feet
diameter. The cells have doors both of wire and glass, and
have small shrubs in them. The plains of the Rhine on this
side are twelve miles wide, bounded by the Bergstrasse mountains. These appear to be eight hundred or a thousand feet
high; the lower part in vines, from which is made what is
called the vin de Nichar; the upper in chesnut. There are
some cultivated spots however, quite to the top. The plains
are generally mulatto, in corn principally; they are planting
potatoes in some parts, and leaving others open for maize

and tobacco. Many peach and other fruit
trees on the lower part of the mountain.
The paths on some parts of these mountains are somewhat in the style represented in the margin.

   Manheim. Kaeferthal. Manheim. Just beyond Kaeferthal is
an extensive, sandy waste, planted in pine, in which the elector has about two hundred sangliers, tamed. I saw about fifty;
the heavies I am told, would weigh about three hundred
pounds. They are fed on round potatoes, and range in the
forest of pines. At the village of Kaeferthal is a plantation of
rhubarb, begun in 1769 by a private company. It contains

twenty arpens or jourries, and its culture costs about four or five hundred francs a year; it sometimes employs forty or fifty laborers at a time. The best age to sell the rhubarb at is the fifth or sixth year, but the sale being dull, they keep it sometimes to the tenth year; they find it best to let it remain in the ground. They sell about two hundred kentals a year at two or three francs a pound, and could sell double that quantity from the ground if they could find a market. The apothecaries of Francfort and of England are the principal buyers. It is in beds, resembling lettice-beds; the plants four, five or six feet apart. When dug, a thread is passed through every piece of root, and it is hung separate in a kind of rack; when dry it is rasped; what comes off is given to the cattle.

April 15. *Manheim. Spire. Carlsruhe.* The valley preserves its width, extending on each side of the river about ten or twelve miles, but the soil loses much in its quality, becoming sandy and lean, often barren and overgrown with pine thicket. At Spire is nothing remarkable. Between that and Carlsruhe we pass the Rhine in a common skow with oars, where it is between three and four hundred yards wide. Carlsruhe is the residence of the Margrave of Baden, a sovereign prince. His château is built in the midst of a natural forest of several leagues diameter, and of the best trees I have seen in these countries: they are mostly oak, and would be deemed but indifferent in America. A great deal of money has been spent to do more harm than good to the ground—cutting a number of straight allies through the forest. He has a pheasantry of the gold and silver kind, the latter very tame, but the former excessively shy. A little inclosure of stone, two and a half feet high and thirty feet diameter, in which are two tamed beavers. There is a pond of fifteen feet diameter in the centre, and at each end a little cell for them to retire into, which is stowed with boughs and twigs with leaves on them, which is their principal food. They eat bread also;—twice a week the water is changed. They cannot get over this wall. Some cerfs of a peculiar kind, spotted like fawns, the horns remarkably long, small and sharp, with few points. I am not sure there were more than two to each main beam, and if I saw distinctly, there came out a separate and subordinate beam from the root of each. Eight angora goats—beautiful animals— all white. This town is only an appendage of the château, and but a moderate one. It is a league from Durlach, half way between that and the river. I observe they twist the flues of their stoves in any form for ornament merely, without smoking, as thus, *e. g.*

April 16. *Carlsruhe. Rastadt. Scholhoven. Bischofheim. Kehl. Strasburg.* The valley of the Rhine still preserves its breadth, but varies in quality; sometimes a rich mulatto loom, sometimes a poor sand, covered with small pine. The culture is generally corn. It is to be noted, that through the whole of my route through the Netherlands and the valley of the Rhine, there is a little red clover every here and there, and a great deal of grape cultivated. The seed of this is sold to be made into oil. The grape is now in blossom. No inclosures. The fruit trees are generally blossoming through the whole valley. The high mountains of the Bergstrasse, as also of Alsace, are covered with snow. Within this day or two, the every-day dress of the country women here is black. Rastadt is a seat also of the Margrave of Baden. Scholhoven and Kehl are in his territory, but not Bischofheim. I see no beggars since I entered his government, nor is the traveller obliged to ransom himself every moment by a chausiee gold. The roads are excellent, and made so, I presume, out of the coffers of the prince. From Cleves till I enter the Margravate of Baden, the roads have been strung with beggars—in Hesse the most, and the road tax very heavy. We pay it cheerfully, however, through the territory of Francfort and thence up the Rhine, because fine gravelled roads are kept up; but through the Prussian, and other parts of the road below Francfort, the roads are only as made by the carriages, there not appearing to have been ever a day's work employed on them. At Strasburgh we pass the Rhine on a wooden bridge.

At *Brussels and Antwerp,* the fuel is pit-coal, dug in Brabant. Through all Holland it is turf. From Cleves to Cologne it is pit-coal brought from England. They burn it in open stoves. From thence it is wood, burnt in close stoves, till you get to Strasburg, where the open chimney comes again into use.

April 16th, 17th, 18th. *Strasburg*. The vin de paille is made in the neighborhood of Colmar, in Alsace, about ——— from this place. It takes its name from the circumstance of spreading the grapes on straw, where they are preserved till spring, and then made into wine. The little juice then remaining in them makes a rich sweet wine, but the dearest in the world, without being the best by any means. They charge nine florins the bottle for it in the taverns of Strasburg. It is the caprice of wealth alone which continues so losing an operation. This wine is sought because dear; while the better wine of Frontignan is rarely seen at a good table because it is cheap.

Strasburg. Saverne. Phalsbourg. As far as Saverne the country is in waiving hills and hollows; red, rich enough; mostly in small grain, but some vines; a little stone. From Saverne to Phalsbourg we cross a considerable mountain, which takes an hour to rise it.

April 19th. *Phalsbourg. Fenestrange. Moyenvic. Nancy.* Asparagus to-day at Moyenvic. The country is always either mountainous or hilly; red, tolerably good, and in small grain. On the hills about Fenestrange, Moyenvic, and Nancy, are some small vineyards where a bad wine is made. No inclosures. Some good sheep, indifferent cattle, and small horses. The most forest I have seen in France, principally of beech, pretty large. The houses, as in Germany, are of scantling, filled in with wicker and mortar, and covered either with thatch or tiles. The people, too, here as there, are gathered in villages. Oxen plough here with collars and hames. The awkward figure of their mould-board leads one to consider what should be its form. The offices of the mould-board are to receive the sod after the share has cut under it, to raise it gradually, and to reverse it. The fore-end of it then, should be horizontal to enter under the sod, and the hind end perpendicular to throw it over; the intermediate surface changing gradually from the horizontal to the perpendicular. It should be as wide as the furrow, and of a length suited to the construction of the plough. The following would seem a good method of making it: Take a block, whose length, breadth and thickness, is that of your intended mould-board, suppose two and a half feet long and eight inches broad and thick. Draw the lines *a d* and *c d*, figure 1, with a saw, the toothed edge of which is straight, enter at *a* and cut on, guiding the hind part of the saw on the line *a b*, and the fore part on the line *a d*, till the saw reaches the points *c* and *d*, then enter it at *c* and cut on, guiding it by the lines *c b* and *c d* till it reaches the points *b* and *d*. The quarter, *a b c d*, will then be completely cut out, and the diagonal from *d* to *b* laid bare. The piece may now be represented as in figure 2. Then saw in transversely at every two inches till the saw reaches the line *c e*, and the diagonal *b d*, and cut out the pieces with an adze. The upper surface will thus be formed. With a gauge opened to eight inches, and guided by the lines *c e*, scribe the upper edge of the board from *d b*, cut that edge perpendicular to the face of the board, and scribe it of the proper thickness. Then form the underside by the upper, by cutting transversely with the saw and taking out the piece with an adze. As the upper edge of the wing of the share rises a little, the fore end of the board, *b c*, will rise as much from a strict horizontal position, and will throw the hind end, *e d*, exactly as much beyond the perpendicular, so as to promote the reversing of the sod. The women here, as in Germany, do all sorts of work. While one considers them as useful and rational companions, one cannot forget that they are also objects of our pleasures; nor can they ever forget it. While employed in dirt and drudgery, some tag of a ribbon, some ring, or bit of bracelet, earbob or necklace, or something of that kind, will show that the desire of pleasing is never suspended in them. It is an honorable circumstance for man, that the first moment he is at his ease, he allots the internal employments to his female partner, and takes the external on himself. And this circumstance, or its reverse, is a pretty good indication that a people are, or are not at their ease. Among the Indians, this indication fails from a particular cause: every Indian man is a soldier or warrior, and the whole body of warriors constitute a standing army, always employed in war or hunting. To support that army, there remain no laborers but the women. Here, then, is so heavy a military establishment, that the civil part of the nation is reduced to women only. But this is a barbarous perversion of the natural destination of the two sexes. Women are formed by nature for attentions, not for hard labor. A woman never forgets one of the numerous train of little offices which belong to her. A man forgets often.

April 20th. *Nancy. Toule. Void. Ligny en Barrois. Bar le Duc. St. Dizier.* Nancy itself is a neat little town, and its environs very agreeable. The valley of the little branch of the Moselle, on which it is, is about a mile wide: the road then crossing the head-waters of the Moselle, the Maes, and the Marne, the country is very hilly, and perhaps a third of it poor and in forests of beech: the other two-thirds from poor up to middling, red, and stony. Almost entirely in corn, now and then only some vines on the hills. The Moselle at Toule is thirty or forty yards wide: the Maese near Void about half that: the Marne at St. Dizier about forty yards. They all make good plains of from a quarter of a mile to a mile wide. The hills of the Maese abound with chalk. The rocks coming down from the tops of the hills, on all the road of this day, at regular intervals like the ribs of an animal, have a very irregular appearance. Considerable flocks of sheep and asses, and, in the approach to St. Dizier, great plantations of apple and cherry trees; here and there a peach tree, all in general bloom. The roads through Lorraine are strung with beggars.

April 21st. *St. Dizier. Vitry le Français. Chalons sur Marne. Epernay.* The plains of the Marne and Sault uniting, appear boundless to the eye till we approach their confluence at Vitry, where the hills come in on the right; after that the plains are generally about a mile, mulatto, of middling quality, sometimes stony. Sometimes the ground goes off from the river so sloping, that one does not know whether to call it high or low land. The hills are mulatto also, but whitish, occasioned by the quantity of chalk which seems to constitute their universal base. They are poor, and principally in vines. The streams of water are of the color of milk, occasioned by the chalk also. No inclosures, some flocks of sheep; children gathering dung in the roads. Here and there a château; but none considerable.

April 22d. *Epernay.* The hills abound with chalk. Of this they make lime, not so strong as stone lime, and therefore to be used in greater proportion. They cut the blocks into regular forms also, like stone, and build houses of it. The common earth too, well impregnated with this, is made into mortar, moulded in the form of brick, dried in the sun, and houses built of them which last one hundred or two hundred years. The plains here are a mile wide, red, good, in corn, clover, Luzerne, St. Foin. The hills are in vines, and this being precisely the canton where the most celebrated wines of Champagne are made, details must be entered into. Remember, however, that they will always relate to the white wines, unless where the red are expressly mentioned. The reason is that their red wines, though much esteemed on the spot, are by no means esteemed elsewhere equally with their white; nor do they merit equal esteem.

A Topographical sketch of the position of the wine villages, the course of the hills, and consequently the aspect of the vine-yards.

Soil, meagre, mulatto clay, mixed with small broken stone, and a little hue of chalk. Very dry.

Aspect, may be better seen by the annexed diagram. The

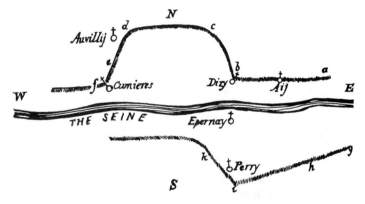

wine of Aij is made from *a* to *b*, those of Dizy from *b* to *c*, Auvillij *d* to *e*, Cumieres *e* to *f*, Epernay *g* to *h*, Perij *i* to *k*. The hills are generally about two hundred and fifty feet high. The good wine is made only in the middle region. The lower region, however, is better than the upper; because this last is exposed to cold winds, and a colder atmosphere.

Culture. The vines are planted two feet apart. Afterwards they are multiplied (provignés). When a stock puts out two shoots they lay them down, spread them open and cover them with earth, so as to have in the end about a plant for every square foot. For performing this operation they have a hook, of this shape, ⅂ and nine inches long, which, being stuck in the ground, holds down the main stock, while the laborer separates and covers the new shoot. They leave two buds above the ground. When the vine has shot up high enough, they stick it with split sticks of oak, from an inch to an inch and a half square, and four feet long, and tie the vine to its stick with straw. These sticks cost two florins the hundred, and will last forty years. An arpent, one year with another, in the fine vineyards, gives twelve pieces, and in the inferior vineyards twenty-five pieces, of two hundred bottles each. An arpent of the first quality sells for three thousand florins, and there have been instances of seven thousand two hundred florins. The arpent contains one hundred verges, of twenty-two pieds square. The arpent of inferior quality sells at one thousand florins. They plant the vines in a hole about a foot deep, and fill that hole with good mould, to make the plant take. Otherwise it would perish. Afterwards, if ever they put dung, it is very little. During wheat harvest there is a month or six weeks that nothing is done in the vineyard, that is to say, from the 1st of August to the beginning of vintage. The vintage commences early in September, and lasts a month. A day's work of a laborer in the busiest season is twenty sous, and he feeds himself: in the least busy season it is fifteen sous. Corn lands are rented from four florins to twenty-four; but vine lands are never rented. The three façons (or workings) of an arpent cost fifteen florins. The whole year's expense of an arpent is worth one hundred florins.

Grapes.—The bulk of their grapes are purple, which they prefer for making even white wine. They press them very lightly, without treading or permitting them to ferment at all, for about an hour; so that it is the beginning of the running only which makes the bright wine. What follows the beginning is of a straw color, and therefore not placed on a level with the first. The last part of the juice, produced by strong pressure, is red and ordinary. They choose the bunches with as much care, to make wine of the very first quality, as if to eat. Not above one-eighth of the whole grapes will do for this purpose. The white grape, though not so fine for wine as the red, when the red can be produced, and more liable to rot in a moist season, yet grows better if the soil be excessively poor, and therefore in such a soil is preferred, or rather, is used of necessity, because there the red would not grow at all.

Wine.—The white wines are either mousseux, sparkling, or non-mousseux, still. The sparkling are little drunk in France, but are almost alone known and drunk in foreign countries. This makes so great a demand, and so certain a one, that it is the dearest by about an eighth, and therefore they endeavor to make all sparkling if they can. This is done by bottling in the spring, from the beginning of March till June. If it succeeds, they lose abundance of bottles, from one-tenth to one-third. This is another cause increasing the price. To make the still wine, they bottle in September. This is only done when they know from some circumstance that the wine will not be sparkling. So if the spring bottling fails to make a sparkling wine, they decant it into other bottles in the fall, and it then makes the very best still wine. In this operation, it loses from one-tenth to one-twentieth by sediment. They let it stand in the bottles in this case forty-eight hours, with only a napkin spread over their mouths, but no cork. The best sparkling wine, decanted in this manner, makes the best still wine, and which will keep much longer than that originally made still by being bottled in September. The sparkling wines lose their briskness the older they are, but they gain in quality with age to a certain length. These wines are in perfection from two to ten years old, and will even be very good to fifteen. 1766 was the best year ever known. 1775 and 1776 next to that. 1783 is the last good year, and that not to be compared with those. These wines stand icing very well.

Aij. M. Dorsay makes one thousand and one hundred pieces, which sell, as soon as made, at three hundred florins, and in good years four hundred florins, in the cask. I paid in his cellar, to M. Louis, his homme d'affaires, for the remains of the year 1783, three florins ten sous the bottle. Sparkling Champagne, of the same degree of excellence, would have cost four florins, (the piece and demiqueue are the same; the feuillette is one hundred bottles.) M. le Duc makes four hundred to five hundred pieces. M. de Villermont, three hundred pieces. M. Janson, two hundred and fifty pieces. All of the first quality, red and white in equal quantities.

Auvillaij. The Benedictine monks make one thousand pieces, red and white, but three-fourths red, both of the first quality. The king's table is supplied by them. This enables them to sell at five hundred and fifty florins the piece. Though their white is hardly as good as Dorsay's, their red is the best. L'Abbatiale, belonging to the bishop of the place, makes one thousand to twelve hundred pieces, red and white, three-fourths red, at four hundred to five hundred and fifty florins, because neighbors to the monks.

Cumieres is all of the second quality, both red and white, at one hundred and fifty to two hundred florins the piece.

Epernay. Madame Jermont makes two hundred pieces at three hundred florins. M. Patelaine, one hundred and fifty pieces. M. Mare, two hundred pieces. M. Chertems, sixty pieces. M. Lauchay, fifty pieces. M. Cousin (Aubergiste de l'hôtel de Róhan à Epernay), one hundred pieces. M. Pierrot, one hundred pieces. Les Chanoines regulieres d'Epernay, two hundred pieces. Mesdames les Ursulines religieuses, one hundred pieces. M. Gilette, two hundred pieces. All of the first quality; red and white in equal quantities.

Pierrij. M. Casotte makes five hundred pieces. M. de la Motte, three hundred pieces. M. de Failli, three hundred pieces. I tasted his wine of 1779, one of the good years. It was fine, though not equal to that of M. Dorsay, of 1783. He sells it at two florins ten sous to merchants, and three florins to individuals. Les Seminaristes, one hundred and fifty pieces. M. Hoquart, two hundred pieces. All of the first quality; white and red in equal quantities.

At Cramont, also, there are some wines of the first quality made. At Avisi also, and Aucy, Le Meni, Mareuil, Verzis-Verzenni. This last place belongs to the Marquis de Sillery. The wines are carried to Sillery, and there stored, whence they are called Vins de Sillery, though not made at Sillery.

All these wines of Epernay and Pierrij sell almost as dear as

M. Dorsay's, their quality being nearly the same. There are many small proprietors who might make wine of the first quality, if they would cull their grapes, but they are too poor for this. Therefore, the proprietors before named, whose names are established, buy of the poorer ones the right to cull their vineyards, by which means they increase their quantity, as they find about one-third of the grapes will make wines of the first quality.

The lowest-priced wines of all are thirty florins the piece, red or white. They make brandy of the pumice. In very bad years, when their wines become vinegar, they are sold for six florins the piece, and made into brandy. They yield one-tenth brandy.

White Champagne is deemed good in proportion as it is silky and still. Many circumstances derange the scale of wines. The proprietor of the best vineyard, in the best year, having bad weather come upon him while he is gathering his grapes, makes a bad wine, while his neighbor, holding a more indifferent vineyard, which happens to be ingathering while the weather is good, makes a better. The M. de Casotte at Pierrij formerly was the first house. His successors, by some imperceptible change of culture, have degraded the quality of their wines. Their cellars are admirably made, being about six, eight or ten feet wide, vaulted, and extending into the ground, in a kind of labyrinth, to a prodigious distance, with an air-hole of two feet diameter every fifty feet. From the top of the vault to the surface of the earth, is from fifteen to thirty feet. I have nowhere seen cellars comparable to these. In packing their bottles, they lay on their side; then cross them at each end, they lay laths, and on these another row of bottles, heads and points; and so on. By this means, they can take out a bottle from the top, or where they will.

April 23d. *Epernay. Château Thieray. St. Jean. Meaux. Vergalant. Paris.* From Epernay to St. Jean the road leads over hills, which in the beginning are indifferent, but get better towards the last. The plains, wherever seen, are inconsiderable. After passing St. Jean, the hills become good, and the plains increase. The country about Vergalant is pretty. A skirt of a low ridge which runs in on the extensive plains of the

Marne and Seine, is very picturesque. The general bloom of fruit trees proves there are more of them than I had imagined from travelling in other seasons, when they are less distinguishable at a distance from the forest trees.

Travelling notes for Mr. Rutledge and Mr. Shippen

June 3, 1788

General Observations.—On arriving at a town, the first thing is to buy the plan of the town, and the book noting its curiosities. Walk round the ramparts when there are any, go to the top of a steeple to have a view of the town and its environs.

When you are doubting whether a thing is worth the trouble of going to see, recollect that you will never again be so near it, that you may repent the not having seen it, but can never repent having seen it. But there is an opposite extreme too, that is, the seeing too much. A judicious selection is to be aimed at, taking care that the indolence of the moment have no influence in the decision. Take care particularly not to let the porters of churches, cabinets, &c., lead you through all the little details of their profession, which will load the memory with trifles, fatigue the attention, and waste that and your time. It is difficult to confine these people to the few objects worth seeing and remembering. They wish for your money, and suppose you give it the more willingly the more they detail to you.

When one calls in the taverns for the *vin du pays*, they give what is natural and unadulterated and cheap: when *vin etrangere* is called for, it only gives a pretext for charging an extravagant price for an unwholsome stuff, very often of their own brewery. The people you will naturally see the most of will be tavern keepers, *valets de place*, and postilions. These are the hackneyed rascals of every country. Of course they must never be considered when we calculate the national character.

Objects of attention for an American.—1. Agriculture. Everything belonging to this art, and whatever has a near relation to it. Useful or agreeable animals which might be transported to America. Species of plants for the farmer's garden, according to the climate of the different States.

2. Mechanical arts, so far as they respect things necessary in America, and inconvenient to be transported thither readymade, such as forges, stone quarries, boats, bridges, (very especially,) &c., &c.

3. Lighter mechanical arts, and manufactures. Some of these will be worth a superficial view; but circumstances rendering it impossible that America should become a manufacturing country during the time of any man now living, it would be a waste of attention to examine these minutely.

4. Gardens, peculiarly worth the attention of an American, because it is the country of all others where the noblest gardens may be made without expense. We have only to cut out the superabundant plants.

5. Architecture worth great attention. As we double our numbers every twenty years, we must double our houses. Besides, we build of such perishable materials, that one half of our houses must be rebuilt in every space of twenty years, so that in that time, houses are to be built for three-fourths of our inhabitants. It is, then, among the most important arts; and it is desirable to introduce taste into an art which shows so much.

6. Painting. Statuary. Too expensive for the state of wealth among us. It would be useless, therefore, and preposterous, for us to make ourselves connoisseurs in those arts. They are worth seeing, but not studying.

7. Politics of each country, well worth studying so far as respects internal affairs. Examine their influence on the happiness of the people. Take every possible occasion for entering into the houses of the laborers, and especially at the moments of their repast; see what they eat, how they are clothed, whether they are obliged to work too hard; whether the government or their landlord takes from them an unjust proportion of their labor; on what footing stands the property they call their own, their personal liberty, &c., &c.

8. Courts. To be seen as you would see the tower of London or menagerie of Versailles, with their lions, tigers, hyenas, and other beast of prey, standing in the same relation to their fellows. A slight acquaintance with them will suffice to show you that, under the most imposing exterior, they are the weakest and worst part of mankind. Their manners, could you ape them, would not make you beloved in your own country, nor would they improve it could you introduce them there to the exclusion of that honest simplicity now prevailing in America, and worthy of being cherished.

The Anas. *1791–1806.*

SELECTIONS

Explanations of the 3. volumes bound in marbled paper

February 4, 1818

In these 3 vols will be found copies of the official opinions given in writing by me to Genl. Washington, while I was Secretary of State, with sometimes the documents belonging to the case. Some of these are the rough draughts, some press-copies, some fair ones. In the earlier part of my acting in that office I took no other note of the passing transactions: but, after awhile, I saw the importance of doing it, in aid of my memory. Very often therefore I made memorandums on loose scraps of paper, taken out of my pocket in the moment, and laid by to be copied fair at leisure, which however they hardly ever were. These scraps therefore, ragged, rubbed, & scribbled as they were, I had bound with the others by a binder who came into my cabinet, did it under my own eye, and without the opportunity of reading a single paper. At this day, after the lapse of 25 years, or more, from their dates, I have given to the whole a calm revisal, when the passions of the time are past away, and the reasons of the transactions act alone on the judgment. Some of the informations I had recorded are now cut out from the rest, because I have seen that they were incorrect, or doubtful, or merely personal or private, with which we have nothing to do. I should perhaps have thought the rest not worth preserving, but for their testimony against the only history of that period which pretends to have been compiled from authentic and unpublished documents. Could these documents, all, be laid open to the public eye, they might be compared, contrasted, weighed, & the truth fairly sifted out of them, for we are not to suppose that every thing found among Genl. Washington's papers is to be taken as gospel truth. Facts indeed of his own writing & inditing, must be believed by all who knew him; and opinions, which were his own, merit veneration and respect; for few men have lived whose opinions were more unbiassed and correct. Not that it is pretended he never felt bias. His passions were naturally strong; but his reason, generally, stronger. But the materials from his own pen make probably an almost insensible part of the mass of papers which fill his presses. He possessed the love, the veneration, and confidence of all. With him were deposited suspicions & certainties, rumors & realities, facts & falsehoods, by all those who were, or who wished to be thought, in correspondence with him, and by the many Anonymi who were ashamed to put their names to their slanders. From such a Congeries history may be made to wear any hue, with which the passions of the compiler, royalist or republican, may chuse to tinge it. Had Genl. Washington himself written from these materials a history of the period they embrace, it would have been a conspicuous monument of the integrity of his mind, the soundness of his judgment, and its powers of discernment between truth & falsehood; principles & pretensions. But the party feelings of his biographer, to whom after his death the collection was confided, has culled from it a composition as different from what Genl. Washington would have offered, as was the candor of the two characters during the period of the war. The partiality of this pen is displayed in lavishments of praise on certain military characters, who had done nothing military, but who afterwards, & before he wrote, had become heroes in party, altho' not in war; and in his reserve on the merits of others, who rendered signal services indeed, but did not earn his praise by apostatising in peace from the republican principles for which they had fought in war. It shews itself too in the cold indifference with which a struggle for the most animating of human objects is narrated. No act of heroism ever kindles in the mind of this writer a single aspiration in favor of the holy cause which inspired the bosom, & nerved the arm of the patriot warrior. No gloom of events, no lowering of prospects ever excites a fear for the issue of a contest which was to change the condition of man over the civilized globe. The sufferings inflicted on endeavors to vindicate the rights of humanity are related with all the frigid insensibility with which a monk would have contemplated the victims of an auto da fé. Let no man believe that Genl. Washington ever intended that his papers should be used for the suicide of the cause, for which he had lived, and for which there never was a moment in which he would not have died. The abuse of these materials is chiefly however manifested in the history of the period immediately following the establishment of the present constitution; and nearly with that my memorandums begin. Were a reader of this period to form his idea of it from this history alone, he would suppose the republican party (who were in truth endeavoring to keep the government within the line of the Constitution, and prevent it's being monarchised in practice) were a mere set of grumblers, and disorganisers, satisfied with no government, without fixed principles of any, and, like a British parliamentary opposition, gaping after loaves and fishes, and ready to change principles, as well as position, at any time, with their adversaries.

But a short review of facts omitted, or uncandidly stated in this history will shew that the contests of that day were contests of principle, between the advocates of republican, and those of kingly government, and that, had not the former made the efforts they did, our government would have been, even at this early day, a very different thing from what the successful issue of those efforts have made it.

The alliance between the states under the old articles of confederation, for the purpose of joint defence against the aggression of Great Britan, was found insufficient, as treaties of alliance generally are, to enforce compliance with their mutual stipulations: and these, once fulfilled, that bond was to expire of itself, & each state to become sovereign and independant in all things. Yet it could not but occur to every one that these separate independencies, like the petty States of Greece, would be eternally at war with each other, & would become at length the mere partisans & satellites of the leading powers of Europe. All then must have looked forward to some further bond of union, which would ensure internal peace, and a political system of our own, independant of that of Europe. Whether all should be consolidated into a single government, or each remain independant as to internal matters, and the whole form a single nation as to what was foreign only, and whether that national government should be a monarchy or republic, would of course divide opinions according to the constitutions, the habits, and the circumstances of each individual. Some officers of the army, as it has always been said and believed (and Steuben and Knox have even been named as the leading agents) trained to monarchy by military habits, are understood to have proposed to Genl. Washington to decide this great question by the army before it's disbandment, and to assume himself the crown, on the assurance of their support. The indignation with which he is said to have scouted this parricid proposition, was equally worthy of his virtue and his wisdom. The next effort was (on suggestion of the same individuals, in the moment of their separation) the establishment of an hereditary order, under the name of the Cincinnati, ready prepared, by that distinction, to be engrafted into the future frame of government, & placing Genl. Washington still at their head. The General* wrote to me on this subject, while I was in Congress at Annapolis, and an extract from my answer is inserted in 5. Marshall's hist. pa. 28. He afterwards called on me at that place, on his way to a meeting of the society, and after a whole evening of consultation he left that place fully determined to use all his endeavors for it's total suppression. But he found it so firmly riveted in the affections of the members that, strengthened as they happened to be by an adventitious occurrence of the moment, he could effect no more than the abolition of it's hereditary principle. He called again on his return, & explained to me fully the opposition which had been made, the effect of the occurrence from France, and the difficulty with which it's duration had been limited to the lives of the present members. Further details will be found among my papers, in his and my letters, and some in the *Encyclop. Method. Dictionnaire d'Econ. politique*, communicated by myself to M. Meusnier, it's author, who had made the establishment of this society the ground, in that work, of a libel on our country. The want of some authority, which should procure justice to the public creditors, and an observance of treaties with foreign nations, produced, some time after, the call of a convention of the States at Annapolis. Altho' at this meeting a difference of opinion was evident on the question of a republican or kingly government, yet, so general thro' the states, was the sentiment in favor of the former, that the friends of the latter confined themselves to a course of obstruction only, and delay, to every thing pro-

*See his lre., Apr. 8, 84.

posed. They hoped that, nothing being done, and all things going from bad to worse, a kingly government might be usurped, and submitted to by the people, as better than anarchy, & wars internal and external the certain consequences of the present want of a general government. The effect of their manœuvres, with the defective attendance of deputies from the states, resulted in the measure of calling a more general convention, to be held at Philadelphia. At this the same party exhibited the same practices, and with the same views of preventing a government of concord, which they foresaw would be republican, and of forcing, thro' anarchy, their way to monarchy. But the mass of that convention was too honest, too wise, and too steady to be baffled or misled by their manœuvres. One of these was, a form of government proposed by Colo. Hamilton, which would have been in fact a compromise between the two parties of royalism & republicanism. According to this, the Executive & one branch of the legislature were to be during good behavior, i. e. for life, and the Governors of the states were to be named by these two permanent organs. This however was rejected, on which Hamilton left the Convention, as desperate, & never returned again until near it's final conclusion. These opinions & efforts, secret or avowed, of the advocates for monarchy, had begotten great jealously thro' the states generally: and this jealousy it was which excited the strong oppositon to the conventional constitution; a jealousy which yielded at last only to a general determination to establish certain amendments as barriers against a government either monarchical or consolidated. In what passed thro' the whole period of these conventions, I have gone on the information of those who were members of them, being absent myself on my mission to France.

I returned from that mission in the 1st. year of the new government, having landed in Virginia in Dec. 89. & proceeded to N. York in March 90. to enter on the office of Secretary of State. Here certainly I found a state of things which, of all I had ever contemplated, I the least expected. I had left France in the first year of its revolution, in the fervor of natural rights, and zeal for reformation. My conscientious devotion to these rights could not be heightened, but it had been aroused and excited by daily exercise. The President received me cordially, and my Colleagues & the circle of principal citizens, apparently, with welcome. The courtesies of dinner parties given me as a stranger newly arrived among them, placed me at once in their familiar society. But I cannot describe the wonder and mortification with which the table conversations filled me. Politics were the chief topic, and a preference of kingly, over republican, government, was evidently the favorite sentiment. An apostate I could not be; nor yet a hypocrite: and I found myself, for the most part, the only advocate on the republican side of the question, unless, among the guests, there chanced to be some member of that party from the legislative Houses. Hamilton's financial system had then past. It had two objects. 1st as a puzzle, to exclude popular understanding & inquiry. 2dly, as a machine for the corruption of the legislature; for he avowed the opinion that man could be governed by one of two motives only, force or interest: force he observed, in this country, was out of the question; and the interests therefore of the members must be laid hold of, to keep the legislature in unison with the Executive. And with grief and shame it must be acknoleged that his machine was not without effect. That even in this, the birth of our government, some members were found sordid enough to bend their duty to their interests, and to look after personal, rather than public good. It is well known that, during the war, the greatest difficulty we encountered was the want of money or means, to pay our souldiers who fought, or our farmers, manufacturers & merchants who furnished the necessary supplies of food & clothing for them. After the expedient of paper money had exhausted itself, certificates of debt were given to the individual creditors, with assurance of payment, so soon as the U. S. should be able. But the distresses of these people often obliged them to part with these for the half, the fifth, and even a tenth of their value; and Speculators had made a trade of cozening them from the holders, by the most fraudulent practices and persuasions that they would never be paid. In the bill for funding & paying these, Hamilton made no difference between the original holders, & the fraudulent purchasers of this paper. Great & just repugnance arose at putting these two classes of creditors on the same footing, and great exertions were used to pay to the former the full value, and to the latter the price only which he had paid, with interest. But this would have prevented the game which was to be played, & for which the minds of greedy members were already tutored and prepared. When the trial of strength on these several efforts had indicated the form in which the bill would finally pass, this being known within doors sooner than without, and especially than to those who were in distant parts of the Union, the base scramble began. Couriers & relay horses by land, and swift sailing pilot boats by sea, were flying in all directions. Active part[n]ers & agents were associated & employed in every state, town and country neighborhood, and this paper was bought up at 5/ and even as low as 2/ in the pound, before the holder knew that Congress had already provided for it's redemption at par. Immense sums were thus filched from the poor & ignorant, and fortunes accumulated by those who had themselves been poor enough before. Men thus enriched by the dexterity of a leader, would follow of course the chief who was leading them to fortune, and become the zealous instruments of all his enterprises. This game was over, and another was on the carpet at the moment of my arrival; and to this I was most ignorantly & innocently made to hold the candle. This fiscal maneuvre is well known by the name of the Assumption. Independantly of the debts of Congress, the states had, during the war, contracted separate and heavy debts; and Massachusetts particularly in an absurd attempt, absurdly conducted, on the British post of Penobscot: and the more debt Hamilton could rake up, the more plunder for his mercenaries. This money, whether wisely or foolishly spent, was pretended to have been spent for general purposes, and ought therefore to be paid from the general purse. But it was objected that nobody knew what these debts were, what their amount, or what their proofs. No matter; we will guess them to be 20. millions. But of these 20. millions we do not know how much should be reimbursed to one state, nor how much to another. No matter; we will guess. And so another scramble was set on foot among the several states, and some got much, some little, some nothing. But the main object was obtained, the phalanx of the treasury was rein-

forced by additional recruits. This measure produced the most
bitter & angry contests ever known in Congress, before or
since the union of the states. I arrived in the midst of it. But
a stranger to the ground, a stranger to the actors on it, so
long absent as to have lost all familiarity with the subject, and
as yet unaware of it's object, I took no concern in it. The
great and trying question however was lost in the H. of Representatives. So high were the feuds excited by this subject,
that on it's rejection, business was suspended. Congress met
and adjourned from day to day without doing any thing, the
parties being too much out of temper to do business together. The Eastern members particularly, who, with Smith
from South Carolina, were the principal gamblers in these
scenes, threatened a secession and dissolution. Hamilton was
in despair. As I was going to the President's one day, I met
him in the street. He walked me backwards & forwards before the President's door for half an hour. He painted pathet-
ically the temper into which the legislature had been wrought,
the disgust of those who were called the Creditor states, the
danger of the secession of their members, and the separation
of the states. He observed that the members of the administration ought to act in concert, that tho' this question was
not of my department, yet a common duty should make it a
common concern; that the President was the center on which
all administrative questions ultimately rested, and that all of
us should rally around him, and support with joint efforts
measures approved by him; and that the question having
been lost by a small majority only, it was probable that an
appeal from me to the judgment and discretion of some of
my friends might effect a change in the vote, and the machine
of government, now suspended, might be again set into motion. I told him that I was really a stranger to the whole subject; not having yet informed myself of the system of finances
adopted, I knew not how far this was a necessary sequence;
that undoubtedly if it's rejection endangered a dissolution of
our union at this incipient stage, I should deem that the most
unfortunate of all consequences, to avert which all partial and
temporary evils should be yielded. I proposed to him however
to dine with me the next day, and I would invite another
friend or two, bring them into conference together, and I

thought it impossible that reasonable men, consulting together coolly, could fail, by some mutual sacrifices of opinion, to form a compromise which was to save the union. The discussion took place. I could take no part in it, but an exhortatory one, because I was a stranger to the circumstances which should govern it. But it was finally agreed that, whatever importance had been attached to the rejection of this proposition, the preservation of the union, & and of concord among the states was more important, and that therefore it would be better that the vote of rejection should be rescinded, to effect which some members should change their votes. But it was observed that this pill would be peculiarly bitter to the Southern States, and that some concomitant measure should be adopted to sweeten it a little to them. There had before been propositions to fix the seat of government either at Philadelphia, or at Georgetown on the Potomac; and it was thought that by giving it to Philadelphia for ten years, and to Georgetown permanently afterwards, this might, as an anodyne, calm in some degree the ferment which might be excited by the other measure alone. So two of the Potomac members (White & Lee, but White with a revulsion of stomach almost convulsive) agreed to change their votes, & Hamilton undertook to carry the other point. In doing this the influence he had established over the Eastern members, with the agency of Robert Morris with those of the middle states, effected his side of the engagement, and so the assumption was passed, and 20. millions of stock divided among favored states, and thrown in as pabulum to the stock-jobbing herd. This added to the number of votaries to the treasury and made its Chief the master of every vote in the legislature which might give to the government the direction suited to his political views. I know well, and so must be understood, that nothing like a majority in Congress had yielded to this corruption. Far from it. But a division, not very unequal, had already taken place in the honest part of that body, between the parties styled republican and federal. The latter being monarchists in principle, adhered to Hamilton of course, as their leader in that principle, and this mercenary phalanx added to them ensured him always a majority in both houses: so that the whole action of the legislature was now under the direction of the treasury. Still the machine was not compleat. The effect of the funding system, & of the assumption, would be temporary. It would be lost with the loss of the individual members whom it had enriched, and some engine of influence more permanent must be contrived, while these myrmidons were yet in place to carry it thro' all opposition. This engine was the Bank of the U.S. All that history is known; so I shall say nothing about it. While the government remained at Philadelphia, a selection of members of both houses were constantly kept as Directors, who, on every question interesting to that institution, or to the views of the federal head, voted at the will of that head; and, together with the stockholding members, could always make the federal vote that of the majority. By this combination, legislative expositions were given to the constitution, and all the administrative laws were shaped on the model of England, & so passed. And from this influence we were not relieved until the removal from the precincts of the bank, to Washington. Here then was the real ground of the opposition which was made to the course of administration. It's object was to preserve the legislature pure and independant of the Executive, to restrain the administration to republican forms and principles, and not permit the constitution to be construed into a monarchy, and to be warped in practice into all the principles and pollutions of their favorite English model. Nor was this an opposition to Genl. Washington. He was true to the republican charge confided to him; & has solemnly and repeatedly protested to me, in our private conversations, that he would lose the last drop of his blood in support of it, and he did this the oftener, and with the more earnestness, because he knew my suspicions of Hamilton's designs against it; & wished to quiet them. For he was not aware of the drift, or of the effect of Hamilton's schemes. Unversed in financial projects & calculations, & budgets, his approbation of them was bottomed on his confidence in the man. But Hamilton was not only a monarchist, but for a monarchy bottomed on corruption. In proof of this I will relate an anecdote, for the truth of which I attest the God who made me. Before the President set out on his Southern tour in April 1791. he addressed a letter of the 4th. of that month, from Mt. Vernon to the Secretaries of State,

Treasury & War, desiring that, if any serious and important cases should arise during his absence, they would consult & act on them, and he requested that the Vice-president should also be consulted. This was the only occasion on which that officer was ever requested to take part in a Cabinet question. Some occasion for consultation arising, I invited those gentlemen (and the Attorney genl. as well as I remember) to dine with me in order to confer on the subject. After the cloth was removed, and our question agreed & dismissed, conversation began on other matters and, by some circumstance, was led to the British constitution, on which Mr. Adams observed "purge that constitution of it's corruption, and give to it's popular branch equality of representation, and it would be the most perfect constitution ever devised by the wit of man." Hamilton paused and said, "purge it of it's corruption, and give to it's popular branch equality of representation, & it would become an *impracticable* government: as it stands at present, with all it's supposed defects, it is the most perfect government which ever existed." And this was assuredly the exact line which separated the political creeds of these two gentlemen. The one was for two hereditary branches and an honest elective one: the other for a hereditary king with a house of lords & commons, corrupted to his will, and standing between him and the people. Hamilton was indeed a singular character. Of acute understanding, disinterested, honest, and honorable in all private transactions, amiable in society, and duly valuing virtue in private life, yet so bewitched & perverted by the British example, as to be under thoro' conviction that corruption was essential to the government of a nation. Mr. Adams had originally been a republican. The glare of royalty and nobility, during his mission to England, had made him believe their fascination a necessary ingredient in government, and Shay's rebellion, not sufficiently understood where he then was, seemed to prove that the absence of want and oppression was not a sufficient guarantee of order. His book on the American constitutions having made known his political bias, he was taken up by the monarchical federalists, in his absence, and on his return to the U.S. he was by them made to believe that the general disposition of our citizens was favorable to monarchy. He here wrote his

Davila, as a supplement to the former work, and his election to the Presidency confirmed his errors. Innumerable addresses too, artfully and industriously poured in upon him, deceived him into a confidence that he was on the pinnacle of popularity, when the gulph was yawning at his feet which was to swallow up him and his deceivers. For, when Genl. Washington was withdrawn, these energumeni of royalism, kept in check hitherto by the dread of his honesty, his firmness, his patriotism, and the authority of his name now, mounted on the Car of State & free from controul, like Phäeton on that of the sun, drove headlong & wild, looking neither to right nor left, nor regarding anything but the objects they were driving at; until, displaying these fully, the eyes of the nation were opened, and a general disbandment of them from the public councils took place. Mr. Adams, I am sure, has been long since convinced of the treacheries with which he was surrounded during his administration. He has since thoroughly seen that his constituents were devoted to republican government, and whether his judgment is re-settled on it's ancient basis, or not, he is conformed as a good citizen to the will of the majority, and would now, I am persuaded, maintain it's republican structure with the zeal and fidelity belonging to his character. For even an enemy has said "he is always an honest man, & often a great one." But in the fervor of the fury and follies of those who made him their stalking horse, no man who did not witness it, can form an idea of their unbridled madness, and the terrorism with which they surrounded themselves. The horrors of the French revolution, then raging, aided them mainly, and using that as a raw head and bloody bones they were enabled by their stratagems of X. Y. Z. in which this historian was a leading mountebank, their tales of tub-plots, Ocean massacres, bloody buoys, and pulpit lyings, and slanderings, and maniacal ravings of their Gardiners, their Osgoods and Parishes, to spread alarm into all but the firmest breasts. Their Attorney General had the impudence to say to a republican member that deportation must be resorted to, of which, said he, "you republicans have set the example," thus daring to identify us with the murderous Jacobins of France. These transactions, now recollected but as dreams of the night, were then sad realities; and nothing rescued us from their liberticide effect but the unyielding opposition of those firm spirits who sternly maintained their post, in defiance of terror, until their fellow citizens could be aroused to their own danger, and rally, and rescue the standard of the constitution. This has been happily done. Federalism & monarchism have languished from that moment, until their treasonable combinations with the enemies of their country during the late war, their plots of dismembering the Union & their Hartford convention, has consigned them to the tomb of the dead: and I fondly hope we may now truly say " we are all republicans, all federalists," and that the motto of the standard to which our country will forever rally, will be "federal union, and republican government;" and sure I am we may say that we are indebted, for the preservation of this point of ralliance, to that opposition of which so injurious an idea is so artfully insinuated & excited in this history.

Much of this relation is notorious to the world, & many intimate proofs of it will be found in these notes. From the moment, where they end, of my retiring from the administration, the federalists got unchecked hold of Genl. Washington. His memory was already sensibly impaired by age, the firm tone of mind for which he had been remarkable, was beginning to relax, it's energy was abated; a listlessness of labor, a desire for tranquillity had crept on him, and a willingness to let others act and even think for him. Like the rest of mankind, he was disgusted with atrocities of the French revolution, and was not sufficiently aware of the difference between the rabble who were used as instruments of their perpetration, and the steady & rational character of the American people, in which he had not sufficient confidence. The opposition too of the republicans to the British treaty, and zealous support of the federalists in that unpopular, but favorite measure of theirs, had made him all their own. Understanding moreover that I disapproved of that treaty, & copiously nourished with falsehoods by a malignant neighbor of mine, who ambitioned to be his correspondent, he had become alienated from myself personally, as from the republican body generally of his fellow citizens; & he wrote the letters to Mr. Adams, and Mr. Carroll, over which, in devotion to his imperishable fame, we must forever weep as monuments of mortal decay.

Conversations with the President

1792. Feb. 28. I was to have been with him long enough before 3. o clock (which was the hour & day he received visits) to have opened to him a proposition for doubling the velocity of the post riders, who now travel about 50. miles a day, & might without difficulty go 100. and for taking measures (by way-bills) to know where the delay is, when there is any. I was delayed by business, so as to have scarcely time to give him the outlines. I ran over them rapidly, & observed afterwards that I had hitherto never spoke to him on the subject of the post office, not knowing whether it was considered as a revenue law, or a law for the general accommodation of the citizens; that the law just passed seemed to have removed the doubt, by declaring that the whole profits of the office should be applied to extending the posts & that even the past profits should be refunded by the treasury for the same purpose: that I therefore conceived it was now in the department of the Secretary of State: that I thought it would be advantageous so to declare it for another reason, to wit, that the department of treasury possessed already such an influence as to swallow up the whole Executive powers, and that even the future Presidents (not supported by the weight of character which himself possessed) would not be able to make head against this department. That in urging this measure I had certainly no personal interest, since, if I was supposed to have any appetite for power, yet as my career would certainly be exactly as short as his own, the intervening time was too short to be an object. My real wish was to avail the public of every occasion during the residue of the President's period, to place things on a safe footing.—He was now called on to attend his company, & he desired me to come and breakfast with him the next morning.

Feb. 29. I did so, & after breakfast we retired to his room, & I unfolded my plan for the post-office, and after such an approbation of it as he usually permitted himself on the first presentment of any idea, and desiring me to commit it to writing, he, during that pause of conversation which follows a business closed, said in an affectionate tone, that he had felt much concern at an expression which dropt from me yesterday, & which marked my intention of retiring when he should. That as to himself, many motives obliged him to it. He had through the whole course of the war, and most particularly at the close of it uniformly declared his resolution to retire from public affairs, & never to act in any public office; that he had retired under that firm resolution, that the government however which had been formed being found evidently too inefficacious, and it being supposed that his aid was of some consequence towards bringing the people to consent to one of sufficient efficacy for their own good, he consented to come into the convention, & on the same motive, after much pressing, to take a part in the new government and get it under way. That were he to continue longer, it might give room to say, that having tasted the sweets of office he could not do without them: that he really felt himself growing old, his bodily health less firm, his memory, always bad, becoming worse, and perhaps the other faculties of his mind showing a decay to others of which he was insensible himself, that this apprehension particularly oppressed him, that he found morever his activity lessened, business therefore more irksome, and tranquility & retirement become an irresistible passion. That however he felt himself obliged for these reasons to retire from the government, yet he should consider it as unfortunate if that should bring on the retirement of the great officers of the government, and that this might produce a shock on the public mind of dangerous consequence. I told him that no man had ever had less desire of entering into public offices than myself; that the circumstance of a perilous war, which brought every thing into danger, & called for all the services which every citizen could render, had induced me to undertake the administration of the government of Virginia, that I had both before & after refused repeated appointments of Congress to go abroad in that sort of office, which if I had consulted my own gratification, would always have been the most agreeable to me, that at the end of two years, I resigned the government of Virginia, & retired with a firm resolution never more to appear in public life, that a domestic loss however happened, and made me fancy that absence, & a change of scene for a time might be expedient for me, that I therefore accepted a foreign appointment limited to two years, that at the close of that, Dr. Franklin having left France, I was appointed to supply his place, which I had accepted, & tho' I continued in it three or four years, it was under the constant idea of remaining only a year or two longer; that the revolution in France coming on, I had so interested myself in the event of that, that when obliged to bring my family home, I had still an idea of returning & awaiting the close of that, to fix the æra of my final retirement; that on my arrival here I found he had appointed me to my present office, that he knew I had not come into it without some reluctance, that it was on my part a sacrifice of inclination to the opinion that I might be more serviceable here than in France, & with a firm resolution in my mind to indulge my constant wish for retirement at no very distant day: that when therefore I received his letter written from Mount Vernon, on his way to Carolina & Georgia, (Apr. 1. 1791) and discovered from an expression in that that he meant to retire from the government ere long, & as to the precise epoch there could be no doubt, my mind was immediately made up to make that the epoch of my own retirement from those labors, of which I was heartily tired. That however I did not believe there was any idea in either of my brethren in the administration of retiring, that on the contrary I had perceived at a late meeting of the trustees of the sinking fund that the Secretary of the Treasury had developed the plan he intended to pursue, & that it embraced years in it's view.— He said that he considered the Treasury department as a much more limited one going only to the single object of revenue, while that of the Secretary of State embracing nearly all the objects of administration, was much more important, & the retirement of the officer therefore would be more noticed: that tho' the government had set out with a pretty general good will of the public, yet that symptoms of dissatisfaction had lately shewn themselves far beyond what he could have expected, and to what height these might arise in case of too great a change in the administration, could not be foreseen.—

I told him that in my opinion there was only a single source of these discontents. Tho' they had indeed appeared to spread themselves over the war department also, yet I considered that as an overflowing only from their real channel which would never have taken place if they had not first been generated in another department, to wit that of the treasury. That a system had there been contrived, for deluging the states with paper money instead of gold & silver, for withdrawing our citizens from the pursuits of commerce, manufactures, buildings, & other branches of useful industry, to occupy themselves & their capitals in a species of gambling, destructive of morality, & which had introduced it's poison into the government itself. That it was a fact, as certainly known as that he & I were then conversing, that particular members of the legislature, while those laws were on the carpet, had feathered their nests with paper, had then voted for the laws, and constantly since lent all the energy of their talents, & instrumentality of their offices to the establishment & enlargement of this system: that they had chained it about our necks for a great length of time, & in order to keep the game in their hands had from time to time aided in making such legislative constructions of the constitution as made it a very different thing from what the people thought they had submitted to; that they had now brought forward a proposition, far beyond every one ever yet advanced, & to which the eyes of many were turned as the decision which was to let us know whether we live under a limited or an unlimited government.—He asked me to what proposition I alluded? I answered to that in the Report on manufactures which, under colour of giving *bounties* for the encouragement of particular manufactures, meant to establish the doctrine that the power given by the Constitution to collect taxes to provide for the *general welfare* of the U.S., permitted Congress to take everything under their management which *they* should deem for the *public welfare*, & which is susceptible of the application of money: consequently that the subsequent enumeration of their powers was not the description to which resort must be had, & did not at all constitute the limits of their authority: that this was a very different question from that of the bank, which was thought an incident to an enumerated power: that therefore this decision was expected with great anxiety: that indeed I hoped the proposition would be rejected, believing there was a majority in both houses against it, and that if it should be, it would be considered as a proof that things were returning into their true channel; & that at any rate I looked forward to the broad representation which would shortly take place for keeping the general constitution on it's true ground, & that this would remove a great deal of the discontent which had shewn itself. The conversation ended with this last topic. It is here stated nearly as much at length as it really was, the expressions preserved where I could recollect them, and their substance always faithfully stated.

July 10. 1792. My lre of —— to the President, directed to him at Mt Vernon, had not found him there, but came to him here. He told me of this & that he would take an occasion of speaking with me on the subject. He did so this day. He began by observing that he had put it off from day to day because the subject was painful, to wit his remaining in office which that letter sollicited. He said that the decln he had made when he quitted his military command of never again acting in public was sincere. That however when he was called on to come forward to set the present govmt in motion, it appeared to him that circumstances were so changed as to justify a change in his resoln: he was made to believe that in 2 years all would be well in motion & he might retire. At the end of two years he found some things still to be done. At the end of the 3d year he thought it was not worth while to disturb the course of things as in one year more his office would expire & he was decided then to retire. Now he was told there would still be danger in it. Certainly if he thought so, he would conquer his longing for retirement. But he feared it would be said his former professions of retirement had been mere affectation, & that he was like other men, when once in office he could not quit it. He was sensible too of a decay of his hearing perhaps his other faculties might fall off & he not be sensible of it. That with respect to the existing causes of uneasiness, he thought there were suspicions against a particular party which had been carried a great deal too far, there might be *desires*, but he did not believe there were *designs* to change the form of govmt into a monarchy. That there might be a few who wished it in the higher walks of life, particularly in the great cities but that the main body of the people in the Eastern states were as steadily for republicanism as in the Southern. That the pieces lately published, & particularly in Freneau's paper seemed to have in view the exciting opposition to the govmt. That this had taken place in Pennsylve as to the excise law, accdg to informn he had recd from Genl Hand that they tended to produce a separation of the Union, the most dreadful of all calamities, and that whatever tended to produce anarchy, tended of course to produce a resort to monarchical government. He considered those papers as attacking him directly, for he must be a fool indeed to swallow the little sugar plumbs here & there thrown out to him. That in condemning the admn of the govmt they condemned him, for if they thought there were measures pursued contrary to his sentiment, they must conceive him too careless to attend to them or too stupid to understand them. That tho indeed he had signed many acts which he did not approve in all their parts, yet he had never put his name to one which he did not think on the whole was eligible. That as to the bank which had been an act of so much complaint, until there was some infallible criterion of reason, a difference of opinion must be tolerated. He did not believe the discontents extended far from the seat of govmt. He had seen & spoken with many people in Maryld & Virginia in his late journey. He found the people contented & happy. He wished however to be better informed on this head. If the discontent were more extensive than he supposed, it might be that the desire that he should remain in the government was not general.

My observns to him tended principally to enforce the topics of my lre. I will not therefore repeat them except where they produced observns from him. I said that the two great complaints were that the national debt was unnecessarily increased, & that it had furnished the means of corrupting both branches of the legislature. That he must know & everybody knew there was a considerable squadron in both whose votes were devoted to the paper & stock-jobbing interest, that the names of a weighty number were known & several others suspected on good grounds. That on examining the votes of these men they would be found uniformly for every treasury measure, & that as most of these measures had been carried by small majorities they were carried by these very votes. That therefore it was a cause of just uneasiness when we saw a legislature legislating for their own interests in opposition to those of the people. He said not a word on the corruption of the legislature, but took up the other point, defended the assumption, & argued that it had not increased the debt, for that all of it was honest debt. He justified the excise law, as one of the best laws which could be past, as nobody would pay the tax who did not chuse to do it. With respect to the increase of the debt by the assumption I observed to him that what was meant & objected to was that it increased the debt of the general govmt and carried it beyond the possibility of paiment. That if the balances had been settled & the debtor states directed to pay their deficiencies to the creditor states, they would have done it easily, and by resources of taxation in their power, and acceptable to the people, by a direct tax in the South, & an excise in the North. Still he said it would be paid by the people. Finding him really approving the treasury system I avoided entering into argument with him on those points.

Bladensbg. Oct. 1. This morning at Mt Vernon I had the following conversation with the President. He opened it by expressing his regret at the resolution in which I appeared so fixed in the lre I had written him of retiring from public affairs. He said that he should be extremely sorry that I should do it as long as he was in office, and that he could not see where he should find another character to fill my office. That as yet he was quite undecided whether to retire in March or not. His inclinations led him strongly to do it. Nobody disliked more the ceremonies of his office, and he had not the least taste or gratification in the execution of it's functions. That he was happy at home alone, and that his presence there was now peculiarly called for by the situation of Majr Washington whom he thought irrecoverable & should he get well he would remove into another part of the country which might better agree with him. That he did not believe his presence necessary: that there were other characters who would do the business as well or better. Still however if his aid was thought necessary to save the cause to which he had devoted his life principally he would make the sacrifice of a longer continuance. That he therefore reserved himself for future decision, as his declaration would be in time if made a month before the day of election. He had desired Mr. Lear to find out from conversation, without appearing to make the inquiry, whether any other person would be desired by any body. He had informed him he judged from conversations that it was the universal desire he should continue, & the expectation that those who expressed a doubt of his continuance did it in the language of apprehension, and not of desire. But this, says he, is only from the north, it may be very different in the South. I thought this meant as an opening to me to say what was the sentiment in the South from which quarter I came. I told him that as far as I knew there was but one voice there which was for his continuance. That as to myself I had ever preferred the pursuits of private life to those of public, which had nothing in them agreeable to me. I explained to him the circumstances of the war which had first called me into public life, and those following the war which had called me from a retirement on which I had determd. That I had constantly kept my eye on my own home, and could no longer refrain from returning to it. As to himself his presence was important, that he was the only man in the U.S. who possessed the confidce of the whole, that govmt was founded in opinion & confidence, and that the longer he remained, the stronger would become the habits of the people in submitting to the govmt. & in thinking it a thing to be maintained. That there was no other person who would be thought anything more than the head of a party. He then expressed his concern at the difference which he found to subsist between the Sec. of the Treasury & myself, of which he said he had not been aware. He knew indeed that there was a marked difference in our political sentiments, but he had never suspected it had gone so far in producing a personal difference, and he wished he could be the mediator to put an end to it. That he thought it important to preserve the check of my opinions in the administration in order to keep things in their proper channel & prevent them from going too far. That as to the idea of transforming this govt into a monarchy he did not believe there were ten men in the U.S. whose opinions were worth attention who entertained such a thought. I told him there were many more than he imagined.

I recalled to his memory a dispute at his own table a little
before we left Philada, between Genl. Schuyler on one side &
Pinkney & myself on the other, wherein the former maintained the position that hereditary descent was as likely to
produce good magistrates as election. I told him that tho' the
people were sound, there were a numerous sect who had
monarchy in contempln. That the Secy of the Treasury was
one of these. That I had heard him say that this constitution
was a shilly shally thing of mere milk & water, which could
not last, & was only good as a step to something better. That
when we reflected that he had endeavored in the convention
to make an English constn of it, and when failing in that we
saw all his measures tending to bring it to the same thing it
was natural for us to be jealous: and particular when we saw
that these measures had established corruption in the legislature, where there was a squadron devoted to the nod of the
treasury, doing whatever he had directed & ready to do what
he should direct. That if the equilibrium of the three great
bodies Legislative, Executive, & judiciary could be preserved,
if the Legislature could be kept independant, I should never
fear the result of such a government but that I could not but
be uneasy when I saw that the Executive had swallowed up
the legislative branch. He said that as to that interested spirit
in the legislature, it was what could not be avoided in any
government, unless we were to exclude particular descriptions
of men, such as the holders of the funds from all office. I told
him there was great difference between the little accidental
schemes of self interest which would take place in every body
of men & influence their votes, and a regular system for forming a corps of interested persons who should be steadily at
the orders of the Treasury. He touched on the merits of the
funding system, observed that there was a difference of opinion about it some thinking it very bad, others very good.
That experience was the only criterion of right which he knew
& this alone would decide which opn was right. That for
himself he had seen our affairs desperate & our credit lost,
and that this was in a sudden & extraordinary degree raised
to the highest pitch. I told him all that was ever necessary to
establish our credit, was an efficient govmt & an honest one
declaring it would sacredly pay our debts, laying taxes for this

purpose & applying them to it. I avoided going further into the subject. He finished by another exhortation to me not to decide too positively on retirement, & here we were called to breakfast.

Feb. 7. 1793. I waited on the President with letters & papers from Lisbon. After going through these I told him that I had for some time suspended speaking with him on the subject of my going out of office because I had understood that the bill for intercourse with foreign nations was likely to be rejected by the Senate in which case the remaining business of the department would be too inconsiderable to make it worth while to keep it up. But that the bill being now passed I was freed from the considerations of propriety which had embarrassed me. That &c. (nearly in the words of a letter to Mr. T. M. Randolph of a few days ago) and that I should be willing, if he had taken no arrangemts. to the contrary to continue somewhat longer, how long I could not say, perhaps till summer, perhaps autumn. He said so far from taking arrangements on the subject, he had never mentioned to any mortal the design of retiring which I had expressed to him, till yesterday having heard that I had given up my house & that it was rented by another, thereupon he mentd. it to Mr. E. Randolph & asked him, as he knew my retirement had been talked of, whether he had heard any persons suggested in conversations to succeed me. He expressed his satisfn at my change of purpose, & his apprehensions that my retirement would be a new source of uneasiness to the public. He said Govr. Lee had that day informed of the genl. discontent prevailing in Virga of which he never had had any conception, much less sound informn: That it appeared to him very alarming. He proceeded to express his earnest wish that Hamilton & myself could coalesce in the measures of the govmt, and urged here the general reasons for it which he had done to me on two former conversns. He said he had proposed the same thing to Ham. who expresd his readiness, and he thought our coalition would secure the general acquiescence of the public. I told him my concurrence was of much less importce than he seemed to imagine; that I kept myself aloof from all cabal & correspondence on the subject of the govmt & saw & spoke with as few as I could. That as to a coalition with Mr. Hamilton, if by that was meant that either was to sacrifice his general system to the other, it was impossible. We had both no doubt formed our conclusions after the most mature consideration and principles conscientiously adopted could not be given up on either side. My wish was to see both houses of Congr. cleansed of all persons interested in the bank or public stocks; & that a pure legislature being given us, I should always be ready to acquiesce under their determns even if contrary to my own opns, for that I subscribe to the principle that the will of the majority honestly expressed should give law. I confirmed him in the fact of the great discontents to the South, that they were grounded on seeing that their judgmts & interests were sacrificed to those of the Eastern states on every occn. & their belief that it was the effect of a corrupt squadron of voters in Congress at the command of the Treasury, & they see that if the votes of those members who had an interest distinct from & contrary to the general interest of their constts had been withdrawn, as in decency & honesty they should have been, the laws would have been the reverse of what they are in all the great questions. I instanced the new assumption carried in the H. of Repr. by the Speaker's votes. On this subject he made no reply. He explained his remaing. in office to have been the effect of strong solicitations after he returned here declaring that he had never mentd. his purpose of going out but to the heads of depnts & Mr. Madison; he expressed the extreme wretchedness of his existence while in office, and went lengthily into the late attacks on him for levees &c—and explained to me how he had been led into them by the persons he consulted at New York, and that if he could but know what the sense of the public was, he would most cheerfully conform to it.

Aug 6. 1793. The President calls on me at my house in the country, and introduces my letter of July 31. announcing that I should resign at the close of the next month. He again expressed his repentance at not having resigned himself, and how much it was increased by seeing that he was to be deserted by those on whose aid he had counted: that he did not know where he should look to find characters to fill up the offices, that mere talents did not suffice for the departmt of state, but it required a person conversant in foreign affairs, perhaps acquainted with foreign courts, that without this the best talents would be awkward & at a loss. He told me that Colo. Hamilton had 3. or 4. weeks ago written to him, informg him that private as well as public reasons had brought him to the determination to retire, & that he should do it towards the close of the next session. He said he had often before intimated dispositions to resign, but never as decisively before: that he supposed he had fixed on the latter part of next session to give an opportunity to Congress to examine into his conduct; that our going out at times so different increased his difficulty, for if he had both places to fill at one he might consult both the particular talents & geographical situation of our successors. He expressed great apprehensions at the fermentation which seemed to be working in the mind of the public, that many descriptions of persons, actuated by different causes appeared to be uniting, what it would end in he knew not, a new Congress was to assemble, more numerous, perhaps of a different spirit; the first expressions of their sentiments would be important: if I would only stay to the end of that it would relieve him considerably.

I expressed to him my excessive repugnance to public life, the particular uneasiness of my situation in this place where the laws of society oblige me always to move exactly in the circle which I know to bear me peculiar hatred, that is to say the wealthy aristocrats, the merchants connected closely with England, the new created paper fortunes; that thus surrounded, my words were caught, multiplied, misconstrued, & even fabricated & spread abroad to my injury, that he saw also that there was such an opposition of views between myself & another part of the admn as to render it peculiarly unpleasing, and to destroy the necessary harmony. Without knowg the views of what is called the Republican party here, or havg any communication with them, I could undertake to assure him from my intimacy with that party in the late Congress, that there was not a view in the Republican party as spread over the U S. which went to the frame of the government, that I believed the next Congress would attempt nothing material but to render their own body independant, that that party were firm in their dispositions to support the government: that the manœuvres of Mr. Genet might produce some little embarrassment, but that he would be abandoned by the Republicans the moment they knew the nature of his conduct, and on the whole no crisis existed which threatened anything.

He said he believed the views of the Republican party were perfectly pure, but when men put a machine into motion it is impossible for them to stop it exactly where they would chuse or to say where it will stop. That the constn we have is an excellent one if we can keep it where it is, that it was indeed supposed there was a party disposed to change it into a monarchical form, but that he could conscientiously declare there was not a man in the U S. who would set his face more decidedly against it than himself. Here I interrupted him by saying "no rational man in the U S. suspects you of any other disposn, but there does not pass a week in which we cannot prove declns dropping from the monarchical party that our governmt is good for nothing, it is a milk & water thing which cannot support itself, we must knock it down & set up something of more energy."—He said if that was the case he thought it a proof of their insanity, for that the republican spirit of the Union was so manifest and so solid that it was astonishg how any one could expect to move them.

He returned to the difficulty of naming my successor, he said Mr. Madison would be his first choice, but that he had always expressed to him such a decision against public office that he could not expect he would undertake it. Mr. Jay would prefer his present office. He sd that Mr. Jay had a great opinion of the talents of Mr. King, that there was also Mr. Smith of S. Carola: E. Rutledge &c. but he observed that name whom he would some objections would be made, some would be called speculators, some one thing, some another, and he asked me to mention any characters occurrg to me. I asked him if Govr. Johnson of Maryld. had occurred to him? He said he had, that he was a man of great good sense, an honest man, & he believed clear of speculations, but this says he is an instance of what I was observing, with all these qualifications Govr. Johnson, from a want of familiarity with foreign affairs, would be in them like a fish out of water, everything would be new to him, & he awkward in everything. I confessed to him that I had considered Johnson rather as fit for the Treasury department. Yes, says he, for that he would be the fittest appointment that could be made; he is a man acquainted with figures, & having as good a knowledge of the resources of this country as any man. I asked him if Chancr. Livingston had occurred to him? He said yes, but he was from N. York, & to appoint him while Hamilton was in & before it should be known he was going out, would excite a newspaper conflagration, as the ultimate arrangement would not be known. He said McLurg had occurred to him as a man of first rate abilities, but it is said that he is a speculator. He asked me what sort of a man Wolcott was. I told him I knew nothing of him myself; I had heard him characterized as a cunning man. I asked him whether some person could not take my office par interim, till he should make an apptment? as Mr. Randolph for instance. Yes, says he, but there you would raise the expectation of keeping it, and I do not know that he is fit for it nor what is thought of Mr. Randolph. I avoided noticing the last observation, & he put the question to me directly. I then told him that I went into society so little as to be unable to answer it: I knew that the embarrassments in his private affairs had obliged him to use expedts which had injured him with the merchts & shopkeepers & affected his character of independance; that these embarrassments were serious, & not likely to cease soon. He said if I would only stay in till the end of another quarter (the last of Dec.) it would get us through the difficulties of this year, and he was satisfied that the affairs of Europe would be settled with this campaign; for that either France would be overwhelmed by it, or the confederacy would give up the contest. By that time too Congress will have manifested it's character & view. I told him that I had set my private affairs in motion in a line which had powerfully called for my presence the last spring, & that they had suffered immensely from my not going home; that I had now calculated them to my return in the fall, and to fail in going then would be the loss of another year, & prejudicial beyond measure. I asked him whether he could not name Govr. Johnson to my office, under an express arrangement that at the close of the session he should take that of the treasury. He said that men never chose to descend: that being once in a higher department he would not like to go into a lower one.* And he concluded by desiring that I would take 2. or 3. days to consider whether I could not stay in till the end of another quarter, for that like a man going to the gallows, he was willing to put it off as long as he could: but if I persisted, he must then look about him & make up his mind to do the best he could: & so he took leave.

"Liberty warring on herself"

Aug. 20. 1793. We met at the President's to examine by paragraphs the draught of a letter I had prepared to Gouverneur Morris on the conduct of Mr. Genet. There was no difference of opinion on any part of it, except on this expression. "An attempt to embroil both, to add still another nation to the enemies of his country, & to draw on both a reproach, which it is hoped will never stain the history of either, that of *liberty warring on herself.*" H. moved to strike out these words "that of liberty warring on herself." He urged generally that it would give offence to the combined powers, that it amounted to a declaration that they were warring on liberty, that we were not called on to declare that the cause of France was that of liberty, that he had at first been with them with all his heart, but that he had long since left them, and was not for encouraging the idea here that the cause of France was the cause of liberty in general, or could have either connection or influence in our affairs. Knox accordg to custom jumped plump into all his opinions. The Pr. with a good deal of positiveness declared in favor of the expression, that he considered the pursuit of France to be that of liberty, however they might sometimes fail of the best means of obtaining it, that he had never at any time entertained a doubt of their ultimate success, if they hung well together, & that as to their dissensions there were such contradictory accts. given that no one could tell what to believe. I observed that it had been supposed among us all along that the present letter might

---

*He asked me whether I could not arrange my affairs by going home. I told him I did not think the public business would admit of it; that there was never a day now in which the absence of the Secretary of state would not be inconvenient to the public.

become public; that we had therefore 3. parties to attend to,—1. France, 2. her enemies, 3. the people of the U S. That as to the enemies of France it ought not to offend them, because the passage objected to only spoke of an attempt to make the U S. a *free nation*, war on France, a *free nation*, which would be liberty warring on herself, and therefore a true fact. That as to France, we were taking so harsh a measure (desiring her to recall her minister) that a precedent for it could scarcely be found, that we knew that minister would represent to his government that our Executive was hostile to liberty, leaning to monarchy & would endeavor to parry the charges on himself, by rendering suspicious the source from which they flowed. That therefore it was essential to satisfy France not only of our friendship to her, but our attachment to the general cause of liberty, & to hers in particular. That as to the people of the U S. we knew there were suspicions abroad that the Executive in some of it's parts was tainted with a hankering after monarchy, an indisposition towards liberty & towards the French cause; & that it was important by an explicit declaration to remove these suspicions & restore the confidence of the people in their govmt. R. opposed the passage on nearly the same ground with H. He added that he thought it had been agreed that this correspondence should contain no expressions which could give offence to either party. I replied that it had been my opinion in the beginng of the correspondence that while we were censuring the conduct of the French minister, we should make the most cordial declarations of friendship to them: that in the first letter or two of the correspondence I had inserted expressions of that kind, but that himself & the other two gentlemen had struck them out; that I thereupon conformed to their opinions in my subseqt. letters, and had carefully avoided the insertion of a single term of friendship to the French nation, and the letters were as dry & husky as if written between the generals of two enemy nations. That on the present occasion how ever it had been agreed that such expressions ought to be inserted in the letter now under considn, & I had accordly charged it pretty well with them. That I had further thought it essential to satisfy the French & our own citizens of the light in which we viewed their cause, and of our fellow feel-

ing for the general cause of liberty, and had ventured only
four words on the subject, that there was not from beginning
to end of the letter one other expression or word in favor of
liberty, & I should think it singular at least if the single passage of that character should be struck out.—The President
again spoke. He came into the idea that attention was due to
the two parties who had been mentd. France & the U S. That
as to the former, thinking it certain their affairs would issue
in a government of some sort, of considerable freedom, it was
the only nation with whom our relations could be counted
on: that as to the U S. there could be no doubt of their universal attachmt to the cause of France, and of the solidity of
their republicanism. He declared his strong attachment to the
expression, but finally left it to us to accommodate. It was
struck out, of course, and the expressions of affection in the
context were a good deal taken down.

Conversations with Aaron Burr

Jan. 26. 1804. Col. Burr the V. P. calls on me in the evening,
having previously asked an opportunity of conversing with
me. He began by recapitulating summarily that he had come
to N. Y. a stranger some years ago, that he found the country
in possn of two rich families, (the Livingstons & Clintons)
that his pursuits were not political & he meddled not. When
the crisis, however of 1800 came on they found their influence
worn out, & solicited his aid with the people. He lent it without any views of promotion. That his being named as a candidate for V. P. was unexpected by him. He acceded to it with
a view to promote my fame & advancement and from a desire
to be with me, whose company and conversation had always
been fascinating to him. That since those great families had
become hostile to him, and had excited the calumnies which
I had seen published. That in this Hamilton had joined and
had even written some of the pieces against him. That his
attachment to me had been sincere and was still unchanged,
altho many little stories had been carried to him, & he supposed to me also, which he despised, but that attachments
must be reciprocal or cease to exist, and therefore he asked if
any change had taken place in mine towards him; that he had
chosen to have this conversn with myself directly & not

through any intermediate agent. He reminded me of a letter written to him about the time of counting the votes (say Feb. 1801) mentioning that his election had left a chasm in my arrangements, that I had lost him from my list in the admn. &c. He observed he believed it would be for the interest of the republican cause for him to retire; that a disadvantageous schism would otherwise take place; but that were he to retire, it would be said he shrunk from the public sentence, which he never would do; that his enemies were using my name to destroy him, and something was necessary from me to prevent and deprive them of that weapon, some mark of favor from me, which would declare to the world that he retired with my confidence. I answered by recapitulating to him what had been my conduct previous to the election of 1800. That I never had interfered directly or indirectly with my friends or any others, to influence the election either for him or myself; that I considered it as my duty to be merely passive, except that, in Virginia I had taken some measures to procure for him the unanimous vote of that state, because I thought any failure there might be imputed to me. That in the election now coming on, I was observing the same conduct, held no councils with anybody respecting it, nor suffered any one to speak to me on the subject, believing it my duty to leave myself to the free discussion of the public; that I do not at this moment know, nor have ever heard who were to be proposed as candidates for the public choice, except so far as could be gathered from the newspapers. That as to the attack excited against him in the newspapers, I had noticed it but as the passing wind; that I had seen complaints that Cheetham, employed in publishing the laws, should be permitted to eat the public bread & abuse its second officer: that as to this, the publishers of the laws were appd by the Secy. of the state witht. any reference to me; that to make the notice general, it was often given to one republican & one federal printer of the same place, that these federal printers did not in the least intermit their abuse of me, tho' receiving emoluments from the govmts and that I have never thot it proper to interfere for myself, & consequently not in the case *of* the Vice president. That as to the letter he referred to, I remembered it, and believed he had only mistaken the date at which it was written; that I thought it must have been on the first notice of the event of the election of S. Carolina; and that I had taken that occasion to mention to him that I had intended to have proposed to him one of the great offices, if he had not been elected, but that his election in giving him a higher station had deprived me of his aid in the administration. The letter alluded to was in fact mine to him of Dec. 15. 1800. I now went on to explain to him verbally what I meant by saying I had lost him from my list. That in Genl. Washington's time it had been signified to him that Mr. Adams, the V. President, would be glad of a foreign embassy; that Genl. Washington mentd. it to me, expressed his doubts whether Mr. Adams was a fit character for such an office, & his still greater doubts, indeed his conviction that it would not be justifiable to send away the person who, in case of his death, was provided by the constn to take his place; that it would moreover appear indecent for him to be disposing of the public trusts in apparently buying off a competitor for the public favor. I concurred with him in the opinion, and, if I recollect rightly, Hamilton, Knox, & Randolph were consulted & gave the same opinions. That when Mr. Adams came to the admn, in his first interview with me he mentioned the necessity of a mission to France, and how desirable it would have been to him if he could have got me to undertake it; but that he conceived it would be wrong in him to send me away, and assigned the same reasons Genl Washington had done; and therefore he should appoint Mr. Madison &c. That I had myself contemplated his (Colo. Burr's) appointment to one of the great offices; in case he was not elected V. P. but that as soon as that election was known, I saw it could not be done for the good reasons which had led Genl W. & Mr. A. to the same conclusion, and therefore in my first letter to Colo. Burr after the issue was known, I had mentioned to him that a chasm in my arrangements had been produced by this event. I was thus particular in rectifying the date of this letter, because it gave me an opportunity of explaining the grounds on which it was written which were indirectly an answer to his present hints. He left the matter with me for consideration & the conversation was turned to indifferent subjects. I should here notice that Colo. Burr must have thot that I could swallow strong things in my own favor, when he founded his acquiescence in the nominn as V. P. to his desire of promoting my honor, the being with me whose company & conversn had always been fascinating to him &c. I had never seen Colo. Burr till he came as a member of Senate. His conduct very soon inspired me with distrust. I habitually cautioned Mr. Madison against trusting him too much. I saw afterwards that under Genl W.'s and Mr. A.'s admns, whenever a great military appmt or a diplomatic one was to be made, he came post to Philada to shew himself & in fact that he was always at market, if they had wanted him. He was indeed told by Dayton in 1800 he might be Secy. at war; but this bid was too late. His election as V. P. was then foreseen. With these impressions of Colo. Burr there never had been an intimacy between us, and but little association. When I destined him for a high appmt, it was out of respect for the favor he had obtained with the republican party by his extraordinary exertions and successes in the N. Y. election in 1800.

1806. April 15. About a month ago, Colo. Burr called on me & entered into a conversation in which he [mentioned] that a little before my coming into office I had written to him a letter intimating that I had destined him for a high employ, had he not been placed by the people in a different one; that he had signified his willingness to resign as V. President to give aid to the admn in any other place; that he had never asked an office however; he asked aid of nobody, but could walk on his own legs, & take care of himself; that I had always used him with politeness, but nothing more: that he aided in bringing on the present order of things, that he had supported the admn, & that he could do me much harm: he wished however to be on differt. ground: he was now disengaged from all particular business, willing to engage in something, should be in town some days, if I should have anything to propose to him. I observed to him that I had always been sensible that he possessed talents which might be employed greatly to the advantage of the public, & that as to myself I had a confidence that if he were employed he would use his talents for the public good: but that he must be sensible the public had withdrawn their confidence from him & that in a government like ours it was necessary to embrace in its admn as great a mass of public confidce as possible, by employing those who had a character with the public, of their own, & not merely a secondary one through the Exve. He observed that if we believed a few newspapers it might be supposed he had lost the public confidence, but that I knew how easy it was to engage newspapers in anything. I observed that I did not refer to that kind of evidence of his having lost the public confidence, but to the late presidential election, when, tho' in possn of the office of V. P. there was not a single voice heard for his retaining it. That as to any harm he could do me, I knew no cause why he should desire it, but at the same time I feared no injury which any man could do me: that I never had done a single act, or been concerned in any transaction, which I feared to have fully laid open, or which could do me any hurt if truly stated: that I had never done a single thing with a view to my personal interest, or that of any friend, or with any other view than that of the greatest public good: that therefore no threat or fear on that head would ever be a motive of action with me. He has continued in town to this time; dined with me this day week & called on me to take leave 2. or 3. days ago. I did not commit these things to writing at the time but I do it now, because in a suit between him & Cheetham, he has had a deposn of Mr. Bayard taken, which seems to have no relation to the suit nor to any other object but to calumniate me. Bayard pretends to have addressed to me, during the pending of the Presidl election in Feb. 1801, through Genl. Saml. Smith, certain condns on which my election might be obtained, & that Genl. Smith after conversing with me gave answers from me. This is absolutely false. No proposn of any kind was ever made to me on that occasion by Genl. Smith, nor any answer authorized by me. And this fact Genl. Smith affirms at this moment. For some matters connected with this see my notes of Feb. 12. & 14. 1801 made at the moment. But the following transactions took place about the same time, that is to say while the Presidential election was in suspense in Congress, which tho' I did not enter at the time they made such an impression on my mind that they are now as fresh as to their principal circumstances as if they had happened yesterday. Coming out of the Senate chamber one day I found Gouverneur Morris on the steps. He stopped me & began a conversn on the strange & portentous state of things then existing, and went on to observe that the reasons why the minority of states were so opposed to my being elected were that they apprehended that 1. I should turn all federalists out of office. 2. put down the navy. 3. wipe off the public debt & 4.

That I need only to declare, or authorize my friends to declare, that I would not take these steps, and instantly the event of the election would be fixed. I told him that I should leave the world to judge of the course I meant to pursue by that which I had pursued hitherto; believing it to be my duty to be passive & silent during the present scene; that I should certainly make no terms, should never go into the office of President by capitulation, nor with my hands tied by any conditions which should hinder me from pursuing the measures which I should deem for the public good. It was understood that Gouverneur Morris had entirely the direction of the vote of Lewis Morris of Vermont, who by coming over to M. Lyon would have added another vote & decided the election. About the same time, I met with Mr. Adams walking in the Pensylve avenue. We conversed on the state of things. I observed to him, that a very dangerous experiment was then in contemplation, to defeat the Presidential election by an act of Congress declaring the right of the Senate to naming a President of the Senate, to devolve on him the govmt during any interregnum: that such a measure would probably produce resistance by force & incalculable consequences which it would be in his power to prevent by negativing such an act. He seemed to think such an act justifiable & observed it was in my power to fix the election by a word in an instant, by declaring I would not turn out the federal officers, not put down the navy, nor sponge the National debt. Finding his mind made up as to the usurpation of the government by the President of the Senate I urged it no further, observed the world must judge as to myself of the future by the past, and turned the conversation to something else. About the same time Dwight Foster of Massachusetts called on me in my room one night & went into a very long conversation on the state of affairs the drift of which was to let me understand that the fears above-mentioned were the only obstacles to my election, to all of which I avoided giving any answer the one way or the other. From this moment he became most bitterly & personally opposed to me, & so has ever continued. I do not recollect that I ever had any particular conversn with Genl. Saml. Smith on this subject. Very possibly I had however, as the general subject & all its parts were the constant themes of conversation in the private *tête à têtes* with our friends. But certain I am that neither he, nor any other republican ever uttered the most distant hint to me about submitting to any conditions or giving any assurances to anybody; and still more certainly was neither he nor any other person ever authorized by me to say what I would or would not do. See a very exact statement of Bayard's conduct on that occasion in a piece among my notes of 1801. which was published by G. Granger with some alterations in the papers of the day under the signature of*

---

*Gaps here and elsewhere in the text reflect unfinished portions of the original manuscript.

Notes on Professor Ebeling's Letter of July 30, 1795

Professor Ebeling mentioning the persons in America from whom he derives information for his work, it may be useful for him to know how far he may rely on their authority.

President Stiles, an excellent man, of very great learning, but remarkable for his credulity.

Dr. Willard. Dr. Barton Dr. Ramsay Mr. Barlow	All these are men of respectable characters worthy of confidence as to any facts they may state, and rendered, by their good sense, good judges of them.
Mr. Morse. Mr. Webster.	Good authorities for whatever relates to the Eastern states, & perhaps as far South as the Delaware.

But South of that their information is worse than none at all, except as far as they quote good authorities. They both I believe took a single journey through the Southern parts, merely to acquire the right of being considered as eye-witnesses. But to pass once along a public road thro' a country, & in one direction only, to put up at it's taverns, and get into conversation with the idle, drunken individuals who pass their time lounging in these taverns, is not the way to know a country, it's inhabitants, or manners. To generalize a whole nation from these specimens is not the sort of information which Professor Ebeling would wish to compose *his work* from.

Fenno's Gazette of the U.S. Webster's Minerva. Columbian centinel.	To form a just judgment of a country from it's newspapers the character of these papers

should be known, in order that proper allowances & corrections may be used. This will require a long explanation, without which, these particular papers would give a foreigner a very false view of American affairs.

The people of America, before the revolution-war, being attached to England, had taken up, without examination, the English ideas of the superiority of their constitution over every thing of the kind which ever had been or ever would be tried. The revolution forced them to consider the subject for themselves, and the result was an universal conversion to republicanism. Those who did not come over to this opinion, either left us, & were called Refugees, or staid with us under the name of tories; & some, preferring profit to principle took side with us and floated with the general tide. Our first federal constitution, or confederation as it was called, was framed in the first moments of our separation from England, in the highest point of our jealousies of independance as to her & as to each other. It formed therefore too weak a bond to produce an union of action as to foreign nations. This appeared at once on the establishment of peace, when the pressure of a common enemy which had hooped us together during the war, was taken away. Congress was found to be quite unable to point the action of the several states to a common object. A general desire therefore took place of amending the federal constitution. This was opposed by some of those who wished for monarchy to wit, the Refugees now returned, the old tories, & the timid whigs who prefer tranquility to freedom, hoping monarchy might be the remedy if a state of complete anarchy could be brought on. A Convention however being decided on, some of the monocrats got elected, with a hope of introducing an English constitution, when they found that the great body of the delegates were strongly for adhering to republicanism, & for giving due strength to their government under that form, they then directed their efforts to the assimilation of all the parts of the new government to the English constitution as nearly as was attainable. In this they were not altogether without success; insomuch that the monarchical features of the new constitution produced a violent opposition to it from the most zealous republicans in the several states. For this reason, & because they also thought it carried the principle of a consolidation of the states farther than was requisite for the purpose of producing an union of action as to foreign powers, it is still doubted by some whether a majority of the people of the U.S. were not against adopting it. However it was carried through all the assemblies of the states, tho' by very small majorities in the largest states. The inconveniences of an inefficient government, driving the people as is usual, into the opposite extreme, the elections to the first Congress run very much in favor of those who were known to favor a very strong government. Hence the anti-republicans appeared a considerable majority in both houses of Congress. They pressed forward the plan therefore of strengthening all the features of the government which gave it resemblance to an English constitution, of adopting the English forms & principles of administration, and of forming like them a monied interest, by means of a funding system, not calculated to pay the public debt, but to render it perpetual, and to make it an engine in the hands of the executive branch of government which, added to the great patronage it possessed in the disposal of public offices, might enable it to assume by degrees a kingly authority. The biennial period of Congress being too short to betray to the people, spread over this great continent, this train of things during the first Congress, little change was made in the members to the second. But in the mean time two very distinct parties had formed in Congress; and before the third election, the people in general became apprised of the game which was playing for drawing over them a kind of government which they never had in contemplation. At the 3d. election therefore a decided majority of Republicans were sent to the lower house of Congress; and as information spread still farther among the people after the 4th. election the anti-republicans have become a weak minority. But the members of the Senate being changed but once in 6. years, the completion of that body will be much slower in it's assimilation to that of the people. This will account for the differences which may appear in the proceedings & spirit of the two houses. Still however it is inevitable that the Senate will at length be formed to the republican model of the people, & the two houses of the legislature, once brought to act on the true principles of the Constitution, backed by the people, will be able to defeat the plan of sliding us into monarchy, & to keep the Executive within Republican bounds, notwithstanding the immense patronage it possesses in the disposal of public offices, notwithstanding it has been able to draw into this vortex the judiciary branch of the government & by their expectancy of sharing the other offices in the Executive gift to make them auxiliary to the Executive in all it's views instead of forming a balance between that & the legislature as it was originally intended and notwithstanding the funding phalanx which a respect for public faith must protect, tho it was engaged by false brethren. Two parties then do exist within the U.S. They embrace respectively the following descriptions of persons.

The Anti-republicans consist of
1. The old refugees & tories.
2. British merchants residing among us, & composing the main body of our merchants.
3. American merchants trading on British capital. Another great portion.
4. Speculators & Holders in the banks & public funds.
5. Officers of the federal government with some exceptions.
6. Office-hunters, willing to give up principles for places. A numerous & noisy tribe.
7. Nervous persons, whose languid fibres have more analogy with a passive than active state of things.

The Republican part of our Union comprehends
1. The entire body of landholders throughout the United States.
2. The body of labourers, not being landholders, whether in husbanding or the arts.

The latter is to the aggregate of the former party probably as 500 to one; but their wealth is not as disproportionate, tho' it is also greatly superior, and is in truth the foundation of that of their antagonists. Trifling as are the numbers of the Anti-republican party, there are circumstances which give them an appearance of strength & numbers. They all live in cities, together, & can act in a body readily & at all times; they give chief employment to the newspapers, & therefore have most of them under their command. The Agricultural interest is dispersed over a great extent of country, have little means of inter-communication with each other, and feeling their own strength & will, are conscious that a single exertion of these will at any time crush the machinations against their government. As in the commerce of human life, there are commodities adapted to every demand, so there are newspapers adapted to the Antirepublican palate, and others to the Republican. Of the former class are the Columbian Centinel, the Hartford newspaper, Webster's Minerva, Fenno's Gazette of the U.S., Davies's Richmond paper &c. Of the latter are Adams's Boston paper, Greenleaf's of New York, Freneau's of New Jersey, Bache's of Philadelphia, Pleasant's of Virginia &c. Pleasant's paper comes out twice a week, Greenleaf's & Freneau's once a week, Bache's daily. I do not know how often Adams's. I shall according to your desire endeavor to get Pleasant's for you for 1794, & 95. and will have it forwarded through 96 from time to time to your correspondent at Baltimore.

While on the subject of authorities and information, the following works are recommended to Professor Ebeling.

Minot's history of the insurrection in Massachusetts in 1786. 8vo.

Mazzei. Recherches historiques et politiques sur les E. U. de l'Amerique. 4 vol. 8vo. This is to be had from Paris. The author is an exact man.

The article 'Etats Unis de l'Amerique' in the Dictionnaire d'Economie politique et diplomatique, de l'Encyclopedie methodique. This article occupies about 90. pages, is by De Meusnier, and his materials were worthy of confidence, except so far as they were taken from the Abbé Raynal. Against these effusions of an imagination in delirio it is presumed Professor Ebeling needs not be put on his guard. The earlier editions of the Abbé Raynal's work were equally bad as to both South & North America. A gentleman however of perfect information as to South America, undertook to reform that part of the work, and his changes & additions were for the most part adopted by the Abbé in his latter editions. But the North-American part remains in it's original state of worthlessness.

A Memorandum (Services to My Country)

[*c.* 1800]

I have sometimes asked myself whether my country is the better for my having lived at all? I do not know that it is. I have been the instrument of doing the following things; but they would have been done by others; some of them, perhaps, a little better.

The Rivanna had never been used for navigation; scarcely an empty canoe had ever passed down it. Soon after I came of age, I examined its obstructions, set on foot a subscription for removing them, got an Act of Assembly passed, and the thing effected, so as to be used completely and fully for carrying down all our produce.

The Declaration of Independence.

I proposed the demolition of the church establishment, and the freedom of religion. It could only be done by degrees; to wit, the Act of 1776, c. 2, exempted dissenters from contributions to the church, and left the church clergy to be supported by voluntary contributions of their own sect; was continued from year to year, and made perpetual 1779, c. 36. I prepared the act for religious freedom in 1777, as part of the revisal, which was not reported to the Assembly till 1779, and that particular law not passed till 1785, and then by the efforts of Mr. Madison.

The act putting an end to entails.

The act prohibiting the importation of slaves.

The act concerning citizens, and establishing the natural right of man to expatriate himself, at will.

The act changing the course of descents, and giving the inheritance to all the children, &c., equally, I drew as part of the revisal.

The act for apportioning crimes and punishments, part of the same work, I drew. When proposed to the legislature, by Mr. Madison, in 1785, it failed by a single vote. G. K. Taylor afterwards, in 1796, proposed the same subject; avoiding the adoption of any part of the diction of mine, the text of which had been studiously drawn in the technical terms of the law, so as to give no occasion for new questions by new expressions. When I drew mine, public labor was thought the best punishment to be substituted for death. But, while I was in France, I heard of a society in England, who had successfully introduced solitary confinement, and saw the drawing of a prison at Lyons, in France, formed on the idea of solitary confinement. And, being applied to by the Governor of Virginia for the plan of a Capitol and Prison, I sent him the Lyons plan, accompanying it with a drawing on a smaller scale, better adapted to our use. This was in June, 1786. Mr. Taylor very judiciously adopted this idea, (which had now been acted on in Philadelphia, probably from the English model) and substituted labor in confinement, to the public labor proposed by the Committee of revisal; which themselves would have done, had they been to act on the subject again. The public mind was ripe for this in 1796, when Mr. Taylor proposed it, and ripened chiefly by the experiment in Philadelphia; whereas, in 1785, when it had been proposed to our assembly, they were not quite ripe for it.

In 1789 and 1790, I had a great number of olive plants, of the best kind, sent from Marseilles to Charleston, for South Carolina and Georgia. They were planted, and are flourishing; and, though not yet multiplied, they will be the germ of that cultivation in those States.

In 1790, I got a cask of heavy upland rice, from the river Denbigh, in Africa, about lat. 9° 30′ North, which I sent to Charleston, in hopes it might supersede the culture of the wet rice, which renders South Carolina and Georgia so pestilential through the summer. It was divided, and a part sent to Georgia. I know not whether it has been attended to in South Carolina; but it has spread in the upper parts of Georgia, so as to have become almost general, and is highly prized. Perhaps it may answer in Tennessee and Kentucky. The greatest service which can be rendered any country is, to add an useful plant to its culture; especially, a bread grain; next in value to bread is oil.

Whether the act for the more general diffusion of knowledge will ever be carried into complete effect, I know not. It was received by the legislature with great enthusiasm at first; and a small effort was made in 1796, by the act to establish public schools, to carry a part of it into effect, viz., that for the establishment of free English schools; but the option given to the courts has defeated the intention of the act.

A Memorandum (Rules of Etiquette)

[*c.* November, 1803]

I. In order to bring the members of society together in the first instance, the custom of the country has established that residents shall pay the first visit to strangers, and, among strangers, first comers to later comers, foreign and domestic; the character of stranger ceasing after the first visits. To this rule there is a single exception. Foreign ministers, from the necessity of making themselves known, pay the first visit to the ministers of the nation, which is returned.

II. When brought together in society, all are perfectly equal, whether foreign or domestic, titled or untitled, in or out of office.

All other observances are but exemplifications of these two principles.

I. 1st. The families of foreign ministers, arriving at the seat of government, receive the first visit from those of the national ministers, as from all other residents.

2d. Members of the Legislature and of the Judiciary, independent of their offices, have a right as strangers to receive the first visit.

II. 1st. No title being admitted here, those of foreigners give no precedence.

2d. Differences of grade among diplomatic members, gives no precedence.

3d. At public ceremonies, to which the government invites the presence of foreign ministers and their families, a convenient seat or station will be provided for them, with any other strangers invited and the families of the national ministers, each taking place as they arrive, and without any precedence.

4th. To maintain the principle of equality, or of pêle mêle, and prevent the growth of precedence out of courtesy, the members of the Executive will practice at their own houses, and recommend an adherence to the ancient usage of the country, of gentlemen in mass giving precedence to the ladies in mass, in passing from one apartment where they are assembled into another.

Epitaph [1826]

could the dead feel any interest in Monuments or other remembrances of them, when, as
Anacreon says   Ολιγη δε κεισομεσθα
               Κονις, οςτεων λυθεντων
the following would be to my Manes the most
gratifying.
On the grave
   a plain die or cube of 3.f without any
mouldings, surmounted by an Obelisk
of 6.f height, each of a single stone:
on the faces of the Obelisk the following
inscription, & not a word more
            'Here was buried
            Thomas Jefferson

Author of the Declaration of American Independance
    of the Statute of Virginia for religious freedom
& Father of the University of Virginia.'
because by these, as testimonials that I have lived, I wish most to
be remembered. to be of the coarse stone of which
my columns are made, that no one might be tempted
hereafter to destroy it for the value of the materials.
my bust by Ciracchi, with the pedestal and truncated
column on which it stands, might be given to the University
if they would place it in the Dome room of the Rotunda.
on the Die of the Obelisk might be engraved

  'Born Apr. 2. 1743. O.S.
  Died _____   '

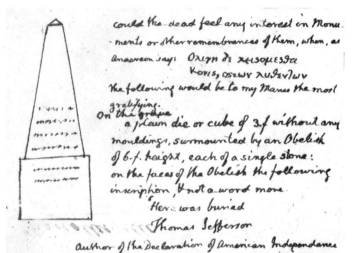

could the dead feel any interest in Monu-
-ments or other remembrances of them, when, as
Anacreon says: Ολιγη δε κεισομεσθα
                    Κονις, οστεων λυθεντων
the following would be to my Manes the most
gratifying.
On the grave   a plain die or cube of 3.f without any
mouldings, surmounted by an Obelisk
of 6.f. height, each of a single stone:
on the faces of the Obelisk the following
inscription, & not a word more.
        Here was buried
            Thomas Jefferson
    Author of the Declaration of American Independance
        of the Statute of Virginia for religious freedom
    & Father of the University of Virginia?
because by these, as testimonials that I have lived, I wish most to
be remembered.   to be of the coarse stone of which
my columns are made, that no one might be tempted
hereafter to destroy it for the value of the materials.
my bust by Ciracchi, with the pedestal and truncated
column on which it stands, might be given to the University
if they would place it in the Dome room of the Rotunda.
on the Die, of the Obelisk might be engraved
        Born apr. 2. 1743. O.S.
        Died ———   ,

Jefferson's Design and Inscription for His Tombstone.
Courtesy of the Library of Congress

381

Chronology

enters Virginia society; begins successful law practice in
Virginia courts following admission to the bar in 1767.

1769   Following his own architectural designs, begins building
            Monticello, his country seat, on a mountaintop that was
            part of his father's original landholdings.

1769–76   Member of Virginia House of Burgesses (until it is closed
            by the Revolution) for Albemarle County; promotes var-
            ious measures intended to resist British authority, among
            them the organization of committees of correspondence.

1772   Marries Martha Wayles Skelton, a 23-year-old widow and
            heiress, on January 1. Brings his bride to the unfinished
            Monticello, where, on September 27, Martha (called
            Patsy), their first child, is born.

1773   Comes into possession of 11,000 acres of land and 135
            slaves upon death of his father-in-law, John Wayles. Im-
            mediately sells over half the lands to meet debts also in-
            herited from Wayles. The purchasers will pay off their
            notes in depreciated Revolutionary currency, and Jefferson
            will struggle for the rest of his life to liquidate his own
            debt to Wayles's creditors.

1774   Writes, in August, proposed instructions for the Virginia
            delegates to the first Continental Congress. These are later
            published in Williamsburg under the title *A Summary
            View of the Rights of British America*, and are reprinted in
            Philadelphia and in England.

1775–76   Attends Continental Congress in Philadelphia as a Vir-
            ginia delegate. Mother dies in March 1776. In June 1776,
            drafts Declaration of Independence, adopted July 4; also
            drafts a constitution for Virginia, not adopted.

1776–79   Member of Virginia House of Delegates for Albemarle
            County.

1777   Correspondence with John Adams begins May 16. First
            and only son dies, unchristened, in June, aged three
            weeks.

1778   Another daughter, Mary (called Maria or Polly), born August 1. Of his six children, two, Martha and Mary, grow to maturity, and only Martha survives him.

1779   Elected Governor of Virginia on June 1. On June 18, the "Report of the Committee of Revisors," on which he has labored during years as a legislator, is submitted to the Assembly. Never enacted as a unit, and not printed until 1784, this revision of the laws of the Commonwealth nevertheless becomes, in James Madison's words, "a mine of legislative wealth"; includes Bills for Proportioning Crimes and Punishments, for the More General Diffusion of Knowledge, for Establishing Religious Freedom, etc.

1780   Elected a member of the American Philosophical Society January 21. Reelected Governor of Virginia June 2. On December 29, a British army under the command of Benedict Arnold invades Virginia.

1781   Term as governor expires June 2; on June 4, along with several members of the Assembly, who are his guests, is driven from Monticello by General Tarleton's troops. The House of Delegates, meeting in Staunton, across the Blue Ridge, resolves on June 12 to conduct an inquiry into the conduct of Jefferson and his Council, responding to allegations that they had been negligent in preparing to meet Arnold's invasion; on December 15, the Assembly accepts the report of the committee appointed to make the inquiry, and votes a unanimous resolution "to obviate and remove all unmerited Censure" for his conduct as wartime governor. On December 20, sends answers (first form of *Notes on the State of Virginia*) to a series of questions posed by François Marbois, secretary to the French legation, relating to the laws, institutions, geography, climate, flora and fauna of Virginia.

1782–83   Martha Wayles Jefferson, in poor health since the birth of their sixth child in May, dies on September 6, 1782, plunging him into deep grief. Appointed commissioner by Congress to negotiate peace with Great Britain on November 12, but winter ice and a British fleet block passage to France. Word of a provisional treaty reaches Congress in February and mission is suspended.

1783–84   Serves as Virginia delegate in Congress, at Princeton and Annapolis.

1784   Submits "Report of a Plan of Government for the Western Territory" to Congress on March 1; when revised, amended, and adopted on April 23, it projects a federal and republican system for the American West. Appointed by Congress May 7 as minister plenipotentiary to join John Adams and Benjamin Franklin in negotiation of treaties of amity and commerce in Europe; travels through eastern states, gathering information on industry and trade in preparation for mission. In Boston on July 5, embarks for England, accompanied by daughter Patsy.

1785   Appointed to succeed Franklin as minister to France in March; signs commercial treaty with Prussia in July. Publishes, in Paris, a private edition of *Notes on the State of Virginia*.

1786   Collaborates anonymously with Jean Nicholas Démeunier on article on the United States for the *Encyclopédie Methodique*, from January to June. Virginia General Assembly enacts Statute for Religious Freedom on January 16. In March and April, visits London and tours English gardens with John Adams (now minister to England). In June, sends model of a new capitol, based on Roman temple, to Virginia. Meets Maria Cosway, an Englishwoman and painter, who becomes his friend and frequent companion in Paris.

1787   Journeys to south of France and northern Italy from March to June. In July, nine-year-old daughter Polly arrives in Paris and *Notes on the State of Virginia* is published in England (Stockdale edition). Receives a copy of proposed United States Constitution in November and supports its ratification, but urges Madison and others to add a bill of rights to the document.

1788   Journeys to Holland and the Rhineland, from March to April. In November, signs a consular convention with France, and writes and has printed *Observations on the Whale-Fishery*. Awarded honorary Doctorate of Laws by Harvard University.

1789   Attends opening of Estates General at Versailles May 5;

observes succeeding events of the French Revolution. When deliberations of the Estates General reach an impasse—the clergy and nobles (First and Second Estates) insisting on preservation of the ancient principle of representation and vote by order, and the commons (Third Estate) demanding a single national assembly—Jefferson suggests that the King come forward with a "charter of rights" including rights of habeas corpus and freedom of the press, giving the Estates General exclusive power to legislate and to levy taxes, and abolishing fiscal privileges and inequities. This compromise solution catches the fancy of the Marquis de Lafayette but avails no further. The King rallies to the nobles and resorts to force; the storming of the Bastille ensues, followed by the King's capitulation and a wave of retributive violence. Jefferson is satisfied with the "legitimacy" of the mobs' actions. In August, Lafayette and other Patriot party leaders meet at Jefferson's house to discuss the formation of a constitution. In September, secures leave of absence from diplomatic post to attend to personal affairs in Virginia and take daughters home. Leaves Paris in October, lands November 23 at Norfolk, Virginia. Upon disembarking, learns that Senate on September 26 confirmed his nomination by President Washington as first secretary of state.

1790   Reluctantly accepts appointment as secretary of state February 14. Martha Jefferson marries Thomas Mann Randolph (her second cousin) on February 23. Takes up duties as secretary of state March 21 in New York. Submits Report on Weights and Measures to Congress July 4. Begins to be disturbed by anti-republican sentiments and courtly forms and ceremonies exhibited in the new administration.

1791   Advises the President on February 15 that the Constitution does not empower the federal government to form a national bank; Washington solicits rebuttal from Alexander Hamilton, secretary of the treasury (who advances the doctrine of "implied powers"), and decides the issue in Hamilton's favor. Administrative rivalry with Hamilton grows steadily more intense. Helps persuade Philip Freneau to come to the capital in Philadelphia to edit an opposition newspaper. Extract of private note of Jefferson's, referring to the "political heresies" of John Adams (vice-president), stirs controversy when it is printed (without permission) as preface to Thomas Paine's *Rights of Man*.

1792   Diplomatic memoir to the British minister, dated May 29, seeks removal of British troops from posts below the Great Lakes and settlement of other issues left unresolved by the treaty of peace; Hamilton's connivance forestalls Jefferson's plan to use commercial discrimination to accomplish these ends. On September 9, appeals to President Washington in dispute with Hamilton, who had attacked him anonymously in the press. Political alignments in Congress begin to take on party character, and Jefferson is widely viewed as leader of the opposition to Federalist policies.

1793   Writes "Opinion on the French Treaties," dated April 28, and prevails upon President Washington to receive the new French minister, Edmond Charles Genet, thus tacitly acknowledging the legitimacy of the Republic of France; also convinces Washington not to renounce the treaties of 1778, which allied the fledgling United States with the French monarchy. Acquiesces in Washington's Proclamation of Neutrality. In August, when Genet's activities and statements threaten to involve the United States in the Anglo-French war, Jefferson prepares papers demanding the diplomat's recall. On December 16, submits Report on Commerce to Congress, urging retaliation in kind against discriminatory British trade policies. Resigns as secretary of state at year's end.

1794   Returns to farming at Monticello.

1795   Denounces Jay's Treaty, which represents the pro-British policies of the Federalists, in private letters.

1796   Begins rebuilding Monticello in February to provide expanded accommodations for family and to conform to his developed taste in architectural design. Writes to Philip Mazzei on April 24 that an "Anglican monarchical aristocratical party has sprung up"; when published a year later, the letter is interpreted as reflecting upon Washington and prompts renewed Federalist attacks on Jefferson. December 7, elected vice-president of the United States, having run second in the electoral balloting to John Adams.

1797   Installed as president of the American Philosophical Society on March 3 at Philadelphia, and inaugurated as vice-president of the United States a day later. On March 10, presents scientific paper on megalonyx, based on recent fossil discoveries in Virginia, to American Philosophical Society. In May, assumes leadership of Republican party at special session of Congress. Mary Jefferson marries her cousin John Wayles Eppes in October.

1798   Anti-Jacobin hysteria envelops Philadelphia, aroused by publication of the "XYZ dispatches," which reveal the attempts by agents of the French foreign minister, Talleyrand, to extort money from the American envoys sent to negotiate for reduction of hostilities. Jefferson strives to prevent war, is calumniated in the press as a traitor and a coward, and retires on June 27 to Monticello. In September and October, secretly drafts resolutions declaring the Alien and Sedition laws (aimed against Republican opposition to Federalist war policy) unconstitutional and arranges for these resolutions to be introduced in the Kentucky legislature, which adopts them in November. In December, the Virginia Resolutions, drafted by Madison in tandem with Jefferson's Kentucky Resolutions, are adopted.

1799   Drafts second set of resolutions in August and September and proposes further actions by Virginia and Kentucky legislatures.

1800   Publishes appendix to *Notes on the State of Virginia* in May, authenticating story of the murder of the family of Logan, a Mingo chief (disputed by Luther Martin, attorney general of Maryland, a political enemy of Jefferson's). Runs for President in first national contest between organized political parties; is vilified by Federalists as an infidel, a Jacobin, and a demagogue, but defeats Adams handily in popular vote. On December 3, however, in the meeting of presidential electors in their respective states, a peculiarity of the electoral system results in a tie vote between Jefferson and his running mate, Aaron Burr, and the election is thrown into the House of Representatives.

1801   *A Manual of Parliamentary Practice*, the product of Jefferson's experience presiding over the Senate as vice-president, published in February. The lame-duck Federalist majority in the House fails in a last-ditch attempt to deny Jefferson the presidency by swinging to Burr, and on the 36th ballot Jefferson is elected President of the United States. On March 4 he is inaugurated, and delivers a conciliatory address. Correspondence with Adams ceases and is not renewed until 1812. Dispatches naval squadron on May 20 to cruise the Mediterranean to protect American vessels against the piracy of the Barbary States. On July 12, replies to the New Haven remonstrance, defending removal of the collector of customs in New Haven (a Federalist holdover) and the appointment of a Republican in his place. On December 8, communicates his First Annual Message to Congress in writing, eschewing the formality of a ceremonial address.

1802   Replies to the Danbury Baptist Association on January 1, affirming his commitment to the separation of church and state. March 8, succeeds in repealing the Judiciary Act of 1801, passed by the Federalists in their final weeks of supremacy, which enlarged the federal judiciary and expanded its jurisdiction. Writes letter to Robert R. Livingston, American minister to France, on April 18, discussing the danger of a rebirth of French empire in the New World posed by the retrocession of Louisiana from Spain to France. In July, James T. Callender, disappointed office-seeker, commences libels of Jefferson, including allegation that he fathered children by his slave Sally Hemings.

1803   Nominates James Monroe on January 11 for extraordinary mission to France to negotiate for purchase of New Orleans and the Floridas. Sends confidential message to Congress on January 18 regarding proposed expedition to the Pacific, to be led by Meriwether Lewis. On February 24, Chief Justice John Marshall of the Supreme Court delivers opinion in the case of Marbury *vs.* Madison. Opinion establishes precedent for judicial review and Marshall issues gratuitous rebuke of the President for refusing to deliver commissions to William Marbury and other "midnight judges" appointed in the final hours of the Adams administration. On April 21, Jefferson sends his "Syllabus . . .

of the Doctrines of Jesus" to Benjamin Rush. Livingston and Monroe conclude treaty of cession of Louisiana in Paris on April 30. In July, believing he had exceeded his constitutional authority in making the purchase, Jefferson drafts an amendment to sanction it retroactively, although for reasons of expedience he does not press it upon Congress. The amendment includes provisions to remove Indian tribes to the far side of the Mississippi and to bar white settlement in the new territory above the 33rd parallel. The policy of removal is abandoned along with the amendment. In September, writes memoir on the boundaries of Louisiana, hoping to make the most of their uncertainty and acquire the Floridas, which had not been part of the bargain. Sends "An Account of Louisiana" to Congress on November 14, and is ridiculed in the press because of the strange, apocryphal tales it includes. Ten days later sends to Senator John Breckinridge an outline of a plan of government for Louisiana, subsequently enacted by Congress.

1804   Younger daughter, Mary Jefferson Eppes, dies April 17; letter of condolence from Abigail Adams leads to brief correspondence with her, which is curtailed when old political animosities surface. Reelected President by a landslide on December 5.

1805   Proposes plan for university in letter to Littleton W. Tazewell on January 5. Supreme Court Justice Samuel Chase, whose partisan attacks on democratic tendencies in the government had led Jefferson to call for his impeachment, is acquitted March 1 in trial in the Senate. Delivers Second Inaugural Address March 4. Peace treaty with Tripoli brings Mediterranean campaign to successful conclusion June 4. Fifth Annual Message to Congress on December 3 offers vigorous defense of American neutrality. Sends confidential message to Congress December 6, hinting at purchase of Floridas from Spain.

1806   With Europe embroiled in war and American neutrality threatened by captures, impressments, and other acts of aggression, Jefferson seeks to exert economic pressure on Britain in particular. He approves the Non-Importation Act, intended to strengthen the hands of James Monroe and William Pinkney, who are nominated joint commissioners to Britain on April 19. In August, lays foundation for Poplar Forest, an octagonal house of his design, on property acquired from father-in-law's estate in Bedford County, Virginia. Lewis and Clark Expedition returns to St. Louis on September 25. Issues proclamation on November 27 warning against Burr Conspiracy, alleged plot of the former vice-president to separate western states from the union and attack Mexico. Sixth Annual Message, on December 2, calls for constitutional amendment to enlarge powers of Congress to undertake internal improvements.

1807   On January 14, offers his collection of Virginia statutes to W. W. Hening for his *Statutes at Large* (1809–23). Sends special message to Congress February 10, calling for the use of gunboats to protect American harbors. On March 3, refuses to submit Monroe–Pinkney treaty to Senate because it contains no guarantee against impressment. Trial of Aaron Burr for treason opens in Richmond May 22; he is acquitted September 1. On June 22, USS *Chesapeake* is fired upon by HMS *Leopard* off Norfolk after American commander's refusal to allow the British to search his ship for deserters. Incident provokes popular clamor for war, but Jefferson retaliates with vigorous commercial measures. The Embargo Act, suspending all foreign commerce, is enacted on Jefferson's recommendation, effective December 22. On December 10, replying to addresses from legislative bodies urging him to continue in office for a third term, he announces his impending retirement from the presidency.

1808   The economy suffers under the embargo, which is regularly violated, especially in the Northeast. On April 19, in response to the smuggling trade carried on across the Canadian frontier, Jefferson issues proclamation declaring the Lake Champlain region to be in a state of insurrection. In July, ships collection of bones of mammoth to National Institute in Paris. Opposition to embargo grows and diplomatic efforts to end the commercial warfare fail. In his Eighth Annual Message, November 8, Jefferson looks to permanent development of domestic manufacturing, which has expanded during suspension of foreign trade. James Madison is elected President December 7.

1809   Signs Non-Intercourse Act March 1, repealing the embargo (which had failed to achieve its ends) and reopening trade with all nations except Great Britain and France. Retires as President March 4 and returns to Monticello, where he spends the remainder of his life entertaining a steady stream of visitors, attending to an extensive correspondence, struggling with mounting debts, planning a university, and engaging in philosophical pursuits.

1810   On May 12 Governor John Tyler invites Jefferson to comment on public education, and on May 26 he responds by affirming his continuing support of the cause "of general education, to enable every man to judge for himself what will secure or endanger his freedom," and by proposing the division of each county into "little republics," each to have a central school.

1811   Destutt de Tracy's *A Commentary and Review of Montesquieu's Spirit of the Laws* is translated and published in July under Jefferson's direction. Suit against Jefferson, brought by Edward Livingston concerning the New Orleans Batture and resulting from order given during Jefferson's presidency that evicted Livingston from a public beach formed by Mississippi silt, is dismissed by federal circuit court in Richmond for lack of jurisdiction. In March, the following year, Jefferson publishes the complex law arguments prepared for counsel in the case.

1812   Resumes correspondence with John Adams at the latter's initiative. War with Great Britain is declared June 18.

1813   August, writes biographical sketch of Meriwether Lewis, published the following year.

1814   Proposes comprehensive plan of public education for Virginia in letter to Peter Carr September 7. Offers his library for sale to the United States on September 21; it becomes the foundation of the Library of Congress. Resigns as president of the American Philosophical Society November 23. War ends with Treaty of Ghent December 24. Andrew Jackson defeats English at New Orleans January 8 of the following year, before word of the treaty arrives.

1815   Contributes to Louis H. Girardin's continuation of John
             Daly Burk's *History of Virginia*, published the following
             year.

1816   Justifies change of opinion on domestic manufactures in
             celebrated letter of January 9 to Benjamin Austin. Calls
             for reform of Virginia constitution in letter of July 12 to
             Samuel Kercheval, widely reprinted. Reads and corrects
             manuscript of William Wirt's *Life of Patrick Henry* in Sep-
             tember.

1817   Virginia Assembly defeats bill that embodies Jefferson's
             general education plan February 20. Develops architec-
             tural plans for an "academical village" in Charlottesville.
             On October 6 the cornerstone is laid for the first building
             of Central College, which will become the University of
             Virginia.

1818   Writes preface to the *Anas* (a collection of partisan anec-
             dotes and memoranda from his years of service in the fed-
             eral government) on February 4, explaining his conflicts
             with Hamilton during Washington's administration; col-
             lection is not published until after his death. August 1–4,
             presides at Rockfish Gap meeting of commissioners
             charged with planning the University of Virginia, and
             writes the Report. In October, Tracy's *A Treatise on Polit-
             ical Economy* is translated and published under Jefferson's
             direction.

1819   General Assembly charters University of Virginia January
             25. Jefferson possibly completes "The Life and Morals of
             Jesus of Nazareth," not published until 1902, but denies in
             private letters that he has converted to any particular de-
             nomination.

1820   Denounces the Missouri Compromise in private letters,
             predicting it will excite sectional prejudices. In this and
             subsequent years, fulminates against the usurpation of
             power by Supreme Court and the tendency toward "con-
             solidation" of authority in federal government.

1821   Writes *Autobiography*, "for my own more ready reference,
             and for the information of my family," from January 6 to
             July 29.

1823   Letter to President Monroe, October 24, contributes to formulation of the Monroe Doctrine, declaring the western hemisphere closed to European expansion.

1824   Makes final preparations in April for Francis Walker Gilmer's mission to Europe to recruit faculty for University of Virginia. Lafayette, on a triumphal tour of the United States, visits Monticello and is feted at the university November 3 to 15.

1825   University of Virginia opens to students March 7. Jefferson drafts "Declaration and Protest" for Virginia legislature, protesting federal usurpations, in December, but suppresses the document.

1826   Writes "Thoughts on Lotteries" in February, asking permission of the legislature to raffle his property to pay his debts, hoping by this means to realize enough money (which could not be done in the depressed market) to save Monticello for his heirs. General Assembly authorizes the lottery, but it is suspended when friends and admirers organize subscription funds in his behalf. Draws his will in March, providing for emancipation of five of his slaves. Dies at Monticello on July 4.

Note on the Texts

Thomas Jefferson published few of his writings during his lifetime. Most of what he wrote served governmental or private purposes: state papers, drafts of legislation, public addresses, autobiographical reminiscences, and letters to a variety of correspondents. The bulk of his writing, therefore, was published only posthumously, and has come down to us mainly through the mediation of several nineteenth-century editors.

Five major editions of Jefferson's writings have been published. The first, *The Memoirs, Correspondence and Private Papers of Thomas Jefferson*, appeared in four volumes in Charlottesville in 1829. Edited by Jefferson's grandson and executor, Thomas Jefferson Randolph, it first published the *Autobiography* and the *Anas* as well as a large selection of personal letters. For previously unpublished material, Randolph worked from manuscript and document sources, but, in accordance with the accepted editorial practice of his time, he made certain changes in spelling, punctuation, and wording.

Henry A. Washington, Librarian of the Department of State, prepared the nine-volume Congress Edition, *The Writings of Thomas Jefferson*, published in Washington, D.C., in 1853–54, following the federal government's purchase of Jefferson's public papers. In addition to these papers, Washington reprinted many items from the Randolph edition, and like Randolph, he routinely made editorial changes.

Paul Leicester Ford's edition, *The Writings of Thomas Jefferson*, 10 vols. (New York, 1892–99), was undoubtedly the best-edited of the nineteenth-century collections. The large majority of the items in this edition were freshly transcribed from Jefferson's manuscripts following conservative editorial principles. Ford indicated the provenance of each manuscript; in the few cases where he reprinted a document from an earlier published source, he indicated that source. For writings not published by Jefferson himself, Ford's edition has been the preferred source of the texts in this volume.

The Writings of Thomas Jefferson, 20 vols. (Washington, D.C., 1903–04), sometimes called the Memorial Edition, prepared by Andrew A. Lipscomb and Albert Ellery Bergh, is the most comprehensive edition and has a highly useful index. Unfortunately, the edition is largely a compendium of reprints. Sources for specific items are not indicated, but comparison with other texts has shown that in most cases Lipscomb and Bergh reprinted documents from Ford, or from Washington, or elsewhere, without reference to manuscripts. Also, Lipscomb and Bergh routinely modernized spelling, punctuation, and orthography. Several documents in their edition, unavailable in any printed source, were newly edited from manuscript: Vol. XVII, comprising the "Miscellaneous Papers," "Thoughts on English Prosody" in Vol. XVIII, and all of Vol. XIX except two letters. The Lipscomb and Bergh edition, therefore, is the only printed source for those items, and has been the source for those texts in this volume that were published for the first time in that edition.

These older editions are destined to be superseded (eventually) by the edition in progress at Princeton University, *The Papers of Thomas Jefferson*, ed. Julian Boyd, Charles Cullen, *et al.*, 20 vols. to date (Princeton, 1950–82). This edition, of which Jefferson's writings form only the core, is still incomplete. Even that edition makes some alterations in spelling and punctuation; its lengthy and detailed historical notes are invaluable.

Jefferson had the *Observations on the Whale-Fishery* (1788) printed in Paris by Jacques-Gabriel Clousier. It appeared in identical format in both English and French. Only a few of the small number of copies printed are extant. The present volume reprints the text from the copy in The Library Company of Philadelphia, which may have been the copy Jefferson kept for his files; several notes in his handwriting which appear at the head and at the end of the printed text are quoted in the *Notes* to the present volume.

In selecting texts of documents not prepared for publication by Jefferson, the order of preferred sources has been: contemporary publications (books, newspapers, published government reports), then the Ford edition, the Randolph edition, the Washington edition (where no other source has

been found), and the edition of Lipscomb and Bergh (only
for selections they transcribed from manuscript). The following is a list of the writings included in this volume, in the
order of their appearance, with the source of each text noted.
The main sources mentioned above are cited here as *Ford,*
Washington, and *L&B.*

LIST OF SOURCES

I. PUBLIC PAPERS

Resolutions of Congress on Lord North's Conciliatory Proposal.
  Pennsylvania Packet, August 7, 1775.
Draft Constitution for Virginia. *Ford*, II, 7–30.
Revisal of the Laws: Drafts of Legislation
    A Bill for Establishing Religious Freedom. *Report of the Committee of*
      Revisors Appointed by the General Assembly of Virginia in MDCCLXXVI
      (Richmond, 1784), 58–59.
    A Bill for Proportioning Crimes and Punishments. *Ford*, II, 203–20.
    A Bill for the More General Diffusion of Knowledge. *Report of the Com-*
      mittee of Revisors . . ., 53–55.
    A Bill Declaring Who Shall Be Deemed Citizens of this Commonwealth.
      Report of the Committee of Revisors . . ., 41–42.
Report of a Plan of Government for the Western Territory. *Ford*, III, 407–10.
Observations on the Whale-Fishery. *Observations on the Whale-Fishery* (Paris,
  1788). Printed here courtesy of The Library Company of Philadelphia.
Plan for Establishing Uniformity in the Coinage, Weights, and Measures of
  the United States. *Washington*, VII, 472–95.
Opinion on the Constitutionality of a National Bank. *Ford*, V, 284–89.
Opinion on the French Treaties. *Ford*, VI, 219–31.
Report on the Privileges and Restrictions on the Commerce of the United
  States in Foreign Countries. *Ford*, VI, 470–84.
Draft of the Kentucky Resolutions. *L&B*, XVII, 379–91.
Report of the Commissioners for the University of Virginia. *Early History of*
  the University of Virginia as Contained in the Letters of Thomas Jefferson and
  Joseph C. Cabell, ed. Nathaniel F. Cabell (Richmond, 1856), 432–47.
Memorial on the Book Duty. *Annals of the Congress of the United States*, 17th
  Congress, 1st Session (Washington, D.C., 1855), 531–32.
From the Minutes of the Board of Visitors of the Commonwealth of Vir-
  ginia. *L&B*, XIX, 413–16, 460–61, 468–70.
Draft Declaration and Protest of the Commonwealth of Virginia. *L&B*,
  XVII, 442–48.

II. ADDRESSES, MESSAGES, AND REPLIES

Response to the Citizens of Albemarle. *The Portable Jefferson*, ed. Merrill Peterson (New York, 1974), 259–60. © 1975 The Viking Press.

First Inaugural Address. *A Compilation of the Messages and Papers of the Presidents*, ed. James D. Richardson, 10 vols. (Washington, D.C., 1907), 309–12.

To Elias Shipman and Others, A Committee of the Merchants of New Haven. *Ford*, VIII, 67–71.

First Annual Message. *Ford*, VIII, 108–25.

To Messrs. Nehemiah Dodge and Others, A Committee of the Danbury Baptist Association, in the State of Connecticut. *Washington*, VIII, 113–14.

Third Annual Message. *Ford*, VIII, 266–74.

Second Inaugural Address, with "Notes of a Draft." *Ford*, VIII, 341–48.

Sixth Annual Message. *Ford*, VIII, 482–96.

Special Message on the Burr Conspiracy. *Ford*, IX, 14–20.

Special Message on Gun-Boats. *Ford*, IX, 23–27.

Eighth Annual Message. *Ford*, IX, 213–25.

To the Inhabitants of Albemarle County, in Virginia. *Ford*, IX, 250.

Indian Addresses

> To Brother John Baptist de Coigne. *Washington*, VIII, 17–76.
> To Brother Handsome Lake. *Washington*, VIII, 187–89.
> To the Brothers of the Choctaw Nation. *Washington,* VIII, 192–95.
> To the Chiefs of the Cherokee Nation. *L&B*, XIX, 146–49.
> To the Wolf and People of the Mandan Nation. *Washington*, VIII, 200–02.

III. MISCELLANY

Reply to the Representations of Affairs in America by British Newspapers. MS, Jefferson Papers, Library of Congress.

Answers and Observations for Démeunier's Article on the United States in the *Encyclopédie Méthodique*.

> 1. *From* Answers to Démeunier's First Queries, January 24, 1786.
>> The Confederation. *Ford*, IV, 141–44.
>> Broils among the states. *Ford,* IV, 146–47.
> 2. *From* Observations on Démeunier's Manuscript, June 22, 1786,
>> Indented servants. *Ford*, IV, 158–60.
>> Crimes and punishments. *Ford*, IV, 169–70.
>> The Society of the Cincinnati. *Ford*, IV, 170–77.
>> Populating the continent. *Ford*, IV, 179–81.
> 3. To Jean Nicolas Démeunier, June 26, 1786. *Ford*, IV, 183–85.

Thoughts on English Prosody. *L&B*, XVIII, 41–51.

Travel Journals

> 1. A Tour to some of the Gardens of England. *Washington*, IX, 367–73.

The standards for American English continue to undergo modification, and in some ways were conspicuously different in earlier periods from what they are today. In eighteenth and nineteenth-century writing, for example, a word might be spelled in more than one way, even in the same work (and sometimes in the same sentence), and these variations might be carried into print. In Jefferson's lifetime the institution of rigid linguistic norms was frequently recommended as a way of halting the process of linguistic change. Jefferson, however, did not spell consistently, nor, apparently, did he care to. Most editors have not been careful to preserve Jefferson's own spellings, which they have characterized as errors; nor have they preserved the punctuation, italics, and capitals that Jefferson used (as was the ordinary practice at the time) to suggest the movements of voice and to give words significances and emphases they might not otherwise have. Most editors have supplied capitals at the beginnings of sentences (a practice that was not Jefferson's), expanded abbreviations, substituted "and" for "&", etc. The texts in the present volume, since they are printed from different editions, represent varying degrees of regularization, according to the policies and habits of their editors.

The presence of brackets at various points in the text calls for brief comment. Some of the previous editions used brackets for different purposes. Ford, for instance, frequently placed his conjectural readings of faded manuscript words or passages inside brackets and in italics. In some cases, however, brackets in the text are Jefferson's own. Usually it is clear from the context whether brackets are Jefferson's or an editor's, and what their function is. Where it is not clear, the information can be sought in the edition from which the text is taken.

The drawings in the text are reproduced from Jefferson's handwritten manuscripts.

This volume is concerned only with representing the *texts* of the various pieces included; it does not attempt to reproduce features of the typographic design of the editions from which the texts are taken—such as the display capitalization and headings of letters, or the exact placement of drawings. The short titles over individual letters have been supplied by the present editor. Typographical errors have been corrected, and a list of these errors follows, cited by page and line numbers: 11.32, privileges; 12.24, to shall; 15.17, anually; 30.34, devant."; 30.42, judgment; 40.10, notice or; 41.7, betwen; 42.1, teacherin; 45.12, mumerical; 46.11, enquie; 46.36, interregatories; 51.6–7, America; 54.12, the; 60.4, in; 61.28, it; 83.34, grain,; 84.2, established (8.); 89.5, it thought; 96.29–30, neutrality.; 99.10, Does; 100.11, party.'; 106.27, word?'; 129.32, (not; 135.17, qualties; 135.20, acquisitions; 144.29, Univresity; 167.12, convulious; 238.3, MANDAR; 248.20, Netherl.^ds; 255.12, &c.'; 256.7, &c.'; 260.37, wealthest; 269.7, question; 297.3, Memorandems; 305.4, peasants; 305.33, brother; 313.22–23, thus a centry; 313.34, twenty-one; 313.35–36, as present; 333.6, go the; 339.15, Hamiltion; 360.20, energy; 373.40, orriginally; 375.7, Adam's.

Notes

In the notes below, the reference numbers denote page and line of the present volume (the line count includes chapter headings). Considerations of space have made it impractical to annotate the vast number of individual names, correspondents, and others mentioned by Jefferson. No note is made for places included in a standard desk-reference book. Notes at the foot of the page in the text are Jefferson's own.

PUBLIC PAPERS

5.1–2   *Resolutions . . . Proposal*]   The resolutions adopted by Congress, printed here, were based on Jefferson's draft submitted July 25.

10.1   *Draft . . . Virginia*]   This is the third and final draft, which was carried to Williamsburg by George Wythe and shown to the delegates. It was first printed in the *Richmond Enquirer,* June 20, 1806. The text here is the MS which Jefferson endorsed with the title "A Bill for new modelling the form of government, & for establishing the fundamental principles thereof in future." Below this he added, "It is proposed that this bill, after correction by the Convention, shall be referred by them to the people, to be assembled in their respective counties and that the suffrages of two thirds of the counties shall be requisite to establish it." Bracketed words in roman were so written by Jefferson; those in italic are Ford's interpolations.

20.2   *A Bill . . . Freedom*]   Jefferson said he drafted the bill in 1777; it was first presented and debated in the General Assembly in June, 1779, when it was also first printed as a broadside. It was enacted on January 16, 1786, but only after considerable deletion by amendment. The statute when passed began, "Whereas Almighty God . . ."

23.1–2   *A Bill . . . Punishments*]   Ford's edition includes Jefferson's notes from the MS, now in the Library of Congress, which were omitted in the published version. In the MS, Jefferson quotes in Anglo-Saxon, Latin, Old French, and English; Ford has transliterated the Anglo-Saxon.

50.1   *Report . . . Territory*]   It was not adopted but led to a revised report, also principally of Jefferson's authorship, which was adopted, after elimination of the prohibition of slavery, on April 23, 1784.

53.1   *Observations . . . Whale-Fishery*]   A manuscript note above the title on the first page of Jefferson's copy of this pamphlet reads: "A Memoire on the Arret of Sep. 8. 1788. prohibiting the importation of whale oils of foreign fishery into France, presented to M. de Montmorin Nov. 19. 1788. by Tho! Jefferson M. P. of the US. at Paris."

66.38   us.]   Another manuscript note appears at the end of the pamphlet:
"In compliance with the above Memoire whale oils of the US. were exempted from the prohibition by an Arret of Dec. 7. 1788."

69.38   (1)]   Numbers in parentheses refer to Appendix beginning on
84.30.

90.28   XIIth. amendment]   The Tenth Amendment as finally ratified by
the states.

123.1   *Draft . . . Resolutions*]   The resolutions in protest against the
Alien and Sedition Laws were adopted by the legislature, after minor amendment, on November 16, 1798.

151.1–2   *From . . . Virginia*]   The reports and resolutions adopted by the
Board of Visitors were written and signed by Jefferson as Rector.

156.1–4   *Draft . . . them*]   The paper, enclosed in a letter to Madison,
December 24, 1825, was withdrawn and never acted upon.

ADDRESSES, MESSAGES, AND REPLIES

165.1   *Response . . . Albemarle*]   The response was delivered to a group of
local citizens after his return from France.

166.2   March 4, 1801]   Date inserted.

167.20–21   We are . . . Federalists.]   In the MS draft, and often in print,
this appears as "We are all republicans; we are all federalists."

168.6–7   thousandth . . . generation]   "Thousandth and thousandth" is
correct. It appears often in other editions as "hundredth and thousandth."

192.1   *Second Inaugural Address*]   In Jefferson's MS is the following outline:

NOTES OF A DRAFT FOR A SECOND INAUGURAL ADDRESS
    The former one was an exposition of the principles on which I thought it
my duty to administer the government. The second then should naturally be
a conte rendu, or a statement of facts, shewing that I have conformed to
those principles. The former was *promise*: this is *performance*. Yet the nature
of the occasion requires that details should be avoided, that, the most prom-
inent heads only should be selected and these placed in a strong light but in
as few words as possible. These heads are Foreign affairs; Domestic do., viz.
Taxes, Debts, Louisiana, Religion, Indians, The Press. None of these heads
need any commentary but that of the Indians. This is a proper topic not only
to promote the work of humanizing our citizens towards these people, but
to conciliate to us the good opinion of Europe on the subject of the Indians.
This, however, might have been done in half the compass it here occupies.
But every respector of science, every friend to political reformation must have

observed with indignation the hue & cry raised against philosophy & the rights of man; and it really seems as if they would be overborne & barbarism, bigotry & despotism would recover the ground they have lost by the advance of the public understanding. I have thought the occasion justified some discountenance of these anti-social doctrines, some testimony against them, but not to commit myself in direct warfare on them, I have thought it best to say what is directly applied to the Indians only, but admits by inference a more general extension.

There are also two papers, as follows:

MADISON'S MEMORANDUM.

Insert

"Thro' the transactions of a portion of our citizens whose intelligence & arrangements best shield them agst the abuses, as well as inconveniences incident to the collection."

substitute

"Religion. As religious exercises, could therefore be neither controuled nor prescribed by us. They have accordingly been left as the Constitution found them, under the direction & discipline acknowledged within the several states."

Indians

"No desire" instead of "nothing to desire."

substitute

Who feeling themselves in the present order of things and fearing to become nothing in any other, inculcate a blind attachment to the customs of their fathers in opposition to every light * example which wd conduct them into a more improved state of existence. But the day I hope is not far distant when their prejudices will yield to their true interests & they will take their stand, &c.

Press—strike out from "their own affairs."

Last page—Alter to "views become manifest to them."

This is endorsed "Dept. State recd Feb. 8, 05 Inaugural."

The second paper reads:

MADISON'S MEMORANDUM.

Is the fact certain that the amt of the internal taxes not objectionable in their nature would not have paid the collectors?

What is the amendment alluded to as necessary to a repartition of liberated revenue amg. the states in time of peace?

Page 3—"in any view" may be better than "in any event" that phrase having just preceded.

Instead of "acts of religious exercise suited to it (religion)" "exercises suited to it" or some equivalent variation is suggested.

Dept. State recd Feb. 21. 05 Inaugural.

MISCELLANY

245.1–2   *Reply . . . Newspapers*] The text is Jefferson's draft. It was translated and published, with some alterations, in the *Gazette de Leyde*, December
7 and 10, 1784.

264.18   13th . . . articles] Article 13 of the Prussian treaty (signed in
September 1785) provided a restrictive definition of contraband; Article 24
offered guarantees for the humane treatment of prisoners of war.

268.1   *Thoughts . . . Prosody*] It is conjectured that this essay was written
in the summer of 1786. The letter to Chastellux was similarly undated, though
Lipscomb and Bergh tentatively date it in October of that year.

278.23   following instance] Quotation from Virgil missing.

297.4   *Whateley*] Thomas Whately, *Observations on Modern Gardening*
(1770).

303.29   axis in peritrochio] Similar to a windless or capstan.

304.8   moolen book] Johannis van Zyl, *Theatrum Machinarum Univer-
sale; of Groot Algemeen Moolen-Boek* (Amsterdam, 1761).

318.16   annexed bill] Not included here.

331.10   pumice] Pomace, the substance of fruit remaining after pressing
of cider or wine.

335.27   only . . . period] John Marshall, *The Life of George Washington*, 5
vols. (1804–1807).

341.14   5/] Five shillings.

352.10   My lre of——] May 23, 1792.

368.26   election] In the House of Representatives.

369.6   4.] There is a gap in the MS between "4." and "That."

370.16   signature of] The MS ends with "of" and the note alluded to
has not been found.

371.1   *Notes . . . 1795*] Christoph Daniel Ebeling consulted Jefferson
while engaged in research for his *Geography and History of North America*, 5
vols. (1796–1816). The MS is undated but was probably written in late 1795.

380.4–5   Ολιγη . . . λυθεντων] "And small we must lie, / A dust of
loosened bones." Not by Anacreon, but one of the Anacreontea, poems in
the style of Anacreon attributed to him until the 19th century.

Index

The Library of America Paperback Classics Series

American Speeches: Political Oratory from Patrick Henry to Barack Obama (various authors)
With an introduction by Ted Widmer
ISBN: 978-1-59853-094-0

The Education of Henry Adams by Henry Adams
With an introduction by Leon Wieseltier
ISBN: 978-1-59853-060-5

The Red Badge of Courage by Stephen Crane
With an introduction by Robert Stone
ISBN: 978-1-59853-061-2

The Souls of Black Folk by W.E.B. Du Bois
With an introduction by John Edgar Wideman
ISBN: 978-1-59853-054-4

Essays: First and Second Series by Ralph Waldo Emerson
With an introduction by Douglas Crase
ISBN: 978-1-59853-084-1

The Autobiography by Benjamin Franklin
With an introduction by Daniel Aaron
ISBN: 978-1-59853-095-7

The Varieties of Religious Experience by William James
With an introduction by Jaroslav Pelikan
ISBN: 978-1-59853-062-9

Selected Writings by Thomas Jefferson
With an introduction by Tom Wicker
ISBN: 978-1-59853-096-4

Selected Speeches and Writings by Abraham Lincoln
With an introduction by Gore Vidal
ISBN: 978-1-59853-053-7

The Call of the Wild by Jack London
With an introduction by E. L. Doctorow
ISBN: 978-1-59853-058-2

≛ The Library of America